The Black Skysc

The Black Skyscraper

Architecture and the Perception of Race

ADRIENNE BROWN

Johns Hopkins University Press

Baltimore

This book was brought to publication with the generous assistance
of the University of Chicago.

Johns Hopkins Paperback edition, 2019
2 4 6 8 9 7 5 3 1

Johns Hopkins University Press
2715 North Charles Street
Baltimore, Maryland 21218-4363
www.press.jhu.edu

*The Library of Congress has cataloged the
hardcover edition this book as follows:*

Names: Brown, Adrienne R., 1983– author.
Title: The black skyscraper : architecture and the perception
of race / Adrienne Brown.
Description: Baltimore : Johns Hopkins University Press, 2017. |
Includes bibliographical references and index.
Identifiers: LCCN 2017007352| ISBN 9781421423838 (hardcover : alk. paper) |
ISBN 9781421423845 (electronic) | ISBN 1421423839 (hardcover : alk. paper) |
ISBN 1421423847 (electronic)
Subjects: LCSH: Architecture and race—United States. | Skyscrapers—
Social aspects—United States.
Classification: LCC NA2543.R37 B76 2017 | DDC 720.1/03—dc23
LC record available at https://lccn.loc.gov/2017007352

A catalog record for this book is available from the British Library.

ISBN-13: 9781421429038
ISBN-10: 1421429039

*Special discounts are available for bulk purchases of this book. For
more information, please contact Special Sales at 410-516-6936 or
specialsales@press.jhu.edu.*

Johns Hopkins University Press uses environmentally friendly book
materials, including recycled text paper that is composed of at least
30 percent post-consumer waste, whenever possible.

HATS, where do you belong?
what is under you?

On the rim of a skyscraper's forehead
I looked down and saw: hats: fifty thousand hats:
Swarming with a noise of bees and sheep, cattle and waterfalls,
Stopping with a silence of sea grass, a silence of prairie corn.
Hats: tell me your high hopes.

—*Carl Sandburg, "Hats," 1920*

CONTENTS

This book exists because of the many people who have extended kindnesses, support, care, critique, generosity, and enthusiasm to both it and me. My dissertation advisers at Princeton University—Diana Fuss, Bill Gleason, and Valerie Smith—were the first to believe in the idea that there was more to the narrative history of the skyscraper than even I knew at the time. Each has expanded my idea of not only what it means to be a scholar of the built environment and of literature but also what it is to be a scholar in general. Thank you. Daphne Brooks taught me to study both what sparks my intellectual curiosity and the things I love. Broad thanks to the Princeton English Department, the Program in American Studies, and the former Center for African American Studies. Thanks to Anne Cheng for her support and cheer. From the Princeton diaspora, I also thank Amelia Worsley, Briallen Hopper, Jess Row, Alicia Christoff, Anne Hirsch Moffitt, Anthony Petro, Alden Young, J. K. Barret, Michelle Coghlan, Ivan Ortiz, and Will Evans for their camaraderie, assistance, and joy in the process of writing this book. Much love to Lindsay Reckson and Nadia Ellis for their brilliant minds and beautiful style, on and off the page. Gratitude to Wendy A. Lee and Jacky Shin for being game to read anything at the drop of a hat and making me laugh at the same time.

Everyone told me when I moved to Chicago that it was the perfect place to be while finishing this book because of its storied skyscraper history. But it is the people within this city who have proved to be far more important to its completion. Thanks to Lauren Berlant for being a generous colleague but also a dear friend—thanks for helping me hold this thing up. Ken Warren's support for this project as it shifted foci was immense. I also want to thank my two department chairs during the course of writing this book, Elaine Hadley and Frances Ferguson. I couldn't have asked for better shepherds. I thank the entire English Department at the University of Chicago, as well as the Center for Race, Politics, and Culture, the Center for the Study of Gender and Sexuality, and the Urban Network. I extend particular thanks to my colleagues Heather Keenleyside, Chicu Reddy, Deborah Nelson, Richard So, Patrick Jagoda, Julie Orliemanski, Maud Ellmann, Rachel Galvin, Edgar Garcia, Tim Harrison, Tim Campbell, John Muse, Raúl Coronado, Bradin Cormack, Adam Green, Cathy Cohen, Jacqueline Stewart, Katherine Fischer Taylor, Theaster Gates, Michael Dawson, Tianna Paschel, Gina Samuels, and Micere Keels. Special love and thanks to Rachel Jean Baptiste, who was one of the first to welcome me to the city and to the university. I also want to thank Lex Nalley, Robert Devendorf, Naomi Patschke, Neesha Oliver, William Weaver, and Hannah Stark for all of their help. Though the following colleagues started at Chicago after me, it feels as if my life here didn't really begin until they arrived—so much affection and gratitude to Sonali Thakkar, Zach Samalin, Christopher Taylor, and especially David Simon for sharing their courage, smarts, warmth, stamina, and solidarity with me.

Chicago would have been so much colder without the light provided by Nasser Mufti, Harris Feinsod, Andrew Leong, Pete Coviello, Emily Licht, Alexis Chema, Tristram Wolff, Jerry Passannante, Thom Cantey, Sarah Pierce Taylor, and Leah Feldman. Shout-out to Andrew Leong and Richard So for beginning the Junior Faculty Writing group. Thanks to Andre Schleife, Yvonne Gower, and Cecelia Leal for their cheer downstate and Tiffany Knight for Boston comfort. Thanks to Bob Michaelson for source assistance. Such deep gratitude to Sonali, Harris, and Rachel for reading parts of this book at the last moment.

Much appreciation is due to Mabel Wilson, who has been not only an amazing cheerleader but also an intellectual model in so many ways. Thanks to Britt Rusert, my collaborator on all things Du Bois and so many other delights.

I had the honor of being part of the first class of the First Book Institute hosted by the Center for American Literary Studies at Penn State University, and it completely changed this book and any books I might write in the future. Thanks to the institute's director, Sean X. Goudie, the intrepid Priscilla Wald, and the wonderful Tina Chen. I also want to thank my FBI cohort, Danielle Heard, Christen Mucher, Samaine Lockwood, Todd Carmody, Sarah Lauro, and Theodore Martin.

The Career Enhancement Fellowship sponsored by the Woodrow Wilson Foundation not only allowed me to take a year of research leave but also introduced me to an outstanding cohort of fellows and gave me the opportunity to work closely with a mentor. Thanks to Ina Noble, Caryl McFarlane, and Koritha Mitchell who helped to make this experience so enriching. And special thanks to my mentor, Priscilla Wald, who has given so much of her time, intellect, and energy to me since first meeting her at Princeton many years ago. I dream of being half of the mentor you are.

Thanks to the reviewers of the two articles drawing from material included here. An early version of chapter 2 was published in *Journal of Modern Literature*: "Between the Mythic and the Monstrous: The Early Skyscraper's Weird Frontiers," 35.1 (Fall 2011) 165–188. A version of chapter 4 appeared in *American Literature*: "The Black Skyscraper" 85.3 (2013) 531–561.

I'm grateful for the three anonymous reviewers at Oxford University Press who helped to shape the book. Thanks to Dianne Harris, who provided me with generous and incisive feedback on the manuscript as my reader for Johns Hopkins University Press. I am grateful to Melissa Gilliam and the Office of Academic Leadership, Advancement & Diversity at the University of Chicago for subvention funds to support this book. So much thanks to Catherine Goldstead, my editor at Johns Hopkins, for all of her help, guidance, and good feeling. You've been such a joy to work with.

Thanks and love to Rachel Karish and Sarah Balagtas for their friendship—no matter how far away I move from Maryland, as soon as I talk to either of you I feel back at home. Much love to the Williams family—Sally, Bob, Jocelyn, Tan, Megan, and Jack. Thanks to my Scottish family, Brian, Marion, Donald, Harriet, Dugald, Violet, Lindsay, and Margaret.

So much love to Brittany Williams, who let me hang out with her at the School of Architecture at the University of Maryland, where some of the first seeds for this project were planted. You've shaped this book and me in so many ways. Thanks, pal.

Sonya Posmentier has probably read more of my prose—from this book and in general—than anyone else. Thank you for all the late-night phone calls, for your willingness to help me think at every level from concept to punctuation, and for all your encouragement. You've been there for all the highs and lows of this thing, and I could not have finished this book without you. I'm ecstatic that we're label-mates. It feels oh so fitting.

Thanks and love to my father, Anthony Brown, for all his support. Love to my brother, Tony Brown, and my niece, Adrianna. To my mother, Marilyn Cohen-Brown, thank you for teaching me that it's okay to think big, ponderous thoughts, to engage with the world even when it disappoints you, to take pleasure in the ordinary as well as the extraordinary, to care deeply and forcefully for ideas, principles, and people. Love you.

Lastly, to Andy Ferguson—this book is for you, with love. You better like it.

The Black Skyscraper

CHAPTER ONE

Introduction

Race in Three Dimensions

In an insurrectionary vision coming near the end of Carl Van Vechten's novel *Nigger Heaven* (1926), skyscrapers appear as tombstones heralding the end of whiteness in New York City:

> Might it not eventually happen, as more Negroes, coming from the South, coming from the West, to take advantage of the opportunities promised by this new metropolis, encroached farther and farther on white territory, that Manhattan, which already had been Indian, Dutch, English, and finally the melting-pot for every nation, become a Negro Island? Byron chuckled aloud as the vision came to him of the last white inhabitant pushing off in a row boat from the Battery while the black flag flew over the Aquarium and from the roof of every skyscraper. (190)

Van Vechten, styling himself as an intimate white witness to New York's veiled black world, intended his book to give readers "such a picture of Harlem, the great walled city, as has not yet been painted."[1] But here we find the novel entertaining the idea of the walls of this "city within a city," as Harlem was colloquially called, one day expanding to encompass the whole island. This scene is in some ways the uncanny inverse of the vision of verdant discovery closing F. Scott Fitzgerald's *The Great Gatsby*, published the year before. Whereas Nick Carraway conjures the wondrous moment when Dutch sailors first glimpsed "the fresh, green breast of the new world" to sustain himself following his experience of urban ruin, Van Vechten's black protagonist gleefully imagines the end of this era of white urban rule as a new beginning.

Van Vechten suggests the skyscraper could stand for blackness only in the extreme event of a coup. But like most things and theories emerging in the late nineteenth and early twentieth centuries, blackness in particular and racial

difference more broadly shaped the skyscraper's material and aesthetic development. The early skyscraper's materiality proves entangled with race on multiple
fronts, from the black and immigrant laborers who riveted girders and dug
foundations while their lives were routinely jeopardized by overzealous managers, to the tactics deployed by steel corporations to exacerbate racial divisions
between workers and weaken unions, up through the architectural debates about
the use of European designs to avoid "miscegenated" façades reflective of the
United States' heterogeneous population.

But whereas Van Vechten wields the skyscraper in this scene as the final
symbol of the vanquished white metropolitan, we find writers, artists, and architects around the turn of the twentieth century conceiving of the early skyscraper as helping to precipitate this disappearance. I argue in this book not
only that race proved crucial to this architecture's inception, but that the skyscraper also impeded the perception of race. In a diverse array of materials from
the turn of the century—pulp fiction and office girl romances, realist travel writings and muckraking journalism, Harlem Renaissance artworks and accounts
of architects slumming in cabarets—skyscrapers are depicted as changing what
it meant to both see and be seen as a racial subject. Tall buildings appear in
these materials as radical reformers of sensory and affective experience, drasti-
cally altering the scale of the city, creating new vantage points within it, and
facilitating denser crowds at street level. As art historian Meir Wigoder insists,
the skyscraper birthed a new kind of spectator.[2] But it also changed what it
meant to be perceived. Bodies looked markedly different, depending on where
one stood in and around these tall structures. They might appear as dark, uniform specks from its apex, blurred or fragmented masses at its base, and variously detailed miscellanies from the many floors and vantage points sandwiched
in-between. Conversely, inside the busy lobbies and elevators of these buildings
and on the crowded streets at their bases, people might appear too close or move
too quickly for steady observation. At stake in these changes to how bodies appeared was the continued viability of perceiving race, a practice heavily reliant
on the believed accessibility of racial evidence on and around the body.

The skyscraper potentially disrupted the ability to perceive race as well as the
capacity to *feel raced*. White metropolitan writers in particular described feeling
less like sovereign agents in the skyscraper's shadow and more like mechanized
automatons or even chattel slaves. Whereas some figures, including a few key af-
filiates of the Harlem Renaissance, embraced these disorienting conditions and
used the skyscraper's effects on perception to imagine how racial hierarchies
might be further dismantled, for those attempting to give voice to the anxieties

of the expanding white middle class, skyscraper architecture—effectively rendering all city dwellers black at a certain height—inspired dread.

In this volume, I recover this architecture's influence not only on the shape of the city but also on the racial sensorium of its residents and readers. Commencing with the invention of the skyscraper in the 1880s and concluding with the 1931 erection of the 102-story Empire State Building, I chart the ways that the skyscraper, which vertically expanded urban environments, mediated processes of racial perception and apprehension in the United States occasioned by the end of Reconstruction, mass migrations, and immigrations. In lesser-known works of apocalyptic science fiction, light romance and Jazz Age melodrama, as well as in more canonical texts by W. E. B. Du Bois, F. Scott Fitzgerald, and Nella Larsen, the skyscraper both absorbs and transforms urban attention. Prompting Henry James to put the verb *seeing* in quotation marks when faced with its overwhelming size, the early skyscraper helped foreground the malleable nature of racial perception. Writers figured this architecture as posing a direct challenge to the nation's concurrent desires in the era of Jim Crow and mass immigration to stabilize, and thus reject, the conditional nature of racial sight.[3] Offering an account of the skyscraper's raced history, as well as charting its effects on racial perception, the materials gathered here allow us to see how all architectures are, inevitably, racial architectures, producing and maintaining site-specific phenomenologies of race.

The "Just Growed" Skyscraper

Given their ubiquity in the cities of the world today, it is easy to forget how radically skyscrapers changed the phenomenological experience of urbanity in the first forty years of their history. Those who funded and designed these structures initially envisioned them as economic and spatial solutions helping to order and contain the new masses crowding into downtown sectors. Both skyscrapers and the masses they choreographed were accused in print of having "just growed"—a phrase turning Topsy's retort about her own development in Harriet Beecher Stowe's novel *Uncle Tom's Cabin* into a cute witticism invoked at the turn of the century to describe the growth of anything deemed to lack a clear guiding agent.[4] As one 1920 article from the New York newspaper the *Independent* insisted, "the wild skyline of New York 'just growed'—like Topsy or the British Empire."[5]

While the term *skyscraper* preexists the tall buildings it now primarily names—used at one point to describe a number of outsized things, from people and horses to sails and even tall tales—it began to be exclusively assigned to structures around the late nineteenth century. But even as the term became solely associated with buildings, what exactly counted as a skyscraper eludes easy categorization given that the term indexes no fixed height or set of construction methods.[6] Although there remains a lack of consensus about what makes a tall building a skyscraper, as well as about this structure's exact origins, there is no denying the impact of this architectural form on both the history of architecture and the history of the city. From the erection of the 10-story Home Insurance Building in 1884 to the 41-story Singer Building in 1908 the height of the tallest inhabitable building more than quadrupled in a single generation.[7] With the completion of the 102-story Empire State Building in 1931, this number would further increase by a factor of two-and-a-half. Although the skyscraper was invented in Chicago, it was New York's permissive building regulations and irregular lot sizes that turned it into a bona fide icon.[8] Manhattan in 1913 boasted approximately one thousand buildings between 11 and 20 stories, and fifty-one buildings between 21 and 60 stories.[9] Housing more than twice the population of Chicago by 1920, New York boasted ten times as many tall buildings.[10] By 1929, the United States had 377 buildings exceeding 20 stories—188 in New York alone.[11] For many Americans, these massive changes to the look and scale of the city occurred within just half a lifetime. As builder William Starrett wondered in 1928, "who can look on the majestic sky-line of New York in sunshine or shadow and not be moved, both by the tremendous power of its mass and the beauty and richness of its detail? Yet if you are forty-three years or more old, your eyes have seen it all."[12] Following historians Asa Briggs and Harold Platt's definition of certain industrial centers as "shock cities," eliciting "the horror and wonder of contemporary society," we might consider the early skyscraper as an example of shock architecture because of the extreme reactions it prompted within architectural discourses and the wider public sphere.[13]

Even for those residing outside this architecture's northern urban domain, the skyscraper's presence loomed large as a frequent topic within mass culture. Stories, cartoons, and photographs of these structures regularly appeared in magazines and newspapers circulating outside urban centers. Despite their association with cities, skyscrapers were referred to in the public sphere as products of the entire nation, touted by at least one critic as "the most distinctively American thing in the world," "all American and all ours in conception," and "the only indigenous architectural product to which we lay claim."[14] Given the astonishing speed of the United States' transformation from Jeffersonian agrarianism to urban industrialism—with the urban population outnumbering the rural for the first time in the nation's history in the 1910s—the skyscraper was part of the immediate and mediated lives of a large number of Americans.

Though the skyscraper affectively "moved" a generation of Americans awed by its size and novelty, others in the period felt estranged by the structure's seeming capacity to "move" their perceptual capacities. The peculiarity of its neck-craning height, its illusory non-load-bearing walls, and its broader effects on the angle, perspective, and scale of urban vision appears in writing about urban life as a challenge to preexisting modes of seeing and sensing within the city. Though the skyscraper's disorienting effects were varied, its consequences for racial perception received persistent attention. As a national reminder of the conditional nature of perception, the skyscraper emerged at a particularly inconvenient historical moment for those looking to codify classifications of racial difference. The skyscraper's invention in the 1880s coincided with the end of Reconstruction, the institutionalized rise of Jim Crow in the South, and the more informal "economic, political and legal regimes" in the North regulating separate but unequal conditions between whites and blacks, as well as between whites and a spectrum of racial others.[15] The racial logics of the late nineteenth century also nourished surging nativist anxiety driven by concerns that the melting pot was cooling, throwing into question the nation's ability to absorb the growing numbers of European immigrants deemed inassimilable to narrowly drawn definitions of whiteness. Although nativist agitators advocated for immigration restrictions as early as the 1880s, their biggest victory came in 1924 when Congress passed sweeping legislation designed to ensure, in the words of South Carolina senator Ellison DuRant Smith, "the preservation of that splendid stock" of "the pure, unadulterated Anglo-Saxon."[16] No mere question of numbers, racial preservation depended on conserving the perceptual conditions under which such "stock" might remain legible. Skyscrapers provided an occasion for many writers to wonder what would happen to race and, by extension, the host of legal, social, and aesthetic forms dependent on its perceptibility in cities where the built environment seemed to have "just growed," pushing preexisting mechanisms of racial perception to their already fragile limits. The skyscraper became a prompt for reconsidering race during a time when both the city's demographics and the means for observing them were in flux.

Before situating the skyscraper's early representational life in relation to changing notions of race, perception, and urban experience in the chapters that follow, I use the rest of the introduction to constellate some of the key contexts essential to apprehending these links: the history of urbanization, immigration, and migration in the United States; its changing legal and social definitions of race; how we have so far imagined racial perception and phenomenology; and the architectural life of race. Viewing the skyscraper in light of architectures, such as the tenement, and perceptual devices, such as the photograph, as I do in the following sections, helps bring this architecture's other functions as a technology, stage, and frame into sharper focus.

The Tenement versus the Skyscraper

Depending on whom one asked at the time, the early skyscraper either symbolized the nation's doomful march into urban disorder or heralded man's impending triumph over aesthetic and infrastructural incoherence. At times, it managed to index both at once. Economist Stuart Chase, for instance, explored the range of associations with the skyscraper by way of a list. Tabling his quantitative training in a 1929 article for *Harper's Magazine,* Chase pursues an analysis of the city "dealing more with the testimony of the five senses than with economics or philosophy of divination."[17] He organizes his testimony into two phenomenological categories—"Positive Reactions—pleasurable" and "Painful Reactions—negative." In the "pleasurable" column, Chase includes several entries that appreciate either views *of* skyscrapers or views *from* them that produce a satisfying experience of unpeopled abstraction. In this category, he includes "the view of the city from a high roof garden, particularly at night," "towers indirectly illuminated," "cube masses against blue sky," and the "corrugated ridges of set-backs" as urban delights. In the "painful" category, Chase only directly references the skyscraper once, singling out a few buildings near Grand Central as "bad bullies," but he includes several other entries that more obliquely index the structure through its deleterious effects on bodily movement and orientation. Material concerns such as "jammed traffic," "the roar of traffic," and "dust, dirt and cinders" associated with the streets surrounding higher-occupancy skyscrapers and greater concentrations of bodies and things constellated around them join more abstract sensations associated with life among skyscrapers, such as "a feeling akin to being at the bottom of a well" and "the insignificance of the sun and moon." If, as Chase concludes, "pleasure is found in sudden glimpses, in certain lights on architectural masses," "pain is found in noise, dust, smell, crowding, the pressure of the clock, in negotiating traffic, in great stretches of dour ugliness, in looking always up instead of out, in a continually battering sense of human inferiority." When isolated as an aesthetic object to gaze at or from, the skyscraper retained the potential for splendor. But when considered a part of the larger material infrastructure impacting one's daily experience of the city, this architecture compounds the sense of Chase and many others of cities as places of chaos, crowding, and shrinking humanism.

To understand how the skyscraper could be perceived as both a refuge from the city and a catalyst for some of its gravest problems and how these functions were tied to the endurance of race, it is helpful to examine the context of urbanization and industrialization in which this architecture developed and that it eventually helped frame. The skyscraper arrived on the American scene at a time when its cities were growing in population, infrastructure, and municipal complexity.[18] This was particularly true of Chicago and New York, the two cities most critical to the skyscraper's development. Whereas the United States began the second half of the nineteenth century as a largely rural nation punctuated by cities, by century's end the urban-industrial core had wrested primacy from the agricultural periphery.[19] Statistics help showcase the intensity of this shift, particularly because the nation's "sensory testimony" about urbanization was likely bolstered by the public circulation of such figures. The number of people living in New York in 1900—3.4 million—roughly equaled the entire population of all American cities fifty years prior. New York became the largest city in the Western Hemisphere in 1850 before surpassing Berlin and catching up to Paris by 1870. Only London remained larger until 1925 when it, too, was eclipsed.[20] Chicago's growth proved similarly dramatic if on a smaller scale. A frontier fort in 1832, Chicago would expand to 109,000 people by 1860 before becoming the nation's second-largest city ten years later. The city gained 600,000 residents in the 1890s, making it one of the largest cities in the world in 1900. Both cities continued to expand well into the twentieth century, with New York City growing by 2.2 million and Chicago by 1 million in the first two decades of the new century.[21]

This boom in urban population was a function of several factors. Horizontally expanding cities swallowed up neighboring towns and districts through acts of municipal annexation. More deliberate acts of migration within the United States in this period proved steadier fuel for urban growth as Americans increasingly flocked to cities in the late nineteenth century in search of employment and culture. Until 1915, African Americans constituted a stable if relatively low number of these migrants. Chicago's African American population grew from about one thousand in the early 1860s to fifteen thousand in 1893, while Manhattan's population of black migrants more than doubled between 1890 and 1900.[22] With the commencement of the Great Migration in 1915, New York and Chicago's black populations expanded by roughly 40 percent between 1910 and 1930. These demographic shifts, along with the emergence of a Jim Crow system whose spatial dimensions were "crucial elements of modern American northern *and* southern commercial industrial cities," meant that "urban territory was racialized in new and more intense ways" during this period, as James Smethurst has noted.[23]

Yet the largest contributor to urban growth in the United States until the Immigration Act of 1924 was foreign immigration.[24] By 1890, Chicago had the greatest percentage of foreign-born residents in the United States, while New York, as the port city through which almost all European immigrants passed, counted the largest number.[25] By 1910, more than three-fourths of New York's population either were immigrants or had a foreign-born parent. Arthur Schlesinger described the city in 1933 as home to "half as many Italians as Naples, as many Germans as Hamburg, twice as many Irish as Dublin and two and a half times as many Jews as Warsaw."[26] By 1920, more than 80 percent of all US immigrants born in Russia, Ireland, Italy, and Poland lived in cities. New York and Chicago were the final destinations of a large fraction of the 17 million immigrants who arrived between 1900 and 1917.

Some Americans around the turn of the century experienced the heterogeneity of American urbanization as a flood that needed to be staunched. Cities were increasingly understood as sites of racial differences, which have only been understood in retrospect as encompassing finer-grade distinctions of ethnicity, as David Roediger has forcefully argued.[27] While blacks and Asians were understood in absolute terms as distinct races, what distinguished ethnic and racial differences was unclear, given the varying definitions of race circulating within scientific, legal, and social spheres. As Michael Omi and Howard Winant argue, attempts to theorize ethnic difference as distinct from racial difference first emerged in the United States in the 1920s, with the scholarship of Chicago School sociologists Robert Park and Louis Wirth.[28] Their efforts were largely in response to the "swarthier" strain of southern and eastern European immigrants arriving in the early twentieth century, who were perceived by some as more alien and harder to assimilate than their northwestern predecessors. These "Atlantic immigrants," as Omi and Winant note, were not fully white but occupied an "intermediate racial status."[29] In a 1901 issue of *Forum* magazine, for instance, one columnist warned readers of "the physical moral, and mental wrecks from Europe of a kind which we are better without," describing this new strain of immigrant as "beaten men from beaten races; representing the worst failures in the struggle for existence."[30] Such sentiments, though never as vicious as the rancor toward Chinese immigrants, drove nativist efforts

to further restrict immigration and curtail the number of "persons of foreign birth" who "seem to seek out cities," as one 1901 study of immigration
insisted."[31]

Depictions of the degenerating city sinking under the pressure of alien immigration and black migrants were countered by assertions that American cities
could and already were absorbing newcomers. For these thinkers and reformers,
as historian Paul Boyer writes, the city was "no mere chance accumulation of
free-floating human atoms," but rather "a cohesive inter-connected social organism that deserved, indeed demanded the dedicated loyalty of all its constituent
parts."[32] Rather than viewing the city as a passive container overwhelmed by irreconcilable difference, urban reformers saw an opportunity to actively wield
city space to transform these arrivals into moral citizens and absorb them
into the larger urban organism. As economist and social worker Edward T.
Devine optimistically declared in 1909, the destitution of the alien poor within
urban centers was "economic, social, transitional, measurable," and, as a result,
"manageable."[33]

Although urban observers expressed divergent opinions as to whether the
concomitant conditions of urbanization and heterogeneity were a danger to the
nation or constitutive of its exceptionalism, almost all agreed that the problem of
the city, as Boston sociologist Frank Parsons wrote in 1899, was now "the problem of civilization."[34] The building type most commonly adopted as the emblem
of urbanization's ills in the late nineteenth century was not the skyscraper but
the tenement. Though we tend to think of these structures in opposition to one
another given their inverse associations with class, occupancy, and the levels of
financial and social investment they elicited, in other ways these structures were
uncanny mirrors of one another as hubs of dense urban verticality. Spending
some time unpacking the nature of Americans' fascination with the tenement—a
space associated with racial containment and, ultimately, racial differentiation—
will help to underscore the skyscraper's divergent reception as an architecture
muddling processes of racial perception and apprehension.

In the American imagination, the tenement evoked racial alterity both in
terms of whom it housed and the neighborhoods it shaped. Black migrants and
marked immigrants arriving in American cities in the nineteenth century largely
settled in dense ethnic enclaves out of necessity. Chicago's Black Belt developed
on the city's South Side, while European immigrants crowded into dwellings in
Old Town, the West Side, and pockets of the South Side. The proximity of these
enclaves served as the laboratory for early Chicago School sociologists studying

how heterogeneous contact shaped urban life and subjects.[35] New York's migrant black population first settled in the city's Tenderloin district, south of Central Park in the late nineteenth century before being pushed north to Harlem soon after. By 1900, New York's Chinatown had a Chinese population of 7,000, while the Lower East Side, which had become identified with immigrant tenements as early as the 1860s, boasted a population of 5 million by 1910. Tenements—substandard buildings specifically built or repurposed to house large numbers of poor families and often badly ventilated with little direct sunlight and few basic amenities—were hastily constructed to shelter these masses within isolated sections of the city. According to the Tenement House Commission of 1894, nearly three in five New Yorkers lived in tenements, which numbered 80,000 by 1900.[36] Although Chicago's tenement problem was less severe than New York's, it nonetheless served as a major civic issue for its residents, with one city report insisting in 1901 that the structural density in certain ethnic neighborhoods of Chicago was "three times that of the most crowded portions of Tokio, Calcutta, and other Asiatic cities."[37] To some, slums were irredeemable sites of degradation, indicating the failings of their inhabitants rather than their lack of resources or means. Journalist Allan Forman wrote in an 1888 issue of *American Magazine*, for instance, that slums were home to "a seething mass of humanity so ignorant, so vicious, so depraved that they hardly seem to belong to our species."[38]

But for reformers like Jane Addams and the more sensationalist Jacob Riis, addressing the condition of derelict tenements was an opportunity to reshape the lives and behaviors of the masses they housed. In 1890, Riis, a Danish journalist and part-time activist, transformed his traveling lantern show exposing the ills of the tenement into the image-heavy book *How the Other Half Lives*, depicting the cramped lives of these "others" in New York. On the one hand, Riis describes the tenement as a site of mixture. In an early introductory chapter titled "The Mixed Crowd," for instance, Riis recalls asking a city official how many people lived in a particularly crowded alley in New York's Fourth Ward.[39] After responding that the alley was home to 140 families, the agent goes on to parse these numbers according to what were for Riis different racial groups—"one hundred Irish, thirty-eight Italian, and two that spoke the German tongue." Riis goes on to insist that within any given slum space in the city "one may find for the asking an Italian, a German, a French, African, Spanish, Bohemian, Russian, Scandinavian, Jewish, and Chinese colony."[40] The plurality of the "queer conglomerate mass of heterogeneous elements" within slum districts, rather than their sheer numbers, serves as the major theme of Riis's chapter, if not his book.[41]

And yet, even as Riis at times depicts tenement sites of mixture, his prose and photography work to isolate its individual strands to bring into focus and, by extension, stabilize the distinct groups constituting this mixture. The very title *How the Other Half Lives* establishes the slums as a segregated space of otherness distant from its intended reader—likely a person of Anglo American extract whose immigration to the country was a comfortable generation or more behind them. The mixture the book indexes, then, is already inherently limited to racial others. But while Riis dramatizes the variety of difference constituting these "others," this difference never threatens to become unclassifiable. Riis continually manages to deconstruct this "conglomerate mass" from the inside, casually describing the innate habits and character traits of each "type" constituting it. The book is filled with adjectival descriptions of racial types intended to telegraph something about their character, from "the Italian scavenger" and "the Chinese coolie" to "the cosmopolitan Irishman," "the thrifty Bohemian," "the dull gray of the Jew" and "the defenceless Black." The book is organized around such groupings, with roughly half of its chapters named after a distinct and examinable part of the larger "mixed" crowd.

Riis's images and captions reinforce the notion that New York's other half is knowable if one zooms in closely enough to view the evidence of their distinction. The captions to his photographs convey his confidence about who his subjects are—"Greek children in Gotham court," "Jewish neighborhood," "Bohemian cigar makers at work in their tenement," "in a Chinese joint," and "boys from the Italian quarter." While the frequent images of young boys sleeping on the street escapes the literal racial categorization Riis deploys in most of his captions, he substitutes a metaphorical racial category—"street arabs"—to incorporate them into his larger system of organization. As Peter Hall writes, Riis's subjects were not examples but "specimens" to be scrutinized.[42] Even Riis's method of producing his photographs—violently charging into dark tenement houses at midnight with "half a dozen strange men," shooting off cartridges from a revolver to illuminate the scene for photographic capture—typifies his faith that with enough light and imposed will even the darkest scenes could be brought into classifiable legibility.[43] In line with broader nineteenth-century photographic practices described by Allan Sekula, Riis's photographs work to "establish and delimit the terrain of the other, to define both the generalized look—the typology—and the contingent instance of deviance and social pathology."[44]

Though the majority of Riis's images in *How the Other Half Lives* are close-ups of individuals or smaller groups, he includes a handful of street scenes meant to illustrate the slum's density. The densest of these scenes is identified as a part of New York's Mulberry Street known as "the Bend," located in the notorious Five Points neighborhood, which Riis refers to in the accompanying chapter as the "foul core of New York's slums."[45] But despite Mulberry Bend's alleged chaotic density, the photograph Riis includes of it in the book is one of surprising orderliness. The scene is framed by buildings roughly three to six stories in height, allowing a good deal of sky to appear in the background. The street itself is well defined by a line of buggies that create a boundary between the mostly empty street and the people contained to the sidewalk. The image appears to have been taken from the second floor of a building, capturing the foreground bodies closest to the camera in detail. While Riis's images of the interiors and closes of tenements more clearly lend themselves to be read in terms of dense squalor, this photograph of the Bend does not readily lend itself to being parsed in those terms.

Jacob Riis, "The Bend." From *How the Other Half Lives: Studies among the Tenements of New York* (1890).
Jacob A. (Jacob August) Riis (1849–1914) / Museum of the City of New York. 90.13.4.117.

Riis's accompanying written narration of the Bend suggests, moreover, that with the right guide and considered attention to its requisite parts, this site is not only easily mapped but can be readily known. Riis initially foregrounds the Bend's disorienting properties, referring to the district at first as "a maze of narrow, often unsuspected passage-ways" he describes as "swarming with unwholesome crowds."[46] "What a bird's-eye view of 'the Bend' would be like," Riis declares, "is a matter of bewildering conjecture." But rather than pursuing this conjectural aerial view, he instead proceeds to break down the scene into its various racial components. He notes, for instance, that while twenty years prior the Bend was primarily Irish, it has since been subject to "the in-rush of the Italian tide." Riis continues to flesh out the current racial map of the Bend by describing it as crossing "the high road to Jew town across the Bowery," where "Hebrew faces, Hebrew signs, and incessant chatter in the queer lingo that passes for Hebrew on the East Side attend the curious wanderer."[47] "But the moment he turns the corner the scene changes abruptly," as Riis marks in the next sentence, preparing his reader for another racial shift. "Before him lies spread out what might better be the market-place in some town in Southern Italy than a street in New York." "Red bandannas and yellow kerchiefs are everywhere; so is the Italian tongue, infinitely sweeter than the harsh gutturals of the Russian Jew around the corner."[48] Riis relies on race—or more precisely the evidence of racial difference he gathers from the face, dress, and tongue of those around him—to orient himself and his reader within these larger slum spaces. By depending on race as a reliable tool for ordering and navigating the slum, Riis reifies race's inherent legibility, finding it everywhere available and evident on the bodies of tenement dwellers and in the distinct atmospherics they produce. Racial mixture, indexing the unhealthful proximity of distinct types, does not devolve into racial confusion for Riis. In fact, the forced intimacy within these crammed spaces often makes these distinctions all the more visible.

Despite debates about whether tenement districts evidenced the inherent degeneracy of immigrant and migrant communities or caused it, almost all agreed with Riis that looking more closely at these places and parsing its details would produce deeper knowledge about its reality and its prospects for improvement. By contrast, urban scenes framed by the skyscraper, either in photographs or descriptions, did not so neatly give way to legibility or categorization. Whereas the tenement proves amenable to the interpersonal scale needed to observe and apprehend race, the skyscraper inaugurates a new scale of perception incommensurate with the more intimate one needed to support discrete acts of racial perception. Compare Riis's 1896 photograph of Mulberry Street in New York to

Frank M. Hallenback, Dearborn Street, Chicago, 1909.
Chicago History Museum, ICHi-04192.

a photograph of Dearborn Street in Chicago taken roughly thirteen years later in 1909. The buildings here exceed the frame, shooting up an unknowable number of stories beyond the photograph's boundary. The sky, visible only in a hazy background sliver, is the only empty space in the entire photograph. The rest of the visual field is crowded with a mixture of men, streetcars, horses, and goods. No single face is legible due to the height at which this photograph was taken, seemingly the third or fourth floor of a building similar in height to the ones captured across the street. Whereas Riis relies on distinctions between the "Hebrew face," the "Italian tongue," and the "guttural of the Russian Jew" to parse Mulberry Street as a landscape of racial details, here it is harder for perceivable signs to orient the viewer.

If Riis brought the allegedly alien space of the tenement into description by relying on the orienting function of race perceived through visible and sensory evidence, in the Chicago street scene framed by the skyscraper the evidence of race is harder to locate either on the body or through its immediate environment. Early skyscrapers, moreover, were largely built in downtown districts that, unlike the tenement districts Riis traverses, did not geographically index any permanent racial group in advance. The skyscraper choreographed the movements of a range of people who moved through and around these structures pursuing the flow of goods, jobs, and spectacle. Skyscraper districts drew a good deal of transient traffic, from clerks and bank presidents to elevator operators, janitors, and furnace workers, to the thousands of men required to dig the foundations and construct steel frames and the numerous spectators desiring to catch a glimpse of these buildings and the men who built them. Although Riis comfortably assumes of the Lower East Side that the people he views there belong to the racial "tribes" known to reside in those parts, the early skyscraper's general location within downtown business districts abutted by tenement districts made it harder for spatial context to help with the work of racial distinction. Shorn of contextual assistance, determining the race of a given body required relying on its perceptible evidence. Yet this too proved difficult given the trying sensory conditions these structures fostered by drawing more people together at its base and creating new sight lines from which to perceive them.

Riis's desire for racial categorization in the 1890s is echoed by the protagonist of Henry Blake Fuller's 1893 novel *The Cliff-Dwellers*. A recent Chicago transplant from Western Massachusetts acclimating to the Midwest city's "confused cataract of conflicting nationalities" exits a downtown skyscraper and immediately expresses his desire to more successfully use "physiognomies" to distinguish between Chicago's "swarming hordes."[49] At first he is optimistic about this prospect: "It soon came to seem possible that all these different elements might be scheduled, classified, brought into a sort of *catalogue raisonné* which should give every feature its proper place."[50] He is confident in his ability to racially read "skulls, foreheads, gaits, odors, facial angles" but also ears, eyes, hair, noses, and dialects.[51] But he quickly comes up against the limits of his reading comprehension in the dense and diverse city. While he claims to have "disposed as readily of the Germans, Irish, and Swedes as of the negroes and the Chinese," other distinctions continue to elude him at the skyscraper's base. "But how to tell the Poles from the Bohemians? How to distinguish the Sicilians from the Greeks? How to catalogue the various grades of Jews? How to tabulate the Medes, and the Elamites, and the Cappadocians and the dwellers of Mesopotamia?"[52] Unlike Riis, who assuredly guides his readers through the Bend while categorizing its "tribes," Fuller's protagonist doubts his own capacity to do the same amid the skyscraper, lacking both the skill and the sight lines needed to perceive these finer racial distinctions. Failing to categorize all that "swept and swirled around him," he ultimately retreats from the dense downtown skyscraper district to a private home in Union Park, granting him "an opportunity for meeting one or two familiar drops."[53]

Not only did the skyscraper place the prospect of observing racial distinctions in doubt, but what it meant to *feel* oneself to be raced in the wake of the skyscraper was also marked as being in flux in the late nineteenth and early twentieth centuries. White metropolitans attested to having a diminished sense of their own bodies in this architecture's shadow, intuiting Elizabeth Grosz's much later claim that the body "does not have an existence separate from the city, for they are mutually defining."[54] Though Ayn Rand most famously linked the struggle of white male selfhood to the skyscraper in her 1943 novel, *The Fountainhead*, this work was preceded by a host of others describing efforts by white male protagonists to overcome their experience of smallness at the foot of the skyscraper, eventually using these same structures to recover their sense of sovereignty. For instance, in James Oppenheimer's *The Olympian* (1913), the main protagonist arriving in New York City from Iowa is described in terms of his "growing panic" prompted by his first encounter with skyscrapers that "towered above his five-feet-nine of man," causing him to feel as if he were "stand[ing] in the deep pit of a deserted city."[55] But by the novel's end, Kirby becomes the head of a powerful steel syndicate. Once subsumed by these structures, he is described in the novel's final sentence as having become "a skyscraper himself, risen in the heavens of America."[56]

Not all such stories end in triumphal overcoming. Others end in defeat, retreat, or, as in Mary Borden's 1927 novel *Flamingo*, psychic enslavement and suicide. Skyscrapers were often shorthand for the dual forces of industrialization and urbanization that modernists yoked to fears about white ennui peaking in the 1920s. Maxwell Bodenheim's poem "North Clark Street, Chicago" (1921) describes men and women emerging "from the base of these large coffins," who walk "like briskly servile automata." "Some repentant toy-maker," he continues, "has given them a cunning pretense of life."[57] Though primitivists exoticized black culture as the antidote to fears of mechanization and automation, black writers also experimented with forms of skyscraper nihilism. Harlem Renaissance rebel Wallace Thurman's description of his narrator's sensational experience of melting into a skyscraper marks his alienation from both physical masses and black collectives demanding his absorption.[58]

Racialized sensations of diminution and even extinction were also associated with the growing numbers of white women working within skyscrapers. Representations of women who increasingly loved their skyscraper offices more than their spouses perpetuated by light romances in the 1920s reignited older concerns about race suicide tied to declining white birthrates. Feminist architectural critics in the second half of the twentieth century have retrospectively indicted the skyscraper's phallic form as a patriarchal crime. But these more recent arguments about the misogyny guiding the early skyscraper's design have obscured the overwhelming presence of white middle-class women within these structures working en masse as secretaries, saleswomen, and supervisors in the earlier part of the century and shaping their internal cultures.[59] Popular novels featuring plucky white women enamored with their skyscraper workplaces reflect anxieties from the period that these working girls, redirecting their maternal energy from the homestead to the corporation, were ceding the country's demographic future to black and immigrant women figured by these texts as instinctually content to stay home and reproduce their races.

To return to Stuart Chase's assessment of the skyscraper that opens this section, he ominously concludes of expanding urban centers that "these mile-high walls are everything," while "man is nothing." The *nothing* Chase invokes here is seemingly manifold. It marks how man now *feels* amid the hard materials surrounding him within urban centers, inducing what Chase describes as the "continually battering sense of human inferiority." But the sensation of nothingness here also marks the difficulty of perceiving one's fellow man within a city scaled to serve the masses over and above the singular subject. Figures at the turn of the century wondered whether racial categories, too, were fated for extinction given the pressures skyscrapers placed on what it meant to both see race and feel raced. The various ways the early skyscraper threatened to reveal the "nothingness" of race is the subject of this book. This is not a material history of the skyscraper, despite being deeply interested in materiality. I offer instead an account of the role the skyscraper played in shaping what Anne Cheng calls the material history of race.[60] Skyscrapers were produced at the intersection of engineering, architecture, and aesthetics and shaped by economic necessity, spatial limitations, and municipal regulations.[61] But more important to this book is the skyscraper's reception as a technology of perception and sensation, leading writers to confront race as conditionally rather than ontologically true. The early skyscraper disrupted the operation of racial perception precisely when the nation most desired to assert and extend the meaningfulness of race.

Reading Race at the Turn of the Century

A number of historical factors influenced the early skyscraper's reception as a mediator of race. Notions about what race was, where it resided, and how to read it were all in flux following Reconstruction. Not only was the line between *ethnic* and *racial* difference contested in the arenas of science, law, and culture, but so, too, did the question of how much blood was required to claim someone as one race or another remain up for grabs. The disorienting experience of racial perception in urban centers drew attention to the nation's competing racial definitions. Throughout much of the South, race had historically been a matter of ancestry. Part of Jim Crow's formal institutionalization at the turn of the century involved the passage of new legislation designed to shore up a two-tiered system of racial segregation rooted in bloodlines. The "one-drop" rule—the assertion that any degree of black ancestry classified one as black—had been the informal racial doctrine throughout much of the United States since its inception, ensuring that the children of white owners and black slaves remained property. Before 1900, however, these rules were neither universal nor legal statute.[62] With the legal institution of the one-drop rule in most Southern states, the definition of blackness in both the North and South considerably narrowed.[63] Virginia, for example, changed its definition of blackness in 1910 from a one-eighth measure—defining a person with one black grandparent as black—to one-sixteenth—legally rendering as black anyone with a great-great-grandparent of African descent. In 1930, the state dropped the pretense of fractional measurement altogether, stating that having "any Negro blood at all" qualified a person as black in the eyes of the state.[64]

And yet, to claim knowledge to a person's ancestry in such detail required the possession of either a deep hereditary archive or a shared pool of colloquial knowledge. Both proved harder to come by in the parts of the country to which people were moving in record numbers, namely, the western frontier and the industrial North.[65] While the one-drop rule was, in theory, the dominant definition of race in the United States in both the North and the South in the early twentieth century, the lack of ready ancestral information about new arrivals caused visual determinations of race to predominate in places with large numbers of migrants and immigrants. Given centuries of miscegenation under slavery, as well as new types of racial difference accumulating within the United States from abroad, the idea that one could determine race by sight was fraught even in the most stable perceptual conditions. Within perceptually complex urban environments hosting denser groups of people and higher groups of buildings, the capacity to sort nonwhites from whites—categories continually contracting and expanding—was further tested.

A series of court cases in the early twentieth century foreground the contortions of blood and skin courts deployed to maintain an exclusionary definition of whiteness.[66] Whiteness frequently appeared as an object of litigation in citizenship cases. A series of legislative acts starting in the 1870s limited naturalization to whites and those of African descent in order to restrict the numbers of people seeking American citizenship. But the definition of whiteness for immigration purposes faced continual legal contestation, with two such cases reaching the Supreme Court. Takao Ozawa, an immigrant from Japan residing in the United States for twenty years, applied for American citizenship in 1914. He argued that because his skin was lighter than most native-born "white" American citizens, he should be counted as white and thusly granted citizenship. The Supreme Court ruled against Ozawa in 1922 on the grounds that "the test afforded by the mere color of the skin of each individual is impracticable" given the "imperceptible gradations . . . even among Anglo–Saxons."[67] A few months later, the Supreme Court also ruled against Bhagat Singh Thind, a Sikh man also seeking citizenship. Singh had argued that as a high-caste Indian, he qualified as an Aryan and, therefore, a Caucasian, classifying him as white under US law. The court rejected Thind's claims first by insisting that experts were split on the status of the "Caucasic division of the human family," cherry-picking the fungible and self-serving claims of scientific racism to suit their liking.[68] But even more significantly, the court declared in a unanimous opinion that race should "be interpreted in accordance with the common man" as "a matter of familiar observation and knowledge" based on "physical group characteristics."[69] Since Thind looked South Asian in the eyes of the common man, the court's logic went, he could not be white. The judges determined that "racial difference is of such character and extent that the great body of our people instinctively recognize it."[70] Whereas courts in the South focused on regulating the boundaries of blackness using knowledge of blood and ancestry, federal courts responding to more global claims on whiteness invoked a policy of "you know it when you see it" to disqualify those who might technically fit legal definitions of whiteness, predicated on blood or appearance, but whose classification as such threatened to open the category of whiteness far wider than was politically and socially palatable.

But what the "common man" could "interpret," "observe," "know," or "recognize" by "instinct"—terms used by the Supreme Court to describe acts of racial perception and discernment—were marked by American writers as fragile operations within urban environments, where buildings grew tenfold seemingly overnight, boulevards hosted thickening masses, and sight lines were interrupted by bodies and buildings. Ozawa's and Thind's legal cases suggest the slipperiness of precise racial definitions anchored in both blood and perception within even the most neutral of hypothetical environments, let alone in expanding cities where genealogical knowledge was scarce and acts of perception required complex negotiation. By putting its faith in the capacities of the hypothetical "common man," the Supreme Court reified a normative account of racial perception without examining its changing mechanics. But concurrent representations of the skyscraper from this period highlight the major discrepancies regarding "common" sight and the identity of the "common man" within the American city.

The skyscraper, of course, was not the first architecture to disturb perceptual norms. From the Eiffel Tower to the postmodern Bonaventure Hotel, structures built both before and after the skyscraper incited their share of public consternation. French architect Charles Garnier's vitriolic assessment of the Eiffel Tower, for example, could easily pass as a complaint about the skyscraper, referring to the French landmark as a "tower of ridiculous vertiginous height" whose "barbarous mass" most resembled a "gigantic black factory chimney."[71] But what differentiates the early skyscraper from these other infamous architectures is the simultaneity of its rise to power with the sweeping changes to protocols for perceiving and stabilizing racial identity in the United States, granting the early skyscraper's specific brand of disorientation its racial stakes. Whereas Fredric Jameson observed of the thirty-six-story Bonaventure Hotel in 1984 that "this new architecture stands as something like an imperative to grow new organs to expand our sensorium and our body to some new, yet unimaginable, perhaps ultimately impossible, dimensions," writers representing the early skyscraper describe an opposing sentiment, desiring in many cases to *reduce* rather than to expand their organs and sensoria they experienced as being wrenched open against their will by growing cityscapes.[72] The collision between the rapidly changing perceptual conditions emblematized by the early skyscraper and competing legal and social efforts to stabilize racial apprehension in the late nineteenth and early twentieth centuries created the conditions that made the early skyscraper a site of racial formation and deformation.

The title of this book, *The Black Skyscraper*, indexes the distinct position that blackness holds within the American imaginary, as well as how the sign of blackness shapes other racial categorizations. While methods for distributing, tallying, and perceiving racial difference changed in the forty years this book covers, the hierarchical ordering of these differences relative to one another remained remarkably stable. Whether someone subscribed to a model of racial difference based on three distinct racial typologies or sixty-three, the presumption within the United States that blackness was the most inferior racial position governed all other distinctions. In mapping the logic various figures deployed when defining and accounting for race, what it means to be deemed a racial other remains mobile throughout this book; sometimes it means anyone surmised to fall short of the ideal of whiteness, as imagined by certain writers, and at other times it takes on more specific and narrow configurations. But these differentiations always take place in relation to the broader spectrum of racial difference overdetermined by blackness on one end and whiteness on the other, even as the means for defining and perceiving these anchoring categories shifted. In other words, the potential presence of blackness persistently haunted concerns about the inability to perceive racial difference of all varieties.[73]

If one of the most pressing question about blackness as a racial category at the turn of the century was how best to measure it, discussions of whiteness were framed by whiteness's seeming elasticity—marking both its pliability at moments and also its durability.[74] Ozawa's and Thind's legal assertions of their right to whiteness were two of the dozens of cases brought to the courts in the late nineteenth and early twentieth centuries by defendants looking to claim whiteness as a means of obtaining citizenship. But the right to whiteness was just as fiercely waged within the social field. Scholars of white racial formation have traced how Jews, Catholics, and Irish, Italian, and Eastern European immigrants both sought out and were conscripted into whiteness, eventually broadening this category, if fitfully so, during the early twentieth century from a more narrow conception of Anglo American ancestry.[75] "The contest over whiteness—its definition, its internal hierarchies, its proper boundaries, and its rightful claimants," as Matthew Frye Jacobson summarizes, "has been a fairly untidy affair."[76] Contributing to this untidiness was the dual status some European immigrants held as "both *white* and racially distinct from other whites" that Jacobson and others have described—a problem I insist was exacerbated by the perceptual conditions in urban centers where many of these recent immigrants resided.[77]

This book builds from historical scholarship on white racial formation to insist that the paradoxes, dualities, and expansions specific to whiteness in this period not only were matters of social reorganization involving labor and migration, as scholars have importantly foregrounded, but were also shaped by the expanding physical landscape in urban centers remaking the conditions for its apprehension. Racial categorizations rely on processes of recognition historically rooted in feeling, genealogy, and visual perception that have allowed whiteness to be conferred upon some and figured as needing defense from the encroachments—spatial, sexual, social—of others. Writers perceived the early skyscraper to complicate the differentiation of white subjects, but it also catalyzed writers to imagine new procedures for detecting race in the case of its continued visual negation. The skyscraper did not, after all, ultimately herald the end of race, as the writers featured in the following pages varyingly welcomed and feared. And yet, as I argue in the epilogue, the constellation of its effects on urban space and perception impacted later revisions to the definition of whiteness, its alleged detection, and its geographical embedment into the midcentury.

In pursuing the question of what it meant to see whiteness in turn-of-the-century cities, I am indebted to scholars of visual culture, such as Richard Dyer and Martin Berger, as well as theorists of critical whiteness studies, including Ruth Frankenberg, Mike Hill, and others, who have emphasized whiteness's particularly paradoxical visuality—what Richard Dyer has termed whiteness's capacity to be both "everything and nothing," marking how whiteness organizes the aesthetic and social field while remaining discursively unmarked. But this project also follows from more recent work by Sara Ahmed, Eva Cherniavsky, Hamilton Carroll, and Robyn Wiegman, putting pressure on whiteness's presumed invisibility as the universal position against which all others are delineated, by attending to what Carroll describes as the "extraordinary labor" required to sustain this unmarkedness.[78] "Whiteness is only invisible," as Sara Ahmed further notes, "for those who inhabit it," foregrounding its hypervisibility to those denied its privileges. "Seeing whiteness," she continues, "is about living its effects, as effects that allow white bodies to extend into spaces that have already taken their shape, spaces in which black bodies stand out, stand apart."[79] I add to Ahmed's formulation that space not only is the setting where whiteness's effects are realized, but shapes the material life and effects of whiteness.[80] The early skyscraper was a symptom—and occasionally a facilitator—of the mass migrations and industrial modernizations in the late nineteenth and early twentieth centuries that reshaped white racial formation in this period. But descriptions of the early skyscraper paint this architecture as an instrument of racial *deformation* threatening whiteness's visibility and recognition. By placing pressure on both the presumed visibility of corporeal whiteness and the capacity for subjects to "feel" white amid buildings rendering everything at their feet as identical matter, skyscrapers emerge as one of the factors causing whiteness to bend—if not break—around the turn of the century.

Racial Perception as Process

The desire for race has resulted in the construction of Rube Goldberg–like systems composed of various apparatuses, criteria, and techniques designed to ensure its detection.[81] Though certain measures of race fall in and out of use over time depending on their perceived efficacy, all leave their mark on the process of racial perception. We tend to talk about racial perception as a singular and instantaneous act, but it is better understood as a complex series of procedures involving judgment, reading, rationalization, and conjecture that normally go undescribed. I use the term *racial perception* to index the varying combinations of techniques, processes, structures, and convictions that allow a subject to believe they are having an experience of race. To follow Nicole Fleetwood, "seeing race is not a transparent act; it is itself a doing."[82] Though there is never one way to perceive race, certain practices prove more or less prevalent in certain historical periods, social systems, and material environments. To point out the constructed and relative nature of racial perception is not to diminish its power or its effects. It is, rather, to mark this "doing's" capacity for adaption and transformation in order to consistently deliver race despite race's immateriality.[83]

Since race is *produced* through its perception rather than merely *apprehended* in the course of this act, the stakes for codifying the procedures for its verification have historically been quite high. Further complicating our ability to map these processes is that fact that many of them manage to operate in excess of empiricism. There is little difference between an intuitive reading of race and an evidential one. Practices of racial perception are designed to locate race regardless of whether it exists. And because racial perception is rarely taught in any explicit fashion but is acquired through socialization and habit—functioning as an ideology rather than a skill—its operations tend to be concealed even from subjects themselves. For these reasons, processes of racial perception tend to become most visible in their breach. This book claims the emergence of the early skyscraper as such a violation, tracking how this architecture instigated explicit reckonings with these processes that tend to remain invisible. The chapters that follow most persistently address epistemologies of racial perception that have produced race, approaching race as a matter of phenomenology rather than ontology.

Racial perception is also always a process of racial differentiation. That is, that part of the work of racial perception is to seek and assemble racial evidence residing on and near the body in order to produce a judgment about what race or combination of races a given person represents. The emergence of ethnicity as a category in the twentieth century, embraced by social scientists such as Franz Boas and Robert Park as a way of marking socially and environmentally determined identities in opposition to the biological notion of race, was the outgrowth not only of political and scientific discourses and changing immigration patterns but also of new material conditions.[84] As cities grew in size, complexity, and scale, it was increasingly hard to maintain faith in the kind of hyperdifferential racial perception Jacob Riis demonstrated in the 1890s. The adoption of ethnicity laid the groundwork for what were once racially indeterminate Europeans to be absorbed into whiteness, their "finer" distinctions no longer needing urgent apprehension.[85]

In insisting on the conditionality of racial perception, I am indebted to work by Martin Jay, Jonathan Crary, and David Michael Levin historicizing perception in relation to philosophy, technology, and art history.[86] Robyn Wiegman in *American Anatomies* situates the importance of this work to the study of race in particular, insisting that "examining the history, function, and structure of visibility" made it possible to treat the creation of raced bodies as part of a historical process.[87] Scholarship mapping the racial genealogies of the senses, as well as a large body of work in performance studies that considers the multiple frequencies on which bodies perceive and are themselves perceived, have linked the development of Western Enlightenment theories of aesthetics and perception to the emergence of racial hierarchies, while also recovering alternative modes of perception operating beyond normative bounds of sense and sensation.[88]

Beyond attending to the perceptual practices and material conditions that make race apprehensible in various places and periods, we also must attend to the environments in which these perceptual and material practices develop and, potentially, degenerate. To tell this story, I rely on an understanding of perception that, following Jonathan Crary, is "definable in terms of more than the single-sense modality of sight, in terms also of hearing and touch and, more importantly, of irreducibly mixed modalities."[89] Like Crary, I use perception to refer to a wide range of strategies and systems for sensing, feeling, and knowing phenomena that are both external to the self and also constitutive of it. That said, visual understandings of race have historically played an outsized role in its definition and perception, and this remains true for many of the materials in this book.[90] We encounter figures throughout *The Black Skyscraper*, however, who work to detect race through other means when the skyscraper interferes with the apprehension of the visual racial detail. In light of the proliferating descriptions at the turn of the century of bodies seen from the tops of skyscrapers as dots, specks, and ants, we find subjects attempting to sense, to feel, or to intuit themselves into racial knowing when bodies fail to divulge their alleged evidence.

When considering the development of racial perception at the turn of the century, photography has often been the go-to medium for understanding its operations. "Photography has not only been deployed in the pursuit of scientific truths about race," as Coco Fusco argues, but "it has played an absolutely fundamental role in the construction of racialized viewing as a positive, pleasurable, and desirable experience."[91] Part of the pleasurable nature of the photographic encounter with race has historically derived from the observer's faith in photography's capacity to shore up the operations of racial perception. By freezing the body in time and space, photographs have the power to offer it up for inspection and, by extension, detection.[92] But the discursive history of American architecture proves no less entwined with race. From nineteenth-century architectural theory attempting to separate "primitive" buildings from enlightened ones to the use of architecture as a force of colonization, the history of architecture is multiply marked by race. In addition to being *shaped* by race, architecture, like photography, is also a medium that has helped to shape race's observation and perception. This book considers the skyscraper's function as the perceptual frame for urban life at various scales and levels in order to better describe architecture's contributions to the perceptual life of race. Whereas photography can freeze the scene of racial perception, enabling viewers to linger on its perceived operability, skyscraper architecture framed kinetic scenes of movement that threatened to overwhelm its observers.[93] If the urban viewer was imagined in the nineteenth century as "increasingly active, vigilant, discriminating," as Joseph Entin writes, this upswing in visual intelligence was countered by the sense that "urban space was increasingly opaque," a sense frequently attached to the skyscraper as a sign of its perceptual indeterminacy.[94] We might understand the early skyscraper's effect on perception in the terms Nicholas Mirzoeff ascribes to certain contemporary photographic practices—as threatening to make the indexicality of race incoherent.[95] The early skyscraper impelled a discussion about race's endurance and, even, its necessity, in light of the environmental pressures placed on its signification within modernizing cities.

Race in Three Dimensions

The skyscraper has received much scholarly attention in the century and a half since its invention. A recent search for "skyscrapers" in the Library of Congress catalog resulted in 391 listings for books situating this architecture in relationship to capitalism, gender, engineering, construction, economics, façade design, the fine arts, and cinema.[96] Of this wide-ranging scholarship, this book draws most extensively from efforts to understand this structure "less as an individual product than a social one," as architectural historian Daniel Bluestone endeavors.[97] In pursuing such a project, this book most heavily engages works such as Robert Bruegmann's account of the architectural firm Holabird and Roche, Katherine Solomonson's scholarship on the Chicago Tribune Building, Carol Willis's history of early skyscrapers as "vernaculars of capital" shaped by financing mechanisms and real estate cycles, Joanna Merwood-Salisbury's reading of early Chicago skyscrapers as reflective of the city's social and cultural turmoil, Roberta Moudry's edited volume foregrounding the skyscraper's cultural history, and Gail Fenske's study of the Woolworth Building.[98] These scholars do not approach skyscrapers as the creation of a single architect, patron, or school but trace the nexus of conditions and forces helping to forge this architecture, including finance, design ideologies, building regulations and land use laws, labor organization, consumer culture, print media, and, most significantly for my study, new patterns of urban movement that these structures both responded to and shaped. These works variously echo Gail Fenske's insistence that "architectural issues cannot be separated from urban issues—especially when the subject is the skyscraper," a claim orienting this study as well.[99]

Of these accounts, works by Gail Fenske, Katherine Solomonson and Joanna Merwood-Salisbury most insistently situate the skyscraper's emergence in New York and in Chicago in relation to these cities' distinctive heterogeneity, understanding this architecture as being fashioned in various ways by the density of difference defining the American city at the turn of the century. Whereas these scholars focus primarily on architecture's production, noting how the diverse demographics of urban centers shaped debates about what architecture's mission should be in relation to these mixed-up masses, my focus is more persistently on the experience and reception of skyscrapers seen to mediate the experience and reception of race.

If we zoom out from the skyscraper to consider the fields of architectural history and criticism, scholars in these fields have been relatively slow to think about race as it shapes either architecture's production or reception. If, as Juhani Pallasmaa writes, "understanding architectural scale implies the unconscious measuring of an object or a building with one's body, and projecting one's bodily scheme on the space in question," the bodily scheme that architecture has most insistently, and unselfconsciously, reified has been white.[100] Like most professional fields in the United States emerging in the late nineteenth century, architecture was and still remains primarily the domain of white practitioners.[101] While architecture's race problem still permeates the histories told by the field, this situation is starting to change because of the efforts of historians such as Dianne Harris, Mabel Wilson, Charles Davis, Irene Cheng, and Dell Upton, the contributors to edited volumes by Craig Barton and Lesley Naa Norle Lokko, and literary critics William Gleason and Anne Cheng closing the gap between history, critical race studies, and architecture.[102] To date, much of the scholarship on architecture and race has focused on recovering race's influence on architecture's design and imagined functionality, and this work remains vital given the neglect historically accorded to race within the field. When looking at writing from the industries and professions most responsible for the skyscraper's materialization—as I do in parts of this book's first two chapters—the role of race in its physical emergence is a fact hidden in plain sight, pervading period accounts of steel mills, architectural design practices, and skyscraper construction. These findings affirm William Gleason's central claim in *Sites Unseen: Architecture, Race, and American Literature*: "The built environment is always shaped in some way by race whether such shaping is explicitly acknowledged or understood."[103] The early parts of *The Black Skyscraper* buttress and build on his argument, linking vernacular literary genres to architectural examples of vernacular design as racialized aesthetic forms in the late nineteenth and early twentieth centuries.

The more persistent intervention I make in the chapters that follow inverts Gleason's argument. While his book explores the built environment's racial marks, I most pressingly insist that *race is always shaped in some way by the built environment*. I focus on the historical specificity of racialized responses to the early skyscraper, but I also intend this argument to suggest the broader ways that race and racial perception are shaped by their environmental context in any number of historical periods and locations. While the humanities has gone through a "spatial turn," embracing an analysis of space as a way to understand the production of the social, scholars have been slower to explore the ways that, as Dianne Harris writes, "space is equally significant in the construction of ideas about race and identity."[104] The racial disorientation the skyscraper invoked at the turn of the century had far-reaching consequences for the course of both American cities and race, setting the stage for a slew of reactionary spatial strategies to resolidify racial knowing. As I argue in the epilogue, the skyscraper was a key precursor to the midcentury emergence of mass suburbanization, redlining, and urban renewal, actions designed to preserve the category of whiteness in the aftermath of its destabilization in the earlier part of the century. To tell this longer story of "white flight" requires understanding the earlier perceptual conditions that first sent white metropolitans looking for exit ramps.

We can further generalize this claim about the built environment's importance to racial perception to places and periods beyond the United States and the turn of the century. Understanding practices of racial perception in any time or place necessitates considering the built environment shaping its conditions and operations. The texts explored in this book, when taken together, produce an understanding of racial perception as a three-dimensional process, framing race as a matter of volume, something that exists in, and can be altered by, space. As built environments change, so do the measures of race, a fact that should encourage us to think about race in more site-specific terms—decentering national and regional contexts in order to attend to the more immediate types of spatial landscapes that condition racial experience. The Parisian street on which Frantz Fanon famously walked when hailed as a Negro by a white child, for instance, highlights the site specificity of racial perception. The white gaze may be inescapable, as Fanon ultimately concludes upon moving through various colonial landscapes, but its mechanisms necessarily change across environments that variously call into question the process of perceiving as a stable or a reliable act. Contrast Fanon's sense of overexposure situated within the relatively level heights of a European street, for example, with Ralph Ellison's invisible protagonist from roughly the same historical moment, who experiences race not just in light of different regional attitudes but also in their attendant built environments. Though seeing for both of these writers transcends a perceptual act to shape an existential understanding of blackness, the built environment matters to both of these experiential modes, carving out the possibilities for both looking and feeling like a subject.

W. E. B. Du Bois's writings about the built environment provide a useful case study in the multidimensional nature of racial perception. W. J. T. Mitchell uses Du Bois's famous theory of the metaphysical veil separating the Negro from the wider white world to claim race as "a *medium*, an intervening substance, to take the most literal definition. Race, in other words, is something we *see through*, like a frame, a window, a screen, or a lens, rather than something we *look at*."[105] Mitchell situates race's conditionality not in the exterior world harboring racial traces but within internal mechanisms of racial interpretation that accrue and move with us through the worlds we inhabit. But in claiming race as a medium, Mitchell potentially diminishes the importance of race's site specificity, not only to Du Bois's theory of the veil but also to his broader oeuvre exploring the interdependencies between the built environment and processes of racial perception and feeling. We find Du Bois insisting on the multidimensionality of acts of racial perception throughout his 1901 *The Souls of Black Folk*, a book that could be described as an account of post-Reconstruction racial perception. While his famous declaration that "the problem of the Twentieth Century is the problem of the color-line" suggests a two-dimensional model of race premised on a single permeable boundary, Du Bois's metaphor of the veil approaches racial perception as a process unfolding in three dimensions.[106] His well-known definition of double consciousness as "this sense of always looking at one's self through the eyes of others, of measuring one's soul by the tape of a world that looks on in amused contempt and pity" relies on not only visual processes, as Shawn Michelle Smith has argued, but also spatial features of scale and vantage point that condition these acts of seeing and measurement within a multi-dimensional setting.[107] Race may be a medium, but it is experienced within discrete spatial environments that affect the kinds of racial measuring, both perceptual and affective, that can be sustained within them.

The skyscraper's disorienting scale, unsettling many nineteenth-century habits of perception, would come to appeal to Du Bois later in his career in light of the entrenched landscapes and, by extension, the entrenched forms of racial relations he experienced in the South. In the Black Belt chapters of *Souls*, he approaches the built environment as shaping not just the specific scene of double consciousness but of racial looking more broadly. Du Bois catalogs the "remnants," "half-ruins," "scarred land," "rotten" buildings, "fallen" bricks, and "phantom gates and falling homes," defining his progression through this world.[108] Whereas Henry James converses with buildings in *The American Scene*, Du Bois compulsively enumerates them a few years later, leveraging their quantities and conditions to narrate the story of race and exploitation in ways its inhabitants cannot. He insists that there can be little hope for the emergence of a new subject of any color amid the material and perceptual conditions designed for enslavement.

If the southern landscape helped produce the conditions of double consciousness, granting the veil part of its materiality and racial perception its constitutive volume, Du Bois turns to the skyscraper to imagine other forms of consciousness and social measurement. In two of his short stories, which I examine in detail in chapter 4, the skyscraper provides him with a tool for disturbing the operations of the veil by changing the scale and scope of perception. Du Bois embraces the skyscraper's disorienting height as it unsettles the alleged civic horizontality that modernizing cities claimed democratized spatial access. He ultimately throws his lot in with the eruptive verticality of the skyscraper as a potential antidote to the exclusionary realm of the horizontal. The skyscraper disorients—and potentially reorients—those around it. Du Bois uses this architecture's capacity to unfix subjects from legible racial regimes to speculate about the spatial conditions that might facilitate race's eventual dismantlement.

The Skyscraper's Archive

This book considers a range of mostly print materials representing the skyscraper in its earliest era. From labor histories of steelworkers, office managerial manuals, and architecture journal articles on the skyscraper's form, function, and design, as well as "low-brow" fictional works of pulp, romance, science fiction, and children's literature and the work of better known realist and modernist writers, such as Henry James, William Dean Howells, Nella Larsen, and F. Scott Fitzgerald, the many genres in which the early skyscraper appeared differently mark its racial effects. To recount the racial story of the skyscraper is, in fact, to recount several stories rooted in the many renderings of its material and symbolic life, from mimetic depictions to openly fantastical ones.

In following the many manifestations of the racialized skyscraper as a physical object, perceptual obstacle, and affective catalyst, I variously invoke modes of social history, cultural studies, visual studies, and literary criticism. The book's opening chapters tilt toward social history in order to document the skyscraper's material indebtedness to racialized processes of labor and design, an important part of the skyscraper's racial history it remains imperative to recount. The later chapters more persistently move within a register of literary and cultural history to consider how the skyscraper's effects on racial perception and apprehension altered the shape of various narrative forms. While my primary intervention across this book is to illustrate the ways the built environment affects the perceptual and affective life of race, most of my chapters also trace the consequences of race's perceptual fragility in the wake of the skyscraper for the genres and aesthetic forms representing these conditions. Each of the chapters foregrounds, to a different degree, the specific tools writers and artists used within a particular genre to either stabilize race as a viable category or further press upon its limits. The skyscraper disturbed realists such as William Dean Howells and Henry James for reasons beyond its size; they found in its obfuscation of race a potential end to narrative forms revolving around social and spatial intimacy. In contrast, writers Nella Larsen and W. E. B. Du Bois, respectively, embraced modernism and speculative fiction as more suitable forms for representing these structures.

Though I read a range of materials, narrative serves a special function in the book as a particularly generative tool for apprehending racial perception's complexities. In prose, we encounter figures attempting to narrate the experience of perceiving and feeling in the city as a story that could be circulated on mass scales, describing conventions for how acts of racial perception might now work—even when they fail to work—in built environments of vacillating scales, fragmented sight lines, and disparate vantage points. This is not to say that racial perception always operates narratively, linearly, or rationally, but that it is in narrative where we find attempts to make these processes seem so. Just as the skyscraper called the reliability of perceived racial symptoms into question, it also raised concerns about the durability of narrative as a genre historically anchored by observable individual subjects depicted in close detail. Many of the writers I focus on link the survival of racial distinction—a categorization imagined to be vital to the very rendering of a subject—to the survival of narrative itself.

A word about the selection of literature included here. This project was originally fueled by an aesthetic question about why prose from the late nineteenth and early twentieth centuries was relatively disinterested in the skyscraper in comparison to its abundant representation in photography, film, painting, and even poetry. Plumbing this architecture's narrative life beyond the canons of American realism and modernism—which involved recovering and analyzing its more frequent presence in less-familiar works of pulp literature, children's stories, and romance novels—made it clear that its unique representational challenges across media and genres were entangled with concerns about what it meant to see and experience race in dense urban centers. In the years spent searching digital databases, archives, and library stacks, I discovered more literature engaging the early skyscraper before 1931 than I could include here—but not an overwhelming amount more. What I've included here does not represent all the literature about the skyscraper; but I do consider the selections I focus on here to be largely representative of the questions and concerns this architecture raised for certain artists, genres, and movements.

This book begins by foregrounding the ways race shaped the skyscraper's material and aesthetic histories. Chapter 2, "Architecture and the Visual Fate of Whiteness," charts the defensive strategies white metropolitan writers developed to imagine how whiteness might continue to endure within America's increasingly dense, diverse, and scaled-out cities. While fears about the insolvency of the white race in this period have typically been linked to evolutionary and biological discourses of eugenics and race science, the skyscraper narratives featured in this chapter foreground the material and perceptual circumstances that also conditioned the white metropolitan's experience of racial vanishing. Bringing together two seemingly disparate genres from the turn of the century—weird tales and realist narratives—this chapter considers their shared apprehensions about the waning visual specificity of whiteness amid denser cities and multiplying sight lines associated with the growing number of skyscrapers in the United States. The chapter opens by looking at two pulp stories from the 1910s that fantastically transport the skyscraper to sites resembling the recently closed American frontier. Resituating the skyscraper within these "natural" border spaces, harboring little density and clearer sight lines, allows the authors of these weird tales to imagine how the skyscraper might support acts of racial perception and distinction favorable to whiteness's preservation rather than its deterioration. The second half of this chapter focuses on a series of late writings by realists William Dean Howells and Henry James suggesting that they harbored similar anxieties about the continued visual endurance of whiteness in the wake of the skyscraper. While Howells articulates in one of his *Harper's* editorials his concerns that the skyscraper facilitated racial mixture, marking how this architecture potentially diluted the visual crispness of the discrete "American" type, James proves more concerned, in works such as *The American Scene* and the short story "The Jolly Corner," with the possibility of race's negation within the growing scales of the American city. The skyscraper stands accused in James's texts of denying the restless analyst access to the ambiguities of the racial detail I argue was vital to his conception of narrative.

Chapter 3, "Miscegenated Skyscrapers and Passing Metropolitans," considers how skyscrapers could both be described as miscegenated and be perceived as agents of miscegenation. The chapter begins by tracing the curious history of the usage of the term *miscegenation*—a word invented in the 1866s to define interracial sex—within nineteenth-century architectural discourses about the skyscraper. I chart the various ways architects used theories of miscegenation first circulated in the United States in the sphere of scientific racism to make aesthetic arguments for certain skyscraper designs over others. Whereas architects in the late nineteenth century accused certain skyscrapers of being miscegenated, by the early twentieth century, America's obsession with racial passing—increasingly understood as an urban phenomenon—led to this same architecture being marked as a catalyst of miscegenation. Considering a range of meditations on passing, the chapter concludes with a reading of Nella Larsen's *Passing* (1929) and its interest in skyscrapers as sites of racial deception. Detailing the effect dense cities were having on the ability to read the race of others, Larsen's fiction ultimately insists we attend to passing as more than an embodied individual performance, highlighting the material and spatial conditions that also undergird this act. The skyscraper ultimately emerges in this chapter as a dually "mongrel" architecture—a structure both shaped by discourses of miscegenation and perceived as miscegenation's agent.

Whereas realists and fantasists alike found the forms of perception unleashed by the skyscraper racially threatening, chapter 4, "The Black Skyscraper," explores how writers W. E. B. Du Bois, Wallace Thurman, and Rudolph Fisher and painter Aaron Douglas embraced the skyscraper's disruptive facets to critique

platitudes of a horizontally oriented civic culture that claimed, but failed, to offer universal access to all. These black modernists unravel the racially homo-
genized popular history of the skyscraper by fashioning new origin stories, utopian
visions, and messianic calls for American democracy through architecture.
Chapter 5, "Feeling White in the Darkening City," explores the difficulties expressed by white metropolitan writers working in the 1920s and 1930s of
maintaining an affective sense of one's whiteness in the shadow of the skyscraper. In three Jazz Age narratives invoking New York's cold glamour—Mary
Borden's *Flamingo*, F. Scott Fitzgerald's *The Great Gatsby*, and Le Corbusier's
When the Cathedrals Were White—whiteness appears to be "on the run," as the
skyscraper makes feeling white, a sensation commonly treated in these works
as synonymous with an experience of bodily sovereignty, increasingly hard to
attain. White metropolitans are rendered in these novels as modernity's new
slaves, emotionally and corporeally constricted in comparison to joyously primitive blacks, depicted as affectively immune to the forms of physical and psychic
diminishment linked to skyscrapers. The second half of this chapter turns to
popular "working girl" novels written by women in the 1920s and 1930s that
repurpose female affect as particularly well suited for corporate skyscraper offices as sites of both work and modern love. These novels illustrate the skyscraper's
role as site and symbol for reorganizing workplace rhetoric around attributes of
white womanhood as the lingua franca of what Eva Illouz has called "emotional
capitalism." I show how these novels relied on black female laborers to serve as
countermodels of an inefficient feeling, enabling white women to distinguish
their own brand of efficient emotionalism as a corporate asset in ways that were
interwoven with the look and feel of the skyscraper. The book concludes with a
brief epilogue that links the early skyscraper's disorienting effect on racial categories to efforts to reconsolidate whiteness through mass suburbanization in
the middle of the twentieth century. I insist here that the skyscraper's failure
to make room for whiteness in the city ultimately helped to steer white metropolitans at midcentury toward built environments such as the suburbs that
proved more accommodating.

Mirroring the skyscraper's disruption of stable perception, this book moves
around its subject and maps the multiple ways racial perception moved in,
around, on top, and beside the skyscraper. To return to the Carl Sandburg poem
serving as the epigraph to this book, *The Black Skyscraper* locates itself at various points between the "skyscraper's forehead" and the "fifty thousand hats"
arrayed below, dwelling in the complicated interstice where the question of who
or what to address from the skyscraper directs the poem first as a question and

then as an unanswered demand. I gather these attempts to ask and to answer the question of "where do you belong?" in the face of the simultaneous "swarming" and "stopping" that the skyscraper frames, dismantles, and frames again from greater and greater heights. In the wide-ranging responses to being afoot and atop the skyscraper, we encounter both the difficulty and the creativity with which questions of perceiving and knowing were explored. Emulating the many modes of seeing, measuring, and interpreting incited by the skyscraper, I approach its archive from multiple vantages and scales, forsaking a totalizing view of the monolith in favor of the fragmented and partial views of race it framed for a generation of Americans newly learning how to see and sense within the modernizing city.

CHAPTER TWO

Architecture and the Visual Fate of Whiteness

To study race, as scholar Matthew Frye Jacobson insists, requires attending to both its conception and perception—analyzing not just how race has been historically constructed but how these constructions have been made to appear as natural facts. "The awesome power of race as an ideology," Jacobson writes, "resides precisely in its ability to pass as a feature of the natural landscape."[1] When one set of racial features are proven unstable—threatening to disclose race's fictionality—racial conceptions mutate to fit another set. But landscapes— which I take to designate physical worlds of varying types—are more than scenes onto which racial concepts are projected. Landscapes also help to determine which concepts of race become viable in certain contexts and less so in others. Attending to race's historical perception, then, means not only attending to how bodies perceive race and are perceived as raced but also considering the physical conditions that make racial perception possible.

This chapter recovers representations of the early skyscraper as one of the physical conditions imperiling racial perception, particularly in relation to whiteness. While scholars of white racial formation, including Jacobson, David Roediger, and others, have studied the economic and ideological conditions that led to the expansion of whiteness at the turn of the twentieth century to more firmly encompass groups including Jews, Italians, and the Irish, this chapter focuses on perceptual concerns about whiteness's potential disintegration should its alleged features prove harder to recognize in expanding urban centers.[2]

Concerns about whiteness's visual endurance, however, were not fully reducible to fears of racial difference. Take, for instance, the touting of New York's Central Park as "the people's park," serving the many rather than the few. In a paper delivered in 1870 to the American Social Science Association, the park's designer, Frederick Law Olmsted, outlined the kinds of diverse sociality he believed his park facilitated. As one of the foremost boosters of what has since been called Victorian urbanism, Olmsted believed a city could be engineered to improve its citizenry. He and his planning peers insisted that the careful ordering of green spaces could serve as a counterbalance to the more unseemly aspects of crowded urban living, exposing residents to both natural beauty and aspirational examples of social comportment. In his lecture, Olmsted described his parks as incubators of "gregarious recreation," his term for the polite pleasantries exchanged in public between congregations of diverse subjects.[3] In describing this contact, he declares his New York parks, including Central Park, to be

> the only places in those associated cities where, in this eighteen hundred and seventieth year after Christ, you will find a body of Christians coming together, and with an evident glee in the prospect of coming together, all classes largely represented, with a common purpose, not at all intellectual; competitive with none, disposing to jealousy and spiritual and intellectual pride toward none, each individual adding by his mere presence to the pleasure of all others, all helping to the greater happiness of each. You may thus often see vast numbers of persons brought closely together, poor and rich, young and old, Jew and Gentile. I have seen a hundred thousand thus congregated, and I assure you that though there have been not a few that seemed a little dazed, as if they did not quite understand it, and were, perhaps, a little ashamed of it, I have looked studiously but vainly among them for a single face completely unsympathetic with the prevailing expression of good nature and light-heartedness.[4]

Central Park's diversity was a relatively recent development at the time of Olmsted's speech. Rising wages and the invention of the eight-hour workday had only recently allowed more working-class families of various backgrounds to make regular use of the park, perhaps explaining the intensity of Olmsted's attention in this lecture to the variety of people enjoying it.

But even as he boasts of the diversity of the park's visitors, Olmsted still manages to differentiate between these users. Even with a "hundred thousand" people congregated there, he nonetheless claims to have "looked studiously . . . among them for a single face" untouched by the gathering's good vibe. In the wide expanses within Olmsted's manicured parks, bodies, buildings, and the natural landscape appear comfortably spaced within its ample acreage where no visual impediments unsteadied his analytical gaze. He reports that in Central Park, "you may thus often see vast numbers of persons brought closely together, poor and rich, young and old, Jew and Gentile," marking the closeness of the contact between these groups, while simultaneously indexing the stability of

"Outdoor Life and Sport in Central Park, N.Y.," Stereograph, 1870.
The Miriam and Ira D. Wallach Division of Art, Prints and Photographs: Photography Collection,
The New York Public Library.

the separation between these bodies, reaffirming the sanctity of their visibly distinct identities. Central Park welcomes all, but it is the park's capacity to bring people together while maintaining their discernible differences that makes it ultimately worthy of praise. In the passage that follows, Olmsted celebrates the good it does other men to "come together in this way in pure air and under the light of heaven," but Olmsted himself seems to derive pleasure from Central Park's open spaces and single faces.

As Central Park's users continued to diversify into the early twentieth century, observers remained fascinated by the park as a site of concentrated difference.[5] Henry James in 1905 famously described the pleasure the park's "polyglot" constituency brought him on a busy Sunday. Echoing Olmsted's account of the park thirty years prior, James's enjoyment of the park derives in part from his capacity to view the multitude while still isolating and identifying the individual. The park functions less as a melting pot amalgamating differences and more as a container prettily framing the distinctions between New Yorkers.

But a new danger to the park emerged during the early twentieth century that threatened to spoil its picturesque framing. A larger number of taller buildings began to loom over the southern border of this sacred civic space. Olmsted's son and namesake, also a landscape architect, referred to the growing skyline flanking the park as inherently ugly, restless, and distressing, noting that the park's "visible frame has become hopelessly un-rural and insistently architectural."[6] If

Central Park—declared by the senior Olmsted to be a "democratic development of the highest significance"—embodied what he and many others believed to be the ideal configuration of public space, the skyscraper threatened to overwhelm not only Central Park but also public space more broadly across the city, heralding the degeneration of the urbanist's dream of a managed metropolitan future.[7]

While Central Park was being praised as a polyglot paradise in 1905, retaining the perceptual clarity Olmsted Sr. valorized in 1870, it was proving harder for observers to describe exactly what or whom they were seeing at the base of the skyscrapers rising just south of the park. Take, for instance, Henry Adams's frenzied representation of New York's skyline from a downtown location in 1907. "The outline of the city," Adams explains, "had become frantic in its efforts to explain something that defied meaning."[8] In throwing "great masses of stone and steam against the sky," Adams continues, the city took on "the air and movement of hysteria, and the citizens were crying, in every accent of anger and alarm, that the new forces must at any cost be brought under control."[9] Alan Trachtenberg reads Adams's reaction as primarily figurative, finding the skyscraper to be a structure that for Adams "typified the entire process of change."[10] But even as it enacts the allegorical, Adams's description of the skyline foregrounds the real problems of sensation within and around skyscrapers. The only observable bodies emerging from the agentless mayhem of Adams's scene are "the citizens" swept up into the stone buildings that ultimately subjugate them. He depicts these two sets of "masses," flesh and stone, as similarly mindless, flailing, and out of hand—helpless to the perpetual motion denying each a discernible form. In contrast to some of Central Park's steady sight lines that permit Olmsted and James to frame a portrait of the masses that does not jeopardize perception of the individual, Henry Adams conjures a city madly gesticulating yet still "defy[ing] meaning," a messy collision of organic and inorganic forms failing to add up to a precise sign.

We find a more extreme set of descriptions of how bodies appear—or fail to appear—when framed by the skyscraper in a 1905 O. Henry story, "Psyche and the Skyscraper."[11] The story centers on a philosopher's efforts to woo a simple but good-hearted candy store clerk named Daisy. The philosopher, whose longing for abstraction corresponds with his disconcerting lack of empathy for others, convinces Daisy to accompany him to the top of a nearby skyscraper to take in the view—a relatively novel experience for most Americans in this era before commercial flight and observation decks. Immediately startled and disoriented by the vista, Daisy tremblingly asks the philosopher to identify the "black dots" she spies moving below. He refers to them as "bipeds," insisting that this is what men become "even at the small elevation of 340 feet," causing them to appear as "mere crawling insects going to and fro at random," "irresponsible black water bugs" that "crawl and circle and hustle about idiotically without aim," and "little black specks dodging bigger black specks in streets no wider than your thumb." "From this high view," the philosopher insists, "the city itself becomes degraded to an unintelligible mass of distorted buildings and impossible perspectives," obliterating "all the minutiae of life." Daisy, the story's humanist hero, adamantly counters that what they are seeing are not bugs but "folks" and that "it's awful to be up so high that folks look like fleas." She ultimately flees the skyscraper to seek comfort in the arms of her "cozy" street-level beau.

While race is not the direct focus of the spatial meditations of Olmsted, Adams, or Henry—though Olmsted's reference to Jews and Gentiles marked forms of religious and racial difference in the period we will encounter again later in the chapter—these writers variously dramatize the complications surrounding the act of seeing and classifying bodies within changing urban built environments. Perceiving corporeal details—the visual evidence typically used to support a racial classification—in the midst of these "frantic" forms of architecture was challenging enough. But the capacity to make such assertions was further complicated by the mounting number of immigrants and migrants arriving in the city whose differences were variously imagined in the late nineteenth century to be more racial than ethnic in nature. By 1910, more than three-fourths of New York's population were either immigrants or had a foreign-born parent; and by 1930, more than two million African Americans had migrated from the rural South to northern cities. In light of these demographic changes, we find concerns about perceiving bodies in the wake of the early skyscraper increasingly entangled with concerns about identifying race.[12] White metropolitans—a term I use to refer to those who understood their white racial identity through a narrower conception of Anglo or Nordic American ancestry—were increasingly prone to imagining themselves, in the words of novelist Faith Baldwin in 1928, as the "sprinkling . . . pinch of salt" atop the city's belly "crammed with black men and yellow men and coffee coloured men, with Africans and Chinamen and Slaves and Swedes and Armenians and Germans and Jews."[13] Such an analogy, whose operation depends on a scaled-out vantage point similar to those made available by the skyscraper, points to the spatial and scalar dimensions shaping the white metropolitan's fear of "utter submerge[nce]," as protagonist Tom Buchanan phrased his fears of racial extinction in 1925's *The Great Gatsby*.

Concerns about the visual vanishing of the white metropolitan's distinction within the urban American scene echoed eugenicist theories such as those repeated by the fictional Buchanan as well as real white metropolitans in the early twentieth century who claimed cities to be increasingly inhospitable places for white subjects. These complaints were commonly articulated in visual and spatial terms. Eugenicist Madison Grant wrote in 1916's *The Passing of the Great Race*, for instance, that the "man of the old stock" was "being literally driven off the streets of New York City by the swarms of Polish Jews."[14] His colleague Lothrop Stoddard more precisely dated the beginning of the white urban population's decline in 1920's *The Rising Tide of Color against White World-Supremacy* to "the close of the nineteenth century" when the nation began to be "invaded by hordes" of immigrants. Since then, Stoddard writes, "the Nordic native American has been crowded out with amazing rapidity by these swarming, prolific aliens, and after two short generations he has in many of our urban areas become almost extinct."[15] America may have taken up "the white man's burden" to bring order to the world through colonization as Rudyard Kipling famously wrote on the eve of the twentieth century, but these white metropolitans suggest twenty years later that existence of the white race may increasingly *depend on* sparser peripheral territories granting whiteness firmer visual ground, rather than being *obligated* to the alleged improvement of these frontiers.

The "crowding out" of urban whiteness bemoaned by Stoddard and Grant was as much a spatial and perceptual matter as a demographic and reproductive one. The early skyscraper, identified by urban critics of the time as the primary agent of crowding and congestion in American cities, was one of the factors leading some white metropolitan writers to tentatively conclude that to be *urban* increasingly meant being *racially other*, marking white urban identity as potentially untenable moving forward.[16] The typical story of white insolvency during this period foregrounds eugenicists like Stoddard and Grant, emphasizing their concerns about waning white bloodlines. Accounts of "melting-pot modernism" tracing the connections between American literary aesthetics and the concurrent turbulence surrounding immigration and migration during the first decades of the twentieth century have similarly tended to approach the built environment as the static background framing the dynamic scene of urban difference.[17]

But early skyscraper narratives allow us to see the *material circumstances* conditioning the white metropolitan's experience of his own vanishing, under-

standing this disappearance in perceptual terms fostered by the built environment rather than merely evolutionary or social in nature. Understanding the
dilemma of white metropolitan identity at the turn of the century requires at-
taining a greater sense of what it newly meant to appear within the early skyscraper's mise-en-scène. Given the rapid pace of Eastern European immigration
and black migration to northern industrial cities, coupled with the growing
density of bodies on the streets of these cities and the multiplying vantage
points for viewing these bodies furnished by the increasing verticality of these
environments, what was to become of the white metropolitan if she was no longer sure that her whiteness was self-evidently displayed on her body and legible
to others? And how was she to scour the bodies of others for markers of racial
identification given that, as one 1911 article about passing insisted, the "bleach-
ing process" of miscegenation caused one to constantly wonder "when is a Caucasian not a Caucasian," while the varieties of racial difference ("black men and
yellow men and coffee coloured men, with Africans and Chinamen and Slaves
and Swedes and Armenians and Germans and Jews") took the form of a lengthy
list tentatively held together by a stream of conjunctions?[18] Anxious answers to
these questions emerged from two literary genres that typically reside at opposite ends of the narrative spectrum: (1) the fantastic exploits of weird fiction—a
label encompassing works of fantasy, the supernatural, and horror by writers
mostly forgotten to us today—and (2) more canonical works of American realism
devoted to genuinely drawn characters. Even though realists such as William
Dean Howells and Henry James dabbled in supernatural storytelling, their most
fantastic works differ markedly from the more plot-driven works of popular fantasy writers publishing primarily in pulps. But despite their generic differences,
the realists and weird writers featured in this chapter are bound by a shared
fascination with the skyscraper and its effects on processes of racial perception
and the visual endurance of the white metropolitan subject. Though they reached
different conclusions about the magnitude of the threat the skyscraper posed to
white particularity, the writers I consider here all explored the question of what
was to become of whiteness in the skyscraper's shadow.

   I begin with two fantastic tales from the turn of the century that variously
whisk the skyscraper away to iterations of the frontier. The geographic anchor of
the American imaginary for much of the nation's history, the frontier was strategically reimagined in two weird tales—George Allan England's "The Last
New Yorkers" from 1912 and Murray Leinster's "The Runaway Skyscraper" from
1919—as a spatial counterbalance of sorts to the skyscraper's effects on acts of
racial perception. Both stories stage how perceivable racial evidence as well as

forms of white affiliation feared to be increasingly unsustainable in the city might be preserved in the skyscraper's midst. Despite their similar conceits, these tales ultimately diverge in their conclusions about the visibility of race and its centrality to the white metropolitan's endurance. Whereas England doubles down on the necessity of the visible racial trace, dramatizing moments of its perception, Leinster suggests how racial categories continue to survive in excess of an immediate encounter with visibly raced bodies.

The second half of this chapter focuses on works by two pivotal realists—William Dean Howells and Henry James—and the different relationships each theorized between skyscraper architecture and the visible white subject. The immense skyscraper posed a direct challenge to the intimate scales, both spatial and narrative, on which realism historically operated. Howells and James each drew connections between the dwindling spatial and narrative intimacies they associated with the skyscraper and a waning intimacy with race. I first turn to a little-known editorial by Howells from 1909 linking critiques of the "unsubordinated" skyscraper to an investment in white supremacy. Howells makes this connection only to then distance himself from it and, possibly, his own earlier disparagements of the skyscraper in light of these potent racial stakes. Whereas Henry James shared Howells's general discomfort with the skyscraper, his concern about the structure followed a different racial logic. In both his 1904 travelogue, *The American Scene*, and his 1908 ghost story, "The Jolly Corner," James appears less bothered by the possibility that acts of racial differentiation were being hampered by the skyscraper—at times, he even welcomes this prospect as a point of narrative intrigue. This architecture troubles James not because it prevents racial categorization but, rather, because it impedes his access to race's stimulating ambiguities. Across these two late works, James imagines the scale of race to be continually entangled with the scale of realist narration, each of which the skyscraper threatened with obsolescence.

Lewis Mumford, architectural critic and one of the most vocal decriers of the skyscraper during its earliest era, made the case in 1924 that due to its neck-craning height and the mediocrity of its street-level design, "for the millions who fill the pavements and shuttle back and forth in tubes, the skyscraper as a tall cloudward building does not exist."[19] In the weird and realist stories featured in this chapter foregrounding the question of the white metropolitan's visual endurance, Mumford's claim is flipped and asked anew—how might the "millions" newly appear and disappear amid the towering skyscraper and the expanding city? Fearing it was they and not the skyscraper that might no longer soon exist, these white metropolitan writers found the early skyscraper arbitrating the terms of their survival.

The Frontier Skyscraper

At the same time that the skyscraper was becoming synonymous with the chaotic masses, it was also being figured as an oasis away from them. In a 1901 issue of *Century Magazine,* journalist Cleveland Moffett theorized the rising popularity of "mid-air dining clubs":

> What a wonderful thing it is truly to be able thus by a word and without effort to fly away from the fume and worry of jostling crowds, from the noise and smell of the streets, up, up, over roofs and domes and steeples into the silent skies, where the ledge of your window actually scrapes the sky, as they say! Look! Here comes a man out into Broadway through a door in one of the great stone hives. It is past noon. The man is weary with the strife and strain. Where shall he go for a brief respite and the strengthening of his body? A few years back it must have been to some clattering, bustling restaurant level with the roaring pavement, where there was not respite at all, but crowds always, noise always. Now he walks a few blocks, turns in at another door, and takes an express elevator for the fifteenth, the eighteenth, the twentieth floor, and in ten seconds is as much out of New York as if he had made an hour's journey into the country. The din dies away. He is far above dust and clanging cars. He can breathe pure air. And, sinking back in the arms of a hospitable leather chair, he looks down over the city as a tired traveler might look down from a mountain crag.[20]

If for Henry Adams the skyscraper posed a question that the city was helpless to answer, Moffett marks the ways select citizens could shirk this question by slipping inside of the city's eye for some relief. Described elsewhere in the article as "refuge-places" and "retreats," midair dining clubs are depicted as protecting their members from the street's glaring light, burning cobblestones, noisy "hoofs and wheels," and jammed cars carrying "women and men of all kinds of colors." Moffett figures the clubs as not only providing bodily relief but also seamlessly facilitating "sociability," the antidote to the chaotic *sociality* wearing down both the body and the mind at street level.

Most of Moffett's article stresses the strategic use of such clubs by businessmen and, increasingly, businesswomen looking to make contacts and hash out deals. He provides several anecdotes of young people advancing their careers by using their lunch hour to make connections. The article's accompanying images,

Otto H. Bacher's engravings for "Mid-Air Dining Clubs," *Century Magazine*, 1901.

however, tell something of a different story. Rather than foregrounding the enterprising "sociability" of the club's users, the eight etchings by Otto H. Bacher
that accompany Moffett's article depict the city's landscape engrossing either a
solitary person or, sometimes, no one at all. The etchings vacate the scene of
profitable sociability for more meditative scenes of repose. They share little in
common with the "grand-style urban photography" Peter Hales identifies as the

triumphal mode of architectural urban photography at the time, featuring sky-scrapers isolated from their contexts to emphasize their monumentality.[21] Unlike those photographs or even the soft and more impressionistic urban ren-derings of the Ashcan school of painting, Bacher's etchings focus on the expan-sive immenseness of the surrounding city scenery while excising its street-level inhabitants.

Despite their modern subject matter, Bacher's images of what Moffett de-scribes as diners "looking down over the city as a tired traveler might look down from a mountain crag" strongly favor mid-nineteenth-century examples of American landscape painting popular with wealthy New Yorkers fifty years prior. From their expansive vistas to the ornate window frame surrounding the dining club patron's view, these etchings evoke behemoth landscapes like those of Frederic Edwin Church, whose famed *Heart of the Andes* was dis-played in New York in 1859 within a thickly embellished frame surrounded by heavy drapes. Bacher's sketches of skyscraper windows framing views like those seen from "a mountain crag," as Moffet describes, offer viewers the pleasures of the immense with the promise of containment characteristic of these earlier frontier works. In placing Bacher's etchings in conversation with landscape painting, it is tempting to naturalize the urban skyline by compar-ing its large features to outsized organic structures, such as mountains, crags, and canyons. In fact, historian Angela Blake has recovered the concerted ef-forts of turn-of-the-century New Yorkers to do just this, as they encouraged comparisons between city skylines and frontier vistas in order to fold New York into a broader narrative emphasizing the nation's cohesive landscape en-compassing its natural and built spaces. City boosters touting the skyline as the latest extension of American natural beauty hoped to displace New York City's image as a land of immigrants in the eyes of middle-class Americans newly engaging in native tourism. "By naturalizing the skyscrapers—icons of New York's and America's modernity," Blake argues, "the city was thus turned into an acceptable national metropolis for a people hungry for nationalist symbols but not ready yet to see themselves represented by New York's urban skyline."[22]

But the frontier offered white metropolitans more than just an analogy use-ful for pastoralizing urban immensity. It also seemed to offer useful visual strategies for preserving whiteness's visual impact in crowded American cities. We find some of these strategies at work in Bacher's 1901 etchings. He situates his white metropolitan gazers in the immediate foreground where they appear as towering figures calmly and quietly consuming the cityscape laid flat below

Stereograph of Frederic Church's painting *The Heart of the Andes* flanked by portraits of American presidents in the fine art gallery at the Metropolitan Fair in New York, 1864. Library of Congress Prints and Photographs Division, The Robin G. Stanford Collection, LC-DIG-stereo-1s04584.

and beyond them much like their meals. Gone is Henry Adams's frantic skyline of "anger and alarm" in which no singularities, even Adams's own, can emerge as distinct. Bacher depicts the white metropolitan as firmly rooted within the city rather than on the verge of being dissolved into it. While the body of the viewer is implied in a mid-nineteenth-century landscape like *The Heart of the Andes*— ornately framed to present spectatorship as an interactive event—Bacher concretizes the viewer's presence by etching him or her as a witness to, yet still removed from, the urban tableau. His white metropolitans are granted a heft within the dining club not ensured to them at street level given its "fume and worry." Bacher depicts his gazers so they maintain their claim on both whiteness and metropolitan modernity, preserving their legibility as white *and* urban subjects.

Bacher's etchings primarily operate under the guise of visual realism. But we find surprisingly similar strategies for scripting acts of seeing and appearing in works of science fiction and adventure that also figure the frontier and the skyscraper as correlated perceptual fields. These tales appearing in both pulp magazines and in more mainstream periodicals were read not just by New Yorkers who had direct experience with skyscrapers but also by readers from across the country, whose primary education in how to see these structures took place in print. These stories fall under the large umbrella category of weird fiction, a descriptor for a range of speculative writing in the early twentieth century.[23] The fantastic conditions at play within these tales—featuring sky-scrapers that get transported either forward or backward in time to wildernesses populated by nonwhite natives—defamiliarize this architecture in ways that raise questions about how it conditioned racial perception in the present.[24]

These fantastic tales about skyscrapers emerged in the long wake of the western frontier's closure in the 1890s. These spaces continued to be associated with a mythos of white conquest well into the twentieth century—an attitude popularized by Theodore Roosevelt and Frederick Turner's frontier histories in the late nineteenth century and further elaborated by scores of histories and cultural studies ever since. But the weird frontier skyscraper stories featured in this chapter pose complex and, at times, hesitant responses regarding the frontier's continued usefulness to conceptions of modern metropolitan whiteness. Nick Yablon, the only other critic to consider the two stories featured here, situates them within a rubric of urban ruins, arguing that New Yorkers grappled with the skyline's impermanence by continually imagining its destruction.[25] But rather than reading these stories as managing fears about the built environment's cycles of construction and destruction, I find their material concerns about vanishing buildings to be enmeshed with the white metropolitan's under-standing of his or her own visual vanishing within the urban scene. This section focuses on two examples of frontier skyscraper fiction in which tall buildings are vanished to isolating settings akin to or explicitly named as the frontier—George Allan England's 1912 tale "The Last New Yorkers" and Murray Leinster's 1919 story "The Runaway Skyscraper." Despite sharing a similar conceit of time-traveling skyscrapers, these writers reached different conclusions about the continued viability of whiteness in chaotic built environments mediating its legibility.

"The Last New Yorkers" and the Frontier Preservation of Racial Sight

George Allan England's pulp tale "The Last New Yorkers" first appeared in a 1912 issue of the Frank Munsey pulp *The Cavalier and the Scrapbook*. It was subsequently reprinted in *The New York Daily Mail* and eventually became part of the 1914 novel *Darkness and Dawn*, which incorporated the tale along with two reader-demanded sequels.[26] *New Yorker* writer A. J. Liebling attested in the 1960s to the youthful mania with which he first devoured England's story whose popularity alongside that of the *Tarzan* stories helped make Munsey the leading pulp publisher in prewar New York.[27] Liebling, like almost everyone who has since engaged with England's work, expressed uneasiness with the story's racism. Featuring protagonists driven westward by a devolved black horde to found a white socialist utopia, "The Last New Yorkers" showcases its author's dual commitments to social utopianism and white supremacy. But fantasy structures more than the tale's time-traveling conceits or devolved populations—it also props up mechanisms of racial identification that are simplified by the skyscraper's removal to the frontier. In contrast to the unruly urban skyscraper of his present, England's frontier skyscraper of the future provides a physical shelter for his white protagonists while sustaining the possibility of racial identification in even the most trying conditions.

England's tale opens with engineer Allan and his secretary, Beatrice, awakening from a thousand-year slumber on the forty-eighth floor of the Metropolitan Life Building, a real skyscraper that was one of the largest in the world at the time. The roused duo work out that the building's height has insulated them from an airborne disease that has wiped out the rest of the city. As the lone human survivors of this deadly plague, Allan and Beatrice go to war with the half-Negroid, half-bestial "horde" they encounter in the city's ruins. Later in the trilogy, the pair eventually escapes to the West and discovers the albino tribe of "Merucaans," whom they help civilize, thusly repopulating the nation with its rightful white citizenry to birth a new cooperative society.

But before making it out West, the two must first come to terms with the ruins of New York. Similar to Bacher's etchings, the story begins with its white metropolitans perched high up inside of a skyscraper. Upon surveying the overgrown world surrounding them, Beatrice describes feeling "like Macauly's lone

Image from the "The Last New Yorkers," printed in the March 4, 1912, edition of the *New York Evening Mail*. The caption reads, "No Familiar Hem of the Metropolis Now Rose."

watcher of the world-wreck on London Bridge."[28] This time, however, instead of the altern subject that New Zealander Thomas Macauly imagined in the 1840s to be the final witness to London's ruin, it is the white metropolitan who is left standing as the ultimate foreigner bearing witness to the lost metropolis. From their raised vantage point, the pair surveys the extent to which the world has "gone to ruin" around them, with most of the city now covered with "forests growing thick." To the south, they spy the once-towering structures of "the Park Row, the Singer, the Woolworth, and all the rest," which have since decomposed to mere hollowed-out "steel cages." Beatrice and Allan, rendered as "two castaways on their island in the sea of uttermost desolation," detail their shock at the city's changed material and perceptual conditions. As the lone inhabitable skyscraper still standing, the Metropolitan Tower functions as a version of the Alamo, granting its white survivors a defensive perch against encroaching others lying in wait.

The pair's heightened vista proves critical to their survival, granting them a view of the devolved black horde that soon crests over the horizon and into focus over the course of several pages. I focus on this relatively inconspicuous scene of racial perception in a story filled with more visceral moments of drama, first, to draw attention to the immense imaginative labor required to support the scene's deceivingly simple sequence of events. As fantastic as the prospect of a thousand-year nap or the emergence of a devolved black species may seem, equally fantastic is the level of racial detail its heroes read from the horde given the scene's severe perceptual challenges. But as noteworthy here is the remarkable duration of this scene and the protracted attention England dedicates to detailing a successful practice of racial perception. I read the story's extended interest in this passage as being symptomatic of concerns that perceiving and knowing race from the body was becoming increasingly difficult to do. England depicts racial perception as a process that unfolds over time and in space; the work of deliberate attention rather than an effortless and instantaneous moment of recognition. If the story produces a fantasy of how racial perception might continue to operate within the city no matter the environmental conditions, the amount of time the story spends describing characters attempting to produce an account of race by way of visual evidence may be the story's least fantastical moment, capturing how acts of racial perception required self-conscious effort in cities expanding both vertically and demographically both in the present and in the future.

This extended scene of racial perception, taking up roughly three pages of England's tale, begins with the pair's initial tentativeness about their observations of the horde. "Why, they look black!" one of them notes at first, with the other confirming, "Black—yes, blue-black! They seem so, anyhow." Their hesitancy seems appropriate—not only is the pair five stories above the city, looking down over the now overgrown street level below, but it is nighttime, and the scene is illuminated solely by the horde's torches. The pair's observations soon grow more certain, however, as the horde draws closer. Despite the dense foliage, their heightened vantage point, and the lack of light, Beatrice and Allan gather enough visual evidence to soundly pronounce that "no white thing showed any-where." "All was dark and vague," the narrator notes, as "indistinctly, waveringly as in a vision, dusky heads could be made out."[29]

But even as the pair perceive the blackening details of the group's constitu-ents, the congregation of bodies simultaneously appears to them as a singular blob "without order or coherence"—"a shifting, murmuring, formless, seem-ingly planless congeries of dull brutality." The horde's dark formlessness, un-doubtedly a racist commentary on its mindless animalism, could also be read as a symptom of Beatrice and Allan's removed vantage point from within the sky-scraper. Instead of casting doubt on their racial assessments, however, their vantage point seems to offer the pair an aggregate portrait of the horde, allow-ing them to classify more precisely its generalized hereditary defects. But indi-vidualized racial details of horde members become visible once more in this passage, allowing the pair to theorize their historical origins. Discerning "a naked arm, greasily shining" here and an "outthrust leg, small and crooked, apelike and repulsive" there, Allan diagnoses the horde as being constituted of "malformed human members." He ultimately uses this data to assess that the horde originated from the physical devolution of Haitians unmoored in the ab-sence of white rule, resulting in this hybrid species that is part "Negroid," "sim-ian," and "Mongol." Thus, the skyscraper, rather than making racial perception more difficult, actually facilitates its crystallization, providing these white met-ropolitans with the perfect ratio of aggregated mass portrait to singular details enabling them to not just see this new racial species in the present but to chart its past evolutions.

One of the skyscraper's ostensible functions in "The Last New Yorkers" is to provide its white protagonists with not only physical shelter but a perch from which to establish their visual distinction from the encroaching horde. The sky-scraper grants them a panoptic site above the city from which race can easily and accurately be perceived from the body and even the group. The dark and distant conditions that encompass this scene are conveniently negated over as the overgrown frontier becomes a site of transparency in which the minutest racial detail can be seen and diagnosed. The white protagonists secure the racial identity of the horde with as little as a glimpse of a "dusky" head or a leg. Even gesture is removed from the interpretive equation, as limbs manifest race through sheer materiality alone. The act of perceiving bodies immediately gives way to racial knowledge in the story, allowing Beatrice and Allan to quickly resolve to confront these dark others. The skyscraper's frontier removal simplifies the act of racial seeing, magically enabling the surrounding perceptual conditions to favor those of the pastoral Central Park or midcentury landscape painting over the frantic unformed outline of downtown accused of distorting and displacing the visible and thusly classifiable racial detail. With these conditions in place, England can treat the skyscraper as a racial resource for the white metropolitan rather than as an instrument facilitating his or her growing racial indiscernibility.

But undercutting the simplification of this act of racial perception is the amount of time and space this scene of racial identification takes up in the story. We could understand the slow reveal of the horde's identity through measured glimpses and group observations as reflecting England's belief that racial mixture produces jarring collages, enabling Allan to eventually trace the horde's visual details back to their disparate and discrete racial origins. But this scene also attests to something far simpler—that perceiving and interpreting the racial detail requires time and attention, even in this fantasy world where race can be accurately assessed at the forest floor at night from the vantage point of a skyscraper. Reading bodies in the actual New York City of 1912 where the vantage points were higher, the crowds denser and moving in different directions and containing not a singular horde but a multitude of racial types, seems far trickier in comparison. "The Last New Yorkers" provides its readership a fantastical refuge in which he or she can imagine acts of racial perception operating smoothly in the presence of skyscrapers; but it also belies a curiosity about racial perception as a process impacted by the vertical city.

"The Runaway Skyscraper"

"The Last New Yorkers" was a direct precedent for Murray Leinster's 1919 weird tale "The Runaway Skyscraper," published five years later.[30] Detailing the survival quest of 2,000 white-collar workers occupying the Metropolitan Life Building upon being plunged through the fourth dimension and into precolonial Manhattan, "The Runaway Skyscraper" not only is set in the same skyscraper as its narrative precursor but also transports the structure to the frontier before concluding with its own version of white socialist utopia. But Leinster's story diverges from "The Last New Yorkers" by refusing to fetishize the scene of racial perception, demonstrating instead how whiteness might survive its perceptual derailment through forms of bureaucratic and legal maintenance that endure when other forms of classification may not. Leinster counters the skyscraper's deleterious effects on racial discernment by establishing modes of racial identification that do not rely on the visibility of the physiognomic body.

In contrast to Beatrice and Allan's abrupt awakening in the future, "The Runaway Skyscraper" begins in the present during a seemingly normal workday. The "ordinary course of business" for these white-collar office workers is typified as a general state of "absorption," a term twice used negatively in the story's first few pages. Upon hearing a large crash, the first sign of their impending danger, the office workers do not proactively leap into action or even appear all that startled. They instead "went back to their ledgers and typewriters," too engrossed in their work to note their peril.[31] The story establishes absorption as a plague of modern living through the habits of its protagonists Arthur Chamberlain, a "young and budding engineer" on the brink of financial insolvency, and his secretary, Estelle Woodward. Each suffers from episodes of absorption negatively affecting their work and personal lives. Chamberlain, "fond of pleasant company, and not too fond of economizing," can no longer make the payments on his rented office.[32] Miss Woodward, "too finicky, too fastidious," cannot find a man she likes enough to marry. "She could not understand their absorption in boxing and baseball," the story explains, finding herself "bored" in the face of male sentimentality. Miss Woodward can't even hear Chamberlain's confession of financial troubles because "she was so much absorbed in her own thoughts that she rarely noticed anything he said or did when they were not in the line of her duties."[33] Ennui colors the enterprises of modern work and love, hampering the capitalistic and reproductive capacities of these white metropolitans, which, for race scientists in the 1920s like Stoddard and Grant, portended the slippery slope to race suicide.

Once the hands of the Metropolitan Tower's signature clock revolve backward to transport it and its occupants back in time to precolonial Manhattan, Chamberlain and Woodward shake off their ennui and jump into action. The pair showcase their preparedness for self-reliance as Woodward uses her country training to teach the men to catch birds, while Chamberlain's engineering skills prove perpetually useful. And, yet, the story treats the overzealous embrace of their adventure as it does all states of emotional excess—with suspicion. Rather than embracing frontier exertion as the solution to urban absorption, the story cautions against this orientation. Chamberlain chides hearty bank president Van Deventer, a Theodore Roosevelt stand-in down to his Dutch surname, for the joy he confesses to taking in their predicament, admitting to "enjoying myself hugely" and twice referring to their dilemma as "fun."[34] Chamberlain wearily chastises him by responding, "I'm glad you're enjoying yourself! I'm not." By painting frontier escapism as potentially misanthropic rather than as a heroic or sustainable option, the story deflates the Rooseveltian ethos of aristocratic westward retreat in its search for a solution to the ennui afflicting white metropolitans.

Chamberlain, Woodward, and Van Deventer are all described by the story as being privileged in their capacity to "view the episode as an adventure" because each lacks a family financially dependent on their income.[35] The other 2,000 occupants, by contrast, are continually wracked with worry about their families' abilities to financially weather their sustained absence. The biggest challenge faced by the group is not starvation, weather, or even the natives—ultimately rendered as benign figures who trade food for light bulbs; rather, it is the brewing mass panic of the occupants themselves that most endangers them. The story is conflicted about the nature of their concern. On the one hand, the workers' apprehension for their kin marks their admirable social embeddedness; on the other, it suggests the white metropolitan's pitiful degeneration from rugged survivalist to hapless worrier financially enslaved to his desk. Leinster treats his anxious white metropolitans with a modicum of empathy, but he also shows how their localized familial absorption prevents other types of collectivities from emerging. "You've a family," as Arthur scolds one occupant, "and so have a great many of the others in the tower, but your family and everybody's family has got to wait."[36]

Chamberlain becomes hip to the nature of his peers' panic almost immediately, privately warning Estelle that "we're in no great danger from Indians or from anything else that I know of—except one thing." Faced with the "thronged" crowd, placing him at "the center of a sea of white faces, every one contorted with fear and anxiety," Chamberlain publicly names this fear as starvation. But what presumably goes unsaid in this bait-and-switch is the more threatening danger of mass hysteria, explicitly colored as white, which Chamberlain finds unfavorable to mention in fear of further stoking the crowd's emotional ire. The biggest threat to whiteness is now whiteness itself, suffering not from a lack of visual difference but rather the inability of white subjects to healthfully scale their own attention. From its opening focus on the self-destructive ennui of modern life to the "soft-bodied" panic overwhelming the survival instincts of these "white faces," the story blames capitalist individualism—marked as the specific product of white civilization—for the decline of the same markedly white citizenry. The skyscraper becomes both whiteness's best shelter and also its greatest foe, perpetuating the harmful effects plaguing its occupants. The story's central drama hinges on whether the occupants have the mental stability to rise above their insularly absorptive states.

It is tempting to read the occupants' panic in terms of Rooseveltian proclamations about "the strenuous life" as the cure for flagging white bodies and minds. "Pitifully few" of the skyscraper occupants have any usable skills beyond keeping "a garden in my yard," "grow[ing] peaches in New Jersey," and "raising chickens as a hobby." In their haplessness, the office workers epitomize Theodore Roosevelt's 1897 fear that "a certain softness of fibre in civilized nations, which, if it were to prove progressive, might mean the development of a cultured and refined people quite unable to hold its own in those conflicts through which alone any great race can ultimately march to victory."[37] And yet the story refuses this conclusion, ultimately suggesting a form of managed collectivism rather than spatial retreat or race wars as the solution to the white metropolitan's ennui. The story explicitly avoids Rooseveltian tropes of racial conquest like those found in "The Last New Yorker" by having Chamberlain learn to peacefully manage the native population with the very states of absorption that once dominated his own life. Intellectual conquest displaces physical conquest through the heroic figure of the engineer admired for his brains rather than his brawn. As Arthur proclaims to his stranded comrades, "I'm an engineer. What nature can do, we can imitate. Nature let us into this hole. We'll climb out."[38] Nature no longer remains the healthful other to metropolitan life but a limit for metropolitan vitalism to overcome. The prowess of the white managerial class, cast as the new imperializing agent, defines a healthful form of attention within this modern frontier.

For the first half of the story, the skyscraper primarily features as a symbol of the white metropolitan's narrowed attention, preventing workers from imagining forms of belonging outside of work and home. But this structure soon comes to frame the solution to these limiting habits of attention. As the platform from which to see outward and an object that draws the gaze within the story, the frontier skyscraper proves central to reconfiguring the absorptive modern gaze. This narrative and visual turn begins when Leinster spatially scales out to frame the scope of the occupants' loss not in terms of their individual families but their larger white facial family. "They were alone in a whole continent of savage," without "a single community of people they could greet as brothers." "Few of them," Leinster writes, considered the "terrifying" prospect that there was "no other group of English-speaking people in the world," as "even Rome" was but a dream in Romulus's eye. "No matter where they might go over the whole face of the globe, they would always be aliens and strangers," alone in a "barbarous world."[39] The workers lack the scalar capacity to register the loss of this global white diaspora. But the skyscraper, soon to be recovered as an apparatus for an outward-looking collectivist vision rather than an inward-facing corporate one, helps readjust their vision.

The spirits of the skyscraper occupants finally pick up in the story's final section as Chamberlain senses "strange stirring of emotions" and "queer currents of panic" in his fellow men "strengthened by an increasing knowledge of the need to work." This knowledge soon gives way into a full-fledged operation. The story jumps ahead two weeks after the "now familiar wild landscape" has undergone a radical transformation. We witness the fruits of this change from Estelle's perspective, perched high in the skyscraper looking out onto this new vista of cooperation. In place of the overgrown landscape of two weeks prior, we now spy "a cleared trail" to the waterfront with logs extending "hundreds of feet" into the river. These rafts, lined with busy fishermen of both genders, sit south of the smoking "huge mound of earth," where charcoal is being mined. In exchange for corporate detritus like light bulbs, picture wires, and metal paperknives, the natives provide the occupants with food. Assuming the position of the absorbed that the workers once held, the laboring natives leave the white metropolitans free to work for themselves and each other.

Leinster uses the skyscraper to frame this new scene of production run by the newly focused white metropolitans. This vision of collectivity appears in the middle ground of Estelle's skyscraper view, distant enough to allow us to see all the different operations needed to sustain the group but bringing us close enough for us to understand their enterprise as a collective endeavor. It also happens to be close enough to preserve the perception of racial difference. The story distinguishes between the "number of Indians in the clearing" and "the whites" for whom they now "industriously work." The skyscraper's earlier vistas of immense and alienating urbanity or overgrown uncivilized wilderness has been domesticated into a scalable landscape enabling a vision of collectivity that can still sustain visible racial difference, allowing the narrator to distinguish between those who belong to the collectivity and those made to work for it. Like England's tale preceding it, the frontier skyscraper is once again used to preserve the act of racial perception as one of absolute differentiation.

But just as quickly as the story stages the frontier as the solution to the affective and absorptive problems besetting the white metropolitan, it renounces this solution for an equally successful, if less fantastic, strategy for retaining white particularity. In the course of a few short paragraphs, Chamberlain discovers the wormhole into which they fell and returns the entire group to the present where only a few seconds have passed. Though the white metropolitans remain generally undifferentiated in the frontier as a "sea of white faces," upon their return to the city one of these occupants turns out not to have been as white as their face had first suggested. The idea that the occupants' communal orientation might survive their urban return is quickly dashed by the actions of "a certain Isidore Eckstein, a dealer in jewelry novelties." Having used their predicament to trade a pair of Indians "two pearl necklaces, sixteen finger-rings, and one dollar" for the deed to Manhattan—a nod to the popular myth that the Dutch bought Manhattan from the Lenape Indians in the mid-1600s for twenty-four dollars' worth of trinkets—Eckstein files suit to claim ownership of the island. Angling to be deemed "the sole owner of real-estate on Manhattan Island, with all occupiers of buildings and territory paying him ground rent at a rate he will fix himself," the story ends with Eckstein's claim unresolved with the courts "deliberating the question with a great deal of perplexity."

Eckstein's difference from his fellow white metropolitans at the story's conclusion is established not in the form of his physiognomic body—his features go visually unmarked in Manhattan of both the present and past—but through his assignment by the text of Jewish surname and a stereotypical act of avarice, details contained in the court documents he files. Eckstein might visually pass as an organic member of the "sea of white" occupants within the collective vista of the frontier skyscraper, but his lawsuit brings his "true" racial identity to light when his body fails to do so. The story's investment in denoting Eckstein as Jewish through his surname and his avaricious actions, as opposed to rooting his racial identity in the shape and form of his body, establishes a critical difference between its concluding racial methodologies and those anchoring "The Last New Yorkers." While England renders the horde's visual materialization concomitant with its racial materialization, Leinster pivots away from the perceivable body in these final paragraphs as the paramount site of racial knowledge. Legal performances and written genealogical accounts of race prove just as effective in identifying racial others. Eckstein's "legal" body is more efficient than even his corporeal body, or what Frantz Fanon might call his "epidermalized" body, in establishing his racial difference. Just as Chamberlain was able to manage racial difference in the frontier, coordinating the newfound collectivism of the white metropolitans and their new native "employees," Eckstein too becomes managed and contained, but this time by legal and cultural systems.

His Jewish last name and his act of greed become consolidated into a racial sign circulating in excess of visual proof of his Jewishness rooted in, say, the shape of his nose. Even as the story devotes a disproportionate three of its four concluding paragraphs to Eckstein's real estate saga, this episode can be treated with the lightheartedness of a joke rather than as a grave impediment to the white metropolitan since Eckstein has been framed in extravisual terms, making his race detectable and thusly manageable. A system of racial classification more akin to the one-drop rule becomes newly feasible within New York when it is imagined to be an effect of the broader bureaucratization of urban operations. In this scenario, the material conditions of the congested, visually fractured, and scaled-out city fail to do any long-term damage to processes of racialization circulating in excess of perceptibly raced bodies.

Eckstein's unsavoriness is further tempered by the story's final paragraph ensuring the ability of "legitimate" white metropolitans to achieve a more healthful distribution of attention. If local absorption is their biggest threat at the story's start, preventing grander visions of romance and ambition from emerging, Estelle and Arthur's union at the story's conclusion finds the couple enacting an optimized ratio of attention akin to the scene of collectivity framed by the frontier skyscraper. The story ends with a description of Arthur as "extremely busy" with "two very important matters," the first being the "the reinforcement of the foundations of the building," while the second involves caring for "his new wife Estelle." These closing lines feature Arthur maintaining a broader outward-looking intellectual drive benefiting others along with a more inward-looking gaze ensuring their domestic and reproductive happiness. In comparison to Eckstein who wants to use skyscrapers to generate ground rent for his personal gain, Arthur finds in the skyscraper a resource worth saving now that he has figured out how to manage it rather than to be managed by it, making it an asset and not a foil to white metropolitan endurance.

"The Runaway Skyscraper" revises the embattled tone of "The Last New Yorkers" through its managerial protagonists who learn to healthfully scale their attention within the city's absorptive delights. Leinster's tale replaces England's fears about miscegenation as well as his attendant eagerness for race war with a technic of racial management. Whereas the skyscraper frames the extremity of difference in "The Last New Yorkers," allowing England to fetishize the moment of visible racial revelation, "The Runaway Skyscraper" imagines racial difference enduring even in the absence of visible evidence. Forms of white racial affiliation like that between Estelle and Arthur or the Met Life occupants and a spectral white diasporic community are imagined to be strengthened by the skyscraper rather than weakened by it, assuring whiteness's endurance in the face of both geologic and perceptual threats. Where racial distinction anchored in visual interpretation fails, Leinster introduces a second mode of racial knowing disaggregated from the visual that allows racial knowledge to continue to accrue and circulate. In both of the weird time-traveling tales featured here, the frontier enables the skyscraper to be imagined as a resource for seeing whiteness rather than as an obstacle to its future appearance. But "The Runaway Skyscraper" alone imagines the long-term viability of racial difference as untethered from the intimate scales necessary for race's visual identification, protecting white particularity in the face of even the most disorienting of architectures.

The Realist Skyscraper

Whereas large leaps in time and space were common to weird pulp tales, American realism was defined by its more intimate geographies and comparatively gradual temporal progressions. Writer Frank Norris bitingly categorized realism in 1901 as a genre of the "minute" revolving around "the drama of a broken teacup, the tragedy of a walk down the block."[40] Though William Dean Howells, one of American realism's foremost advocates, was the primary addressee of Norris's provocation, Howells described the genre's scalar proclivities in strikingly similar terms a decade prior. Howells wrote in 1891 that American writing tended to "excel in small pieces with three or four figures, or in studies of rustic communities, where there is propinquity if not society." Observing that realism's "grasp of more urbane life is feeble," Howells found that "most attempts to assemble it in our pictures" resulted only in "failures."[41]

It seems fated, then, that realist writers would respond antagonistically to the skyscraper, a structure whose growing dimensions seemed to strain the measured units of spatial intimacy realism held so dear. Unlike weird fiction's capacity to whisk the skyscraper away to more containable provinces, realism was forced to confront the skyscraper when and where it stood. The first realist novel to seriously engage the skyscraper, Henry Blake Fuller's *The Cliff-Dwellers*, represented it as the new ominous center of American life where both personal lives and individual integrity were routinely destroyed. First serialized in 1893, Fuller's tale borrowed its name from the southwestern Pueblos who lived vertically on the mesa hundreds of years before, using this term to now name Chicago's white managerial class whose lives increasingly revolved—and fell apart—around these tall structures. Fuller's early antipathy toward "repelling" skyscraper regions was echoed by Henry James and William Dean Howells, whose infamous descriptions of these structures as "artless jumble" and "brute bulks," confirm realism's base discomfort with its enlarging scale.[42] If realism was minute, with propinquity at the heart of its representational practice, the skyscraper's distanced and distancing dimensions could only prove discomforting.

But the skyscraper troubled realism for reasons beyond its sheer size alone. While the structure's perception as a "monstrous phenomena" in the eyes of its realist detractors certainly had to do with its immensity, the skyscraper also unnerved as an instrument of "multiplication," to borrow a term from Henry James's *The American Scene*, creating an inordinate number of sight lines in its wake.[43] Increasing the number of vantage points from which to see and be seen, the skyscraper spatially modeled a dispersed and potentially fractured demos difficult to collect with or through a shared gaze. Intrigued and, despite their multiple critiques of this architecture, even momentarily enchanted by the skyscraper, realist writers Henry James and William Dean Howells worried about its disruptive effects on intimate forms of both aesthetics and politics. Each wondered what was to become of realism's preferred scale of the dinner table in the age of the skyscraper where distanced bodies and increasingly dispersed publics threatened to bring realism—and perhaps the question of national belonging more generally—to an impasse.[44]

The intimate forms of social and narrative relations that realists favored primarily unfolded between subjects connected at the very least through their shared racial intimacy as white subjects. With Reconstruction signaling the prospect of African Americans gaining access to enlarged social and political spheres, as Ken Warren argues in *Black and White Strangers*, as well as the waves of immigration concentrating a host of racial others in urban centers, realism faced a new set of aesthetic and social dilemmas. Warren demonstrates how the reconfiguration of social space should African Americans in particular be granted full rights and access to the democratic polity was central to realism's project of representation.[45] But realist concerns about the changing shape of social space were deeply entangled with the changing shape of America's physical spaces and the types of perception their dimensions enabled. As the skyscraper's effect on urban scale made it increasingly difficult to perceive details of individual bodies, realism found itself seeking refuge in the more intimate scales of space and, by extension, race that had long fueled its narrative logic.

As I insist throughout this book, questions of measurement, scale, and interpretation were raced concerns at the turn of the century. In addition to being a matter of law, economy, and politics, race was also a matter of scale determining its capacity to be perceived. The question of where race resided in the body and under what conditions it became manifest were entwined with concerns about who gets to count as a citizen and how that counting gets done. As the city grew in both height and population, Howells and James each wondered what forms of measurement would remain possible in cities increasingly rendering obsolete the modes of measurement at which the realist novel was most adept—surveying incremental gradations of interior motives and interpersonal encounters circulating within closed, yet complex, systems.[46] Race was one of the intimate measures potentially unseated by the skyscraper's enlarging scale, threatening to fold everyone into one "muddy medium," as Henry James described.[47] Though Howells and James were both uncomfortable with the extremes of southern racism, race itself, as a sign aligned with the more intimate scales of encounter realism relished, provoked more complex responses from them. Concerns about the skyscraper's effects on racial perception freight their engagements with the skyscraper, carrying large stakes for their own narrative acts.

Though Howells and James both understood the skyscraper to be intimately linked to questions of racial perception, their respective motives for pursuing this line of inquiry diverged in key ways. Howells expresses his unease with the skyscraper's scale through the grammar of racial mixture. He accuses the skyscraper's distancing scale of placing pressure on the possibility of locating and recognizing an implicitly white "American type" distinguishable from racial others. James, by contrast, is concerned with the skyscraper not as a site of racial mixture but as a site of *race's potential nullification,* a possibility deeply connected for him to the limits of realist narrative. He treats the scale of race as concomitant with the scale of the private home—each offering him the right ratio of narrative intrigue. The skyscraper, obliterating the intimacy inherent to the scales of both racial perception and the home, appears to him as an agent of deformation. Though their logics for doing so differ, both Howells and James approach architecture as a site of racial knowing and unknowing, provoking them both to consider what kinds of stories they might tell should the skyscraper portend race's coming illegibility and, even, its irrelevance. If realists treated race as a veritable house of fiction, linking narrative's endurance to the prospect of an enduring form of racial perception rooted in the perceivable body, they sensed their own undoing as both white metropolitans and realists in skyscraper architecture's capacity to confound the legible racial trace.

William Dean Howells and the Subordinated Skyscraper

William Dean Howells was a staunch skyscraper disparager for much of his career. His most frequently cited critique of the structure appears in his 1893 novel, *The World of Chance,* in which a character describes it as "the necessity of commerce and the despair of art."[48] His Altrurian traveler refers to New York's skyline that same year as "a horse's jawbone, with the teeth broken or dislodged at intervals" producing a "hideous effect."[49] In an autobiographical piece from 1901, Howells insisted that New York of the 1860s "was really handsomer then than it is now, when it has so many more pieces of beautiful architecture, for at that day the sky-scrapers were not yet, and there was a fine regularity in the streets that these brute bulks have robbed of all shapeliness." "Dirt and square there were aplenty," Howells writes of the bygone city predating the skyscraper, "but there was infinitely more comfort."[50]

And yet these choice quotes do not speak to the entirety of Howells's engagement with the skyscraper and what he imagined its relationship to the city, citizens, and realism to portend. Howell's final and most definitive engagement with the urban landscape is most commonly taken to be his 1890 novel, *A Hazard of New Fortunes,* after which, as Amy Kaplan claims in *The Social Construction of American Realism,* "Howells stops exploring the dangerously shifting boundary lines of his urban representation, and turns to domestic and utopian fictions that remain within the untested perimeter of the foreground."[51] It is a pronouncement that still stands relatively intact some twenty years later, with Paul Abeln in 2005 similarly insisting on "Howell's retreat in the mid 1890's into psychological, utopian, and eventually autobiographical fiction."[52] And yet *Hazard* did not end Howells's engagement with urban boundaries. He would return to this theme in his Editor's Easy Chair editorials for *Harper's,* revising his claims for realism precisely by pushing them to their limits.

Kaplan belongs to a long critical tradition negatively assessing realism's conservative energies, a tradition as old as realism itself.[53] Recent critics looking to reclaim Howells and James as more than grumpy bourgeois reactionaries insist that these figures were more prescient—and thus worthy of our sympathy—about mass culture's dilemmas than has been acknowledged.[54] But if the tone of Kaplan's conclusions about realism can be argued with, her description of realism's technics remains usefully precise. Kaplan dissects Howells's intricate framing of novelistic visual planes in *Hazard,* as he toggles between background "information" associated with urban difference and foreground knowledge tethered to its immediate characters.[55] However, neither these narrative strategies nor his engagement with the city ended with this novel, where Kaplan ends her assessment. They continue to inform his urban outlook well into the twentieth century. In a little-known Howells editorial from 1909 featuring the skyscraper, we find Howells very much alive to the kinds of critiques Kaplan would later launch upon him, even preemptively distancing himself from some of their worst implications. Staging an encounter between the skyscraper and racial perception, Howells uses his column to amend, revise, and ultimately back away from the racial consequences of realism's most conservative pursuits. While *Hazard*, as Kaplan argues, "fulfills and exhausts the project of realism to embrace social diversity," ultimately welcoming retreat from the city and the multitudes of difference found there, Howells's reflections on the skyscraper some twenty years later find him facing these failures head-on.[56] Rather than retreating from urbanity, the Howells of 1909 decides to use the skyscraper to retreat from realism.

Howells's editorials, if not exactly fiction, are certainly prosaic, featuring characters and exchanges that would not be out of place if encountered in any of his novels. In his February 1909 Editor's Easy Chair column, reprinted in *Imaginary Interviews* a year later under the title "New York to the Home-Comer's Eye," Howells recounts an unnamed friend's reaction to the New York skyline after some time away.[57] As was typical of his Easy Chair pieces, this column was written almost entirely as a dialogue, a tactic that critic Rob Davidson argues granted Howells a way to rhetorically distance himself from his "earlier style of polemical criticism" by adopting a gentler tone tailored for a broader audience.[58] This is the case for the 1909 column, too, as Howells takes up the position of the unnamed, gentler "we" in contrast to his more polemical friend and, perhaps, his more polemical earlier self.

The column opens with Howells's unnamed associate struggling to put his impressions of the city into words for his hosts. After much tortured pondering, the friend eventually comes up with sublimity as a descriptor. His hosts respond with relief, having so often defended New York from this friend's critiques in the past that they "accept sublimity" as a relatively glowing review coming from him.[59] Howells's friend, however, quickly overturns his own verdict when it comes to the city's most seemingly sublime structure—the skyscraper. After the friend lists a number of the city's sublime qualities as observed from "the top of one of the imperial motor-omnibuses," his hosts notice the skyscraper's absence from his account, prompting them to ask, "Why leave out of the reach of sublimity the region of the sky-scrapers."[60] The friend responds by insisting that "there is a point beyond which sublimity cannot go; and that is about the fifteenth story." As a kind of law of diminishing of returns, Howells's friend notes the "unimpressiveness" of any skyscrapers daring to rise beyond this height.[61] When asked by Howells once more why the skyscraper fails at sublimity, his friend responds at length:

The other day I found myself arrested before a shop-window by a larger photo-graph labeled "The Heart of New York." It was a map of that region of sky-scrapers which you seem to think not justly beyond the scope of attributive sublimity. It was a horror; it set my teeth on edge; it made me think of scrap-iron—heaps, heights, pinnacles of scrap iron. Don't ask me why scrap-iron! Go and look at that photograph and you will understand. Below those monstrous cliffs the lower roofs were like broken foot-hills; the streets were chasms, gulches, gashes. It looked as if there had been a conflagration, and the houses had been burned into the cellars; and the eye sought the nerve-racking tangle of pipe and wire which remains amongst the ruins after a great fire. Perhaps this was what made me think of scrap-iron—heaps, heights, pinnacles of it. No, there was no sublimity there. Some astronomers have latterly assigned bounds to immensity, but the sky-scrapers go beyond these bounds; they are primordial, abnormal.[62]

Howells's friend then goes on to note that "if you want sublimity," forsake these monstrosities for a motorbus tour of Fifth Avenue's more proportional buildings.[63]

Howells's friend describes the skyscraper in this passage as an amalgama-tion of destroyed homes, literalizing its menace to the more comfortable and narratable domestic spaces most associated with realism. Despite the newness of these structures, the friend declares them "primordial" and "abnormal," grouping them with far older forms of deviancy to further punctuate his dis-missal. While the train ridden by the middle-class Basil and Isabel March of *A Hazard of New Fortunes* twenty years prior snakes along to all parts of the city, the motorbus Howells's friends ride is contained to the city's most glamorous street. Howells's associate, to employ Kaplan's terms for describing *Hazard*, de-lights in the contained foreground of Fifth Avenue, while condemning the "bound-less" and inassimilable skyscraper to the immeasurable urban background.

Howells's friend, moreover, dismisses these unseemly skyscrapers, not on the basis of direct experience of their size and mass but through his encounter with a secondhand representation found in the shopwindow, an image curi-ously described as both a "map" and a "photograph." Howells wrote back in 1891 that "realism becomes false to itself when it heaps up facts merely, and maps life instead of picturing it."[64] The realist's aim was to figure out how to frame an urban picture to carefully guide its readers between local detail and urban total-ity. Where the map, synonymous with raw data, threatens to overwhelm, the realist novel offers a balanced and coherent depiction of the city by cropping out much of the confusing and inassimilable data to focus on the selected foreground.

But if the Howells of the *Hazard* era argued that realism should be the domain of the framed picture over the unmediated map, by 1909, with the advance of photographic equipment and the rising popularity of cinema, the picture and the map were harder to situate as antagonistic forms of representation. The difficulty of maintaining their distinction in this later column suggests the strain modernity was putting on Howells's earlier claims for realism's distinct virtues, a strain the skyscraper brings to the foreground despite the desire of Howells's friend to push it to the background.[65]

From the relatively more reasonable position of the "we," Howells treats the friend's hysterical response to the mere image of skyscrapers with mocking curiosity. In response to his rant, Howells and company retort that "you strain for a phrase as if you felt the essential unreality of your censure." But whose unreality is Howells mocking here? If we recall Howells's own skyscraper meditations roughly ten years before in which he juxtaposed the structures with the "fine regularity" of the city's old streets "robbed of all shapeliness" by "these brute bulks," the friend resembles none other than Howells himself. This version of a critical Howells in 1909 putting pressure on his friend's conservative urban opinions disrupts Kaplan's portrait of a post-*Hazard* Howells clinging to parlor tales to avoid the "unreal" city. Here we find Howells poking fun at a position that is more Howellsian than Howells himself.

Howells's "we" not only distances himself from his earlier critiques of the skyscraper but also rebukes Howellsian realism's sacred cows of contained foreground and domestic retreat. What drove Howells to stage this reversal so theatrically? As the column goes on to hint at some of the unseemly social consequences of the friend's bounded gaze, the motive for this disassociation slowly materializes. Howells begins to plant these seeds halfway through the column by foregrounding the conceit of subordination structuring his friend's aesthetic judgments. When asked how he can profess to love Fifth Avenue when it "abounds in sky-scrapers," the friend replies that this street harbors skyscrapers with a difference—"sky-scrapers in subordination, yes," that keep themselves limited to "one to every other block."[66] Singling out the Flatiron as one of these "very good and kind giants," the friend argues that the skyscrapers along Fifth Avenue have "somehow harmonized," separating themselves "from the barbarous architectural discords of lower New York."[67] The Flatiron, sinking back into "measurable inconspicuity" since its flashy arrival on the scene, serves as the epitome of a kindly building as the friend claims to "thrill with their grandeur and glow" and bask in their "condescension."

Subordination becomes a key word for the friend, reveling in his own subordination to skyscrapers that subordinate themselves to the larger skyline. Terms of measurement positively pepper the friend's descriptive vocabulary throughout the column—from figuring New York and London's differences according to their comparative "magnitude" and precisely identifying sublimity's "assigned bounds" at exactly fifteen stories, to favorably describing the Flatiron in terms of its "measureable inconspicuity" and insisting skyscrapers defer to the skyline's quantifiable "line of progress." By contrast, the brutal skyscrapers represented by "The Heart of the City" refuse to be subordinated to measurement and reason—even in a picture they manage to produce a "nerve-racking tangle." These structures negate the terms of the Kantian sublime, defined as reason's ability to scale and contain overwhelming immenseness where the senses fail to do so. If the Kantian sublime figures the body's failures as the mind's triumphs, both the body and mind equally collapse for Howells's friend in the face of these behemoths.

But the challenges to measurement posed by the city, the column goes on to suggest, prove to be merely symptoms of another, more pressing concern. The friend's delight in subordination up to this point could be either dismissed as the out-of-touch views of a harmless aesthete or embraced as a laudable, if over-the-top, enthusiasm for managed cities. But as the piece pivots from the realm of architecture to that of bodies, the friend's position appears more pernicious as he edges closer to his final topic of racial perception. From his upward focus for most of the column, the friend suddenly turns his gaze down to "the shining black roofs of the cabs" now "obeying the gesture of the midstream policemen."[68] He celebrates the street's newfound order, delighting that "the means of traffic and transportation have been duplicated in response to the demand of the multiplying freights and feet."[69] If crossing the city of old required him to take "my life in my hand," the subordinated city of traffic wardens divvies up the street into "gentle eddies," where "one may pause in the midst at will."[70] Subordination here, too, brings comfort.

But Howells's "we," seemingly sensing something else lying behind the friend's revelry in controlled buildings and traffic, impatiently cuts him off, crying, "enough of streets!" before asking one final question: "Now, what of men? What of that heterogeneity for which New York is famous or infamous?" Howells's "we" catalogs the racial groups engulfing the city, from "the tribes of Israel, lost and found" to the alliterative "swart stranger from our sister continent to the southward." Howells ends his question by referring to this racial conglomeration within New York City as those "who so sorely outnumber us." If Howells has distanced himself from his friend for much of the column, his reference here to their cohesive unit as a "we" bound by racial commonality suddenly reestablishes their intimacy.

The friend responds with surprise at the tenor of Howells's inquiry, suggesting that rather than being overwhelmed by racial difference, "in Fifth Avenue the American type seems to have got back his old supremacy." After jokingly referencing fears about Anglo American "race-suicide," the visitor remarks that on this particular street, "it is as if our stirp had suddenly reclaimed its old-time sovereignty." "I don't say that there are not other faces, other tongues than ours to be seen, heard, there; far from it," he insists. "But I do say it is a sense of the American face, the American tongue, which prevails. Once more, after long exile in the streets of our own metropolis, you find yourself in an American city." He concludes by proclaiming that "your native features, your native accents, have returned in such force from abroad, or have thronged here in such multitude from the prospering Pittsburgs, Cincinnatis, Chicagos, St. Louises, and San Franciscos of the West, that you feel as much at home in Fifth Avenue as you would in Piccadilly, or in the Champs Elysees, or on the Pincian Hill."

In contrast to the unfriendly skyscrapers confusing the body and the mind, the friend posits the return of the pure "American" and his implicitly white body and tongue as the triumphal ending to his story of urban experience. Just as the Fifth Avenue skyscrapers subordinate themselves to the greater elegances to be found on the street, so too have racial others subordinated themselves to the "American type" within the friend's favored corner of the city. These "native features" make themselves visually available from within the architecturally subordinated spaces in which he feels most at home. By placing racial perception at the core of urban interpretative practices, Howells's friend explicitly links the two as correlated processes.

Howells's "we," however, gets the column's final word. In a one-line response that appears conflicted, ambivalent, and hard to parse in both content and tone, the column's last line reads as follows: " 'Perhaps,' we suggested, after a moment's reflection, 'it isn't true.' "[71] It remains unclear what exactly the "it" refers to here. Howells could be questioning his friend's sincerity, his facts, or his method, or a combination of all three. It is impossible to ascertain definitively what exactly he wants to refute. But even without the interpretive surety of its content, the quiet resistance of this brief rebuttal's phrasing and the drama of its column-ending placement suggest that Howells felt the need to rescue the reader from a potentially unwanted identification with the friend on disclosing the racial implications behind what at first seemed to be merely an eccentric take on urban architecture. In playing out the friend's urban logic to its conclusion, linking his taste for architectural subordination to his desire for racial subordination, Howells's "we" suggests that this is not the realism he signed up for.[72]

But how should one have responded to Howells's question of what to make of the "them" "who so sorely outnumber us?" If the friend answers wrongly, the column ends without positing a right or a corrective response. In an earlier novel from 1891, *An Imperative Duty*, Howells destabilizes vision and blood as useful symptoms of race through the plight of his protagonist, Rhoda, who discovers she is one-sixteenth black.[73] Upon its initial revelation, this racial secret threatens to destroy her. But by the novel's end it is treated as an inside joke between Rhoda and the white doctor who knows her secret and marries her anyway. The serious notion of "native stirp" in the 1909 column similarly devolves into farce, as the "native features" of the American type are ultimately conflated with those found in English, French, and Italian cities, bankrupting his assertion about the particularity of national type. Perhaps the best answer to Howells's question of "what of them" is, in fact, well, what of them?— because the line between *them* and *us* increasingly failed to congeal or stabilize in the unsubordinated city of the skyscraper, turning everything into background *we* rather than a bifurcated *us* and *them*.

But the column's concluding interest in racial type has one final result—it allows Howells to continue to evade the question of class difference he most concertedly tried and, by most accounts, failed to grapple with in *Hazard*. Divvying the city into racial types, even if it is to then complicate their division as I have interpreted it, seems to be the more thinkable feat for Howells than seeing or measuring class difference, a typing that no level of spatial scaling can obfuscate through perceptual mediation alone. Even if Howells uses the skyscraper to refuse some of realism's most conservative tendencies, the Howells of 1909 nonetheless repeats the strategies of refuge and removal he adopted in relationship to class Kaplan finds him enacting in *Hazards* twenty years prior. But this time, instead of fleeing into the domestic space of the apartment to avoid the "unreality" of class conflict, Howells takes shelter in what becomes for him the more narratable encounter with race, rescued from the skyscraper's disorienting scale to once again anchor his prose in racial perception's more intimate register.

Henry James and the Race-Negating Skyscraper

In addition to favoring a younger Howells, the fictive friend of Howells's 1909 column could also be said to resemble Henry James—particularly the James of

The American Scene published two years prior. Not only do the two "analysts" share a fondness for what James called Fifth Avenue's "elegant domiciliary" but they harbor a similar distaste for buildings James termed "grossly tall and grossly ugly," referring to New York's skyline as an overplanted pincushion and a toothless comb.[74] James briefly approaches the skyscraper in *The American Scene* as a fantasia of narrative intrigue, finding that "each of these huge constructed and compressed communities [. . .] testified overwhelmingly to the character of New York—and the passion of the restless analyst, on his side, is for the extraction of character."[75] But he ultimately finds the skyscraper to have reneged on its promise, declaring it a "compromised charmer" failing to convince that "she is serious, serious about any form whatever, or about anything but that perpetual passionate pecuniary purpose which plays with all forms, which derides and devours them." Ruling their end "effect" one of "insincerity," James damns skyscrapers for lacking history or depth, making them useless to the "restless analyst" searching for meaning.

James's rebuke of the skyscraper should come as no surprise to any reader even passingly familiar with his work. Given realism's penchant for intimate scales and James's own particular investment in houses and histories harboring hidden depths, his skyscraper aversion is to be expected. But if James's response to the skyscraper is predictable, the racial logic behind it is less so. Unlike Howells's friend, James's distaste for the skyscraper does not stem from its capacity to interrupt the perception of the "American type." Valuing good stories over pure races, James is, to the contrary, continually fascinated throughout *The American Scene* by the numerous iterations the "American type" may one day take following the expansion of citizenship. He may not always be sure of the democratic worth of forms of racial mixture, either reproductive or social, but he is much more certain of their narrative worth. James approaches sites of interracial encounter throughout *The American Scene* as kinetic spaces presenting the restless analyst with satisfyingly complex puzzles ripe for narrative exploration. Where the skyscraper "derides and devours" forms and resists representation, interracial spaces and mixed bodies mark for James the elastic possibilities of biological and narrative forms to come.

This does not mean, however, that James's engagement with the skyscraper is without racial stakes. Less concerned with the empirical verification of race as a matter of taxonomy, James's racial anxiety about the skyscraper revolves around securing the pleasurable ambivalences housed by the visible racial trace that this architecture threatens. James differentiates between *race's recombination*, a reordering of the American demos he found conducive to narrative, and *race's negation*, an obliteration of the racial detail harmfully denying the "restless analyst" a discursive medium to puzzle over, shutting down avenues of narration. The skyscraper disturbs James because it threatens to make racialized forms of gazing—a mode of narrative intimacy propped up by spatial intimacy—obsolete. He demonstrates the connection between architecture, perception, and race throughout *The American Scene*, contrasting the skyscraper's negative capacity for narration with the positive capacities he assigns visibly raced bodies. In what follows, I consider how this text stages the problem of perceiving race across various spaces before turning to James's late ghost story "The Jolly Corner," in which he uses race to repair the narrative fissures initiated by tall buildings. If the skyscraper disrupts processes of racial perception in *The American Scene*, this later story posits the reconsolidation of racial perception as the white metropolitan's solution to the optic and psychic traumas produced in this architecture's wake.

James's journey through New York City in *The American Scene* is a drama of arrested communication across a range of sensory registers, including sight and hearing, as Bill Brown has elucidated, but also taste ("there is yet more of the bitterness of history to be tasted") and smell ("the illiteracy seemed to hover like a queer smell").[76] He longs to "commune" with the architectural "survivor[s] of the clearer age," but finds it increasingly difficult to do so in a city whose sight lines, or rather sense lines, are increasingly obstructed.[77] James's lament about the city's diminishing capacity for history, the most-cited reason for his disaffection with the skyscraper, correlates to his concern about its multiplication of perceptual vantage points. In the famous Washington Square scene where James finds that his "birthhouse" has been replaced by a "high, square, impersonal structure," he outlays the difficulties of memorializing this lost site within the current cityscape. "Whereas the inner sense had positively erected there for its private contemplation a commemorative mural tablet," James writes, "the very wall that should have borne this inscription had been smashed as for demonstration that tablets, in New York are unthinkable."[78] Bill Brown, acknowledging the speed with which architecture was being razed and erected at this time, notes how New York made visceral the idea that "object[s] cannot be depended on as a source of continuity in the midst of human flux."[79]

But even the most permanent of skyscrapers would still concern James, who worries not only about their transience but also about the numerous new vantage points they make possible. Even if James could erect a "mural tablet" for his lost birthhouse, the city's erratic topography made concentrated remembrance near impossible. He begins by asking the reader "where, in fact, is the point of inserting a mural tablet, at any legible height, in a building certain to be destroyed to make room for a sky-scraper?"[80] But his second question takes on further urgency: "And from where, on the other hand, in a façade of fifty floors, does one 'see' the pious plate recording the honor attached to one of the apartments look down on a responsive people?"[81] James places the word *see* in quotation marks, noting his doubtfulness that such a verb captures the perceptual experience associated with skyscrapers. So, too, does the notion of a "responsive people" as a comprehensive collectivity fall into doubt without a singular vantage point from which to read this memorial needle in a haystack. What holds the responsive people together as either *responsive* or *a people* in light of the skyscraper's perspectival scattering? At stake here is the status of *the people* itself— denoting some unit of commonness—versus the uncollectable vantage points of discrete subjects failing to cohere in their scaled-out redistribution around the skyscraper. These subjects who fail to "see," let alone know, also fail to be seen and known by James. They cannot be collected into a demos of even the most tenuous fabric.

James's relationship to the skyscraper reaches its greatest impasse when he tries to describe the "state of the streets" produced around it, finding them to be saturated with

> the consummate monotonous commonness, of the pushing male crowd, moving in its dense mass—with the confusion carried to chaos for any intelligence, any perception; a welter of objects and sounds in which relief, detachment, dignity, meaning, perished utterly and lost all rights. It appeared, the muddy medium, alone with every other element and note as well, all the signs of the heaped industrial battlefield, all the sounds and silences, grim, pushing, trudging silences too, of the universal will to move—to move, move, move, as an end in itself an appetite at any price.[82]

Lacking the framing devices of stage, scene, or illumination, James's rendering of the streets surrounding skyscrapers suggests the uncontainability of this scene, if one could even call it a scene. In the place of discrete subjects, we find only a "welter of objects and sounds." There is no nod here to the "privileged citizen" who can comfortably move from an outward gaze to an inward act of processing and back again to make sense of it all. We have no idea where James is even situated in this description, as the "confusion carried to chaos" disrupts "any intelligence, any perception" from latching hold. There are no delineated spaces for the viewer and the viewed in this description. Everything becomes one "muddy medium" whose motions produce silence rather than representable sound. The "state of the streets" can only be defined in terms of lack as James focuses on the sensory, affective, and cognitive "rights" denied the restless analyst in the form of "relief, detachment, dignity, meaning." *The American Scene* typically features James finding some sort of thrill in ambivalence, sensation, and otherness within a given scene, even if he ultimately comes to a negative opinion about it. This is not one of those scenes. The skyscraper is definitively unpleasurable for James here, unmaking form to such an extent that preexisting tropes of containment fail to be adequate to it.

The skyscraper's formlessness sits in contrast to the ancient house composed of insular and isolating nooks and crannies where secrets—one of James's favorite words in *The American Scene*—can favorably reside, awaiting the author's extraction. James laments the openness of the modern home, increasingly defined by "the indefinite extension of all spaces and the definite merging of all functions," making them utterly "visible, visitable, penetrable" from every angle. The loss of "room-character" in modern homes, according to James, handicaps the possibility of a magnitude of "social relation" less than a "shriek or shout."[83] If the storied house of old functioned as an enveloping vessel capable of assembling a "seeing" group of subjects ripe for narrative extraction, the modern home increasingly symbolized a radical exteriority around which nothing coheres. The "indefinite" modern home threatens to turn the once intimate space of the domestic into a virtual skyscraper, negating the home's prized interiority until nothing but scattered and uncollectable subjects remain. The formlessness of urban architecture gestures for James toward the future deformations of space and the social relations it configures.[84]

But lest we imagine formless skyscrapers and form-making old homes to constitute a stable binary across the text, a third architectural regime emerges in *The American Scene* to complicate this coupling: civic architectures, including Ellis Island, the Boston Public Library, New York City Hall, and Harvard Yard. These sites remain open to the public while still retaining some sense of containment and, as a result, narratability. James does not always know how to render these places with which he is not entirely comfortable, but he also does not imagine them to be beyond the limits of representation as he does the skyscraper. The amenability of these civic spaces to social democracy and, possibly, civic democracy is a prospect he treats with more ambivalence than he is usually credited. Critic Jane Wolf Bowen, for instance, paints James's response to the Boston Public Library as one of mere disgust, reacting to what she finds him describing as the building's "huge, hermaphroditic body in which the invasive American public circulates en masse."[85] But James does not entirely dismiss buildings that embrace public access at the expense of "private penetralia"—James's term for recessed inner sanctum-like spaces that facilitate isolation. Rather, we find him almost giddy upon glimpsing these civic spaces he deems "unfriendly to the preservation of penetralia," a trait he finds characteristic of "social democracies, like that of America."[86]

Although James mourns the loss of private nooks for isolated reading within the Boston Library, he also finds within them a "detail of the personal port" of American democracy, which, "unlike the English, is social as well as political."[87] James never suggests that the building's alignment with social democracy is necessarily a bad thing. There seems to be a bit of pride in his statement, finding a potentially lucrative political trade-off for this aesthetic loss in America where "everyone is 'in' everything, whereas in Europe so comparatively few persons are in anything." James, otherwise quick to pronounce his distaste when he encounters things not to his liking, does not deploy such language here or in other like sites. In contrast to the skyscraper that makes bodily perception impossible, the Boston Public Library still allows James to latch onto a legible "detail" that quickens rather than unnerves him. Bodies may mix here, but they conjure a containable form ("everyone is 'in' everything") rather than the negation of one.[88]

This language of stimulation and thrill carries forward to other public sites in *The American Scene* where his self-proclaimed "perverseness" in enjoying these spaces is more openly yoked to their racial heterogeneity. In considering Ellis Island, another penetralia-less site, James conflates "the ceaseless process of the recruiting of our race" he witnesses there with "the plenishing of our huge national *pot au feu*," casually placing the processes of racial mixture and national expansion together in the same sentence—a conflation that would have sent many of his contemporaries insistent on strict racial classifications into hysterics. Furthermore, in both Harvard Yard and Ellis Island, we find James treating with "haunting wonder" the future of a mixed-race America. In Harvard Yard, faced with what Gary Levine has identified as the first generation of Jews admitted to the Ivy League, James asks "what might be becoming of us all, 'typically,' ethnically, and thereby physiognomically, linguistically, *personally*," as he speculates regarding these students, "*whom did they look like the sons of*?"—a question of paternity James treats as a "game" he finds "positively thrilling to play out."[89] These ghostly future progeny tantalize "the restless analyst" with new forms and, potentially, new stories. Rather than worrying about the identifiable "stirp" of the American type as Howells's grumpy friend does, both James the storyteller, longing, in the words of Martha Banta, to "scale the walls of forbidden gardens in order to get at good secrets intended for public display as great stories," and James the democrat, a persona unmarked by Banta but which I find emerging in moments when he is momentarily enraptured by the possible expansion of civic and social democracy in America, become aroused here as he imagines the new "types" that might populate the future nation.

Even when James is most nervous about the prospect of racial difference, he manages to frame interracial contact in terms of shared and containable intimacy rather than as an epic process of disintegration, as he does the skyscraper. Unlike the tall building type, which had "got the start, got ahead of, in proper parlance, any possibility of poetic, of dramatic capture," James expresses far more confidence in his ability to capture Ellis Island, which he describes as "the refuge and stage of patience for the million or so of immigrants annually knocking at our official door."[90] Despite the seeming similarities between Ellis Island and skyscrapers, each playing host to masses of people, James succeeds in bringing Ellis Island into a knowable frame, which he fails to do with the skyscraper. While narratively incapacitated by the skyscraper, James treats Ellis Island as a theater presenting him with a "whole watched drama poignant and unforgettable." He has a front row seat to the "visible act of ingurgitation on the part of our body politic and social." By rendering Ellis Island as both the enclosed space of the theater and the enclosing act of eating, James renders it quantifiable, scalable, and knowable. Ellis Island evokes a stage with clear focal points, a stark contrast to the skyscraper's disavowal of vantage point. James notes that the "sensitive citizen" may find "the intimacy of his American patriotism" shaken on the island by the presence of "the inconceivable alien."[91] But this sentence also suggests that this relationship will endure as one of intimacy. Ellis Island may project a "lurid light" on the nation's new demos, inducing a "new chill" in the heart of the native citizen, but it nonetheless illuminates a concrete *something* capable of being brought into view—a far cry from the skyscraper's negation of the very possibility of "seeing" itself.[92] He describes the theoretical citizen spectating within the theater of Ellis Island as having "seen a ghost in his supposedly safe old house."[93] If the intimate house of the nation is shaken, it ultimately remains intact. Ross Posnock notes James's "uneasy commitment to diversity" in this scene but overlooks the relative narrative ease James exudes while rendering this epicenter of American difference.[94] Instead of trying his narrative capabilities, Ellis Island is rendered by James in the fashion of one of his favorite narrative sites—the haunted house.[95]

James's lack of narrative equipment for rendering the deracinating skyscraper as part of a scene, however, is most graspable when we compare it to the

narrative exuberance he feels when inhabiting a scale that allows him to properly "commune" with discernible racial traces. When James travels in the second half of *The American Scene* to the South populated with old homes and
legible archetypes, there is a marked difference in his narrative voice as James
the storyteller fully holds court. In the North, the question of racial mixture
"haunts" the restless analyst with the exciting promise of an unknown future,
which James himself may or may not be able to render. He thrills in the democratic and narrative possibilities of racial mixture but is constantly marking
how these possibilities sit slightly beyond his current narrative comfort zone.
But James's southern encounter with a mixed-race body, rather than marking
an uneasy thrill, is treated as a sign of comforting stability, presenting James
with a mark of the past he already knows how to excavate. In the following passage from his chapter on Charleston, we find James dwelling in a chain of comfortable containment triggered by the figure of a tragic "mulattress":

> Prismatically, none the less, they had shown me the 'old' South; in one case by the
> mere magic of the manner in which a small, scared, starved person of color, of
> very light color, an elderly mulattress in an improvised wrapper, just barely held
> open for me a door through which I felt I might have looked straight and far
> back into the past. The past, that of the vanished order, was hanging on there
> behind her—as much of it as the scant place would accommodate; and she knew
> this, and that I had so quickly guessed; which led her, in fine, before I could see
> more, and that I might not sound the secret of shy misfortune, of faded preten-
> sion, to shut the door in my face.[96]

This is not the ambivalent James titillated and made uneasy among the mixed-
up masses moving through Boston Public Library or New York's City Hall; nor
is it the James that tentatively imagines the "physiognomic future" of the nation
to come. Instead, the James of the South openly desires the secrets the mulattress
both guards and represents. She epitomizes his ideal ratio of legible sign to withheld story, serving as the living remnant of the complicated past responsible for
her being. She is less a subject here than a part of the home's architecture, con-
joined with the door through which James looks to glimpse the past "hanging"
in the background. Whereas William Dean Howells's 1891 novel *An Imperative
Duty* features the family of the mixed-race protagonist, Rhoda, recoiling from
her body as the bearer of shameful familial and national secrets, James, by contrast, "thrills" in encountering this evidence of slavery in the "magic manner" of
this mulattress gatekeeper. When Martha Banta describes the longing of James
as storyteller to "scale the walls of forbidden gardens," she makes no explicit

reference to this scene involving a walled garden or its hovering mulattress. But I insist that the mulattress cannot be separated from the garden, as both sit at the heart of James's narrative enterprise. Together, they represent the inseparable racial and spatial intimacies undergirding his sense of American identity. Unlike the skyscraper, obfuscating processes for perceiving race, or the other heterogeneous civic spaces of the North conjuring a racial future James acknowledges but cannot quite narrate, the southern home flanked by the mulattress offers him a foundational form of racial mixture generative both in its elusiveness and in its familiarity.

James does not tell us how he makes it past the "elderly mulattress," but the next time we see him, he has slipped into the garden to revel in its narrative possibilities:

> Fresh altogether was the air behind the garden wall that next gave way to my pursuit; there being a thrill, for that matter, in the fact that here at last again, if nowhere else over the land, rose the real walls that alone make real gardens and that admit to the same by real doors. Close such a door behind you, and you are at once within—a local relation, a possibility of retreat, in favor of which the custom of the North has so completely ceased to discriminate. One sacrificed the North, with its mere hard conceit of virtuously meeting exhibition—much as if a house were just a metallic machine, number so-and-so in a catalogue—one sacrificed it on the spot to this finer feeling for the enclosure.[97]

Where the "muddy medium" begotten by the skyscraper represents a "welter of objects and sounds" so voluble it produces a negation of sound and vision, the mulattress—another type of "muddy medium"—serves as a gateway for James to more preferable proportions of withholding to revelation, surface to interior, secrecy to transparency. James notes the "starved" nature of her body in the preceding passage, but she poses no enduring concern for him as she gives way to the prize of the gated southern home in which "local relation" and "retreat" enable the kind of "discrimination" James most enjoys. While race scientists at the time worried that miscegenated persons would irreparably disrupt racial categorization, James's mulattress induces in him a "finer feeling" associated with comforting enclosure. The perpetually open doors of northern civic spaces prove less satisfying for James than the presence of the southern door that he can open and close at will—an agency coming at the direct expense of the mulattress, who is unable to hold the door shut in order to keep James out. In his willingness to sacrifice the motion of the North for the comforts of southern enclosure, James also suggests his willingness to sacrifice the mulattress and

Reconstruction's promises of agency to her via citizenship, freezing her into place as the doorframe on which the South's "enclosing" architecture—and its attendant intimate circuits of narrative possibility James so relishes—remains eternally propped open, ripe for James's penetration. Dwelling on the racialized pleasure James takes in the southern home makes visible the racial discontent informing James's disdain for the skyscraper.[98]

The correlation between architecture and race in *The American Scene* emerges in a sprawling and at times haphazard manner. Discovering its relation requires tracking James's sensual responses to the different dimensions and scales of the numerous spaces he traverses across hundreds of pages. But simultaneous to *The American Scene*'s publication, James conducted another, more controlled, experiment in narrative scale, architecture, and the possibilities of racial sight. He wrote the short story "The Jolly Corner" only a few months after the initial publication of the New York sections of *The American Scene* while he was finalizing the manuscript version.[99] "Corner" reads in many ways like a condensed microcosm of many of *The American Scene*'s spatial juxtapositions, excising its sprawling civic spaces to focus on the outsized skyscraper and the intimate narratability of the old house as warring binaries. But where the "restless analyst" of *The American Scene* abandons the skyscraper, deeming it impossible to represent, "The Jolly Corner" approaches acts of racial perception as a corrective to the skyscraper's dispersing scale. Unifying his white protagonists through their shared vision of the story's ghostly and miscegenated "black stranger," James re-collects the fractured vantage points dispersed by the skyscraper by way of a mutual act of racial perception that reifies white metropolitan affiliation and counteracts the skyscraper's abstracting optics.

"The Jolly Corner" centers on the haunting of protagonist Spencer Brydon upon his return to New York after a decades-long absence abroad. Brydon has returned to America to survey his two properties financing his life in Europe. The first is the "good" and "consecrated" space of his ancestral home, while the other is the "not quite so 'good' [. . .] mass of tall flats" that Brydon is renovating in the hopes of reaping even greater profits.[100] Despite his claims to detest his tall buildings, Alice, his quasi-love interest, upon witnessing the adeptness of his management of their construction, remarks that if "he had but stayed at home he would have anticipated the inventor of the sky-scraper." It is this "bad" space that initiates the eventual emergence of Brydon's ghostly American "double"—the man he would have become had he stayed in New York. Though most of Brydon's haunting by his double unfolds during late-night prowls in the "jolly corner" of the good home, the first "vibration" of the double's emergence is felt on the construction site when Alice insinuates Brydon's deeper complicity with the skyscraper, initiating a string of deformations against which Alice and Brydon must defend themselves.

As in *The American Scene*, the racial stakes framing the protagonists' derision of the skyscraper comes into focus when juxtaposed with the racial salve associated with the domestic home. Brydon's jolly corner, like the southern home guarded by the elderly mulatress, is similarly propped up by a series of bodies bearing perceivable racial traces, bodies that mark the spatial and racial intimacies central to a realist narrative practice. Unlike *The American Scene*, which features the solitary wanderings of the "restless analyst," the racial traces in this latter story become a shared site of gazing reaffirming forms of white affiliation the modern city threatens to erase. This reconsolidation begins abstractly as Alice and Brydon position themselves as a waning band of survivors united by their common orientation toward the past. As members of the fraying elite white metropolitan networks of old New York, they imagine themselves to form an intimate circle perpetually under assault. In contrast to the "dreadful multiplied numberings" of New York reducing the city to "a vast ledger-page" of overwhelming difference, Brydon revels in the "small still scene" he finds in Alice's weathered yet regal old home.[101] Alice is described as going to "battle" in defense of the "spirit [. . .] of the better time, that of *their* common, their quite far-away and antediluvian social order."[102] They are the fading remainders of "communities of knowledge, 'their' knowledge (this discriminating possessive was always on her lips) of presences of the other age."[103] Although the story eventually concerns itself with a more concrete type of haunt, Alice and Brydon's relationship is defined by their ghostly past bulwarking them against the present's "awful modern crush."

But it takes an act of mutual racial perception to fully concretize their "their" into a binding form. This act takes place in Brydon's ancestral home where he spends night after night stalking the ghost of his other self. The empty house allows Brydon to engage in an act of total narrative possession increasingly difficult to attain in the vertical city, as he, a singular storyteller, reads what the narrator terms "value" from an old and enclosed space. Much like the "finer feeling" of enclosure in the southern garden, and in stark contrast to the ineffectual memorial plaque marking James's demolished birth home, Brydon's home is spring-loaded with details activated by its inhabitant-turned-narrator— from the "large black and white squares" of the marble hall, which Brydon sets in motion with the steel point of his cane that sends a "dim reverberating tinkle" into the house's depths, to "the multiplication of doors—the opposite extreme to the modern," which allows Brydon to "rejoice so" in his game of chase by creating "clear vistas" to bolster the suspense of his doppelgänger hunting.[104] In "The Jolly Corner," the story is the house and the house is the story. The tale's power derives from James's ability to turn a nothing—a bare house—into a narrative something of epic proportions. To use an architectural maxim here, less is more.

It is in the enclosed home where the ghost, bearing a mixture of racial signs, is eventually glimpsed. The haunting game of chase at the center of "The Jolly Corner" resembles the earlier scene of ghost hunting from *The American Scene* similarly entangled with the visibility of the racial traces. Let us recall the "positively thrilling" game James plays following his visit to Ellis Island in which he imagines with "haunting wonder" "what might be becoming of us all, 'typically,' ethnically, and thereby physiognomically, linguistically, *personally*" before asking of this crowd "whom did they look like the sons of?" Brydon, too, faces an American ghost of uncertain paternity who harbors a physiognomy that cannot be predicted or guaranteed. As in *The American Scene*, James proves to be less concerned here with answering the question of what this ethereal American son actually looks like. He is more concerned in both texts with stabilizing the scene of perception that would allow him to pose this question, presuming the viability of racial apprehension.

Race matters in "The Jolly Corner," not for the answers to paternity it provides but for its power to unite subjects in the project of perceiving it. When Brydon finally spies his ghost, decked out in full evening dress and missing two fingers, he describes this "evil, odious, blatant, vulgar" other as having "the face of a stranger."[105] Alice, who has suspected Brydon's late-night activities, has a simultaneous vision of this crippled "black stranger," causing her to rush over to his house and rescue Brydon from himself. The story culminates with the pair's communion over their shared vision, while the markedly Irish housekeeper, Mrs. Muldoon—the other believer in haunts in the story—stands by as a witness to, but ultimately excluded from, the couple's union. Although Brydon describes the ghost as having "white masking hands," both Alice and Brydon refer to this man as "a black stranger," a coloring mirroring the "black and white squares" earlier described as lining the floors of the ancestral home. Alice insists to Brydon that the stranger "isn't—no he isn't—*you!*"[106] Brydon then "drew her to his breast," physically reconsolidating their vantage points as the story's closing gesture. As with James's earlier game of physiognomic roulette in *The American Scene*, the pair's shared glimpse of the ghost gives them enough material to speculate on the ghost's paternity, reinforcing the strength of "their" collective unit in this act of shared pondering. And yet the story does not provide enough concrete material to ever solve the puzzle of the ghost's paternity. The ghost's representational collage of white hands and black stranger never fully adds up to something that can be definitively catalogued. Race makes itself just legible enough to mark the ghost, along with the brogue-speaking Mrs. Muldoon, as different from and outside of Alice and Brydon's "their." Much like the elderly mulattress, these two racial specters—the ghost and Mrs. Muldoon, both contained within the protagonist's jolly corner—become the gateways through which Alice and Brydon pass to re-consolidate their enclosed and excluding sense of shared racial affliction at the story's conclusion.

"The Jolly Corner," already composed with the bare minimum of narrative gestures—its biggest plot point rests, after all, on the drama of whether the protagonist opened a door—further enacts its minimalist maxim by evoking race in the slightest way possible while still granting it maximum impact. The trace of race circling the stranger allows the story, as Ken Warren argues, to "simultaneously acknowledge the power of, while establishing the means of control over, the Other."[107] But it is important to point out how little James has to do in order to establish this control. With this black-and-white ghost, James conjures *race* while refusing to conjure *a race*. He uses racial rhetoric to gesture toward difference without defining it as such. Like with the southern mulattress, James the storyteller finds racial ambiguity delivering the best story of all. In contrast to the skyscraper, which threatens to subtract race, the house's intimate closed scale—most synonymous with the scale of racial intrigue—provides James the storyteller the ultimate setting for narration. Race, functioning like the literal black-and-white flooring underneath Brydon's ancestral home, becomes the "immense material" knitting the sovereign self and his acts of gazing, scattered by the skyscraper, back together.

Ken Warren finds the ghost enabling the story's white protagonists "to distance [themselves] from black strangers." But I find James here wielding blackness as a remedy to the toll of distance rather than a distancing mechanism itself. Across both works, the skyscraper proves to be far more harmful to James than the racially indeterminate apparitions whose presences cause him to narratively "thrill" time and time again. James conveniently displaces the question of sustained civic and social intimacy with racial others to a distant moment of futurity, deferring the full flowering of this democratic promise to another time. But James as storyteller recognizes race's more immediate use-value as an anchoring interpretive structure. Far from unwanted specters, the appearance of racially othered bodies serves as the bedrock of narrative possibility.

Although James leaves the ghost's paternity an open question, inviting our ongoing interpretive engagement with the ghost's "muddy" visage, I want to posit an identity for this haunt that, in line with James's anxieties across these two texts, might have been for him the most terrifying haunt of all. While critic Nicola Nixon reads the broken hand of Brydon's double in light of Adam Smith's invisible hand of the market, finding the double's crippling symptomatic of the market-based degeneracies wrought on him by the American adulthood Brydon dodged, I find the injured eye and hand of Brydon's ghostly double to signal James's fear of his own artistic degeneration had he stayed in the United States, with the nation's perceptual, civic, and racial confusions hobbling his faculties rather than sharpening them.[108] James experiences awe within American spaces that evoke an enrapturing feeling of democracy. But, like Brydon, he cannot ultimately recognize himself in any figure capable of surviving them fully intact, let alone narrating them.

The disabled white metropolitan of "The Jolly Corner" encapsulates many of the broader concerns featured in this chapter about the perceptual and narrative degeneration associated with the skyscraper and its effect on racial perception. From the attention-deficient office workers of "The Runaway Skyscraper" and the war-minded survivalists of "The Last New Yorkers" to Howells's visitor hungry for subordination and James's ghostly black specters, the white identities of these protagonists are continually threatened by the skyscraper's presence. I end this chapter not by dwelling on the stories' similarities, however, but by returning to the one that stands out from the rest in its prescience about the possible endurance of race beyond an encounter with the visible racial trace. Whereas George England, William Dean Howells, and Henry James all continued to connect the white metropolitan's survival to the preservation of environments favorable to the apprehension of the racial detail, Murray Leinster's "The Runaway Skyscraper" foregrounds an alternative strategy for circulating racial knowledge that does not rely on visual access to the body. By containing the avaricious Jew, Isidore Eckstein, within the abstract space of litigation, "Runaway" points to the ways white metropolitan identity might weather the perceptual storm of urbanization through more impersonal means. Anchoring racial knowledge in the indirect and ongoing collection of data, records, deeds, and maps over the active event of the embodied encounter, Leinster's "Runaway Skyscraper" suggests how practices of racial identification might endure. If the skyscraper exposed the perils of trying to identify race solely through visual access to the body, access that was increasingly hard to guarantee or legitimate in dense urban centers, then Leinster's rendering of the property-seeking legal body of the racial other signals the new frontiers to which white metropolitans would increasingly look in the suburban midcentury while seeking to maintain the privilege of their particularity.

CHAPTER THREE

Miscegenated Skyscrapers
and Passing Metropolitans

In the preceding chapter, I approach fears about whiteness's vanishing as a matter of scalar change rather than tarnished blood. But racial definitions emphasizing the preservation of allegedly pure bloodlines, which ultimately depended on the belief that one could successfully apprehend the race of a potential partner, underscore the reliance of both visual and hereditary notions of race on trustworthy perception. Stories at the turn of the century about undetectable 'white Negroes' intensified the public's long-standing concerns about inadvertent racial mixing. Though omnipresent throughout much of US history, fears about *miscegenation*, a term coined in the 1860s to name interracial sexual contact, and *racial passing*, which described the choice of the children of miscegenation to live as white, sharply intensified between the turn of the twentieth century and the late 1920s. This intensification was partially due to the exponential growth of American cities in both population and physical scale. As more people flocked into urban centers, whose physical infrastructures seemed to further compromise the capacity to perceive race, writers and journalists increasingly cast acts of miscegenation and racial passing as byproducts of urbanization.

This chapter traces how miscegenation shaped both the inception and reception of the early skyscraper. I begin by mapping the ways architects in the late nineteenth century wielded the term *miscegenation* and its related vocabulary of *mongrelization, hybridity*, and *amalgamation* as aesthetic rebukes for certain skyscraper designs. Evolutionary-based discourses rooted in race science casting miscegenation as a crime against nature served as a lingua franca of sorts for the late nineteenth century, its terminology migrating between the biological sciences and various aesthetic and social fields.[1] In architectural journals in this period, architects and critics invoked miscegenation to describe what skyscraper design must avoid emulating at all costs.

Upon recovering the skyscraper's "miscegenated" origins in architecture, I attend in the chapter's second half to the skyscraper's "miscegenating" effects on racial perception as described by Nella Larsen in her 1929 novel *Passing*. Unlike the white metropolitans in the previous chapter eager to shore up the operations of racial perception, Larsen used the dense congestion associated with tall buildings to demonstrate race's fragility. *Passing* depicts the skyscraper choreographing several visual economies that variously expedite, impede, and suspend the practice of racial detection. By illustrating the skyscraper's multifaceted effects on the capacity for subjects to perceive race and be perceived as raced, Larsen gestures toward what Anne Cheng calls "the material history of race"—which I also take to be the history of that material's perception—to undermine race's "facticity."[2] By reframing racial perception not as a melodrama of hidden blood but as a matter of spatial perspective and material context, Larsen renders race in *Passing* as an *effect* of the built environment rather than as something merely *framed* by it. Although the end of *Passing* suggests how the psychic and physical infrastructures built to reify race may outlast its demystification, Larsen's depiction of miscegenating skyscrapers asserts architectural history's centrality to the history of race.

The Miscegenated Skyscraper

> It represents hodge-podge crowded on hodge-podge.
>
> —*"The American Skyscraper,"* The Craftsman, 1913

Though less celebrated than the skyscraper's more tangible precursors such as the elevator, the telephone, and electric lighting, the new circulation patterns of both raced bodies and changing racial ideologies following Reconstruction and rapid urbanization in the United States proved just as crucial to this architecture's materialization.[3] Take, for instance, the use of race-based competition in steel manufacturing that provided the material for the skyscraper's internal supports.[4] By actively recruiting a racially diverse field of workers managers knew would have difficulty unionizing, steel conglomerates organized the workforce according to a three-tiered racial hierarchy featuring better-paid Anglo-descended "Johnny Bulls" at the top, semiskilled Eastern European immigrants known as "Hunkies" in the middle, and African Americans and Mexicans at the bottom, who were often employed as strikebreakers and assigned the most grueling jobs and received the lowest pay. These cultivated race-based divisions, deferring the unionization of steelworkers until 1937, helped set the low steel prices in the nineteenth century that enabled the early skyscraper to become a staple of urban architecture.[5]

A similar racial hierarchy organized skyscraper construction sites. As a 1911 magazine profile recounts, the laborers hired to dig the structure's foundations— one of the most dangerous on-site jobs—were most often "Dago, niggers, and Hungarians," who, this journalist charges, were treated as "unintelligent, sweating workers who could be killed without counting."[6] But many more periodical pieces from this period trained their attention upward to offer readers a closer look at the more visually spectacular work of ironworking "beamwalkers" balancing on high to connect the skyscraper's girders. Here, too, we find journalists emphasizing the racial taxonomy of these workers, cataloging the "Americans, Scotchmen, Irishmen, Englishmen," as one article describes, primarily hired for these positions. These profiles only begrudgingly acknowledge the presence of a "few Canadian Indian half-breeds" or the occasional "nigger-head man" who fails to "know his business" laboring alongside these otherwise Anglo heroes.[7]

While racial differentiation ordered the early skyscraper's material development in steel and construction, racial mixture and miscegenation haunt its aesthetic development through the rhetoric architects and critics used to describe how best to clad it. The term *miscegenation* was first coined in 1863 as part of a political hoax designed to cast New York Republicans as fervent advocates of marriage between whites and blacks.[8] Combining the Latin words *miscere* (to mix) and *genus* (kind), this scientific-sounding fabrication gave interracial sex, looming large in the national imagination, its first dedicated terminology. But while the originators of the term *miscegenation* intended it to narrowly describe acts of sexual reproduction between blacks and whites, by the time of the skyscraper's invention roughly twenty years later it was being used to describe a host of mixed-up and undesirable material, social, and aesthetic forms emerging from or associated with interracial contact.

The expanding application of the word *miscegenation* to mark a variety of relationships between not only members of different races but also any generally unlike entities coincided with the emergence of denser and more racially diverse US cities raising new concerns about miscegenation both strictly and loosely defined.[9] With the growing numbers of various racial groups working and living in greater proximity to one another in urban centers, efforts to understand and represent the effects of their contact also intensified. New theories about interracial relations and racial classifications emerged in fields such as sociology, urban planning, forensics, and public health, as well as in specializations within anthropology, including anthropometry, craniology, phrenology, and physiognomy. Prevailing opinion within these disciplines generally corroborated the notion that interracial contact was to be regulated and avoided where possible and was used to justify everything from immigration quotas and forced sterilization to educational practices and aesthetic principles.[10]

Architecture was one of many fields in this period interested in what new hybrid forms—reproductive, social, and aesthetic—might emerge from the expanding circuits of interracial intimacy within modernizing cities. Although the skyscraper is often positioned within the long modernist twentieth century, situating it within the context of the postbellum long nineteenth century makes visible the connections between the burgeoning discourse emerging around this new architecture and the changing legal and scientific language of race appearing within aesthetic debates about skyscraper form.[11] If the skyscraper were to be the preeminent canvas for a budding American aesthetics, which version of the United States and its citizenry should it reflect? Though architects and critics disagreed about which styles were best suited to this task, they drew from the same language and theories of scientific racism—particularly suppositions about the dangers of sexual contact between incompatible racial types—to justify a variety of aesthetic programs.

This chapter follows from recent efforts by architectural historians to describe the fuller range of economic, social, and material forces shaping the early skyscraper beyond the singular heroic architect or client.[12] Carol Willis, for instance, importantly foregrounded the key role economics played in determining skyscraper form, while Donald Hoffmann, pushing this claim even further, insists that for famed skyscraper architect Louis Sullivan, "the function of what he called the metallic frame construction was neither aesthetic nor philosophic, but entirely economic."[13] But as the racial histories of steel and construction suggest, the economic is often entangled with the aesthetic, the philosophic, and the social in ways that make it hard to cleanly extricate these spheres of influence.[14] Critics such as Willis and, more recently, Thomas Leslie have embraced the porousness of these spheres, persuasively making the case for deemphasizing the figure of the valiant architect as the ultimate mediator of architectural form to instead "recognize the productive interplay between architectural, engineering and constructive activity" shaping the early skyscraper's materialization.[15] Leslie notes that it is more accurate to think of the early skyscraper as the product of a "collective of designers, engineers, consultants and contractors," who together act as the "the orchestrators of the complex and often contradictory influences" determining its final form.[16]

Though my focus here is on the aesthetic debates surrounding the early skyscraper rather than its physical materialization, Leslie's approach to the skyscraper as a collective product proves useful for analyzing its aesthetic theory, which, too, is best understood as a mashup of ideas and influences derived from multiple origins and sources. Focusing on race science as a key source from which critics derived aspects of the skyscraper's aesthetic theory, this chapter builds from the efforts of architectural historians, including Mabel Wilson, Joanna Merwood-Salisbury, Charles Davis, Philip Steadman, and Christina Cogdell to contextualize nineteenth-century architectural discourse in relation to the changing racial discourse that helped shape it. After engaging the broader landscape of race, architecture, and nativism through discussions of architectural styles emerging primarily in the late-nineteenth-century Midwest, I focus on how more specific anxieties about racial mixture came to shape debates about the visual appearance of the skyscraper.[17] The discursive emergence of the miscegenated skyscraper at the turn of the century was the product of complex negotiations between scientific, social, and aesthetic racial schemas invested in the look of bodies, both flesh and steel.

The practice within architecture of drawing analogies between bodies and buildings long precedes the skyscraper, dating back to architectural theory's inception.[18] Starting with Vitruvius's 15 BC claim that a building's elements should have the same "precise relation" as those of a "well shaped man," the design of the human body has been a persistent model for architecture.[19] And like most evocations of the body in Western discourse, the bodies most commonly singled out as ideal analogues for building have historically been or presumed to be white. American architecture would prove no different. For architects in the United States in the late nineteenth century seeking a distinct national style, the American character they strived to represent was synonymous with Anglo American exceptionalism. Nonwhites most frequently appeared in American architectural writing either as problematic bodies requiring special management or as negative images to the autonomous modern white users with whom this writing was most concerned.[20]

In addition to determining which bodies American architecture should serve in the future, race also acted as a lens through which architects analyzed architectures of the past. As architectural historian Joanna Merwood-Salisbury has observed, prominent American architects in the late nineteenth century believed the history of architecture to be synonymous with "the history of civilization, which was, in turn, the history of race and expansion."[21] This attitude was prominently on display, for instance, in the built environments created for the World's Fairs in this period. Organizers of the Paris and Chicago exhibitions in 1889 and 1893 designed them to offer visitors a narrative of architectural evolution reflective of Western notions of progress. Fairs offered the public a story of development moving, as one fair official wrote, from "the primitive shelters of savages to the elaborate dwellings of barbaric times, and finally to the early classical architecture."[22] Nathan Clifford Ricker, architect and professor of architecture at the University of Illinois, made similar claims about the concomitant evolution of architecture and civilizations in order to emphasize just how much rested on the development within the United States of an admirable native architectural style. In a paper delivered at the second convention of the Western Association of Architects in 1885 and published shortly after in *Inland Architect*, Ricker insists that "architecture, when properly studied, presents the history of the human family in different stages of civilization from time immemorial, its degrees of perfection or imperfection plainly show the state of the country's civilization."[23] He proceeds in his paper to list "different degrees of human abodes" as evidence of a hierarchy of various racial civilizations, moving from the wigwam of the American Indian and the "half hole, half hut" associated with "the Australian savage" to the "skin tents of the Arabs and Tartars" and the "bamboo dwellings of the Chinese" before finally arriving at the "Caucasian race" whom he deems "preeminent" in "refinement, religion, art and architecture." Ricker uses this chronology to insist that America's claim as the next great world civilization depended in part on the development of its architecture: "Our country stands at, or near, the head in both architecture and civilization, and to uphold the fame and purity of the former we should spare no pains to effect the removal of all incompetent men from our profession."

At least one architect in this period argued that the link between architecture and civilization went beyond a correlation rooted in culture, insisting more explicitly on a biological conception of race as the origin of architectural difference. Irving K. Pond, a student of architect William Le Baron Jenney and a contemporary of Frank Lloyd Wright, worked prolifically not only as an architect but also as a writer. As a forty-year member of the Chicago Literary Club and its onetime president, Pond wrote everything from poems, detective fiction, and travel essays to a cheeky study of the whale. The ranginess of Pond's interests in natural history, regionalism, and architecture inform his 1891 article in *Inland Architect*, "Architectural Kinships," in which he correlates the bodily traits and native fashions of different ethnic and racial groups to the shape of their architectures.[24] In the article and accompanying sketches, Pond insists that the surfaces of buildings, like the surfaces of bodies, can be read symptomatically for information about the inherent intelligence and values of the races who built them. Juxtaposing three "race types"—"an old Greek," a "moor from Tangiers," and "a Mongolian type"—with the buildings associated with these types, Pond ultimately rules that "so subtle is the relationship between man and architecture that it shows where blood is weak or wanting," as well as "where social customs have served to mark the character of the man."[25] In line with what Joanna Merwood-Salisbury describes as the "almost eugenicist approach to the development of architectural form" punctuating the work of Irving Pond and his brother Allen Pond, here and elsewhere the Ponds connect the evolution of architectural designs not only to the habits and needs of distinct populations and climates but also to their distinct physiologies—approaching bodies *and* buildings as bearing evidence of racial difference to perpetuate hierarchies rooted in white supremacy.[26]

While the Ponds most egregiously pursued connections between the developments of various architectural forms to the racialized civilizations from which they emerged, race more frequently appeared within architectural discourse in more oblique and indirect ways. This is particularly true of debates about the direction of skyscraper façade during the late nineteenth and early twentieth centuries. As Christina Cogdell notes in *Eugenic Design*, "evolutionary thought in its numerous guises served as a common ideological foundation upon which modernists in almost every field constructed their work, arguments, and perceptions of the world and themselves, either consciously or unconsciously."[27] And the skyscraper was a particularly ripe subject for the evolutionary imagination. As a new architectural form lacking both aesthetic and structural precedent and emerging in a nation seeking to join the pantheon of great civilizations, evolution offered critics a useful analogue for imagining this new structure as not instituting a break with tradition but expressing its next progression. Unlike architecture of the past imagined to have been the result of centuries of slow aesthetic evolution—a process Pond claimed to have been coeval with the social and biological progression of their makers—the skyscraper emerged with relative haste following the advent of stronger structural steel and the growing demand by businesses to locate their offices in urban centers. The sudden arrival of the steel skeleton in the 1880s—described by architectural historian Carl Condit as the most radical transformation in the structural art since the twelfth century—along with the technologies of the elevator, telephone, and electric

Sketches from Irving K. Pond, "Architectural Kinships," *Inland Architect and News Record* 17.2 (Mar 1891) 28.

lighting, made the skyscraper a point of pride and a source of angst for American architects needing to decide with relative haste how best to dress this new engineering innovation.[28]

Making this task even more difficult was the fact that, unlike previous building types whose designs were largely dictated by structural necessity, the skyscraper's steel skeleton could increasingly carry more of its weight load internally, liberating

its exteriors to adopt almost any style imaginable. "Freed of its load-bearing responsibilities," as architectural historian Scott Charles Murray writes, "the exterior
became a blank canvas."[29] Renowned architectural critic Montgomery Schuyler
summarized in 1894 the predicament in which American architects found
themselves when attempting to design for this new vertical architectural form: "an
architectural problem absolutely new was imposed upon them, a problem in the
solution of which there were no directly available and no directly applicable precedents in the history of the world."[30] He goes on to insist that "the problem is by no
means yet solved." When searching for "an architecture expression" for "these
towering buildings," Schuyler concludes, "we look in vain."

The aesthetic freedom accompanying the skyscraper's steel skeleton at the
same time threatened to serve as a gateway to stylistic anarchy. There were no
clear historical precedents for cladding buildings of the skyscraper's magnitude, shape, or function or for designing façades not intended to bear structural
loads. If structural concerns were not to determine the look of the skyscraper's
newly emancipated exteriors and, as Montgomery Schuyler further wrote in
1894, "the structure cannot be expressed in terms of historical architecture," it
was unclear what would ultimately determine its expression. Should American
architects attempt to develop a new "native" style to cover these buildings? Or
should they instead clad them using European precedents originally developed
for towers and cathedrals? One argument against pursuing a native style was
that America was too racially heterogeneous to produce a pleasing aesthetics.
In the 1891 inaugural issue of the landmark architectural journal *Architectural
Record*, critic Barr Ferree pursues a version of this claim, explaining the challenges America's racial diversity posed for the development of a national style.
"The important phenomena" historically influencing the emergence of style,
Ferree explained, were the "national or ethnographic qualities" of the place in
which it emerged. Given the plethora of "ethnographic qualities" housed within
the United States, he found it impossible to imagine a national style emerging
from its mixed-up populace:

> A people composed of English, French, Germans, Italians, Spaniards, Russians,
> Austrians, Hungarians, Danes, Swedes, Norwegians, Poles, Turks, Armenians,
> Portuguese, Greeks, black, white and Mongol, Christians, heathen, infidel, cannot
> assimilate such diverse elements without many years of intermixture and solidifi-
> cation. We have ideas that are representatively American; we have American cus-
> toms and methods, none of which can be mistaken for anything else, but we have
> not that quality which will give us an architecture of our own.[31]

Ferree concludes that the distinct heterogeneity of the United States "render[s] it altogether impossible for us to hope to evolve a genuine and national style of Architecture."[32] In the absence of a cohesive demographic base, American architects should instead "mould architectural ideas and forms to the varied conditions of our national life and situation," creating, if not "an Architecture that may be American in outward aspect," then one that "will be American in purport and adoption."[33] Ferree's insistence that it was better for buildings to 'feel' American in spirit rather than *look* like the unassimilated American public in their "outward aspect" was one way to avoid a discordant skyscraper aesthetics from taking hold. Ferree's concerns echo those expressed by the more outré Allen Pond three years prior that the emergence of "the American architectural type or style" relied on the development of "a truly distinctive national spirit" that could only be the "outgrowth of a homogenous national life."[34]

Many architects heeded such warnings. Except for the relatively small number of Commercial-style buildings erected in Chicago in the 1880s and 1890s bearing exteriors that accentuated their steel frames, the most widely embraced strategy for cladding America's newest architecture until the first decade of the twentieth century was to give up on the dream of a national style and model the skyscraper's exteriors on established European styles held in high regard—an ethos further facilitated by the Beaux-Arts training emphasizing classical, baroque, and gothic historical styles that many of the most prominent skyscraper architects received either at the Ecole des Beaux-Arts in Paris or from one of the many American architecture schools that adopted its curriculum.[35] Adapting the historical styles of the Western tradition to cover the skyscraper was in keeping, as one architect wrote in 1893, with an understanding of the United States as "a new Anglo-Saxon empire across the Atlantic."[36] Proponents of a European-inflected eclecticism, sometimes called academic eclecticism, urged skyscraper architects to borrow from a mixture of tried-and-true styles handed down by "our architectural ancestors"—implicitly understood to be European—styles that, as one architect at the 1898 convention of the American Institute of Architects insisted, had been "perfected by long series of experimental efforts to attain to beauty."[37] "The most truly legitimate of all architectural designs," this architect continued, "is the one which has survived, in its various modifications through the wreck of the Roman Empire, the untoward influences of the Vandals and the Goths, and has come to us strangely modified," yet "still intact in spirit."[38] In bolstering the case for embracing European design precedents, American architect Henry Van Brunt went so far in 1875 as to argue that only primitive cultures strived for originality in their art: "It must not be forgotten that the most essential distinction between the arts of primitive barbarism and those of civilization is that, while the former are original and independent, and consequently simple, the latter must be retrospective, naturally turning to tradition and precedent, and are therefore complex."[39]

Advocates of a European-oriented eclecticism invoked the relatively young language of evolution to endorse a mode of skyscraper design based on an ethos of slow adaptation. John Root, an architect central to the skyscraper's early articulation in Chicago, claimed that the relationship between skyscrapers and older forms of architecture were as "related as the poetry of Darwin's evolution is to other poetry."[40] Critic Montgomery Schuyler similarly insisted in 1894 that "architectural forms are not invented" but rather "are developed, as natural forms are developed, by evolution," supporting arguments that American architects should not move too quickly away from historical styles lest they risk producing a potentially abhorrent style for the sake of novelty.[41] The supporters of this conservative mode of eclecticism generally believed, as one architect outlined in a 1908 issue of *Architectural Record*, that "the theory of the evolution of styles, as generally stated, is that our style is copied from another preceding it, and is so modified by differing conditions of climate, custom, and function that it eventually achieves an individuality of its own that is recognized as a style."[42] Given that America was home to "a mixed race, descended from the most enterprising individuals of the various European races," as N. Clifford Ricker argued in 1886—tellingly leaving out the other geographic origins of America's distinct mixture that concerned Barr Ferree in 1891—so too, Ricker believed, would an American architecture similarly emerge from the carefully sanctioned mixing of appropriate historical styles.[43] Covering tall buildings using recognizable and legitimated Western skins, these architects maintained, was more likely to lead to a favorable aesthetics over time than the hasty pursuit of a potentially degenerative national style.

The language of evolution, development, and inheritance that eclecticism's advocates used when insisting that when it came to the skyscraper, as one architect wrote, "there is more hope for a good copy than there is for a bad original," was first widely circulated in the United States beginning in the mid-nineteenth century by esteemed naturalists such as Louis Agassiz, Samuel George Morton, and Edward Cope, who co-opted theories from Charles Darwin, Herbert Spencer, and Jean-Baptiste Lamarck to support the idea that certain races had evolved more quickly than others, resulting in superior and inferior races.[44] American advocates of scientific racism sanctioned the mixture of European races they deemed more evolved and thusly superior while condemning the mixture of races they believed to produce weakened offspring. Prominent Harvard biologist Agassiz and the first chair of the Lawrence Scientific School—one of the first US engineering schools and, incidentally, attended by a young William Le Baron Jenney, one of the inventors of the skyscraper—posited as scientific fact in 1863 that "the population arising from the amalgamation of two races is always degenerate." "Everywhere, in fact," Agassiz continues, "history speaks as loudly in favor of the mixture of clearly related nations as she does in condemnation of the amalgamation of remote races."[45] The aesthetic arguments made by American architects promoting "legitimate" designs borrowed from evolutionarily sanctioned architectural ancestors mirrors the arguments Agassiz and other naturalists in the late nineteenth century made when endorsing the mixture of "clearly related nations," while reproaching the mingling of "remote races" as repugnant and unnatural. Believing that "the production of half-breeds constitutes a sin against nature," Agassiz wrote, "no efforts should be spared to check that which is abhorrent to our better nature, and to the progress of a higher civilization and purer morality."[46] Edward Cope, the nation's leading paleontologist at the turn of the century, similarly insisted in 1890 that "the highest race of man cannot afford to lose or even to compromise the advantages it has acquired by hundreds of centuries of toil and hardship, by mingling its blood with the lowest."[47] Decades of naturalist arguments in the United States attesting to the purity of white civilizations perfected over centuries informed architectural rhetoric insisting that perfected European styles inform skyscraper design. As architect C. H. Blackall warned his colleagues, those obsessed with pursuing a distinct American style for the skyscraper "would have us cast aside tradition" to "cover our gaunt and ugly skeleton of steel with something which in a mysterious, unheard-of way shall be peculiarly metallic, and peculiarly sui generis."[48] Just as Agassiz "shudder[ed] at the consequences" of a civilization overrun by racial mixture, Blackall in 1898 appears similarly unnerved by the prospect of a "sui generis" skyscraper style that, unanchored from tradition, may take a "peculiar" form.

By the 1930s, forms of European eclecticism had largely fallen out of fashion as American architects began championing the antihistorical ethos of modernist styles. But in a brutal twist of irony, modernists looking back on this earlier period—dominated by buildings that drew from European design precedents and precluding the development of a distinctly American architecture—ruled these more conservative buildings just as guilty of perpetuating miscegenated design as the native architecture whose development it was meant to stanch. In 1930, architectural critic Sheldon Cheney pejoratively painted this entire earlier era of American eclecticism as one of "architectural miscegenation," neglecting the finer-grained arguments made by these earlier architects vis-à-vis race science that distinguished between good and bad mixtures to instead emphasize what Cheney deemed to be the regrettable embrace of stylistic mixture of any kind, sanctioned or unsanctioned, evolutionary or devolutionary.[49]

We find similar denigrations of stylistic mixture explicitly deploying the language of miscegenation even earlier than Cheney's. In his 1908 treatise *Architectural Composition*, architect and anarchist John Beverley Robinson, for instance, demonstrated the dangers of eclecticism's brand of what he, like Sheldon Cheney twenty years later, deemed "architectural miscegenation." Robinson included a sketch of an example of a "miscegenated" design practice that "purports to connect two equal individuals of equal race" but "fails to do so."[50] Such a practice, he insists, "joins together an unequally matched pair, of hostile race and alien feeling." In analogizing aesthetic dissimilitude to miscegenation, Robinson gives his claims about architectural style a sense of urgency as well as the veneer of scientific truth.

But it was Louis Sullivan, one of the most famous architects of the early skyscraper era and perhaps the most outspoken critic of eclecticism and Beaux-Arts-style training in the period, who first used *miscegenation* to refer to skyscraper

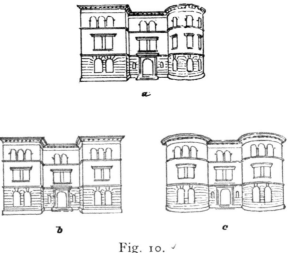

Fig. 10. ✓
Similarity and dissimilarity of parts.

John Beverley Robinson's diagram of "architectural miscegenation" from *Architectural Composition* (New York: D. Van Nostrand, 1908) 35.

architecture he found deficient, equating the fondness for mixing historical styles of any origin to this allegedly degenerative act. Sullivan's interest in the language of miscegenation appears throughout his 1901 book, *Kindergarten Chats*, a collection of philosophical, and often bombastic, musings on American architecture, originating as a column in the Cleveland journal *Interstate Architect and Builder*. In a section titled "An Oasis" that praises H. H. Richardson's thirteen-story Marshall Field Building completed in 1887, Sullivan's fictional stand-in explains to his student that "in a world of barren pettiness" Richardson's building is a rare triumph, describing the structure as "a real man, a manly man; a virile force" that "sings the song of procreant power as others have squealed of miscegenation."[51] Sullivan uses similar language in a later column when the professor, in the course of describing his frustrations with bad architecture, proclaims that "when we, in place of a fertile unity which we had hoped for, come suddenly upon miscellany and barrenness, we are deeply mortified, we are rudely shocked" before noting the "remarkable perversity" of "artificial" architecture.[52] Contrasting fertile architecture of unified design with displeasing architectural "miscellany" affiliated with sterility and perversity, Sullivan invokes rationale germane to late nineteenth-century naturalist theories about the aberrant consequences of interracial sex. Because some hybrids in nature were incapable of reproduction, these theories went, the reproductive offspring of blacks and whites—thought to belong to different racial "species"—would also eventually exhibit diminished fertility.[53] For Louis Sullivan, searching for a language with which to describe his hopes for a nascent national architectural style, the discourse of miscegenation—associated with impurity, infertility, perversity, and unnaturalness—proved useful for critiquing a "mongrel" form of design he hoped to discourage.

Whereas advocates of eclecticism borrowed the evolutionary language of race science to advocate for the slow development of an American skyscraper architecture from historical precedents, Sullivan, enamored with the distinctiveness of the nation's democratic principles as well as its landscape, encouraged his peers to turn to its native nature rather than to European history for evolutionary precedent. Evolutionary theory, as David S. Andrew notes, was a leitmotif running throughout Sullivan's writing, ideas he culled from the work of Charles Darwin, Herbert Spencer, John Draper, and Max Nordau, whose work on degeneration Sullivan owned in translation.[54] Although Sullivan's personal design philosophy is perhaps best understood, as Andrew suggests, as "an often baffling admixture of unintegrated streams of thought," his investment in the language of evolution and, more specifically, miscegenation and mixture remained relatively consistent across his writing if not his aesthetic practice.[55]

Sullivan drew upon tropes of miscegenation to describe not only eclecticism's failures on the level of surface appearances but also its aberrant relationship to underlying structure.[56] Drawing from the principles of architectural
theorists Viollet-le-Duc and, more principally, John Ruskin, Sullivan subscribed to
the program of what Ruskin termed "honest architecture."[57] Proponents of this
idea maintained that a building's exterior should convey how it was put together
and that there should be no discrepancies between the structural story commu-
nicated by a building's exterior and its underlying internal supports. Honest
architecture folded easily into Sullivan's organicist philosophy based on the
principle, as he wrote in his famed essay "The Tall Office Building Artistically
Considered," that "the pervading law of all things organic and inorganic" was "that
the life is recognizable in its expression."[58] "All things in nature have a shape"
or "outward semblance," as Sullivan argued, "that tells us what they are."[59]
Just as the surfaces of biological organisms reflected their internal structure—
or, as physiognomy would have it, as the surfaces of the human body indexed
underlying intelligence and character—so, too, Sullivan insists, should exterior
envelopes reflect a building's essential form. To transform the skyscraper from
"this sterile, this crude, harsh brutal agglomeration" into something with the
"graciousness of those higher forms of sensibility and culture," Sullivan insists
architects "seek the solution" in the analogous process of "natural law."[60]

Applying the theory of honest architecture to the skyscraper, Sullivan describes the idea of cladding "a steel form function in a masonry form" in a 1900
essay as being as "queer" a combination to him as the idea of "pumpkin-bearing
frogs," "tarantula potatoes," or "sparrows in the form of whales, picking up crumbs
in the street."[61] Taking his reproductive metaphors a step further, Sullivan declares a few sentences later that "American architecture of today is the offspring
of an illegitimate commerce with the mongrel styles of the past." While he does
not explicitly invoke the word *miscegenation* in this passage, Sullivan's reliance
on natural metaphors of mixture to mark unnatural forms of architectural hybridity follows the same argumentative logic that race scientists had long used
to depict miscegenation as improper and abnormal, dating as far back, as Philip
Steadman notes, to naturalist George Cuvier's 1817 claim regarding the "innate
repugnance in all species to such illegitimate alliances."[62]

Several architects joined Sullivan in reinforcing the association between
"honest" exterior design and a natural ethics. Journals from the period are filled
with writings by architects using terms like *truthfulness, honesty, fact-based,
frank,* and *rationalistic* to describe exterior designs that "confessed" their steel
skeletons. By comparison, hybrid structures that gaudily "masked" their skele-

tons in egregious ornament were disparaged as *sins, fictions, concealments, simulations,* and *irrelevances.* Though there was much about skyscraper construction that fascinated turn-of-the-century Americans both in person and in print, seeing incomplete skyscrapers allowed their beholders to catch one last glimpse of their internal structure that might or might not be indexed by its external surfaces.[63]

While European-inflected eclecticism proved to be the prevailing style for skyscraper exteriors in the late nineteenth and early twentieth centuries, debates about skyscraper style continued to consume the profession for years after. Critic H. W. Desmond wrote in 1904 that "whenever the subject comes uppermost, at convention, or meeting, or elsewhere, among two or among a hundred, there is inevitably in a short time a shrugging of shoulders and finally a dismissal of the matter as one of the impossibilities of life." Reports of these disputes about skyscraper design circulated beyond the field of architecture into the public sphere even as the general public found the exact stakes of these debates hard to parse. As the author of a 1907 article in *Harper's Weekly* titled "Modern Towers of Babel in New York" attests, "there is no use trying to discuss the artistic side of modern tall buildings" because "there are too many critics of rival camps to make the work pleasant. No two agree, or at least if they have any point on which they can favorably compare notes they obscure their words or praise or condemnation by terms too technical for the ordinary reader to comprehend."[64]

But the ultimate irony of the earliest disagreements about skyscraper style in the nineteenth century was that both the architects advocating for "honest" organicist design central to a nativist aesthetic program and their adversaries favoring the adaptation of European historical styles to clad this new structure were each indebted to the language and ideas of evolution and miscegenation emerging from scientific racism. Beaux-Arts-oriented architects drew from the language of evolution to gird their preference for skyscraper designs borrowing from established European forms perfected over time. And yet Louis Sullivan, Beaux-Arts eclecticism's greatest opponent, was just as quick to use the rhetoric of racist science to insist on the impurity of such an ethos, accusing skyscraper exteriors modeled after European precedents of "squeal[ing] of miscegenation."[65]

Although there were no articles by African American architects published in the mainstream architectural journals of the late nineteenth and early twentieth centuries, one article on skyscraper form printed in a black newspaper suggests its author's awareness of, and even a resistance to, the use of these evolutionary-based arguments in opinions about architectural style. The anonymous author of the 1912 *Chicago Defender* article "Poetry in Skyscrapers"

Reliance Building, 1890 (*top*). New York Life
Insurance Building, 1894 (*bottom*). Both
Chicago steel-frame buildings, under construc-
tion in the midst of receiving external walls.
Images of skyscrapers under construction
regularly appeared in books and periodicals
around the turn of the twentieth century.
Top, Joseph Kendall, *Architectural Engineering with
Special Reference to High Building Construction*
(New York: John Wiley & Sons, 1909) 48.
Bottom, E. Benjamin Andrews, *History of the
United States,* vol. 5 (New York: Charles Scribner's
Sons, 1912) 108.

critiques classicism as an American façade style, recognizing the racial stakes of these aesthetic arguments and proposing an aesthetic intervention of his or her own. "It is a mistake," the author writes, "to think we must go back a thousand years or more for genuine poetic inspiration or that the poet of today must necessarily confine himself to the veins that the Greeks worked to create their lasting vogue. There is poetry in the big modern institutions where twentieth-century life pulsates, if only there be the imagination that can treat it in a masterly way."[66] Criticizing Beaux-Arts eclecticism as a form of "confinement," the author of this *Defender* piece pushes against ideas about the intrinsic superiority of European forms without seeking recourse in Sullivan-esque organicism. Belying this writer's insistence that architects turn away from an exclusionary past and harness the "poetry" of modernity capable of bringing new modes of seeing into being attests to a belief in architecture's power to engender new aesthetic and social hierarchies.

As architectural critic H. A. Caparn noted in the *Craftsman* in 1906, "the skyscraper forces a crisis in what we expect from our structures and how we find surface correlating to our structures."[67] Today, accustomed to the gravity-defying exteriors of Frank Gehry, Rem Koolhaas, and Renzo Piano, as well as postmodernism's gleeful cannibalism of historical styles, it is hard to imagine a time when such fanciful exteriors were denounced. Resituating debates about skyscraper style within their rhetorical contexts makes visible the racial anxiety animating concerns about mixed-up façades and deceptive surfaces at the turn of the century. "What appears to be the building is a mask, a make-believe, in which an imaginary construction has to be more or less resorted to."[68] For this critic writing for *Architectural Record* in 1909, architectural façade could no longer be approached as a natural outgrowth of its structure nor its history but as a manipulable covering untethered from any orienting anchors. In this portrayal of skyscrapers harboring false façades masking their structural truths, however, we hear not so much the language of miscegenation but an echo of the growing concern in the early twentieth century that skin, too, might be an "imaginary construction" masking deeper racial truths.

Passing and Skyscrapers

The "mongrel" nature of America's march to modernity feared by nineteenth-century naturalists was seen by many to find actualization in Manhattan in the 1920s.[69] Home to the simultaneous renaissances of racist science and black arts, Jazz Age Manhattan was where a growing number of white metropolitans expressed feeling simultaneously fascinated by and fearful of the growing number of racial others redefining urbanity. By 1920, one out of every four residents in New York State was foreign born, most of whom resided in New York City. Joining these immigrants were the hundreds of thousands of African Americans who arrived in the city during the Great Migration.[70] Melting-pot theories of assimilation once promising a harmoniously blended citizenry seemed quaintly outdated by the 1920s in the wake of the first Red Scare, the bombing of Wall Street allegedly carried out by anarchic European immigrants, and the rise of Garveyism.

Skyscrapers were the structural anchors around which the city's tumultuous events and diverse populations were frequently plotted. And yet, for all the academic interest skyscrapers have garnered, their effect on the lived experience of race in New York and other dense American cities has received scant attention. Ann Douglas's landmark history of interracial Manhattan, *Terrible Honesty: Mongrel Manhattan in the 1920s* is particularly instructive in its treatment of this architecture. Douglas discusses skyscrapers at length but in isolation from her broader investigations of race relations in the city, ultimately approaching the skyscraper as sharing a time frame with "black arts" but not any actual contact.[71] However, Nella Larsen's 1929 novel *Passing*, set in the skyscraper meccas of New York City and Chicago, paints a very different portrait of the relationship between black arts, passing bodies, and tall buildings. Whereas the language of miscegenation helped shape the early skyscraper's aesthetic development, Larsen's novel marks the ways the skyscraper exacerbated the "miscegenating" perceptual conditions of American cities, making it hard to see and be seen according to fixed racial rubrics. *Passing* represents racial perception not as a single linear act but as a collection of sensations and calculations conditioned by the built environment. Disrupting the ability to approach race as an empirical symptom, skyscrapers in *Passing* help induce other phenomenologies of race.

Although passing has a history at least as long as America itself, as Allyson Hobbs chronicles in her history of this phenomenon, the first published use of the term in reference to a person of black ancestry living as a white person only dates back to Carl Van Vechten's 1926 Harlem novel *Nigger Heaven.*[72] Nella Larsen's *Passing* is one of several texts exploring this theme in the late 1920s when this act was imagined to be increasingly germane to modern urban living. Racial passing is treated as an epidemic, for instance, in the 1929 pamphlet *From Negro to Caucasian, or How the Ethiopian Is Changing His Skin.* Approaching passing as a distinctly urban phenomenon, the pamphlet's author insists on the existence of countless numbers of passers hiding amid the "millions of salesmen and saleswomen," the "other millions of stenographers or telephone operators," and the "millions of street-car motormen and conductors" needed to engine the urban economy.[73] This pamphlet's lone pair of illustrations further dramatize passing as a phenomenon yoked to urbanization. The first image depicts a more pastoral scene featuring a young girl named Ethel whose status as black is derived from the darker-skinned playmates surrounding her in the sparse foreground, while the skyline looms ominously in the distance. The second image depicts an adult Ethel ten years later now firmly ensconced within the city and passing as white. She is shown selling hosiery in a downtown department store to a white man whom the accompanying text suggests she will marry under false racial pretenses. Together these images correlate the rising interest in passing and accelerating trends of urbanization.

With the revived interest in passing in the 1920s, the country's worst anxieties about the severance of indexical surfaces from deeper anchoring structures seemed to be coming true. Historian Karen Halttunen has detailed how urbanization altered the faith middle-class Americans placed in surfaces to convey trustworthy information.[74] In her work on advice manuals from the late nineteenth century, Halttunen examines the hypocrisy of Americans both wanting to maintain a belief in the honest transparency of surfaces and, at the same time, welcoming guidance about how to manipulate their own exteriors using clothing, makeup, and manners. Urbanization intensified this surface paradox as those moving to cities had to learn to navigate the conditions of anonymity common to urban experience. In his 1915 essay on the city, sociologist Robert Park recapitulates growing discomfort with surfaces as the primary vehicles for knowing others in urban centers: "The individual's status is determined to a considerable degree by conventional signs—by fashion and 'front'—and the art of life is largely reduced to skating on thin surfaces and a scrupulous study of style and manners."[75] As fashioned "fronts" seemed to be displacing more indexical forms of authentic surface in the wake of urbanization, writers and journalists bemoaned the diminishing capacity to successfully perceive, and by extension, know others. Such concerns about deceitful surfaces, consistently shadowed by concerns about inadvertent racial intermixture, culminated in the obsession with passing engulfing urban centers in the early twentieth century.

The modern city was seen as both facilitating interracial contact, resulting in the birth of more "passers," and providing a haven for mixed-race persons desiring to pass. *Century Magazine* reported in 1925, for instance, that "literally

Images from the 1929 pamphlet *From Negro to Caucasian*: "Our attention was called to cases of 'PASSING' in dozens of cities throughout the country, and after interviewing scores of the older colored residents of several Eastern seaboard states, a recent tour of investigation was made, in an attempt to locate some of those children whose parents had told of how 'Ethel got a job in a Department Store and married one of her white customers.'" Note the change of setting from the more rural schoolyard in which her context surrounded by several more pronouncedly black children announces Ethel's blackness, with the city looming ominously in the background, to the urban scene of passing.

Louis Fremont Baldwin, *From Negro to Caucasian, or How the Ethiopian Is Changing His Skin* (San Francisco: Pilot Publishing Company, 1929) 14.

thousands" of passing African Americans existed in New York City alone.[76] Another article from the same period insisted there were "hundreds of men and women in New York City who, although fully aware of their racial affiliations have gone over on 'the other side' and feel highly elated over being able to practice deception."[77] Southern states ratified racial purity laws more firmly defining racial categories with the twinned hope of preventing interracial marriage and barring the children of those unions from claiming whiteness through passing's "back door method."[78] But in northern cities of growing density and genealogical anonymity, few had faith that there was a law strong enough to combat savvy passers leveraging the perceptual and genealogical confusion associated with urbanization to their benefit.

As the public became increasingly fascinated by the possibility of "secret" urbane African Americans in their midst, writers such as Nella Larsen, Walter White, and Jessie Fauset created fictional characters who wielded their bodies in ways that destabilized the logic of the racial symptom. Their novels rendered passing as more than just an individual's prerogative, yoking this act to longer trajectories of American racism as well as the more recent demographic, perceptual, economic, and material transformations wrought by industrialization and urbanization. Nella Larsen's *Passing* is particularly cogent in the way it demonstrates the failures of traditional racial classifications, depicting the larger perceptual economy formed by modern bodies, buildings, and objects whose disorienting surfaces and estranging scales disrupted assumptions about the empirical reality of race.

Larsen spends much of *Passing* exploring whether race could ever be as fungible as modernity's other miracle surfaces and what forms of liberation a material approach to race might bring about. And, indeed, for much of the book's duration, skin joins what Anne Cheng has described as a broader category of modernist surfaces capable of arresting meaning rather than stabilizing it.[79] Cheng correlates the dream of the skyscraper—its impenetrable surface functioning as a prosthesis of sorts for the human body—to the desire for a second skin, a fantasy that " reveals the profound and perhaps utopic desire to refabricate human geography as bodies, places, and nations."[80] But by the novel's end, Larsen differentiates between the desire to perceive race from the body—a task subject to perpetual confusion—and race itself, a category more ephemeral and elastic than the physical racial symptoms to which it is often linked. Even if racial perception falters within America's growing cities, Larsen's novel suggests, there is no building tall enough, no street dense enough to permanently decommission the desire for race or to dismantle the economic and social systems built on and maintained by racial hierarchies—structures that ultimately endure in the novel in ways no physical material could.

Though the skyscraper plays a large role in the mechanics of the novel's opening and closing scenes, *Passing* contains only a single explicit reference to this structure. It comes over halfway through the book, after protagonist Irene suspects her estranged friend, Clare, raised black but currently passing as a white woman, of sleeping with her husband. In considering how to proceed with her suspicions, Irene contemplates giving in to her husband's long-standing desire to move their family to Brazil to escape the racism of the United States. She ultimately rules against this action through a jingoistic appeal: "She belonged in this land of rising towers. She was an American. She grew from this soil, and she would not be uprooted. Not even because of Clare Kendry, or a hundred Clare Kendrys."[81]

The analogy Irene constructs between herself, a black woman light and wealthy enough to pass, and the skyscraper—approaching them together as two like products forged from the American soil—was the kind of pairing inspiring dread within the hearts of white metropolitans who worried about their own racial uprooting in cities increasingly framed by "rising towers" helping "a hundred Clare Kendrys" or Irene Redfields to pass undetected in their midst. Irene claims the skyscraper with ease in these lines as a personal symbol of triumph, rhetorically reifying the concerns of American architects at the turn of the century that the skyscraper might favor the nation's racially heterogeneous population rather than the white European architectural precedents they preferred. Irene's analogy vividly encapsulates the connection between racial determinacy and the skyscraper found in both its material and cultural histories.

But *Passing*'s lone explicit reference to the skyscraper is something of a red herring. Despite its suggestive appearance in this dramatic declaration, the skyscraper does not appear anywhere else in the novel either as a discrete object of direct reference or of descriptive importance. Tall buildings make up a good deal of the novel's settings, but Larsen rarely draws our attention to their presence directly. This does not negate the skyscraper's influence within Larsen's text but suggests, rather, that this architecture's most meaningful role in the novel is as a background catalyst of urban experience, shaping the physical and spatial conditions framing many of the novel's foreground events. The skyscraper appears most forcefully in *Passing* as the sum of its effects on perceiving and feeling in the city, both directly and indirectly instigating a host of actions contributing to the breakdown of racial discernment occurring across the novel.

Larsen highlights the racial consequences of the skyscraper's secondary effects on density, sight lines, and the limits of attention by rendering both the immediate failures of older methods for perceiving race in cities shaped by skyscrapers and the more gradual forms of dissensus accruing around the act of racial perception within legal and social spheres. In *Passing*, the skyscraper appears less as an icon and more like an agent producing a slew of effects on urban density and perception cumulatively transforming the material and perceptual idioms of race.

Larsen's light touch in rendering the skyscraper's impactful presence is representative of her larger interest during this period in developing new tactics for capturing the tenor of contemporary lived racial experience. Her meditations on modernist prose in 1926, a few years prior to writing *Passing*, foreground her sense that writers needed new ways to render black cosmopolitan life. Responding to Frank Horne's negative review in *Opportunity* of Walter White's 1926 passing novel, *Flight*, Larsen expressed her frustrations to friend and *Opportunity* editor Charles Johnson regarding proponents of realism who refused to seriously engage more experimental forms of writing in relation to race. First confessing to possess a mind "warped . . . by the Europeans and the American moderns," Larsen writes that Horne's disparagement of *Flight* for its "lack of clarity," "confusion of characters," and "faulty sentence structure" were all "sins" that had escaped her.[82] "But then," as Larsen writes, "I have been recently reading Huysmans, Conrad, Proust, and Thomas Mann. Naturally these things would not irritate me as they would an admirer of Louis Hemon and Mrs. Wharton." Larsen suggests that, in contrast to the work of realists such as Hemon and Wharton, within White's novel, "actions and words count less and the poetic conception of the character, the psychology of the scene more." Comparing Horne's literary conservatism with her own "modern" outlook, Larsen implies that readers of realism who refused works like White's failed to grasp not only aesthetic subtlety but also the changing rhythms of modern life increasingly rooted in the ephemeral unsaid over elusive empirical certainty.[83]

Larsen would embrace many of the tenets she ascribes to modernism in this 1926 letter when writing her own novel on the subject soon after. *Passing* could be described as a novel built around poetic characters and psychological scenes as Larsen chooses to narratively privilege unverifiable inferences over securable truths. The novel continually points the reader's attention to the entangled material and mental conditions leading to the deterioration of actions and words as self-evident forms of documentation.[84] As bodies melt, sear, and tear in the midst of dense cities framed by dizzying skyscrapers, Larsen zeroes in on these physical sites where the older logics that had once guided the perception of race start to unravel.

Irene and Clare's initial encounter in downtown Chicago foregrounds the multiple orientations and forms of gazing that the skyscraper influenced both at its street-level base and within its insulated interior. Before immersing the reader within Irene's experience of this encounter, Larsen first provides us with Clare's description of this event in a letter she sends to Irene shortly after their meeting. Clare describes their meeting and her subsequent emotional response to it using fairly standard visual metaphors, writing to Irene that "you can't know how in this pale life of mine, I am all the time *seeing* the bright pictures of that other that I once thought I was glad to be free of" (italics mine).[85] "Seeing" appears again in the letter when Clare explains that her "wild desire" to reconnect with the black community would never have occurred "if I hadn't *seen* you that time in Chicago" (italics mine). In both instances, Clare casually refers to the act of seeing as relatively straightforward, treating it as the obvious catalyst for her eventual emotional revelations.

The rhetoric of seeing becomes strange, however, when we notice Irene's avoidance of this commonplace language when she provides the reader with her account of events. When both citing and summarizing Clare's letter in the next paragraph, Irene circumvents Clare's language of seeing, describing her letter as being in reference to "that time in Chicago" rather than, as Clare phrases it, when they had last "seen" one another. Irene's version of their encounter here emerges as not so much something *seen* but *felt*, inducing in her a "clear, sharp remembrance" of the "humiliation, resentment, and rage" over any finite content triggering these sensations.[86] She treats the empirical substance of their encounter as divorced from the more visceral sensations it evokes within her. This noticeable difference between Irene and Clare's perceptual relationship to the surrounding world continues to define their relationship over the rest of the novel. Clare lives her life according to her faith that seeing is believing, a confidence allowing her to hold firm in the security of her racial performance. Irene, by comparison, most strongly trusts her sense of the things even in spite of perceivable evidence to the contrary. She is constantly pushing against the world of demonstrative "actions and words" that Larsen referred to in her 1926 letter, preferring deferred and inferred knowledge, an orientation that eventually colors her approach to race.

But Irene's hesitation to frame her Chicago outing in perceptual terms is as attributable to the physical context of the city that made perception difficult as to her own penchant for sensing over seeing. When the scene of Irene and Clare's encounter is recounted at greater length in the next chapter, Larsen most strongly paints it in terms of perceptual duress. Though the skyscraper is not explicitly named as the agent of the scene's sensory difficulties, the density of bodies and things Larsen depicts as overwhelming Irene in downtown Chicago—a problem referred to by critics at the time as one of "congestion"—was commonly attributed in the public sphere to the growing number of tall buildings overloading finite downtown spaces. As one defense of the skyscraper published by the American Institute of Steel Construction in 1930 acknowledged, "in the public mind, probably the major count in the indictment of the skyscraper is its alleged effect in increasing traffic congestion," before admitting that "congestion is unquestionably the most serious problem" and a "serious evil."[87] The steel construction intrinsic to the skyscraper that allowed more of a city block's total space to be inhabited than ever before also had the effect of concentrating more and more people onto streets and sidewalks built prior to the skyscraper's invention and not designed to accommodate such heavy traffic. Critics of the skyscraper commonly referred to congestion woes when disparaging this architecture and its effects on everyday life. In his famous 1929 treatise on the city, *The Metropolis of Tomorrow*, architectural illustrator Hugh Ferriss suggested that "going down into the streets of a modern city must seem—to the newcomer, at least—a little like Dante's descent into Hades. Certainly so unacclimated a visitor would find, in the dense atmosphere, in the kaleidoscopic sights, the confused noise and the complex physical contacts, something very reminiscent of the lower realms."[88] Congestion, in his opinion, was "rapidly approaching the point of public danger."[89] "As the avenues and streets of a city are nothing less than its arteries and veins," Ferriss concludes, "we may well ask what doctor would venture to promise bodily health if he knew that the blood circulation was steadily growing more congested!"[90]

No one was more critical of the skyscraper and its effects on crowding and the quality of life in cities than architectural critic Lewis Mumford. In his 1924 book *Sticks and Stones*, Mumford wrote of the skyscraper that "a city so generously planned would have no need for this sort of building whose sole economic purpose is to make the most of monopoly and congestion."[91] Mumford insisted that the skyscraper was not scaled for the realities of urban living, believing it to have been built for the appreciation of "angels and aviators" privy to distant aerial views of the city rather than everyday city dwellers who could hardly see it, or anything else, from their crowded street-level perspective. "In order to accommodate the office-dwellers in the Chicago Loop, for example, if a minimum of twenty stories were the restriction, the streets would have to be 241 feet wide."[92] Mumford maintained that the "obdurate, overwhelming masses" of skyscrapers were responsible for "tak[ing] away from the little people who walk in their shadows any semblance of dignity as human beings."[93] Such structures, he harshly surmises, "have precious little to do with the human arts of seeing, feeling, and living."[94]

It is a congested downtown scene much like the ones described by Ferriss and Mumford that Irene finds herself in the midst of on a hot Chicago afternoon when she first reunites with Clare. The details of Irene's experience of the city leading up to her encounter with Clare generally affirm her belief, as well as Mumford's, that "seeing" was inadequate to capturing the experience of bending buildings, sticky bodies, and dripping skin in vertically oriented urban epicenters.[95] In search of a "mechanical aeroplane" and "drawing-book" for her sons—objects, it is worth mentioning, notable for their manipulable surfaces—Irene describes the oppressive conditions of heat and density impeding her pursuit of them within Chicago's Loop. With the sun beating down "like molten rain," a sensation intensified by the tall buildings synonymous with Chicago's downtown, the cityscape turns into an indeterminate slush.[96] Surfaces appear to melt away from flaccid buildings as dust whips up, "stinging the seared or dripping skins of wilting pedestrians."[97] Buildings "shudder" and "quiver" in ways analogous to bodies, while skins "sear" and "drip" in the fashion of melted materials. In this blurry scene, surfaces oscillate, deflecting interpretation and refusing to stand in as firm markers or stable boundaries.

The city appears in this scene as a morass of congested confusion filled with surfaces that refuse to hold together let alone serve as indices for interior structures. Bodies ensconced in this environment are described as literally "giving out." "Right before her smarting eyes" Irene spies "a man toppled over" into "an inert crumpled heap." A nameless bystander emerging from the crowd that instantaneously springs up around this fallen figure asks Irene if the man has died or merely fainted. Here, and later in the aftermath of Clare's deadly fall from her skyscraper apartment that this scene foreshadows, Irene refuses to look deeper into the incident to know more about this downed person: "Irene didn't know and didn't try to discover. She edged her way out of the increasing crowd, feeling disagreeably damp and sticky and soiled from contact with so many sweating bodies."[98] How Irene "feels"—damp and sticky—trumps her desire to "know" or "discover" what led to the man's fall. She dwells in the realm of unanchored sensation facilitated by the city's perceptual and atmospheric dif-

ficulties, allowing for a gap between her experience of the world and its triggering material contexts to emerge.

In addition to documenting the skyscraper's direct and indirect effects on
the dignity of the sovereign individual, Larsen illustrates this architecture's
ability to shape forms of urban relationality. In this Chicago scene, Irene
moves in and out of groups of people without gaining much knowledge of or
intimacy with them. Larsen's depiction of the social distance accompanying
physical proximity in cities resonates with the findings of urban sociologists
from the period about the limits of interpersonal relations in early twentieth-
century urban centers. Building from the insights of German sociologist
Georg Simmel, Robert Park, along with several of his colleagues associated
with the Chicago School of Sociology, demonstrated how the growing spatial
proximity occasioned by urbanization failed to bring about greater familiarity
between the discrete racial populations living closer and closer together.[99]
Passing reinforces a version of this claim both in Irene's machinations and
those of the novel's narrator who brings the reader in close physical and psychic proximity to characters in these congested settings while refusing to disclose their inner motives or "authentic" feelings.[100] Like Irene on this downtown city street, we as readers can never scale in close enough to get a firm
grasp on its subjects or its settings. We follow Irene from scene to scene but are
given few details about what is in them. The "human arts of seeing, feeling,
and living" Mumford claimed the skyscraper impeded appear further blunted
in *Passing* where characters and readers alike fail to feel or see clearly in urban
centers.

Robert Park and his Chicago students and colleagues pursued their inqui-
ries into disorienting forms of urban sociality primarily along racial lines, mapping and classifying forms of interracial contact to make larger claims about the
nature of urban alienation. But in stark opposition to urban sociology's racialized
interest in measuring the social, *Passing*'s rendition of Chicago's urban density
in this opening street scene contains not a single reference to race. The ability to
see race, a possibility linked in some sense to the ability to first see, appears to
malfunction along with the rest of the perceptual faculties amid the dripping
bodies and stinging hot wind concentrated by the skyscraper. Neither Irene's
race nor the race of anyone else sharing the street with her is explicitly denoted by
the text. When Irene starts to feel like she might faint, she easily solicits a cab to
take her elsewhere without expressing any fear that she may be denied on the
basis of her race. The cab that picks her up takes her to the nearby Drayton

Hotel, a place where she might, as Irene notes, "repair the damage that the heat and the crowds had done to her appearance." It is presumably the cab driver's perception of her class status telegraphed by her modish clothing and grooming, likely informing his understanding of her race as well, that leads him deliver her to the luxurious Drayton.

Once she arrives at the Drayton, Irene's class presentation, facilitating her welcome within this chic hotel, goes unremarked by the novel. Class serves as the stable background against which the fungibility of racial perception, the focus of the scene to come, unfolds. We spend over a dozen paragraphs with Irene as she settles into her surroundings at the Drayton before race enters her consciousness. It is not until Irene tenses up under Clare's steady gaze that we remember the racial trespassing Irene has inadvertently undertaken to arrive here. Until this moment, the racial symptom has had neither the time nor space to cross her mind or to perceptually materialize in front of her on the congested city street. Though her delayed racial consciousness could be ascribed to Irene's more general knack for repression, the anonymity and difficult perceptual conditions of the city grant Irene's racially indeterminate skin even more room to escape examination. The chaos of the urban scene makes it possible for her to "edge" away from downtown's crowds and toward the isolated repose she finds atop the Drayton. Despite almost bringing her to her knees, the street's chaos also enables Irene to flee it.

Irene's rescue from Chicago's dense downtown punctuated by skyscrapers ironically comes in the form of another skyscraper. Though unannounced as such in the novel, the Drayton, the hotel to which Irene retreats from the heat and crowds, would have been considered a skyscraper at the time of *Passing*'s writing. While the sixth-floor New York apartment building from which Clare falls at the novel's end or the seventeenth-story apartment in which Irene resides remain nameless and relatively nondescript in the novel, several analogues for the Drayton exist within the historical record. The likeliest match is the Drake Hotel, built in 1920 on Chicago's Magnificent Mile.[101] At thirteen stories, the Drake was not much of a skyscraper by New York standards, especially in comparison to the fifty-seven-story Woolworth Building. But by Chicago standards, the Drake was massive. As the tallest building east of Michigan Avenue at the time of its construction, it qualified as a tall building of note.

Irene describes her arrival on the Drayton's rooftop café as akin to "being wafted upward on a magic carpet to another world, pleasant, quiet, and strangely remote from the sizzling one that she had left below." In this homogeneous space atop this tall building, Irene, seemingly insulated from the burden of ra-

Postcard of the Drake Hotel soon after its construction.

cial detection, begins to regain her capacity to see as she "surveyed the room around her" before resting her sights on a window view framing "some lower buildings at the bright unstirred blue of the lake reaching away to an undetected horizon." Not only can Irene once again take in what is around her from this raised vantage, but her vision is seemingly infinite, avoiding the mixed-up bodies located below to focus on the lake view extending far beyond the street. This scene of Irene gazing atop a skyscraper exemplifies critiques of panoptic vistas as sites of imperial empowerment, where, as Dianne Harris and D. Fairchild Ruggles write, the distanced viewer "brings a landscape into being but remains unseen, and is therefore is imbued with a globalizing sense of totality."[102] But it is not just the distancing height of this vista that matters to Irene here but the specific view of Lake Michigan it affords her, enabling her preferred mode of immersive gazing without the burden of detecting distinctions. Everything washes together into one blue panorama.

It doesn't take long, however, for the threat of the racial gaze to interrupt this reposeful scene of infinite nonindexical staring. While Irene's lake view from the top of the Drayton grants her the pleasure of perception without the burden of interpretation, the enclosing walls of the hotel framing the staid glances of its occupants start to trigger Irene's concerns about being outed as black in this white space. Noticing the intense gaze of a woman that she only later recognizes as Clare, Irene panics, wondering, "Did that woman, could that woman, somehow know that here before her very eyes on the roof of a Drayton sat a Negro?" The steady gaze required for racial detection, unimaginable a few moments ago, suddenly becomes viable within the Drayton's calm perceptual conditions, a possibility to which Irene must quickly adjust. She brings her suspicions about the detective power of white "eyes" under control by reiterating to herself the idiocies of such a gaze: "White people were so stupid about such things for all that they usually asserted that they were able to tell; and by the most ridiculous means, finger-nails, palms of hands, shapes of ears, teeth, and other equally silly rot."[103] Irene can attempt to debunk the truth of the racial symptom only from within a setting where the symptom is visually viable.

Up to this point in the novel, we have followed Irene from her immersion within a street-level mode of perception too fragmented and dizzying to support acts of racial perception to her perceptual repose atop the Drayton where she inadvertently passes as white—temporarily freeing her from the burdens of both urban fragmentation and racial detection—to finally being jolted back into the world of the racial gaze when faced with the Drayton's white diners. Irene cycles through these different modes of gazing in accordance with the various spaces she inhabits and the types of gazing they support. But Irene's attempt to train her vision on Clare presents the most disorienting moment of gazing in the entire chapter. Once she recognizes Clare and realizes who she is, Irene is momentarily entranced by her theory of the body as a moldable surface. Clare explains to Irene that passing is "such a frightfully easy thing to do," requiring only "a little nerve" if "one's the type."[104] Clare approaches her own body almost like a Model T, manipulating her own surfaces without much concern about the "real" blood that lies beneath. But Irene cannot stop herself from hunting for the "Negro" features she presumes must be legible on Clare's body in some fashion. Despite her protests about the "stupidities" of racial detection just a few sentences earlier, Irene now vigorously works to discover Clare's racial symptoms while simultaneously trying to enjoy Clare's surfaces as nonindexical founts of pleasure, resulting in this confusing and conflicting description:

> And the eyes were magnificent! Dark, sometimes absolutely black, always luminous, and set in long, black lashes. Arresting eyes, slow and mesmeric, and with, for all their warmth, something withdrawn and secret about them. Ah! Surely! They were Negro eyes! Mysterious and concealing. And set in that ivory face under that bright hair, there was about them something exotic.[105]

Referring to Clare not as "her" but "the" in the course of her scopic binge, Irene allows herself within the insulated space at the top of this skyscraper to indulge in contradictory forms of gazing and reading. Adopting the distant analytical eye of race scientists, Irene dissects Clare's "Negro eyes." And yet, at the same time, she approaches Clare's body here as an object expertly engineered to "conceal," radiating a mysterious luminosity that requires no deeper explanatory structure for its appeal. Irene treats Clare as an aesthetic riddle she prefers to puzzle over than to solve. She moves between treating Clare as an enticing object harboring a mesmerizing surface and an undercover Negress genealogically yoked to a blackness that will never fade. At one instance, Irene exults in discovering traces of Clare's hidden racial secret on her body, while in the next we find her reveling in Clare's nonindexical façade, taking pleasure in its status as pure surface. At the end of the passage, Clare's face appears as something artificially "set" rather than a biological bearer of symptomatic racial truth.

Unlike the sensory meltdown she experiences on the dense Chicago street, Irene atop the Drayton has the freedom to indulge in not one form of gazing but several—embracing the pleasures of racial perception when hungrily gazing at Clare, while, at the same time, actively seeking relief from being gazed at in this way. Though the physical conditions of the street she has just left behind are harsh and disorienting, it is the more seemingly neutral and staid conditions of the Drayton achieved through the exclusion of visibly marked racial others and the lower classes, as well as its physical contours where Irene's experience of gazing is most psychically damaging. She feels the threat of racial violence for the first time here in this enclosed space where the patrons have room to engage in acts of racial perception unfeasible on the street of a few moments prior. The more austere chambers of the insulated skyscraper allow a flood of racial information to confront Irene, data she must laboriously decide how to process. The physical discomfort and perceptual disorientation Irene experienced within Chicago's downtown congestion ironically seem to offer her the best chance of repose, freeing her from the burden of both perceiving and being perceived that suddenly engulf her atop the Drayton. When she is on the street, Irene does not have to actively choose whether to racially pass or not; the exterior chaos of urban congestion does not allow for Irene to express a conscious orientation toward race. While Mumford and Ferriss detail the ills of the skyscraper's effects on congestion, Larsen suggests the strange forms of relief that may come from perceptual disorientation for subjects continually at the mercy of the racial gaze.

Though it is more immediately apparent how Irene's experience of the hot Chicago streets is shaped by the presence of skyscrapers, the conflicting forms of racial gazing Irene experiences atop the insulating space of the Drayton are also linked, if more indirectly, to the conditions of congestion and anonymity associated with the skyscraper and urbanization. Whereas *Passing*'s opening pair of chapters dramatize the more direct effects of crowded buildings and bodies on acts of racial perception, slower adjustments to how race was perceived and interpreted were taking place within more formal legal settings as well as informal social systems tasked with adjudicating racial classification in the wake of these perceptual changes. The real-life 1925 *Rhinelander* court case in New York, one of the most followed court cases of the decade, captures some of the transformations to racial perception in this period. *Passing*'s narrator even refers to the trial as an example of what could happen to Clare should her black heritage become publicly known. But more than a reminder of the worst-case scenario facing Clare, the *Rhinelander* trial highlights the various scales of confusion surrounding racial perception following America's rapid urbanization.

The highly publicized case centered on the authenticity of the marriage between Leonard Rhinelander, the wealthy white heir to a Manhattan real estate empire, and the working-class Alice Jones, whose father was part black. Though Leonard almost certainly married Alice with full knowledge of her racial background, his family pressured him into seeking an annulment on the grounds that Jones had deceived him about her black ancestry. The trial arguments revolved around two conflicting modes of racial classification. Leonard Rhinelander's lawyers based their arguments on an understanding of race as a matter of blood, continually pointing to Alice Jones's father in court to reinforce this older model of race as birthright. Alice's fair appearance, his lawyers insisted, deceptively hid the truth of the black blood coursing through her veins.

The defense, on the other hand, as legal historian Elizabeth Smith-Pryor documents, attempted to "shift the logic of the case away from blood," the older hallmark of racial classification, to a more modern understanding of race dependent on vision, urging the jury to blame Leonard for his failure to read the racial signs her lawyers insisted were written all over Jones's body.[106] They argued that even if Alice had used makeup or clothing to cover her skin in her daily life—practices associated with the manipulated fronts in urban and anonymous settings that Karen Halttunen and Robert Park have described—the intimate knowledge Leonard would have possessed of her body as her husband should have been enough to clearly signal her blackness. In addition to submitting private letters detailing their premarital sex life, Alice's lawyers convinced her to submit her own body as evidence to the jury in support of this claim. She was asked to reveal her breasts and upper thighs in the judge's chambers, actions she complied with under much duress. This tactic ultimately worked—the jury agreed that while the man on the street may have found Alice's race indeterminate, her blackness was readily apparent on closer inspection. The court upheld their marriage, forcing Leonard to file for divorce and pay Jones a monthly settlement that she would claim until her death in 1989.

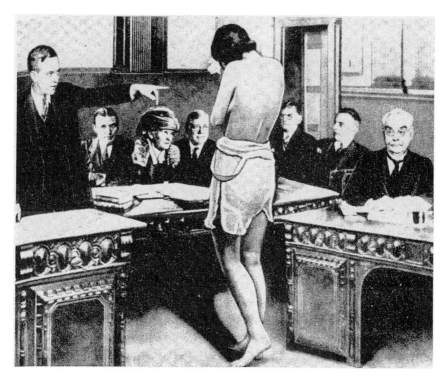

The first composograph, a staged picture made up of montage, appearing in the
Evening Graphic in 1925, allegedly depicting Alice Jones baring her skin to the judge
and jury.

The *Rhinelander* trial made national headlines, receiving daily coverage in
most major newspapers. The doctored "composograph" appearing in the *Evening
Graphic* during the trial further heightened the public frenzy for the case, boost-
ing the paper's circulation by 100,000 the day it ran. The falsified photograph
created through a process of montage—a stripper stood in for Alice—models
the fantasy of perfectly symptomatic skin providing reliable racial knowledge if
one only looks closely enough. The scene portrayed by the composograph is the
polar opposite of the one at *Passing*'s start in which Irene's jostled movements
through Chicago's dense downtown suggest the impossibility of racial gazing.
Contrast that fictional scene of urban chaos with the staid perceptual conditions of racial adjudication the *Evening Graphic* also fictionalizes. All the jurors
in its doctored image occupy the same horizontal sight line as they take a closely
scaled and unobstructed look at Jones's naked physique. The image makes the
case that while acts of racial detection may prove difficult and ineffectual in the

chaotic spaces of American cities, intimate and transparent acts of racial gazing remain both possible and legally viable. *Passing* insistently pushes against such a claim by repeatedly foregrounding the unreliability of racial gazing in a multitude of modern spaces, from base of the skyscraper to its lofty apex and everywhere in between. Even within the relatively restful setting atop the Drayton, Irene's methods of gazing radically shift from moment to moment, messily careening into one another. *Passing* upends the fiction purported by the *Rhinelander* trial and reinforced by the popularity of its accompanying composograph ensuring the ease of racial detection when undertaken in stable enough spatial conditions. In *Passing*, the Chicago street scene dramatizes the malfunctioning of the racial gaze that continually fails across all settings.

Uncertainty about the capacity to perceive race from bodily surfaces highlighted by both *Passing* and the *Rhinelander* trial resonates with earlier architectural debates about aberrant skyscrapers with nonindexical exteriors. In both of these contexts, miscegenated skin becomes a sign for deceptive urban surfaces threatening to upend the dream of simplified symptomatic reading. In fact, when situated next to the images of the half-clad skyscrapers featured earlier in this chapter, the composograph depicting Alice's stripped body visually echoes photographs and illustrations of incomplete skyscrapers capturing some of the last glimpses of their underlying structures before being covered over by their exteriors. These images of "peeled" bodies and buildings evoke different fantasies of surface in the city. Whereas images of incomplete skyscrapers bring the buildings' structural secrets into view, the *Rhinelander* composograph suggests that Jones's body can only be visually exposed to a point. In the *Evening Graphic*'s rendering of the jury's view, Alice's body can be peeled back no further beyond her clothes. If the eyes were to fail in perceiving race from her body, there might be no other viable means for ascertaining the "truth" of her race. Whereas architectural critics in the age of steel-frame construction resigned themselves to the notion that "what appears to be the building is a mask, a make-believe," the American public desperately needed to hold on to the belief that skin could deliver more certainty about racial ontology. It was easier to blame dense cities and good makeup for obstructing the authenticating racial gaze rather than to face the symptomatic limits of race itself.

Most of *Passing* emphasizes the fallacies of racial perception as characters continually fail to correctly connect phenotype to hereditarily informed definitions of race. But as the novel approaches its conclusion, it doubles back on itself, ultimately suggesting the futility of debunking the racial symptom as a means of permanently disrupting the primacy of race. Irene is the primary vehicle for

The *Rhinelander* composograph juxtaposed with an image of the Reliance Building under construction. Whereas images of incomplete skyscrapers bring the buildings' structural secrets into view the *Rhinelander* composograph suggests that Jones's body can only be visually exposed to a point.

this lesson, beginning with a seemingly innocuous exchange late in the novel during a conversation with Hugh Wentworth, a white writer and close friend of hers who casually mentions his inability to detect passers by sight. In her response to Hugh, Irene once more contradicts her earlier claim atop the Drayton that efforts to read race from bodily characteristics were "stupid" and "ridiculous." Instead of secretly pursuing racial detection as she does atop the Drayton, Irene now openly admits to Hugh she believes race can be detected. This time, however, she argues for race's more abstract existence in a realm beyond what can be empirically verified. Irene explains to him that race is not found "by looking" but is rather a matter of sensing "just—just something. A thing that couldn't be registered."[107] Faced with the empirical limits of racial perception across the novel's many settings, Irene ultimately shifts tactics here to reframe its perception as an extrasensory phenomenon, enabling her still to claim to "know" race in the absence of any perceivable evidence or supporting context.

Irene's theory of race as something sensed rather than something seen gives the reader one more theory of racial interpretation in a novel already replete with them. Even though no one in the novel seems to know "what race is," as Irene's husband insists elsewhere in *Passing*, its unknowability fails to stop Irene from both feeling it and seeking it out. Irene's admission that race will always exist for her in excess of the visible racial symptom is an important turning point. Prepared to treat race as a "something" divorced from, and in excess of, the perceivable body, Irene's response suggests that deflating the lie of the racial symptom actually does little to affect the belief in race. The *material* grounding of race and its *lived* experience turn out to be discrete phenomena. The built environment affects the lived experience of race throughout *Passing* in concrete ways, but Irene's described relationship to race as something sensed survives the perceptual disorientations that stress the unreliability of its empirical traces. The novel's experiment in approaching race materially ultimately runs up against Irene's extrarational orientation to race that proves more difficult to challenge.

From this point on in the novel, race functions less like other material surfaces and operates more like a ghost—something immaterial yet present, intangible yet visceral, a phenomenon in excess of any physical body that may host it or any environmental context that could surround it. The novel's opening juxtaposition of the chaotic city street surrounding the skyscraper with the experience of being at rest inside of one initially foregrounds the disparate effects various perceptual environments have on acts of racial perception. But Larsen ultimately suggests through Irene's embrace of the world of intuition over empiricism that, while architecture may alter the perceptual experience of race, the desire for intimacy with race transcends the presence of bodies and buildings framing its material life. If race can endure in excess of its perception as "just something," untethered from any empirical verification, then the tallest building in the world will fail to dislodge the psychic, structural, and economic needs race continues to fill. By the novel's end, race fails to be like the other modernist materials it gets compared to at various points in the book. Unlike the mechanical airplanes, coloring books, French Orientalist couture, and the various tall buildings that waft through the novel—objects representative of newly liberated surfaces disrupting the symptomatic relationship between interiors and exteriors celebrated by modernism—the desire for race supersedes its material reality. The perceptual conditions of urbanization may encourage "miscegenating" modes of vision; but *Passing* suggests in the end that debunking the legitimacy of the racial symptom fails to alter the desire to pursue the confirmation of race.

The two endings of *Passing* drive this conclusion home. Clare's husband arrives at a party that Clare and Irene are attending located on the sixth floor of a Manhattan apartment building. Once there, he proceeds to publicly confront his wife with his recently acquired information about her black heritage. Following this revelation, Clare, perched near an open window and flanked by Irene, mysteriously falls to her death. Larsen leaves it unclear as to whether Clare fell accidentally, intentionally threw herself from the window, or was pushed from it by Irene. Like Irene, we "sense" that there is more to "register" about the immediate causes of Clare's death but are denied concrete answers. Larsen refuses to reward us with any certainty about her fall, leaving the reader stranded in what Ann duCille calls the novel's "surplus of signifiers." Like the novel's opening, which similarly features tall buildings and falling bodies amid chaotic interchanges, this ending gives the reader a lot of sensory information without offering any answers about its sources or meanings.

The original ending of the first and second printed editions of *Passing*, however, leaves open the possibility of a deferred moment of empirical clarification regarding Clare's fall.[108] After the partygoers rush to the street to discover Clare's corpse, all of the editions of the novel note a "strange man, official and authoritative" arriving on the scene. In the novel's earliest editions, this man gets the last word, declaring Clare's fall a "death by misadventure" before imploring everyone to "go up and have another look at that window."[109] This initial ending dangles the possibility of definitive answers about her death gathered from empirically available clues that reveal the sequence of actions leading to this event. With the appearance of this mysterious bystander, a stranger arriving with objective clarity from beyond the known terrain of the novel, its original ending concludes with the promise of detection based on the reliability of looking and looking again. Like the *Rhinelander* trial and its affiliated composograph, this version of *Passing* reinforces the belief that a closer look can deliver knowledge of the truth. Literary critics Ann duCille and Miriam Thaggert have approached this ending in terms of its ambiguity, but I wish to call attention to the ways this original ending seems to actually forsake ambiguity for the dream of rescuing an empirical mode to bring Clare's fall into the realm of the known.[110]

The authoritative man promises to clear the congested scene and, like the Rhinelander composograph, reify the possibility of using empirical methods to discover the "truth."

Given the novel's repeated attempts to disrupt empirical certainty, this first ending rings false. And either Larsen or one of her editors at Knopf must have agreed. Though it remains unclear who authorized the changes made to the third printing, it and subsequent reprintings of *Passing* deemphasize the unknown man's arrival. Much more in keeping with the tenor of the novel preceding it, the revised second ending highlights the absence of illumination rather than its impending messianic arrival. In both versions of the novel, Irene meets the fate she had earlier avoided on that hot Chicago day by finally collapsing on the ground. But where the first edition cuts away from Irene's descent into unconsciousness to make away for the strange man promising forthcoming clarity, the second edition follows Irene into darkness. The final lines of the novel's subsequent editions read as follows: "Through the great heaviness that submerged and drowned her she was dimly conscious of strong arms lifting her up. Then everything was dark."[111] Plunging the reader into the darkness associated with both Clare's death and Irene's collapse, this second ending not only refuses empirical verification but also refuses surfaces and seeing all together, plunging us into a final and encompassing darkness. No authority emerges to take over the story from the unreliable and now unconscious Irene. This ending erases landscape entirely, stranding us literally nowhere. It is a simultaneously transcendent and bleak ending, as Irene's final relief from symptomatic surfaces derives from her entrance into nonrelation with the world. Relief from both the legible racial symptom and the extrasensory burden of race comes only from absenting oneself from the world rather than finding an endurable orientation to it. Like Irene's pleasurable suspension when staring at the infinite and submerging view of the lake atop the Drayton, it is the suspension of detail that brings about the greatest reprieve.

In light of popular strategies for perceiving, knowing, and organizing race used to steady publics and economies in the wake of an increasingly more "mongrel" United States at the turn of the century—conditions exemplified by the skyscraper's material origins in steel and architecture—*Passing* captures the perceived fraying of racial certainty in the 1920s in cities filled with congested crowds and obfuscated sight lines. City dwellers concerned about the growing number of secret passers in their midst imagined few solutions to this growing problem of interracial intimacy and its various effects as cities seemed to only be growing more and more unmanageable. "Unless therefore there are distinct evidences that the individual in question is a Negro," as the 1929 pamphlet *From Negro to Caucasian* shruggingly concludes, "he may go his way without interference."[112] Larsen's novel points to the role the material conditions of modern cities played in unsteadying the "distinct evidence" of race, rendering acts of racial gazing as being intimately tied to the physical and spatial conditions that frame them.

But in *Passing*, the fraying of racial perception ultimately does little to fray race, which endures as the "just something" that Irene cannot manage to shake. While both Irene and Clare benefit at times from the "miscegenating" conditions of the modern and congested city that make it more difficult to stop to deliberate over racial phenotype in the manner dreamed of by the *Rhinelander* composograph, both these characters fail to outrun the other sites, animate and inanimate, physical and psychical, that race emerges from and colonizes in excess of the empirical body. The material history of the skyscraper and the phenomenological experiences it molds in *Passing* not only suggest how race shapes architecture and the ways architecture shapes understandings of race—they also point to aspects of racial experience that, despite being framed by architecture, continue to exist for a character like Irene in excess of the evidential body, as race endures for her in realms beyond the empirical.

CHAPTER FOUR

The Black Skyscraper

In his 1955 essay "Notes of a Native Son," James Baldwin arrives at an understanding of himself as "a kind of bastard of the West" by way of a series of failed recognitions. Discovering that the masterworks of the Western tradition "were not really my creations" and "did not contain my history," Baldwin describes the "special attitude" of disinvestment he learned to adopt toward "Shakespeare, Bach, Rembrandt," "the stones of Paris," "the cathedral at Chartres," and, last, the lone American cultural object in his list, "the Empire State Building." Of these items, Baldwin writes that "I might search in them in vain forever for any reflection of myself. I was an interloper; this was not my heritage."[1]

Baldwin's midcentury failure to see himself or his heritage reflected in American skyscraper architecture seems at first to recall a moment of architectural dissonance expressed by another black writer three decades prior. In the original 1921 preface to *The Book of American Negro Poetry*, James Weldon Johnson famously made the case for the artistic superiority of African Americans:

> [The Negro] has the emotional endowment, the originality, and artistic conception, and, what is more important, the power of creating that which has universal appeal and influence. I make here what may appear to be a more startling statement by saying the Negro has already proved the possession of these powers by being the creator of the only things artistic that have yet sprung from American soil and been universally acknowledged as distinctive American products.[2]

Johnson lists the cakewalk, the spiritual, and ragtime as examples of these "distinctive products" of American art produced by Negro artistry.

Roughly ten years later, however, Johnson would twice acknowledge the skyscraper as the single exception to his original "startling statement" about the Negro's singular contributions to American culture. As both an exemplary object of American artistry and a cultural product seemingly divorced from African American craft, the skyscraper was viewed by Johnson as a challenge to his initial formulation. In the preface to the 1931 edition of the anthology, Johnson writes in a footnote that "this statement should probably be modified by the inclusion of American skyscraper architecture."[3] He reiterates this correction in his 1933 autobiography *Along the Way*: "I modified that statement by excepting American skyscraper architecture. . . . In all that white groups have wrought, there is no artistic creation—with the exception noted above—born of the physical and spiritual forces at work peculiarly in America, none that has made a universal appeal as something distinctively American."[4]

While Baldwin in his 1955 essay seamlessly groups together in one sentence the twenty-year-old Empire State Building with far older European artists and art forms, treating them as the collective canonical objects of a white Enlightenment tradition, it would take Johnson more than a decade to try to disaggregate the skyscraper from a black artistic ontology. The protracted duration of his attempts to acknowledge the skyscraper as an exception to his earlier theory, along with the rhetorical strangeness of these statements, suggests that Johnson's claim of nonrelation is more conflicted than it might first appear. At the time of the original 1921 publication of Johnson's anthology, when he first articulates the Negro's unique relationship to American culture, skyscraper architecture was not new or even novel, having been a part of the nation's urban landscape since the 1880s. When Johnson amends his thesis about the centrality of African Americans to the development of American aesthetics, it is to acknowledge the, by then, forty-year-old skyscraper. Even more confusingly, Johnson approaches the skyscraper not simply as a technological innovation marking the nation's economic and engineering prowess—an observation in line with the cool admiration for the skyscraper's structural ingenuity that even its harshest critics conceded—but as a product of "physical and spiritual forces" with broad cultural appeal, framing the architecture as the product of a country of artists engaged in a soaring humanistic project. Though Johnson, following writers such as Henry James and William Dean Howells, could have easily cast the skyscraper as a blight, he chooses to frame it as an "artistic creation" of national pride, further amplifying the sting of the Negro's nonrelation to it. In contrast to Baldwin's celebration of his disinheritance in relation to the skyscraper, Johnson's orientation toward this architecture is far more abstruse.

The awkward phrasing of Johnson's multiple nods to the skyscraper further suggests a hesitation. In both the 1931 footnote in the reedited preface and his 1933 statement from *Along the Way*, Johnson syntactically contorts his concession to never directly attribute the production of the skyscraper to white artisans. In the 1931 preface, Johnson places his acknowledgment of skyscraper architecture at the bottom of the page, spatially isolated from the statement he intends to modify. In the body of the footnote, Johnson writes that his original statement "should probably be modified," but stops short of discussing how such a concession changes his original thesis. The same creative syntax appears in *Along the Way*, in which dashes offset the skyscraper in the text, leaving his insertion unassimilated into the sentence. In both instances, Johnson never places "white groups" next to their alleged product in the same sentence, building spatial and rhetorical distance into his amendment.

Given that *The Book of American Negro Poetry* makes the case for African American contributions as *constitutive of* rather than *supplementary to* national aesthetics, Johnson's reluctance to fully incorporate this architectural exception into his argument makes sense. But what firm counterargument could Johnson have possibly mounted at the time? Though black architects were trained at Tuskegee and Howard, no known black architects or engineers contributed to skyscraper design. Furthermore, if the skyscraper were a product of the spiritual force of America, the structure seemingly benefited the souls and pocketbooks of white Americans alone. In 1908, African American sociologist Kelly Miller wrote that "the city Negro grows up in shade [. . .] completely overshadowed by his overtowering environment. As one walks along the streets of our great cities and views the massive buildings and sky-seeking structures, he finds no status for the Negro above the cellar floor."[5] And even the cellar remained a questionable space for black employment. Mary White Ovington, white sociologist and a cofounder of the NAACP, details the labor situation of African Americans in Manhattan in her 1911 study *Half a Man: The Status of the Negro in New York*. She notes that while elevator operation in residential buildings was mostly an "occupation [that] is given over to the Negro," within spaces such as "office buildings, large stores and hotels"—building uses often associated with downtown skyscrapers—blacks were rarely hired.[6]

The syntactical knottiness of James Weldon Johnson's concessions, disrupting their spatial and temporal unraveling, should urge us to slow down and consider the racial history of the skyscraper intuited by Johnson through these compositional speed bumps. In investigating his grammatical hesitations regarding the skyscraper's white provenance, as well as more concrete refutations of this exclusionary genealogy, my work joins the emerging body of scholarship by critics to rethink (or think for the first time, in many cases) the relationship between black subjects and architecture, illuminating their exchanges across a multitude of genres, places, and periods.[7] Referring to the possible forms these exchanges took within modernism in particular, architect Melvin Mitchell in his book *The Crisis of the African-American Architect* proposes a broader cultural lineage for modern architecture that includes blues and jazz as tangible influences. Echoing and amplifying Johnson's syntactical suspicion of the skyscraper's white lineage, Mitchell advocates for "new realizations throughout black America that presumptively 'white' Modern architecture can be no whiter than today's American music and other cultural art forms."[8] Where architectural and labor histories have generally remained silent on this matter, literature from the period corroborates and even expands Mitchell's claims. Accounting for a fuller range of raced bodies that worked on and in the skyscraper, literature intercedes to repopulate the skyscraper in ways that complement and exceed the existing historical record.

Mitchell, in widening the possible types of cultural contact between black subjects and architecture, casts the relationship between architecture and race as moving primarily in one direction, marking black cultural influence on modern architecture as the privileged vector of impact. But African Americans were not only helping to shape the skyscraper—they were also being shaped by it. Literary criticism foregrounding shock and diminution as the primary registers of black urban migration has yet to account for the fuller range of engagement between black writers and the modern built environment. While literary scholars of the Great Migration such as Farah Jasmine Griffin and Lawrence Rodgers, echoing Kelly Miller's 1908 claim about the overshadowed Negro, have described the black migrant's relationship with the urban landscape as estranging and phenomenologically violent, black modernist narratives involving the skyscraper reveal the range of dialogues between black subjects and architectural modernity.[9]

Part of what has obscured the broader spectrum of these exchanges is the supposition that black modernist writing of the city maps cleanly onto the borders of black enclaves. Though transnationalist accounts of the period have decentered Harlem's place within the larger network of black Atlantic movement to include Paris, London, Chicago, Washington, DC, and the Caribbean, black writers' simultaneous regional movements beyond the black enclaves of these locales have gotten shorter shrift. Black accounts of New York undoubtedly centered Harlem, but writers such as W. E. B. Du Bois, Jessie Fauset, and Rudolph Fisher were also navigating, in person and in print, sites such as Wall Street, Greenwich Village, and the Chrysler Building. Even as they were drawing Harlem in distinct shades, black writers simultaneously challenged its borders by engaging structures, both literal and metaphorical, to which they were figured as external or nonconstitutive.

As a technology for envisioning the city and its masses, the skyscraper was a key site where black subjects positioned themselves within the landscape of modernity. The literary and artistic works by African Americans I focus on here feature the skyscraper as a useful tool for imagining the racial reorganization of the city at a time when its citizenry was feared to be unmanageably dissimilar. Although Du Bois and writer Wallace Thurman vehemently disagreed on the utility of both black art and the black public sphere during the 1920s and 1930s, they shared a textual fascination with the skyscraper that counters Johnson's and Baldwin's claims about its nonrelation to black life and thought. Du Bois wrote at least two short stories, both speculative in nature, set atop skyscrapers. In his earliest skyscraper story, "The Princess Steel," Du Bois depicts the skyscraper as fostering a kind of grand social vision he found wanting in traditional sociology. When he returns to the skyscraper roughly a decade later in his 1920 book *Darkwater*, Du Bois more readily condemns the structure as a symbol of capitalism's ills. And yet, despite this critique, he nonetheless sets the collection's final story atop a skyscraper, staging this space as one of vertical rupture in contrast to the false civic promises associated with horizontal infrastructure. Harlem Renaissance writer Wallace Thurman criticized Du Bois for advocating an ethos of black respectability he found smothering. Yet he, too, reclaimed the skyscraper in strategic ways, ending his second novel, 1932's *Infants of the Spring*, with an image of a black skyscraper signaling the ongoing potential of the black subject to regroup and thrive. Their representations of skyscrapers, as well as those of Harlem Renaissance contemporaries Rudolph Fisher and painter Aaron Douglas, make visible the manifold forms of belonging the skyscraper suggested to African American artists.

From Du Bois's appropriation of "double consciousness" as an explicitly visual relationship, Ralph Ellison's use of invisibility as a trope of raced seeing, and Toni Morrison's treatment of blue eyes as powerful sites of black loathing, black writers have used narrative to denaturalize the processes of racial perception. The early skyscraper proved to be a generative tool for black writers theorizing the new ways of seeing and moving this architecture might foster. In contrast to Max Horkheimer and Michel de Certeau's disparaging readings of the skyscraper's totalizing view, which they argued granted its beholders apex God-like autonomy, black writers and artists such as Du Bois, Thurman, Fisher, and Douglas were more ambivalent about what practices of perception the skyscraper made possible.[10] The totalizing flatness that Horkheimer and de Certeau found inherent within the view from the skyscraper is displaced in the work of Du Bois and Thurman, who consider what its disorientations might positively provoke. Lynching and minstrelsy have been the primary vehicles for thinking about race, crowds, and visions during the early twentieth century, but Thurman and Du Bois explore what role the skyscraper might play in creating new racial imaginaries for modern modes of vision. In contrast to Baldwin's traumatic disidentification with the skyscraper at midcentury, this chapter not only finds black thinkers describing other possible relationships between modern architecture and black subjects; it shows them experimenting with the benefits of racial misrecognitions they found the skyscraper to forge.

W. E. B. Du Bois's Abstracting Skyscraper

W. E. B. Du Bois expressed reservations about the utility of abstraction in both his sociology and his fiction. In his 1899 study *The Philadelphia Negro*, Du Bois mixed quantitative and qualitative methods to analyze this city's black communities up close and in person, bucking the trend within sociology at the time for more universalizing theories of human action. With the publication of *The Souls of Black Folk* in 1901, as the narrative of his intellectual trajectory commonly goes, Du Bois began to move away from statistical empiricism toward what Ronald Judy has called a more "direct engagement through propaganda," preferring the role of impassioned activist over reserved observer and crisp calls to action over more plaintive appeals.[11] Believing that "all Art is propaganda and ever must be," Du Bois was wary of edgy or experimental work that risked ideological clarity for the sake of art and called instead for aesthetic works that were openly instrumental in their intent.[12] In 1926's *The Criteria of Negro Art*, he describes his own fictional practice—"whatever art I have for writing"—as being "always" in the service "for propaganda for gaining the right of black folk to love and enjoy."[13] Though his fondness for speculative science fiction caused him to fall short of the narrow definition of realism that Marxist aesthetician Georg Lukacs insisted was the most effectual genre for politically engaged art, Du Bois made it clear that, like Lukacs, his preference was for art imparting legible messages.[14]

It is curious, then, that the skyscraper—viewed by a host of artists and thinkers in the early twentieth century as a vehicle of dehumanization—would feature so prominently as a force for good in at least two of Du Bois's short stories. As I've argued in chapter 3, the skyscraper was commonly perceived as an abstracting architecture that muddled urban perception. Leftist writers lodged critiques of the skyscraper similarly rooted in scalar concerns, finding the distancing views of people it offered to line up with capital's abstracting tendencies that reduced men to their labor power. This anxiety was codified in the stock villain of the evil industrialist relishing his view from the skyscraper's apex that appeared in many a labor novel during the 1920s and 1930s.[15]

Given Du Bois's increasingly leftward trajectory, we might expect him to similarly lambast the structure not only as a symbol of capitalist triumphalism but also for the estranging and reductive view of humanity it made available.[16] But Du Bois finds a use for the skyscraper's capacity for abstraction and perceptual disorientation. These structures appear in his fiction as versions of what Fredric Jameson calls "utopian enclaves," which he describes as closed worlds cordoned off from the "forward momentum of differentiation" within broader social space where "new wish images of the social can be elaborated and experimented on."[17] As versions of utopian enclaves, Du Bois's skyscrapers serve as clarifying tools of rupture. The abstract vistas they offer temporarily disrupt the urgency of racial differentiation that normally organizes urban perception, helping its beholders disturb the racial mandates that typically orient their behaviors. In these stories, birthing a new society involves birthing a different kind of racial optics. The skyscraper is an integral, if overlooked, part of Du Bois's early program of countervisuality, to borrow Nicholas Mirzoeff's term, challenging forms of visuality that historically supplemented the violence of authority.[18]

Understanding Du Bois's attraction to the skyscraper in the early 1900s requires contextualizing this interest in relation to his concurrent writings about sociology, the field with which he was heavily engaged at the time and whose rhetoric shadows this architecture's emergence in his first skyscraper story, "The Princess Steel." In a short essay Du Bois wrote in 1905 but never published, titled "Sociology Hesitant," he admits to harboring "a real confusion of mind as to the field and method of Sociology."[19] Upon discovering this piece in the Du Bois archives at University of Massachusetts, Amherst, and publishing it for the first time in 2000, Ronald Judy classified "Sociology Hesitant" as a provocative challenge clarifying Du Bois's own sociological methodology in contrast to the European fathers of the field.[20] Du Bois describes sociology, coming of age in the nineteenth century alongside "the Novel, the Trust, and the Expansion of Europe," as responding to an emerging need for a science of human deeds.[21] But from the very start, he insists, sociology erred by forsaking the study of men for the more abstract concept of 'Society.'[22] He accuses Auguste Comte, the field's founding father, of neglecting the direct observation of "men or cells or atoms" for the study of more abstract social structures.[23] Du Bois finds similar fault with Herbert Spencer leading the next generation of sociologists after Comte. Spencer based his notion of society on what Du Bois described as "woefully imperfect" historical data taking the form of "hearsay, rumor and tradition, vague speculations, travellor's tales, legends and imperfect documents, the memory of memories and historic error."[24] Sociology of this era, consequently, "could only limn a shadowy outline" of the social built on faulty historical gossip rather than offer a deductive picture of the present. More obsessed with the *why* behind society rather than the *what* constituting it, traditional sociology seemed to Du Bois more like a science for science's sake rather than a field serving real people and their problems.

Whereas sociology had historically dedicated itself to "reduc[ing] human action to law, rule, and rhythm," Du Bois argued that the field must now learn to attend to the "something incalculable" inherent to the world of men that may not conform to a universal rule.[25] Sociology needed a way to deal with the paradox of, on the one hand, "the evident rhythm of human action" and, on the other, "the evident incalculability in human action" in order to eventually plant itself somewhere in between to study the "Hypothesis of Law" while honoring "the Assumption of Chance." Sociology's true students, Du Bois insisted, would come to temper the radical positivism of Comte and Spencer by "adopt[ing] the speech and assumption of humanity" even when it was at odds with traditional sociological wisdom.[26]

In this relatively short essay, Du Bois establishes a model of toggled scalar observation capable of moving between the zoomed-out scale of the abstract laws of "Society" and the close-up details of singular individuals. Tempering sociology's abstract tendencies requires finding a mobile perspective that allows the analyst to move between these differing scales. Du Bois would ultimately use the skyscraper to model a version of this scalar toggling in a short story he wrote roughly three years after "Sociology Hesitant" titled "The Princess Steel," written sometime between 1908 and 1910 during his final years at Atlanta University.[27] Scholars have yet to acknowledge, let alone analyze, this story, a strange omission from the body of Du Bois scholarship given the story's eccentricities and its engagement with sociology that both complements and exceeds what we currently know about his changing relationship to this field during this time.[28]

Never published during Du Bois's lifetime, "The Princess Steel," which exists in the Amherst archives in the form of two drafts, revolves around the encounter between an aged black sociologist and a young white couple who arrive at his skyscraper lab to try out his mysterious invention called the megascope. Most of the story recounts the husband's epic experience of seeing with this contraption, allowing him to glimpse the centuries-long story of modern steel featuring battling knights, kidnapped African queens, and tragic princesses.

The skyscraper serves as the perch for this experimental and estranging vision connecting modern steel to centuries of primitive accumulation. In moving from a single viewer to a metaphorical tableau, from the local actions of a few to a transnational epic of global oppression, Du Bois practices the kind of toggled scalar vision he advocated sociology adopt just a few years earlier in "Sociology Hesitant." He renders the skyscraper as an optical technology capable of bringing historical abstraction into focus as well as contemporary relevancy, enabling the kind of seeing he hoped sociology would more commonly come to facilitate. But Du Bois also uses the skyscraper to suggest the limits of even the most ideal sociology to eradicate racial prejudice, a project requiring more expansive correctives if deeply ingrained habits of perception were to be dislodged.

"The Princess Steel" opens with a white couple arriving at the forty-third story of "the new Whistler building, or rather tower, on Broadway" in search of Professor Hannibal Johnson, a sociologist who promises in a newspaper ad to "exhibit the results of his great experiments in Sociology by the aid of the megascope."[29] Having recently married after meeting as sociology students at the University of Chicago, the honeymooning couple decides on a whim to follow up on Johnson's ad. "We had, too, certain pet theories in regard to sociological work and experiment and it certainly seemed very opportune to hear almost immediately upon our arrival of a great lecturer in Sociology albeit his name to our chagrin was new to us."[30]

Upon entering the sociologist's office, the white husband-turned-narrator describes "scarcely looking at the man at the door" because he is so overtaken by the wonders of the room. Immediately attracted to a dramatic wall "dark with velvety material shrouding its contents in a great soft gloom," the couple next turns to the adjacent wall featuring "one vast window full 40 by 20 feet" through which "burst suddenly on us the whole panorama of New York."[31] The husband describes how they "rushed forward and looked down on seething Broadway," his wife enraptured by "the river and cliffs of Manhattan!"[32] Swept up by the room and its view, the newlyweds suddenly realize they have ignored the professor. They turn around to discover, to their great surprise, that the professor is a black man with "a certain air of ancient gentility about him."[33] The husband notes that "one would not for a moment have hesitated to call him a gentleman had it not been for his color," given that "his voice, his manner, everything showed training and refinement."[34] While he describes his wife as "naturally" having "stiffened and drew back" upon realizing his race, the husband describes himself as being "struck with curiosity."

The white couple's disorientation in this opening scene derives from the juxtaposition of the modern New York vista with this black man's presence, whom they deem the antithesis of modernity. Their shock deepens once they find this man to be refined and knowledgeable, not the "uncle" the wife initially mistakes him for but the professor running the show. Du Bois layers these assumed contradictions all within the space of the story's first two pages, first making a black man the keeper of modernity's prized view and, second, rendering him as an intellectual rather than a clown or a savage. What is "perfectly absurd" to the couple's first glimpse becomes if not "perfectly clear" after this exchange, then a reality with which they must deal while occupying this space. Du Bois's skyscraper, rather than negating race or making it indistinguishable, as white metropolitan genre writers and realists feared, upends their raced presumptions. Du Bois uses this architecture to delay race's impact, making the grand view of the city it offers so enticing that it temporarily displaces the scripts of racial interaction to which the couple is accustomed. It throws them off kilter just enough that they remain to see what will happen next. Despite common assumptions, both now and then, about the black migrant's shock at the height and speed of modernity, Du Bois figures the skyscraper as astounding only the story's white protagonists hardened by their visual habits. The spectacle of the skyscraper vista allows these white visitors to settle into the room with the black sociologist, an unlikely scenario without the distracting pull of the awesome view.

The husband is soon distracted by another visual oddity. On closer inspection, the velvety wall initially drawing his gaze turns out to consist of a multitude of bound books. The professor identifies this collection as "the Great Chronicle" detailing "everyday facts, births, deaths, marriages, sicknesses, houses, schools churches, organizations, the infirm, insane, blind, crimes, travel and migration, occupations, crops, things made and unmade."[35] Kept by "a silent Brotherhood for 200 years" the Chronicle corresponds to the sort of data Du Bois called for a few years earlier in "Sociology Hesitant." In both works, we find Du Bois seeking the collection of "everyday facts" anchored in an empiricism of the particular as a corrective to older sociological methods producing vague formulations about society from the speculative evidence of "hearsay, rumor and tradition, vague speculations, travellor's tales, legends and imperfect documents, the memory of memories and historic error." With the Great Chronicle, Du Bois conjures his ideal data set that includes information not just about normative structures, such as schools and churches, but information about the more marginalized populations of the "infirm, insane and blind." If "Sociology Hesitant" details the field's methodological flaws, in "Princess Steel" Du Bois uses genre fiction to invent the kind of data he believed all sociologists should seek.

Using the Chronicle's complete empirical observations, the professor describes his past efforts to construct a device described as "a great frame over which was stretched a thin transparent film, covered with tiny rectangular lines, and pierced with tiny holes" upon which he had plotted the Chronicle's data, "plane on plane, dot over dot."[36] Transcribing the Chronicle's written records into a two-dimensional model rendered this data "infinitely more accurate and extensive," according to the professor. But he has since taken this data set even further by curving these flat planes to plot what he calls the "the Law of Life" in three dimensions. The professor reveals this second device to his visitors, using a series of levers to lower a "vast solid crystal globe" fifty feet in diameter in front of the large window. On this globe, the professor has plotted the curves of the sociological "laws" he has so far uncovered in pursuit of the ultimate discovery—"the Great Curve" governing all of society's machinations.

The advancement of knowledge charted in these passages corresponds to progressing spatial dimensions. Moving from the "flat" empiricism of the Chronicles to the scaled-out analysis of the globe allows Professor Johnson to see both the calculable laws and the incalculable "shadows" behind the data. From the globe's shadowy curves, Johnson has gathered that "human life is not alone" but is heavily determined by "a social Over-life" run by "Over-men, Super-men, not merely Captains of Industry but field marshalls of the *Zeit-geist*, who today are guiding the world events and dominating the lives of men."[37] To see this other realm, which exists on a scale inaccessible to either naked human sight or any known optical inventions, the professor has invented a new optical device. He explains that although "we can see the great that is far by means of the telescope and the small that is near by the means of the microscope," we have no such apparatus for seeing what he calls "the Great Near."[38] He proceeds to lower from the ceiling a contraption he calls the megascope, described as "a great tube, like a great golden trumpet" wrapped in "silken cords like coiled electric wire" with "handles, globes and collar-like appendages" through which the gazer peers. The megascope is trained upon the crystal globe upon which sits a "thin dark curve" Professor Johnson identifies as "the Curve of Steel—the sum of all the facts and quantities and times and lives that go to make Steel, that modern skeleton of the Modern World."

Once the couple puts on the megascope's "head and eye and ear and hand pieces," the experiment commences. The professor urges his visitors to "look—feel—see!" Broadway as it newly appears viewed through the megascope. The husband notes that everything looks "darker, and yet strangely more intense" before everything suddenly turns black. Winds whip, crickets chirp, and waters rush as "great crags" with castles atop them surge into view, each linked together by "little silver threads that went out through the broad empty country side, out far, far away," eventually leading to "the hills of Pittsburg."[39] The rest of the story largely recounts the battle between the two knights to acquire the African Princess's valuable steel threads of hair.

Whereas "Sociology Hesitant" remains relatively neutral in its politics, pitched primarily as an intervention in methodology, "Princess Steel" finds Du Bois using those methods to relay the ominous history of materialism underlying the unequal conditions of the present. The megascope further instrumentalizes the scaled-out and abstracted view of Manhattan the skyscraper makes available by turning historical materialism into a viewable epic. But in addition to enabling the visual estrangement necessary to see "the Great Near," the skyscraper also plays a key role within the nested tale of primitive accumulation as a product constructed with the princess's prized steel hair. With this detail, Du Bois also acknowledges the skyscraper's embeddedness within material history, contextualizing the breathtaking view it offers at the story's start as part of the increasingly tragic tale of steel and theft that unfolds in the story's body.

And yet, rather than ending the story on a triumphant note of revelation—with the skyscraper bestowing world-changing knowledge of the Great Near that transforms the pair's consciousness—Du Bois ultimately undercuts this outcome, suggesting that it will take more than this new vision to provoke lasting change. Just as the husband's historical vision reaches its climax, leaving the imprisoned princess in limbo, it abruptly ends. He looks to his wife to gauge her reaction to what he assumes has been their shared vision. But rather than sharing his shock, she explains she has merely been "watching Broadway" through the megascope all this time. The husband haplessly describes "the cliffs and castles and the Lord" he has just witnessed through the instrument. But his wife counters that all she saw was "the great towering cliff-life buildings" of the city's present day.[40] As they leave his office, the professor whispers to the husband that the machine "was not tuned delicately enough" for his wife and the story concludes with their brisk exit.[41] While the megascope has the potential to deliver potentially life-changing knowledge, even the most powerful empiricism cannot raise the veils of those who refuse to see.

In "The Princess Steel," Du Bois creates his ideal version of sociology, combining the Chronicle's perfect data and a scientific apparatus granting access to an abstracted explanatory realm. Yet the fruits of these observations are withheld from the white wife—the one who initially drew back from the professor because of his race—presumably because of her lack of readiness to accept them as true. The skyscraper enables the husband's experimental sight to a point, but Du Bois pulls up before granting such gazing its full utopian power, tempering the deep vision facilitated by the skyscraper with his characters' limited capacities for understanding its content. The moral seems to be that even when sociology is equipped with ideal data and methods, this science may still fail to alter the lived habits of racial seeing of a disinterested public.

When Du Bois next returns to the skyscraper in fiction over a decade later, he would replicate certain aspects of "The Princess Steel," once more freighting the skyscraper with utopian potential before deflating this potential at the story's conclusion. But if "The Princess Steel" refuses to offer us any solace in the aftermath of its disappointments, Du Bois's second skyscraper story refashions the structure into a medium for consolation, rendering the skyscraper a site of black solidarity and survival when efforts to produce a meaningful and sustainable interracial solidarity fall spectacularly flat.

Like its more famous predecessor, *The Souls of Black Folk* (1901), W. E. B. Du Bois's *Darkwater* (1920) features an array of topics, genres, and disciplines.[42] Incorporating autobiography, poetry, prose, sociology and history, *Darkwater* enacts what Susan Gillman and Alys Weinbaum call a "politics of juxtaposition" that allows Du Bois to thread together a variety of oppressions under a common banner of capitalist injustice.[43] While Du Bois in 1901 could rely on a largely monolithic construction of black folk as southern, rural, and without regular access to formal education to steer his investigation into the race problem, by 1920 he faced a much more fragmented legion of souls situated amid ever-widening coordinates of region, gender post-suffrage, and class. In accounting for the demographic shifts redefining not just African Americans but the global oppressed in the aftermath of World War I, Du Bois retreats from the trope of double consciousness in 1920 for that of dark water, a more multitudinous model of vision. Always in search of a fuller analogic model for social relations, Du Bois's imagery of dark water complicates the binary paradigm of double consciousness, allowing him to evoke a conglomerate body made up of an infinite number of smaller drops and subject positions rather than a mere two.

But despite the term's top billing in the collection's title, Du Bois ends *Darkwater* with yet another model of vision that, rather than revealing the shadowy flipside to modernity's bright lights, co-opts its technologies to deconstruct racial ideologies from above. In the penultimate chapter of *Darkwater*, Du Bois bitingly refers to the Woolworth Building, the most iconic New York skyscraper at the time and colloquially known as the "Cathedral of Commerce," as "that Cathedral of the Purchased and Purchasing Poor."[44] But in the apocalyptic fictional short story "The Comet" that follows it, Du Bois disrupts the skyscraper's symbolic association with capitalist reproduction by staging a speculative fantasy of interracial reproduction atop one. Even as this fantastic vision collapses in "The Comet," much as it does in "The Princess Steel," Du Bois stages a second brief vision atop the skyscraper that situates a fractured image of blackness at the center of modernity's largest triumph.

Like much of Du Bois's fiction, "The Comet" uses generic conventions of fantasy to imagine the conditions capable of dismantling racial discrimination. This time, these conditions come in the form of a comet collision. After a comet strikes Earth, the last two people left alive in Manhattan are Jim, a black bank messenger, and the unnamed white daughter of a businessman. When the pair fail to find any survivors in Manhattan, they resign themselves to their fate on the top of the Metropolitan Life Insurance Building, where the woman's father once worked. Atop one of Manhattan's tallest structures, the pair transforms into quasi-mystic deities ready to beget a mixed-race future free of the past's racial intolerances. Just as they turn to embrace as an interracial Adam and Eve, the woman's father and fiancé suddenly reappear to reveal that only Manhattan was destroyed by the collision. As an angry crowd pours onto the skyscraper's roof, the old racial order quickly reinstates itself as Jim is accused of rape and coldly dismissed. The story ends with Jim's quiet reunion with his black wife atop the skyscraper as they sob with both joy and grief at finding one another while holding their dead child.

One of the reoccurring themes of "The Comet" is Jim's alienation from the urban masses. The story opens with Jim standing on the steps of the bank where he works, "watching the human river that swirled down Broadway." Isolated from the crowd that passes him by, Jim is described as being "outside the world—'nothing!' "[45] Du Bois frames his black protagonist's nihilism as resulting from what James Smethurst calls the "territorial racialization of the city" fostered by Jim Crow at the turn of the twentieth century.[46] Jim continually feels his difference from the urban crowd, unable to dissolve into the mass consciousness others theorized as inescapable within growing urban centers. This opening scene underscoring Jim's separateness extends the questions explored in the book's preceding chapter, "Of Beauty and Death," about the raced assumptions belying neutral-seeming constructions such as mass consciousness and mass culture. In this earlier chapter, Du Bois attempts to understand the "tantalizing contradictions" composing modern life, a topic of particular concern for African Americans, according to Du Bois, whose joys were so often spoiled by the sorrows of lurking discrimination. He recalls his own daily experience of alienation as he is skipped over by the milkman, prevented from lunching at Marshall's, and, in the ultimate slight, denied recognition as a member of the masses when attempting to enjoy its greatest delight, the cinema. The precise place where the masses allegedly flee into fantasy, during a Charlie Chaplin film no less, Du Bois must face "matters of life, death and immortality" when an usher challenges his right to a ticket.[47] Instead of losing himself within the cinematic space of group experience, Du Bois is made to feel his difference psychically and physically, his "tissue burn[ing]" as a part of "the miserable wave of reaction."[48]

While Jim's sense of isolation at the beginning of "The Comet" echoes Du Bois's earlier claims about the false universality of mass culture, his remoteness turns out to be his saving grace. Sent into the bank's underground vault on an errand, Jim survives what turns out to be a comet strike that destroys much of the city above. Emerging from the vault to survey the damage, he discovers the animated urban masses of a moment earlier replaced by "the stillness of death."[49] In a refracted image of the exclusionary "human river" that opened the story, Jim now experiences the "universal" crowd not with bitterness but horror as he finds "in the great stone doorway a hundred men and women and children" lying "crushed and twisted and jammed, forced into the great, gaping doorway like refuse in a can—as if in one wild frantic rush to safety they had crushed and ground themselves to death."[50] If Du Bois was made to feel not only his own social death but the "despoiled" futures of "millions of unborn children, black and gold and mauve" in the movie theater of the previous chapter, this second image of mass death emerges in "The Comet" as a morbid alternative form of mass collectivity.[51]

The mass death of the urban crowd clears the way for a reimagining of the social, a task set into motion when Jim meets the only other survivor of the comet, an unnamed white woman. Recalling the moment in "The Princess Steel" when the discombobulating architecture of the professor's office temporarily allows his visitors to overcome entrenched racial rituals, the comet produces enough disorientation to allow the pair to get over their initial repulsion to each other. They soon embark together on a search for their respective "ghostly kin." They drive to Harlem first, where Jim briefly takes leave of his new companion to confirm the loss of something or someone, the specificities of which are denied to both her and us as readers. After Jim's private errand, he and his companion return to the car, driving "up and down, over and across, back again" through Manhattan looking for survivors.[52]

Jim's drive through New York with his white companion emphasizes the loss of the horizontal networks that previously determined their experience of the city; but it also suggests new possibilities for urban movement freed from these spatial precedents. Historian Thomas Bender has argued that turn-of-the-century New Yorkers associated the city's horizontal planes with civic-oriented notions of parity. From its colonial grid to its broad avenues and subway lines, New York's horizontally oriented modes of mapping and mobility, Bender argues, corresponded to ideas of cohesive democracy based upon equal and eased access.[53] "The Comet" showcases, however, how New York's horizontality fell short of these equitable virtues for black subjects. Jim's street-level exclusion at the story's beginning, set alongside Du Bois's own alienating accounts of Manhattan in the preceding chapter, contrarily suggests that the civic orientation of horizontality in New York was not universally enjoyed by all. It is only after the catastrophic comet strike that Jim can move seamlessly through the city, unburdened of his continual sense of exclusion. Driving between Harlem and Wall Street, the interracial pair reengraves the city's grid with their physical bodies, symbolically negating older racial codes that once regulated urban mobility. Only with the city's destruction can horizontality begin to live up to its civic ideals.

Upon failing to reach anyone through horizontally based modes of communication such as telephones, telegraphs, and cables—a scene that includes a brief interlude during which Jim's companion briefly imagines the black telephone he talks on to be a black phallus, unleashing in her a wave of racial panic she ultimately overcomes—the pair moves on to vertical solutions.[54] They proceed to climb to the top of the Metropolitan Tower, where the woman's father once worked, to get an unimpeded view of the city and launch flares. While the horizontal vectors orienting New York fall short of their civic promises when it comes to black subjects, in the second half of the story Du Bois imagines the skyscraper as a positive disruption to the city grid's pretenses of inclusivity, figuring this architecture as a potential site of civic rebirth. He crucially stages the sexual awakening between Jim and his white partner atop the Met Life Tower, appropriating the highest vantage point within the city to stage their interracial fantasies about transforming urban social space.

On the observation deck of the Met Life Tower, Jim's companion increasingly relinquishes her racialized fear of him for a growing sense of comfort. As Jim wraps her in a shawl, she looks up at him with "thankfulness in her eyes," noting that, as opposed to only a few moments earlier, Jim now "seemed very human—very near now."[55] At the top of the skyscraper, she waxes lyrical about "how foolish our human distinctions seem—now."[56] The skyscraper lends a romantic air to their situation as the horizontal space of the city fades below. Removed from the gridded street level and its entrenched modes of seeing, she now claims to view Jim as human for the first time. The woman does not forget Jim's race but learns to interpret it differently from this space of removal ironically situated at the city's epicenter. In both stories, Du Bois imagines changing racial perception through large scalar shocks to the bodily system, as experienced by the white husband of "The Princess Steel" and the white woman of "The Comet" atop their respective skyscrapers. Their fantastic setups suggest just how monumental Du Bois thought this shock needed to be to make even a dent in these established conventions.

Jim cannot embrace his companion's softening vision just yet. He holds onto the refrain that, "yet—I was not—human, yesterday" first uttered during his solo explorations of the empty city earlier that day.[57] Unlike his enamored companion, Jim evokes "death, the leveler" with more bitterness than glee. His thoughts remain withheld from us atop the skyscraper as hers become increasingly infused with desire. But as Jim eventually starts to warm to his companion, the skyscraper transcends its infrastructural role to become the symbolic stage for begetting a new world. In "The Comet," the skyscraper not only looks like an inkwell, a metaphor Du Bois develops earlier in *Darkwater*, but functions as one, too, becoming a site for rewriting the future of the human race in interracial terms. As the city below them remains frozen as a memorial of the past's hatred and exclusion, atop the skyscraper, figured as outside time and space, a vision of a new racial future takes hold. Jim fires rockets into the night while his companion indulges in such imagining:

A vision of the world had risen before her. Slowly the mighty prophecy of her destiny overwhelmed her. . . . She was no mere woman. She was neither high nor low, white nor black, rich nor poor. She was primal woman; mighty mother of all men to come and Bride of Life. She looked upon the man beside her and forgot all else but his manhood, his strong vigorous manhood—his sorrow and sacrifice. She saw him glorified. He was no longer a thing apart, a creature below, a strange outcast of another clime and blood, but her Brother Humanity incarnate, Son of God and great All-Father of the race to be.[58]

Jim's companion envisions their particularity melting away atop the skyscraper as the two come to form a new primal pairing ensconced in the rhetoric of epic myth. Racial difference is not undone, but is remade to fit a new legend.

But Jim's blindness to his companion's ecstasy undercuts her fantastic vision. Rather than joining her in rapture, Jim "did not glimpse the glory in her eyes but stood looking outward toward the sea and sending rocket after rocket into the unanswering darkness."[59] Amid the phallic imagery of rockets being unleashed atop the erect skyscraper, Jim is recast by his white companion as the virile "All-Father of the race to be." While the tenor of the scene oscillates between sexual innuendo and mystic enrapture, the rhetoric of an intimate, tender, or distinct romance remains strikingly absent. Alys Weinbaum, the only critic to read this scene in depth, analyzes their union as one of "interracial romance" offering the final "utopian" solution to racial antagonism as they experience between them a "deep longing, a wish, the realization of which will enable civilization to continue in the face of imperial destruction."[60]

While the term *romance* describes the story's generic strivings, it works less well as a descriptor of the actual feelings between Jim and his companion.[61] An experience of romance, as something separate from lust or mysticism, remains difficult to locate in their encounter. Even in the face of the alleged leveling of humanity that both the comet and the skyscraper conspire to bring about, Jim never becomes fully humanized in her eyes as an individual—only more freely sexualized as a generically virile race-begetter. Their new context does not inaugurate Jim and this woman into a space of pure humanism where they can commune as equals; rather, it reduces them to the reproductive ciphers of "primal woman" and "Pharaoh."

Du Bois's interest in interracial romance as a vessel for utopia, an idea that recurs throughout his long oeuvre, further complicates this particular failure of interracial romance in the "The Comet." While Du Bois's investment in the idea of interracial utopia is strongest in what he identified as his favorite of his books, the novel *Dark Princess*, Du Bois fails to exhibit the same level of authorial conviction in his depiction of the interracial relationship here. Even as Jim begins to have his own utopian corporeal awakening to his companion's form, joining her in ecstatic feeling, nothing particularly romantic guides his turn. As "the shackles seemed to rattle and fall from his soul," causing him to rise "as though some mighty Pharaoh lived again," Jim and his companion lock eyes as "their souls lay naked to the night."[62] Yet Du Bois goes on to describe what arises between them as "not lust; it was not love—it was some vaster, mightier thing that needed neither touch of body nor thrill of soul. It was a thought divine, splendid."[63]

Romance requires a certain sentimentality of the particular, but Jim and his partner are not smitten with each other's characters or individual "true souls." Rather, their union revolves around the more abstract romance of race. More than they desire each other, they lust for their powerful new roles within their glimpsed interracial utopia. While Du Bois does not discount a romance *with* race (in contrast to a romance *despite* race) as a valid catalyst for a utopian future, he illustrates its weaknesses once the story's apocalyptic conditions dissipate.

As soon as it begins, the fantasy comes crashing down. Jim and his companion cry out to each other in a singular voice, "the world is dead." They get as far as pronouncing "long live the—" before a car horn from below interrupts.[64] Noise floods the scene as "the roar and ring of swift elevators shooting upward from below made the great tower tremble."[65] As the woman's white fiancé arrives atop the Met Life Tower, he reveals her name to be Julia. Just a few moments ago, she was "Bride of Life" and "primal woman," ready and willing to repopulate the world with a new interracial race; now firmly reembedded within the order of white hegemony, she regains her old name. The old racial order falls swiftly back into place. Julia's family accuses Jim of "harming" her. Though she defends him "quietly," we are told "she did not look at him again."[66] Her father thrusts a roll of bills into Jim's hand, utters a hollow offer of employment, and sweeps Julia downstairs as he reassumes his occupation of the Met Life building. A crowd now "poured up and out of the elevator" to confront Jim at the top of the skyscraper and repeat the story's originary exclusion, whispering threats of lynching. As Jim stands alone "beneath the glare of the light," shrinking into himself, he reaches into his pocket and brings out "a baby's filmy cap."[67] Suddenly, a woman, described as "brown, small, and toil-worn," walks toward Jim with "the corpse of a black baby" in one arm. As "the crowd parted and her eyes fell on the colored man," Jim "whirled, and with a sob of joy, caught her in his arms," ending the story.[68]

Alys Weinbaum interprets the ending of "The Comet" as a "failure of spirit" in which the vision of the interracial future is "foreclosed by the decimation of interracial romance and the reestablishment of intraracial reproductive imperatives." She suggests that the black couple's dead baby represents "the corollary of the white couple's fecundity," arguing that "without the promise of interracial romance as catalyst and reproducer of global interracial unity, the consolidation of white racial nationalism and the related decimation of black reproductivity together hold sway."[69] And yet, in light of Julia and Jim's abstract longings, the strongest moment of intimate and personal romance belongs to Jim and his wife at the story's conclusion. Despite the death of their child, Jim's "sob of joy" at discovering his wife to be alive constitutes the story's final words. Though their child has died, Jim's reunion with his wife leaves open space for black reproductivity rather than signaling just its decimation. Du Bois builds many strategic gaps into Jim's narrative, denying the reader trespass into his private loss: from the refusal to follow him into his Harlem apartment where he most surely discovered his child's corpse, to the brief but full love Jim displays toward his wife, Du Bois excludes the "human river" of readers from these intimate moments of black feeling. While the traumatic reestablishment of the old racial order causes Jim to shrink into himself much like at the story's beginning, this ending offers a repetition with a difference. Rather than being singled out from the human river as on Wall Street, Jim is now joined by his partner, revising his earlier status as the singular exclusion to the "universal" space of the crowd. The veil drops down around Jim and his wife as their sob of joy cues us to the fact that their reunion transcends a singular sensation of grief or trauma.

In the aftermath of lost utopia, the Met Life Tower becomes a setting for a powerful alternative to the racial exclusion Jim experiences at the story's opening. While Julia's father may still have the most official attachment to the building as an employee within it, Du Bois repurposes the skyscraper as a stage for black love in the story's final moments. The crowd watches Jim and his wife embrace at one of the city's highest points, momentarily recoding the white skyscraper as a site of black unification even amid loss. Their joy and grief escapes ghettoization in Harlem, where it would remain invisible to the wider world. Long after Julia and her family have descended from the skyscraper, Jim's fractured black family recolonizes the skyscraper in front of the masses, displacing the structure's previous associations with capitalism with an embodied performance of intraracial love.

Following Du Bois's deflation of Jim and Julia's utopian fantasies of interracial regeneration, Jim's simultaneously joyous and sorrow-filled reunion with his wife presents a complicated picture of redemption. Coming at the end of a book about the evils of segregation and the need for a new world order, the story's final scene reifying intraracial black love seems to question the very usefulness of utopian imagining in a world where habits of seeing impair the possibilities for even the most progressive optics. Both "The Princess Steel" and "The Comet" suggest that even the most ideal conditions for disrupting habits of racial perception and apprehension—conditions Du Bois aligns with the skyscraper's reorienting presence—may not be able to undo what took centuries of oppression to instill as gleamed from the megascope in "The Princess Steel." And yet, despite its ultimate failure to remake racial sight, the skyscraper, hosting this less dramatic but nonetheless vital act of black survival at the end of "The Comet," still has a utility for Du Bois's black subjects in the imperfect world of the present.

Wallace Thurman's Undelineated Skyscraper

Roughly ten years after *Darkwater*, the skyscraper would make a string of appearances in works associated with the more rebellious arm of the Harlem Renaissance. Rudolph Fisher and Wallace Thurman both drew the ire of Du Bois, the elder statesman of black America, for their more ambivalent and often seedier representations of black urban living. Despite his critique of sociological abstraction, Du Bois would have taken the most abstruse work of fiction over the representations of rent parties, gin heads, and the "dicty" black bourgeois in vogue with the younger set of writers in the 1920s and 1930s. Lascivious representations of black spaces particularly irked Du Bois. Many of his strongest rebukes to writers of the period were directed toward those creating depictions of Harlem he found to be overexotic and dehumanizing. Declaring Carl Van Vechten's *Nigger Heaven* a "caricature" that mistook the whole of Harlem for one giant cabaret and Claude McKay's *Home to Harlem* "filth" whose depiction of "black Harlem" made him feel "distinctly like taking a bath," Du Bois was quick to attack novels he felt exploited Harlem and its denizens by sensationalizing their basest elements.[70]

Du Bois's battles in print over Harlem's representation are by now legendary, with few critics (myself included) being able to resist quoting his snarkiest rebuttals to representations he deemed harmful to the race. Garnering much less attention, however, has been the less dramatic but equally dynamic dialogue between black writers about spaces other than Harlem, as well as other black enclaves. While Du Bois publicly clashed with Fisher and Thurman for their various portrayals of Harlem, the three found much more common ground in the skyscraper, each representing black subjects finding value in its size, its distance, or its scale. This is not to say their representations of this architecture were similar. Fisher wielded the skyscraper as the ultimate tool of urban orientation, while Thurman, with help from his friend the painter Aaron Douglas, depicted it as a harbinger of productive disorientation. But when taken together, all of these writers suggest that the skyscraper had more to offer the black subject than antagonism.

Rudolph Fisher, physician and X-ray researcher by day and writer by night, belonged by all accounts to the Talented Tenth whom Du Bois identified earlier in his career as the educated leadership class destined to uplift the race. But Fisher would fall short of this ideal in Du Bois's eyes, a sting Du Bois felt all the more sharply due to the promise Fisher's class and education seemed to portend. In a review of Fisher's novel *The Walls of Jericho*, Du Bois wrote with disappointment of Fisher's depiction of the black middle class, insisting that "the glimpses of better class Negroes which he gives us are poor, ineffective make-believes."[71] While far from the devastating critiques he penned for *Nigger Heaven* and *Home to Harlem*, Du Bois's review of Fisher's novel hints at his higher expectations for this young doctor turned writer with the credentials and talent to produce the kind of racial "propaganda" Du Bois favored.

For all their differences, Du Bois and Fisher shared an interest in writing about black subjects moving beyond the borders of black enclave. Like the black sociologist's downtown skyscraper office in "The Princess Steel" or Jim's movements between Wall Street, Harlem, and the Met Life Tower in "The Comet," Fisher used geographical placement to trouble the notion of the antimodern black subject. In scripting black southerner Miss Cynthie's first glimpse of the Chrysler Building in her grandson's robin's-egg-blue Packard or describing the experience of moving northward from Fifth Avenue's lower white neighborhoods into Harlem's "dark shadow," Fisher took care to recount not just discrete spaces but also the spatial transitions marking black experiences of the city.[72] We find him foregrounding the expansiveness of the urban black subject's movements in a 1933 children's short story he published in *Junior Red Cross News*, "Ezekiel Learns."[73] Intending the story to be the second part of a trilogy about a black child's experience of migration from Georgia to New York, Fisher died at the age of thirty-seven before completing the third installment.

Unlike the fantastic occupations of the skyscraper in W. E. B. Du Bois's fiction, Fisher's scripts black experiences atop the skyscraper as a regular ritual of urban assimilation. "Ezekiel Learns" opens by describing how in less than a month upon moving to New York from Georgia, the young black migrant Ezekiel "had become accustomed to the strange sights of the city."[74] The story credits Ezekiel's quick assimilation to his uncle's shepherding of his nephew around the city to view "all the miracles of greater New York." The first of these miracles involves a subway trip downtown to see "the tallest buildings in the world." They climb one to its apex, where they view "all of Manhattan isle, spreading away below them like a relief map."[75] Although the story goes on to juxtapose this spectacular scene of perceptual revelation with the less-spectacular but equally impactful epiphanies awaiting Ezekiel back in Harlem, this brief invocation of the skyscraper matters precisely because of its relative casualness. In contrast to Michel de Certeau's reading of the skyscraper's apex as a site where one goes "to leave behind the mass," transfiguring the subject into distant voyeur with God-like designs, Fisher figures the skyscraper as democratizing access to modern looking.[76] Ezekiel claims a position in the city, in part, by occupying this position above it. While there are no comet collisions or epic fairy tales in Fisher's folksy tale, Ezekiel's comparatively more modest experience of the city atop the skyscraper as a "relief map" helps to knit this young migrant into the city's fabric.

Both Du Bois and Fisher depict the skyscraper enabling forms of belonging. Ezekiel becomes a New Yorker, and by extension modern, through his spatial explorations that allow him to orient himself in a city that at first seems only to offer shock. Du Bois, moreover, despite staging conflicting versions of solidarity in "The Comet," continued to believe in its value as a conduit for survival, if not quite equality. Even as Jim and Julia's interracial fantasy of regeneration depends on Manhattan's destruction, their coupling presents an opportunity not to escape the masses but to remake them through sexual reproduction. When this grouping fails, Du Bois provides an alternative model of regeneration through the small but powerful collective unit of Jim and his wife atop the Metropolitan Life tower. Skyscrapers appear in the work of both Du Bois and Fisher as spaces allowing black subjects to imagine their membership within broader communities, be it a community of two or two million.

The skyscrapers appearing in the work of writer and journalist Wallace Thurman, however, serve no such unifying function. Thurman fiercely criticized Du Bois and the broader New Negro movement for promoting a homogenizing group politics. In his final novel, *Infants of the Spring* (1932), Thurman expresses his wariness of such movements as inevitably exclusionary and restrictive, a subject of particular concern for Thurman, whose own ambiguous sexuality, bohemian mores, and dark skin excluded him from the Talented Tenth model of racial uplift that his friend Rudolph Fisher seemed to so neatly fit.[77] Thurman's version of the black skyscraper in *Infants* emphasizes the limits uplift movements place on individual expression, ultimately encouraging readers to envisage for themselves a form of belonging also capable of embracing difference. Whereas Du Bois's megascope grants its viewer a look into the past from its vertical perch, Thurman casts the skyscraper as an instrument for future-gazing, figuring it as a site for imagining if not utopia, then a more inclusive configuration of affiliation to come.

Before his death at age thirty-two, Wallace Thurman published two novels, several plays, and numerous pieces of journalism during his seven years in

Harlem. He is best remembered today as one of the cofounders of the literary journal *Fire!!* Despite its early collapse (only one issue was published in 1926), *Fire!!* remains a key text of the Harlem Renaissance, marking the generational break between younger artists, such as Thurman, Langston Hughes, Zora Neale Hurston, and Aaron Douglas, and the older academic statesmen of the Renaissance, such as Alain Locke, affiliated with the more conservative New Negro movement, and the art-as-propaganda dictum of W. E. B. Du Bois, of whom Thurman wrote that "the artist in him has been stifled in order that the propagandist may survive."[78]

Thurman continued his assault on the oppressive aspects of New Negro ideology in *Infants of the Spring*, a work often cited as marking the Harlem Renaissance's dissolution. The novel certainly views itself as such a signal, evidenced by its relentless focus on the failures of interracial Harlem rent parties and black literary salons alike to bring about either racial progress or great art and the tragic endings the novel assigns to nearly all its characters. The novel centers on the world of the autobiographical aspiring novelist Raymond and his roommates occupying a Harlem commune informally known as "Niggeratti Manor." Joined by Stephen Jorgenson, a Nordic-Canadian onlooker, the bulk of the story tracks the decaying relationship between these men amid racial and social pressures. Thurman signals the dissolution of black artistic unity in quick succession with an abortion, a character deciding to pass as white, another character's imprisonment, and finally, the suicide of Paul Arbian, the queer black painter based on Richard Bruce Nugent whom the novel marks as one of Harlem's few real talents. Thurman locates the failure of the New Negro movement in its dogmatic belief that cultural work should advance a singular ideology of racial solidarity. In Thurman's contrasting view of a successful Renaissance, voiced by his fictional mouthpiece Raymond, "individuality is what we should strive for. Let each seek his own salvation."[79] If the New Negro movement could not be a home for various forms of generative difference, Thurman questioned the need for a movement at all.

Infants is plagued with the same problems of other novels centered on ideological debates: wooden dialogue, thin characters, and patchy plots.[80] The striking exception to the novel's generally stiff prose, as noted by critics Judith Brown and David Levering Lewis, is the novel's climatic ending featuring the spectacular suicide of the queer black artist Paul Arbian.[81] I share their fascination with this ending but want to shift focus from the penultimate discovery of Paul's body to the novel's actual closing lines—a brief description of Paul's last remaining legible possession, a drawing of a "distorted, inky black skyscraper."[82]

As one of the first fictional portrayals of an openly gay black man, *Infants* has been understood as Thurman's "refusal to legitimate any particular construction of racial identity as authentic."[83] Critics have rightfully read the novel's critiques of conservative notions of black authenticity primarily through the lens of its decadent sexuality.[84] Thurman undoubtedly upends normative models of racial authenticity by way of the bohemian, intraracial homoeroticism steering *Infants'* modes of sociality. Yet in his struggle to articulate a blackness that can include queerness, he also offers us a way of thinking through the perpetual dilemma of affiliation—how to make articulative space for difference while also retaining an operative sense of unity. Within the novel, the skyscraper's massiveness serves as part symbol and part setting used to evoke how individuals become absorbed into larger structures. Far more ambivalent in his depiction of the skyscraper than either Du Bois's or Fisher's, Thurman stages black relationships to this icon of modernity all while remaining skeptical about the benefits of relationality of any sort.

The skyscraper's first appearance in *Infants* dramatizes the novel's larger ambivalence about assimilation—the process of integrating the self into a larger group—as a process of both safety and estrangement. Already on the verge of impending mental collapse due to the implosion of his inner circle of friends, Raymond finally breaks down after visiting his imprisoned roommate Pelham, whose attempts to emulate the suave lifestyles of his artist roommates land him in jail for statutory rape. Overwhelmed by the tragedy of the situation, Raymond flees the prison and finds relief in the city streets, whose "fresh air and the intermittent shafts of skyscraper-obstructed sunshine were tonic in their effect."[85] However, this tonic does not last long, and Raymond becomes increasingly agitated as the obstructing buildings morph into something more ambiguous:

> The sidewalks were crowded. Raymond walked in confused circles. He had lost all sense of direction. [. . .] He grew dizzy, distraught, and unexpectedly found himself leaning against a building. He felt an urge to bore into its surface and lose himself in its chilled immunity. Then the noises of the street began to recede into the distance. The people passing became inflated and floated haphazardly above the surface of the sidewalk. The buildings on the opposite side of the street leered from their multitudinous windows, and leaned precariously, a flashback to the Cabinet of Dr. Caligari.
>
> He pressed harder and harder against the surface of the building. After what seemed hours of effort, it gave way, and his body began to penetrate into its stone. He became chilled. The buildings across the way toppled crazily downward. Let

them fall. He was safe in his cranny. The protective stone had entombed him. He had achieved Nirvana, had finally found a sanctuary, finally found escape from the malevolent world which sought to destroy him. He sank back into his protective nook. The opening through which he had bored closed as if by magic and shut him out from insensate chaos. Oblivion resulted. His body was slumped to the pavement, lay inert, lifeless, and was booted by the careless, rushing feet of passing pedestrians.[86]

Raymond's existentialist-like moment of nausea amid New York's skyscrapers seems to support the understanding of the black subject as failing to find purchase within the modern built environment, reifying James Baldwin's later act of disidentification. However, as with James Weldon Johnson's syntactical hesitation, Raymond's scene of structural entombment, with its language of sanctuary and protection, exceeds this interpretation. The skyscraper appears here as a dually loaded object; though it contributes to the urban chaos in which Raymond finds himself, it also crucially provides him with a thick-walled sanctuary for dropping out. In referencing the 1920 Robert Wiene silent film *The Cabinet of Dr. Caligari*, Thurman conjures its expressionistic architecture, where jagged, flat, and slanted buildings constantly threaten to envelop nearby subjects in intimate proximity. With this reference, Thurman keys us into the importance of considering his work within the broader context of expressionism, a critically underexamined lens for thinking black modernist prose. While Ralph Ellison claims to inaugurate this tradition with *Invisible Man*, rendering his protagonist's move North "expressionistically" in contrast to the naturalist and realist styles he respectively brought to the South and the Brotherhood, Ellison's take on the Great Migration story finds its roots in the work of modernists like Thurman experimenting with expressionist representation decades prior.[87]

But rather than using expressionistic techniques to depict the black subject's estrangement from the city, Thurman uses them to render this relation as something more like absorption, a more indeterminate type of exchange. Such an understanding of Raymond's descent thickens when placed alongside the work of Thurman's friend and collaborator Aaron Douglas, who was introduced to expressionist painting by his mentor Winold Reiss in the early 1920s. Douglas incorporated skyscrapers into many of his early paintings, from his 1925 advertisement for Carl Van Vechten's *Nigger Heaven* and his 1927 dust jacket for James Weldon Johnson's *The Autobiography of an Ex-Colored Man*, up through his most famous work, the 1934 mural "Song of Towers." In his most iconic works, skyscrapers appear either as dwarfed background structures distant from the towering black figures in the foreground or, as in "Song of Towers," ghostly progressive and intangible. Critics have largely contextualized Douglas's skyscrapers through the lens of artistic movements such as Cubism or Precisionism, interpreting his skyscrapers as vague metaphors for modernity.[88]

But in several of Douglas's covers commissioned for black magazines from the late 1920s, he renders skyscrapers as mirrors of, and even as sliding into, black bodies. For the cover of the May 1929 edition of the *Crisis*, then under the editorship of W. E. B. Du Bois, and the first and only volume of *Harlem: A Forum of Negro Life*, edited by Wallace Thurman in 1928, Douglas created two stylistically similar spreads engaging the relationship between black bodies and tall buildings. For the May 1929 *Crisis* celebrating the magazine's twenty-year anniversary, Douglas created a bold illustration of a black woman that foregrounds the figure's dark skin and thick neck in a restricted color palette of red and white. To the figure's back sit a pair of small skyscrapers located on the horizon, while facing her and in much closer proximity sits a single skyscraper extending beyond the picture frame's borders. The woman sandwiched between these skyscrapers has her eyes closed, suggesting their mutual indifference to one another. And yet she is rendered in such a way to suggest a visual parallel between her tall rising neck and those of the skyscrapers that surround her. Her red body and the red skyscraper visually echo one another in Douglas's illustration to suggest a more indeterminable relationship between the two than her closed eyes admit. The skyscrapers and the woman's head erupt from the thick red border framing the image, their shared base intimating their correlated origins.

A year earlier, Douglas drew a similar illustration for Wallace Thurman's latest upstart journal. Despite Thurman's insistence in a letter to Claude McKay about *Harlem* that the *Crisis* was "dead," to be replaced by his own "independent, fearless and general" magazine, the covers of these two magazines by Douglas share many elements.[89] Both covers emphasize the visual synchronicity between black bodies and big buildings. In the cover for *Harlem*, Douglas more explicitly blurs the line between black subjects and the skyscraper than on his May 1929 *Crisis* cover. For Thurman's journal, Douglas illustrated two black heads, one male and one female, sprouting from elongated black skyscraper bodies, followed by two black feet at the cover's bottom. These two figures—half-person, half-building—frame the cover's text situated between them. Where his earlier *Crisis* cover suggests the intimacy between black subjects and tall buildings through size, shape, and orientation, here Douglas creates an explicit hybrid marrying these fixtures of urbanity into one sleek form.

Magazine covers designed by Aaron Douglas: the *Crisis*, May 1928; the *Crisis*, May 1929; Wallace Thurman's upstart journal, *Harlem: A Forum of Negro Life*, 1928. *Top left and right,* The publisher wishes to thank the Crisis Publishing Co., Inc., the publisher of the magazine of the National Association for the Advancement of Colored People, for the use of this material first published in the May 1928 and May 1929 issues of the *Crisis* magazine. *Right,* Beinecke Rare Book and Manuscript Library, Yale University.

Douglas's May 1928 cover for *The Crisis* also renders the relationship between black subjects and tall buildings in terms of resonance and intimacy. But where the first two covers depict this intimacy in hard lines and sharp colors, representing this association in sharp visual terms, the 1928 *Crisis* cover, drawn in varying gradations of a slate blue-gray color and featuring various architectures and bodies overlapping and blending into one another, illustrates the intimacy between black bodies and tall buildings in a softer and even dreamlike tenor. The slanting, almost swirling, arrangement of pictorial elements evokes a sense of dizziness, as well as striving. Douglas biographer Amy Helen Kirschke describes the May 1928 *Crisis* cover as featuring "the typical profile Douglas face with slanted Dan Ivory Coast eyes."[90] But rather than situating this cover as "executed in a style identical to the previous covers," as Kirschke suggests, I insist on this cover's sharp difference from both Douglas's early or late works *and* the other covers featuring skyscrapers he produced in the late 1920s.[91]

With its softer lines and the jumbled directional orientations of its subjects and objects, the 1928 *Crisis* cover looks less like his other covers and more like the scene of Raymond's urban descent that his collaborator Wallace Thurman would publish a few years later. Douglas's 1928 illustration, in which it is unclear whether its bodies are rising from or falling into the buildings, mirrors the spatial ambiguity of Raymond's architectural fever. Raymond, "dizzy," "distraught," and having "lost all sense of direction," leans against the skyscraper to feel his body "penetrat[ing]" into this immediate structure's stone while simultaneously imagining the buildings around him as having "toppled crazily downward" around him. Douglas's cover depicts similar slippages of spatial orientation and between markers of interior and exterior. The faces on Douglas's cover, rather than "looking upward" as Kirschke insists, could just as easily be described as falling backward. These bodies are not neatly situated behind or between the skyscrapers but appear amorphously blurred into them due to their diagonal slant. Neither a sense of civic horizontalism nor of corporate verticality emerges in the slanted axis of either Douglas's figures or Raymond's slumping body. Unlike the strong statuesque figures featured in Douglas's other covers placing black bodies in direct visual conversation with the similarly upright skyscrapers, the May 1928 cover depicts the comingling between the black body and the skyscraper as a more vulnerable and precarious position, its black subjects and tall buildings caught between the acts of rising and falling. Anticipating the duality of Raymond's response to the skyscraper eliciting his desire and repulsion, Douglas's figures haunt the skyline in ways that look both aspirational and ghostly.

Returning to *Infants* in light of Douglas's work, if expressionism employs distortion to better depict interior states (as opposed to the mimetic impulse behind impressionism's blurred aesthetics), we might understand Raymond's expressionistic fall into the skyscraper as corresponding to his broader suspicion of absorptive masses—both architectural and social in nature—swallowing up individual subjects. The disparate feelings of both lifelessness and safety Raymond describes from inside his skyscraper tomb resemble his similarly conflicted response to black aesthetic and social movements he treats as dispiriting shelters. While a powerful black public sphere can potentially deliver a sense of empowering solidarity, Raymond struggles with feelings of inadequacy, repression, and spiritual death that emerge when the tone of this sphere is set by race men and women with constrictive ideas of belonging. Raymond declares his fear of being "too easily seduced by the semblance of security" group movements offer him, unwilling to "risk the loss of creature comfort." But as with his experience of first relenting to and then fighting his absorption into the skyscraper, the comfort of group movements becomes increasingly elusive for him.[92] Just as the skyscraper fails to serve as a haven, ultimately leaving Raymond "slumped on the pavement," the safe space of the black public sphere proves to be an illusory type of assimilative sanctuary.[93] Both kinds of "masses" eventually become urban chimeras within *Infants*, seemingly possessing the power and safety of bulk solidarity while purging individual elements whose difference threatens their stability.

When the image of the skyscraper returns in *Infants'* closing pages, it reframes the relationship between blackness and buildings once more. The novel completes the destruction of Raymond's inner circle with Paul Arbian's suicide. Raymond arrives at Paul's apartment to discover that for his final performance piece, Paul has lined his bathroom with pages from his unfinished novel before slitting his wrists. Although most of the manuscript pages have been turned into a "sodden mass" by Paul's overflowing tub, the title sheet remains legible. Below the title (*Wu Sing: The Geisha Man*) and the inscription (To Huysmans' Des Esseintes and Oscar Wilde's Oscar Wilde), is the following image, whose description ends the novel:

> Beneath this inscription, he had drawn a distorted, inky black skyscraper, modeled after Niggeratti Manor, and on which were focused an array of blindingly white beams of light. The foundation of this building was composed of crumbling stone. At first glance it could be ascertained that the skyscraper would soon crumple and fall, leaving the dominating white lights in full possession of the sky.[94]

This last doomed image of a crumbling black skyscraper viewed under blinding white lights seems to suit a novel that ends so calamitously. Critics have taken for granted the last line's "dominating white lights" as marking the total collapse of the black artist in the spotlight of the white public sphere.[95] With the exception of Judith Brown, who reads Paul's disintegration into posthumous objecthood as a sacrificial move, leaving behind "a vision of the self that is enduring, even as the self itself does not endure," critics have read *Infants'* ending as one of mere disintegration.[96] But in light of Thurman's interest in the experience of modern massness as one of both refuge and refuse, the novel's faith in enduring narrative extends further than even Brown acknowledges. If at "first glance" Paul's skyscraper appears on the verge of destruction, Thurman leaves open an unnarrated, inferred *second glance* maintaining space for a divergent "possession."

Paul's "distorted, inky black skyscraper" has several potential local antecedents. In addition to Aaron Douglas's various paintings, Harlem socialite A'lelia Walker's famed salon, which played host to Thurman's circle of upstarts, was known as the Dark Tower. And though we tend to associate skyscrapers with downtown Manhattan, Harlem was no stranger to tall buildings, the most famous of which was located at 409 Edgecombe Avenue on 154th Street. During the 1920s and 1930s, W. E. B. Du Bois, Rudolph Fisher, Jessie Fauset, James Weldon Johnson, Countee Cullen, and Aaron Douglas all lived in this thirteen-story-tall building.

But the structures that most strikingly correspond to Paul's "inky black skyscraper" are the most iconic skyscraper sketches of the era: Hugh Ferriss's dark, gothic—and inky-looking—illustrations for the 1929 book *The Metropolis of Tomorrow*.[97] Ferriss was not an architect but a delineator; instead of designing original buildings, his job was to create perspectival sketches for architectural projects. His gray-scale sketches of cities both real and imaginary, constituting the bulk of *The Metropolis of Tomorrow* and featuring images of dark skyscrapers either lit up at night or rendered as if cloaked in a light haze, influenced a generation of architects who were inspired by Ferriss's monumental imagination of towering cities to come. With the character of Paul, Thurman provides us with a counter-delineator of sorts to Ferriss and his famous soft-focus sketches of dark buildings. Paul's black skyscraper crumbling under white spotlights remobilizes Ferriss's iconic images of the dark city as symbols of black artistic potential, "distorted, inky" things of uncertain dimensions and borders that do not permit clear or totalizing legibility. Paul's perspectival drawing of the skyscraper could be read as bestowing the black coloring of Ferriss's drawings with racial heft, intimately linking these structures to black life (and death) in the city.

If at "first glance," Paul's skyscraper offers a seemingly pessimistic theorization of both the city and its surrounding social milieu as crumbling followed by the coming white repossession of the sky, Thurman invites the reader to take a revisionary second glance. This narrative opening at the novel's close remains true to Thurman's belief in heterogeneous vision that fails to cohere into a sin-

From Hugh Ferriss's *Metropolis of Tomorrow.*
Hugh Ferriss, *Metropolis of Tomorrow* (New York: Dover, 2005) 135.

gular ideology or movement. The inherent second glance requires the reader to become her own delineator, to fashion a perspective out of an unnarrated invitation to look again. Although Paul's skyscraper appears to be crumbling, it has not crumbled yet. While a crumbling foundation gestures toward structural collapse, its collapse also suggests renewal, freeing the skyscraper from its historical base and leaving the question of the successes or failures of this "black mass" unsettled. The multiple perspectives for viewing the skyscraper become the optimal place for finding a potentially more sustainable relationship between the irreconcilable social positions of group and individual identities.

While Thurman's inky skyscraper challenges Du Bois's vision of this architecture in "The Comet" recolonized by black heterosexual reproduction, what links these writers' skyscraper representations is their mutual insistence on this architecture's correspondences with the contentious and incomplete project of affiliation. For Thurman, all solidarities should be "inky" and perpetually motile, welcoming divergent and incoherent positions. In *Infants of the Spring*, the weakening hegemony of group movements improves the prospect of all kinds of other affiliations. As Raymond proclaims at the first and last salon of the novel's black literati, "there is no necessity for this movement becoming standardized." The infinite number of glances the skyscraper both invites and makes possible models Thurman's attraction to anti-standardization, with this architecture simultaneously signifying as a tombstone for group movements, as well as a totem for the eruptive cohesion to come. Thurman's skyscraper remains ambivalent, but he embraces this ambivalence as flexibility, giving the black subject the gift of inconsistency.

But Du Bois, too, chooses to leave his vision of the black skyscraper strategically incomplete, with Jim and his wife's living emotions of joy and grief working against the suggestion of a foreclosed future evoked by their child's corpse. Du Bois and Thurman, with assists from Rudolph Fisher and Aaron Douglas, leave us with a distorted and sketchy vision of black skyscrapers as alternatives to the urban, scientific, and aesthetic optics of the status quo as well as prescribed utopias that also prove too difficult in Du Bois's case or too singular in Thurman's for implementation. Transcending their infrastructural roles and confirming James Weldon Johnson's suspicion of their singularly white ontology, skyscrapers emerge within this body of work as projections of yet-unrealized modes of affiliation premised on the elastic skin and "inky" indeterminacies within blackness itself.

I end this chapter with one final image. In her book *Picturing the New Negro*, Caroline Goeser reprints a little-known image of a publicity stunt staged by the publisher Harper and Brothers in support of Claude McKay's 1928 novel *Home to Harlem*. The company hired a black horse-and-carriage man to drive a six-foot version of Aaron Douglas's cover illustration around parts of Manhattan, Brooklyn, and Harlem for two weeks. An article from *Publishers Weekly* covering the advertising ploy claims it to be "the first time as far as the publishers know" that such a tactic had been used to sell a book.[98] Goeser reads this event as a contradictory assemblage. "The contrast between Douglas's highly modern jacket design and the outmoded horse and buggy" suggests for her the "disjuncture between the modernist product and an advertising stunt drawn from old stereotypes."[99] She cites the dialect-riddled transcription of the carriage driver's in the *Publishers Weekly* interview to corroborate further the tonal unevenness of this production.

But as with the conclusion of *Infants of the Spring*, this image of a black skyscraper requires a second glance. Douglas's cover for *Home to Harlem* that Harper and Brothers had blown up and then driven across the city was itself already a "blown-up" image of the city. The front jacket features a black man of seemingly giant proportions standing between a skyscraper and what appears to be a church, gesturing to the surrounding buildings as if to signal his proprietary relation to them. His left hand stretches out toward the cathedral—perhaps modeled after the Cathedral of St. John the Divine on the border of Harlem— but doesn't quite reach it, while his right hand manages to graze the skyscraper

The 1928 cover for Claude McKay's *Home to Harlem*, illustrated by
Aaron Douglas.
Reprinted by permission of HarperCollins

to his right. Because both the figure's body and the skyscraper are rendered in the
same black color, this light touch institutes a seamless connection between
the two as these black silhouettes meet. As with his magazine covers, Douglas's
book jacket renders a black subject's intimate relationship with these icons of
modernity, an intimacy that was then projected onto the real skyline during its
journey through Manhattan's streets.

This fleeting ethereality of the billboard's movement through the city has
left few historical traces, paving the way for Baldwin's midcentury claim that
such a relation was no longer imaginable. But rather than reading the buggy
and the image as working at cross-purposes to one another, as Goeser does, I
read the work of this black carriage driver, identified in the article as sixty-eight-
year-old William Robinson, in light of Du Bois's Jim retracing the streets of
Manhattan, Fisher's Ezekiel traveling to the top of a skyscraper, and Thurman's

Publisher Harper and Brothers hired William Robinson to drive a six-foot version of Aaron Douglas's cover around Manhattan to promote Claude McKay's book *Home to Harlem*.

Republished with permission of *Publishers Weekly*: "William Sells Books to Harlem," *Publishers Weekly* (15 Apr 1928) 1623; permission conveyed through Copyright Clearance Center, Inc.

Paul and his counterdelineation of the black skyscraper. In the *Publishers Weekly* article, Robinson describes driving through "de mos' aristocratic streets in de city—Fifth Avenue an' Broadway an' Washington Squah an' Wall Street. Ah travel aroun Hahlem too." He is even invited at one point to join the Saint Patrick's Day parade with McKay's cover in tow.[100] Robinson's carriage, juxtaposed with the oversized book jacket illustration he carted through the streets of Manhattan, may suggest a collision of the modern and the antimodern. But it also suggests Robinson's assertion of his place within urban modernity one block at a time, beaming the specter of not one but two black bodies into the interstices of the city's most symbolic spaces. To return to a well-known claim of Michel de Certeau's, by reading Robinson's movement through the city as an inscription we find him writing a relation to modern architecture by way of his urban navigation.[101] Ensconced in this publicity stunt, then, are dual responses by black subjects to the built environment—Douglas's depiction of a skyscraper and Robinson's maneuvering within one skyline while literally maneuvering with another. Rather than being excluded from the city's infrastructural modernity, Robinson is at the helm of this avant-garde image, charged with carefully guiding it through this space. Instead of finding a disjuncture between the old and new Negro here, I find in this image a more unified assemblage suggesting the depth of the racial history both informing and informed by skyscraper architecture. Robinson is not outside of this story but squarely within it.

CHAPTER FIVE

Feeling White in the Darkening City

So far this book has primarily focused on the early skyscraper's role in disrupting how race is perceived from the surfaces of the body. The narratives examined up to this point either have detailed strategies for overcoming the skyscraper's perceptual hindrances in order to maintain an evidentiary relationship to race or have tactically pushed these disorienting conditions to their limits with the aim of dismantling norms of racial perception. The nature of the raced concerns surrounding the skyscraper, however, start to change the further we move away from the immediate aftermath of its invention in the late nineteenth century and into the later end of the early skyscraper era in the late 1920s and early 1930s. As the skyscraper transitioned from an architectural novelty that might soon fall out of fashion to an accepted, permanent fixture of American urban life—a reality cemented by the erection of the 102-story Empire State Building in 1931—white metropolitan writers in particular became interested in this architecture's effects not just on how race looked as a matter of external perception but also on how race was felt as a matter of lived experience.

Whereas earlier writers of skyscraper narratives worried the structure was eroding the visual distinction of white bodies, a group of white authors writing during the end of the Jazz Age and the beginning of the Great Depression expressed concern that the skyscraper was also wearing away the affective distinctiveness of whiteness as a discrete category of experience. These writers describe the difficulties white metropolitans experienced in not only maintaining whiteness as a visual category but also *feeling* themselves to be white—an identity historically yoked to self-sovereignty and a heightened capacity for bodily and emotional control—in cities seemingly built for their subjugation. In Jazz Age tales of suicidal white men plunging from the exterior of the skyscraper, as well as light romances featuring plucky "office wives" managing its interiors, the skyscraper stands accused of turning once self-sovereign virile white agents into dwarfed and distracted subjects whose personal breakdowns in and around skyscrapers foretell whiteness's broader impending collapse as a category alleged to be exceptional, superior, or even distinct. Whereas racial minorities, viewed by these texts as purely corporeal beings, are rendered immune to the skyscraper's mesmerizing presence, white metropolitans appear swallowed, disoriented, disarmed, entranced, and unnerved by it. With "the spidery steel monster" taking "so many white men in its claws," as one writer refers to the skyscraper, these later skyscraper narratives urgently pose the question of how to affectively distinguish the experience of whiteness in the wake of its subjects' architectural captivity.[1]

The first half of this chapter focuses on Jazz Age narratives featuring white metropolitan men who experience the skyscraper as an agent of racial alterity. Looking closely at two novels—F. Scott Fitzgerald's *The Great Gatsby* (1925) and the lesser-known *Flamingo,* by Mary Borden (1927)—as well as modernist Swiss architect Le Corbusier's American travelogue, *When the Cathedrals Were White* (1937), this section explores the analogues these writers forged between the experience of living amid skyscrapers and the sensation of racial marginalization. Although Le Corbusier was one of the world's most famous modernist architects and not a novelist, his energetic journal-like account of New York, published in French in 1937 and in English in 1947, shares deep affinities with the modernist prose of Fitzgerald and Borden. Despite their differences in genre, in training, and in language, all three of these writers considered themselves cosmopolitans shaped by a transatlantic modernist culture anchored by primitivism that shaped their notions of how whiteness felt within an allegedly darkening world.

The modernist skyscraper narratives written by Fitzgerald, Borden, and Le Corbusier—rendering white subjects akin to chattel slaves in the skyscraper's outsized presence—imagine the performance of whiteness to fail in a number of ways in relation to the massive architecture. The self-sovereignty of the white men in these narratives, historically imagined to be their special providence, appears frayed by the overwhelming vertical built environments of Jazz Age cities. Whereas Louis Sullivan imagined American architecture to become an increasingly masculine affair in both spirit and shape at the turn of the century, prophesizing that the fertile architect of tomorrow will "be as a man active, alert, supple, strong, sane" and "a generative man," nearly thirty years later these writers insist architecture was depleting male virility rather than better enshrining it.[2] The protagonists of these texts ultimately envision strategies for escaping the vertical city of the present—either by planning a managed urban utopia in the future, retreating into an imagined past of the unconquered city, or in death.

From the awe induced by the skyscraper's exterior, the second half of this chapter turns its focus to its interior office spaces housing the growing class of professional white women working as secretaries, clerks, and saleswomen for the corporate enterprises generally occupying them. The skyscraper's attraction for this growing demographic of white-collar women found description in the popular novels of Faith Baldwin, a writer little known to us today but who was one of the best-selling authors in the United States during the 1920s and 1930s. The white working female protagonists of Baldwin's novels struggle to succeed in both their careers and their romantic lives, spheres colliding in her books in tempestuous ways. Baldwin frames whiteness as both the catalyst for the unruly ambitions of these women—gifting them with a distinct and, at times, unhealthy "drive" attracting them to the workforce—and the foremost victim of their ambition, foregrounding the consequences for the category of whiteness should white women continue to choose the exciting environments of corporate skyscrapers over starting families. Calling on older fears about white race suicide and "vanishing Americans" emerging at the turn of the century in response to declining white birthrates, Baldwin juxtaposes the "racial instincts" of Italian and black women orienting them away from the skyscraper and toward the domestic sphere, with the "drive" of working white women too enamored with the skyscraper office's mass and abstract intimacies to tend to their more immediate familial relations. Despite their different gendered interests, all the writers in this chapter depict white subjects as specifically vulnerable to the overwhelming and, ultimately, injurious feelings deriving from their interactions with skyscrapers. Not only did vertical cities make it difficult to obtain racial knowledge about others but, as these white metropolitan writers attest, these spaces also altered the affective coordinates thought to anchor race from the inside out.

Between the Skyscraper and the Cabaret

Whereas the white metropolitan appears drained and defeated in representations from the 1920s, the Negro was imagined to have been remade anew during this same era following decades of migration to northern urban centers. Alain Locke observed in his introduction to the 1925 landmark anthology *The New Negro* that African Americans "shifting from countryside to city" had recently "hurdl[ed] several generations of experience at a leap," resulting in the positive spiritual and artistic transformation of the race.[3] Locke's optimism about the fate of the urbanized Negro stands in stark contrast to depictions from this same decade of lost and restless young white metropolitans seemingly depleted of mind, body, and spirit. "Americans were getting soft," F. Scott Fitzgerald wrote of his implicitly white countrymen in the 1920s in the essay "Echoes of the Jazz Age," reflecting on the tumultuous decade just passed in 1931.[4] Fitzgerald recounts that "by 1927 a wide-spread neurosis" affecting his white metropolitan peers had made itself known. "By this time," he writes, "contemporaries of mine had begun to disappear into the dark maw of violence," a statement he follows by listing the dark endings met by acquaintances who did not survive the Jazz Age. Of the seven deaths he recounts, two involve skyscrapers as Fitzgerald describes how one classmate "tumbled 'accidently' from a skyscraper in Philadelphia, while another falls purposely from a skyscraper in New York."[5]

The picture Fitzgerald paints of debilitated Jazz Age white metropolitans dropping off of skyscraper cliffs contrasts not only with Locke's image of the enervated New Negro but with turn-of-the-century portrayals of Anglo American vanquishers destined by both genetics and evolution to rule the century to come. Theodore Roosevelt insisted in 1892, for instance, that the descendants of the Anglo-Saxon and Teutonic races were by nature "bold and hardy, cool and intelligent, quick with their hands and showing at their best in emergency."[6] Roosevelt added a nationalist twist to broader transatlantic theories of white supremacy by insisting that Anglo Americans in particular, reared for the past two centuries in the harsh environs of the frontier, were genetically and environmentally engineered for greatness. As fearsome warriors, he claimed, Anglo Americans would continue to conquer and rule lesser races; and as innately moral and measured managers, he further insisted, whites would better the lives of conquered races who lacked the self-control required for self-rule.[7] From Roosevelt's historical monographs to Edgar Rice Burroughs's *Tarzan*, the depictions of the Anglo American's racially determined gifts that widely circulated in the United States during the early twentieth century helped support arguments for the hard and soft expansion of American global power.

The figure of the rugged white frontiersman circulated well past the 1920s and 1930s. But this iconography proved more escapist than aspirational for the multitude of Anglo Americans moving to cities to stake their bets on the nation's urbanizing future.[8] As American cities surged in population and size into the twentieth century, the western frontier was increasingly supplemented by the romanticization of the eastern urban frontier as the new seat of a business-driven Anglo American triumphalism symbolized by the skyscraper. Guy Emerson, head of the National Bank of Commerce and an amateur frontier historian himself, cast his eastern banking associates in 1920, for instance, as the "true pioneers of the new frontier."[9] The frontier tenets of rugged individualism and unlimited expansion perpetuated by Turner and Roosevelt appealed to boosters of American business who, anticipating Ayn Rand's 1943 testament to the virile corporate skyscraper architect in *The Fountainhead*, viewed the corporate office of the East and the frontier battlegrounds of the West as sister spaces of hypermasculinity that lucratively rewarded competitive individualism.

But while the landscape of American exceptionalism shifted back East, many of the racialized tropes used to romanticize the West remained intact, just transposed onto new terrains. Nationalist accounts of the skyscraper like this one published in *Harper's* in 1910 proclaiming this architecture "exclusively American, an expression of American enterprise, American inventiveness, American impatience and daredeviltry, American workmen" recycled many of the same characteristics Roosevelt and others had earlier posited as being inherent to Anglo American superiority.[10] Architects and businessmen alike viewed this architecture as the latest evidence of American exceptionalism.

Triumphal explanations of the skyscraper as the product of robust Anglo Americans in the early twentieth century were shadowed by competing portraits of atrophying white metropolitans, usually male, who appeared depressed and even suicidal under the skyscraper's umbrage.[11] Though the image of men throwing themselves from tall buildings is most commonly associated with despairing businessmen at the onset of the Great Depression, the skyscraper's association with suicide is as old as this architecture itself. The observation deck of the Singer Building, which briefly held the title of world's tallest building in 1908, was known as "Suicide Pinnacle" during the 1910s due to the frequency of jumpers. The author of a 1916 book about the history of Chicago declared the "gorges and canyons of its central district" to be "the most convenient place in the world for the establishment of a Suicide Club."[12] Fitzgerald's melancholic descriptions of skyscrapers in both 1931's "Echoes of the Jazz Age" and his 1932 essay "My Lost City" only deepened the long-standing associations of the skyscraper with death. The skyscraper offered Fitzgerald and other Jazz Age writers a dramatic backdrop for highlighting the white metropolitan's growing propensity for violence, depression, and death.

In select texts from the 1920s and 1930s, however, the skyscraper appears as more than a mere setting for demonstrating the depths of the white metropolitan's despair. These narratives frame the skyscraper as actively contributing to the white metropolitan's declining affective state, implicating this architecture in speeding his transformation from hardy vanquisher to vanquished subject. This section looks closely at three such narratives from the late 1920s and 1930s—

the novels *Flamingo* by Mary Borden (1927) and *The Great Gatsby* by F. Scott Fitzgerald (1925) and Swiss architect Le Corbusier's nonfiction treatise on the American city, *When the Cathedrals Were White* (1937)—that depict the skyscraper as a foil to the white metropolitan's capacity to feel himself to be white in the out-sized city. If one of the hallmarks of Anglo American whiteness, as argued by Roosevelt and others at the turn of the century, was the capacity of its subjects to *feel* sovereign—granting them an allegedly enhanced level of bodily and emotional control in relation to racial others perceived to lack the same instincts—the skyscraper stands accused in these texts of wearing away the inherent emotional and behavioral advantages theorized to belong to white subjects. Skyscrapers leave the protagonists in these narratives feeling stripped of their agency and emotionally unequipped to manage the modern city's spatial and affective land-scapes. The authors featured in this section describe the white metropolitan's experience of waning self-sovereignty in the wake of the skyscraper using a tan-gle of racialized terms, connecting the spatial dispossessions their protagonists experience in towering cities with the sensation of racial dispossession.

The affective and sensory traffic between the experience of one's own racial identity, the experience of the raced bodies of others, and the effects of tall buildings on the body is multidirectional and erratic in these Jazz Age narra-tives, presenting a fitful landscape of white feeling in the modern city. All of these narratives rehash well-trod primitivist imagery, depicting white metro-politans looking to "rooted" black bodies for instruction as to how they might hold their ground in the city without losing their minds. Various white metro-politans in the period admitted, as white novelist Edna Worthley Underwood wrote in 1925, to turning "more and more to the black races for art, because joy—its mainspring—is dying so rapidly now in the Great Caucasian Race."[13] Whereas whites seem to have lost the ability to enjoy their own bodies in the skyscraper's wake, black bodies often emerge in these texts as models for resisting this archi-tecture's effects.

But the racialized sensations associated with the experience of skyscraper are not reducible to primitivism alone. Blacks might appear resistant to the sky-scraper in one moment in these texts while emerging in another as part of a broader racial coalition writhing under the skyscraper's influence. At other times, white metropolitans declare themselves to be modernity's new blacks, imagining themselves as being enslaved by the skyscraper and the organizational structures they housed, whereas blacks, aware of the value of their hard-fought freedom, remain cannily distant from this architecture. Black bodies are even figured at times as being like skyscrapers, imagined to induce a similar mixture of horror and desire capable of bringing white metropolitans to their sensory limits. The feeling of being "moved" by something beyond the self, as Sianne Ngai writes in *Ugly Feelings*, has long been imagined to be the domain of "the overemotional racialized subject," historically figured as exceptionally receptive to external control.[14] But who gets cast as the overemotional racialized subject in these skyscraper narratives proves exceedingly mobile, pinned at various points in these texts on a host of subjects, objects, and performances within the urban landscape. The skyscraper emerges in these works as an agent of racialization, mediating not just the racial experience of one's own body but the imagination of how others feel, behave, and perform race.

Mary Borden and the Skyscraper's New Slaves

More so than any other novel from the early skyscraper era, Mary Borden's 1927 *Flamingo* is thoroughly obsessed with skyscrapers. This novel, largely ignored by literary critics, has been overshadowed by Borden's better-known career as a war memoirist.[15] Born to a wealthy Chicago businessman, Borden left the United States for England as a young woman and eventually opened a field hospital there during World War I. She recounts this experience in her 1929 war memoir, *The Forbidden Zone*, which has since been called one of the most powerful and experimental pieces to emerge from the war. Borden continued to live overseas until her death, publishing novels well into the 1950s, including the controversial *Mary of Nazareth*, fictionalizing the Virgin Mary as an ordinary woman, and *The Techniques of Marriage*, in which Borden advocated for making the legal hurdles to marriage higher and divorce lower.

In contrast to these more polemical writings, *Flamingo*, published in the United Kingdom as *The American Tower*, deals with far less radical content. Peter Campbell, New York architect extraordinaire and the novel's protagonist who is battling to build his next great skyscraper, reconnects with his childhood sweetheart and fellow skyscraper enthusiast, Englishwoman Frederika Joyce. Despite Joyce's love of structural engineering, her British bureaucrat husband has stymied her dreams of doing this work, deeming it an improper interest for a diplomat's wife.[16] Her entwined passion for Peter Campbell and the skyscraper are rekindled when she and her husband arrive in New York on state business. Campbell and Joyce's love for one another along with their mutual love for the skyscraper drives most of *Flamingo's* plot.

While the skyscraper's form initially reignites the connection between Joyce and Campbell, form is precisely what the *New York Times* found lacking in the novel in a 1927 review, asserting that "the themes and elements of 'Flamingo' are so numerous and often so irreconcilable that the book eludes all sense of form, all basic unity."[17] And this criticism is certainly justified—the book's multiple plots and subplots veer throughout its 400 pages, as the novel moves between corporate intrigue, tragic romance, high-society exposé, and backwoods romp. Much of *Flamingo*'s formal instability derives from its deep interest in skyscraper form. The novel's descriptive faithfulness to this building hinders its own unfolding, stifling the plot's momentum and the development of its characters. *Flamingo* seems premised on the belief that, like its skyscraper-obsessed protagonists, the reader, too, wants nothing more than to consume descriptions of the skyscraper's arresting horror. Its skyscraper descriptions fluctuate between rebuking the structure as a "spidery steel monster" turning the city into a hellish site of subjugation and praising its inspiring possibilities marked by its "beautiful clear angles, geometric masses, walls that stream up, stream down, breathless, straining, the architecture of suspense, of aspiration."[18] Rather than ascribing it a meaningful semantic structure, Borden's compulsive description of the skyscraper makes it all the more unstable as a symbol.

The skyscraper's erratic representation in *Flamingo* has much to do with its positioning within a broader matrix of racialized feeling running throughout the novel. Skyscrapers and black bodies appear in the text as linked sites of optic fascination, similarly arresting the gazes of their white metropolitan beholders and threatening to shatter their increasingly fragile sense of themselves as sovereign subjects. These same black bodies, however, also possess the antidote to these dizzying effects, becoming models of liberation for white metropolitans who describe feeling like modernity's new slaves in the skyscraper's presence. When it is finally revealed that black art forms also serve as the aesthetic inspiration for the skyscraper's architectural design in the novel, there seem to be no available modes left for relating to the skyscraper that are not fundamentally structured by the experience of blackness. In *Flamingo*, the affective hallmarks of whiteness yoked to an inherent sense of bodily and emotional control are increasingly difficult to attain in the skyscraper's shadow.

Flamingo's opening lines immediately foreground the link between the skyscraper and blackness. Its first scene, utilizing third-person omniscient narration, sets the dual tones of grandeur and angst that run throughout the entirety of the book:

> Sometimes, when I think of Peter Campbell standing at his high window in that
> breathless American tower and looking out at the panorama of New York City, a

figure so minute in the great flat façade of the building as to appear an indistinguishable speck across the precipitous cañon of the street, I remember that space is black, and I think of the eternal night of space with little lighted worlds spinning in it, a thousand million or so, tracing across the void a faint luminous trail that is no bigger in the immensity than the whisk of the tail of a firefly. The darkness seems to be undisturbed by their passing.[19]

From the start, existential fear has a color, and this color is black—from the unhinged feeling of floating in dark space from within the skyscraper to the sudden image of the world suspended in a sea of darkness. *Flamingo* continues to associate the skyscraper with blackness in this atmospheric way, noting the black gaping holes of its construction dotting the city and, as in this passage, associating blackness with the sensation of diminishment as Campbell, the agent of space, transforms into an "indistinguishable speck" lost within it. Despite helping to build this landscape, Campbell now seems to be swallowed up into it. *Flamingo* opens with the visual vanishing of the white metropolitan as the normal state of things.

As the novel continues, the skyscraper's power to vanish, to diminish, to estrange, and to fascinate the white metropolitan all at once becomes increasingly linked to a more corporeal form of darkness. With descriptions like those of the "black rollicking giants" in Harlem's dance halls or the dastardly Jewish financier for Campbell's newest skyscraper described as "a big black Jew with beautiful brown hands," the novel figures the white metropolitan as physically contracted in relation to both skyscrapers and racial others that all seem to tower over him.[20] When the white metropolitan's body is not being dwarfed by racial others, it is rendered as indistinguishable from them, particularly from the point of view of the skyscraper's heights. The book describes the "black creatures no bigger than midgets" that are ejected each day from the skyscraper's "great intestines." A similar passage analogizes the skyscraper to an Egyptian obelisk causing a man to appear in its midst as "a little black insect like a flea running about on its hind legs."[21]

Lending this more general imagery of visually blackening its specifically racial charge is its similarity to descriptions of how bodies look and feel in Harlem in a subterranean cabaret known as The Crib. Borden figures this space as "the draughty basement of her terrible American city" where "this dark, uprooted fragment of a race" goes to "rot away." African Americans, deemed to lack "guts and no sense," are described as having "died off like flies in these cellars of theirs."[22] Rendered in similar shades of darkness, dehumanization, and a decayed sense of will, the "dark race" described within the Harlem cabaret is not all that different from how the novel depicts New York's broader population in which all subjects appear similarly diminished, blackened, and stripped of agency under the skyscraper. *Flamingo* figures the city at times as one large subterranean basement populated by a single devolved and degraded "dark" population. Couched here within a Jazz Age idiom of melancholy and enchantment, anxieties about waning white distinction remain just as palpable in *Flamingo* as in the more explicitly violent parables of white urban extinction analyzed in the first chapter of this book.

Not only do the visual landscapes of the skyscraper and the Harlem cabaret share a descriptive language but the experience of encountering these modern hallmarks of urban experience are also rendered in like ways, with each causing the novel's white metropolitans to physiologically vibrate in compulsive fits of both awe and terror. On entering The Crib, one of Frederika Joyce's attendants is described as having "just had time to gape, to feel his eyes bulging and strain greedily at the weird, wild scene" filled with the "awful beauty of the African camp-fire dances going on round them."[23] The description of the Harlem cabaret's "awful beauty" mirrors the "awful logic" Peter Campbell ascribes to the experience of the skyscraper, which he accuses of inciting "inspired terror" in metropolitans of a magnitude "so strange that a lot of people felt uncomfortable at the sight of it, and said it was ugly." The "distant, hypnotic, inaccessible tower" causes its spectator to feel "the breathless feeling that one has when one is being driven at a terrific speed," as if being "hoisted up suddenly by the neck and flung with a twang into the blue."[24] Encounters with the cabaret and the skyscraper, respectively, paralyze the white metropolitan in episodes of bodily shock, flooding the white metropolitan's body with a sensation of pulsating excess that comes to define the feeling of the "modern."[25]

Campbell eventually sharpens the link between the skyscraper and the cabaret as twinned space of sublimity when he imagines his life in the city according to a three-tiered model. At the top sits "his working life . . . lived in the air," while on the bottom layer resides the underground space of the Harlem cabaret, described by him as "another world, subterranean, the world of blazing night cellars where the Negros gather." Campbell describes being "irresistibly drawn" to both these top and bottom layers stimulating him. In between the skyscraper and the Harlem cabaret lies Campbell's "married life" on the middle tier, which he associates with the formal rules of "Society." Campbell yokes the skyscraper and the Harlem cabaret together as dual substantiations of modernity breaking with the affective, institutional, and architectural forms of the past he connects to ossified forms of white sociability. The skyscraper and the cabaret together frame the experience of modernity in contrast to the white status quo sandwiched between these two layers, depicted as having little room for spatial or spiritual expansion.

But if blackness produces sensations of existential crisis and titillating danger akin to the experience of the skyscraper, blackness also provides the novel's white metropolitans with a model for how to survive the most oppressive of the sensations associated with vertical living. Beyond the experience of pleasurable estrangement they find in Harlem, Campbell and his friends slum in Harlem to learn from the cabarets' black denizens how to, in the novel's own words, make their own "flesh-and-blood bodies" feel "good again" in light of the skyscraper's dehumanizing domination.[26] Borden depicts the crowded spaces of the underground cabaret as allowing white bodies to accrue a level of presence no longer deemed possible at street level where the skyscraper continually reminds them of their speck-like insignificance. *Flamingo*'s narrator draws upon fashionable tropes of primitivism to figure blacks as unthinking founts of joy, mindlessly liberated from the white man's modern burdens. Negroes, Borden writes, "paid no attention to those straining skyscrapers on top of them. They went on breeding and singing and laughing and yelling and dancing and being lazy and getting religion just as if they were in Africa with no clothes on." The primitivist language Borden uses here to describe black joy is unsurprising given the prevalence such descriptions during this period. What makes Borden's use of these tropes distinct, however, is the way she uses them to respond to the spatial disorientations distinct to urban modernity. The black body, figured as nothing but body and incapable of attending to anything beyond the body's immediate sphere, appears powerfully immune to the kind of skyscraper malaise overwhelming Campbell and *Flamingo*. Simultaneously hyperactive (breeding, singing, laughing, yelling, dancing) and inactive ("being lazy"), Borden's blacks are both too busy and not busy enough to be bothered by skyscrapers. As ahistorical subjects, they prove unsusceptible to modernity's particular dramas.

In this final published version of *Flamingo*, Borden anchors black urban invulnerability to a timeless African otherness. But in an earlier draft housed in her papers at Boston University, Borden provides an alternative account of black skyscraper resistance. In a sentence ultimately edited out in the final draft, the narrator explains that rather than perceiving "darkies" as "dangerous to his race," Campbell saw them instead as "the one human power in America, strong enough, rich blooded enough, to save the human race from being enslaved by the machinery of Industrial Development. They had been slaves once so they knew. Once bitten twice shy."[27] The word "darkies" and the reference to slavery were cut in the final manuscript, with the paragraph ending instead with the sentence about Negroes "breeding and singing and laughing" their way out of skyscraper subjugation. We can only speculate as to why Borden made this choice. She may have cut the nod to slavery for the same reason she edited out the term *darkie*—concerns that these references crossed a line of offense. And yet it is hard to imagine this deleted sentence as any sort of real tipping point, given the novel's heavy investment in flat black stereotypes elsewhere, even within this same paragraph. A more compelling way to understand this edit would be in terms of its inconsistency with the more corporeally jocular depictions of black frivolity she prefers throughout the rest of the novel. By tying the skyscraper wariness of African Americans to historical memories of enslavement, Borden situates modern blacks *not* as a carefree and unknowing race happily "breeding and singing and laughing" into oblivion but as knowing subjects hip to the pitfalls of modernity and choosing to opt out. This deleted line, figuring blacks as having learned to mistrust the physical and ideological structures of modernity after the "lesson" of slavery, positions them less like joyful subordinates and more like subterranean subversives. And this is what may have been a bridge too far for Borden, whose finished novel ultimately positions white metropolitans as feeling at times *like* the previously enslaved, while still maintaining their real-time superiority to blacks in the present. Blacks can serve as models of feeling, but approaching them as models of thought, as this earlier draft does, ultimately becomes unthinkable.

But the novel has another incentive for framing blacks as indifferent to the skyscraper—their scripted unresponsiveness allows Campbell to openly claim black art as a direct inspiration upon his skyscraper designs, a borrowing he can then frame as an innovative repurposing rather than as an egregious act of appropriation. In addition to the physical and psychic release he receives from Harlem's hedonistic pleasures, Campbell describes the ways his powers of design are heightened by his acts of slumming. As the narrator explains of Campbell, "all those black men stimulate his creative power."[28] Within the "black continent, that subterranean Africa blazing under the city's pavement," as the narrator notes, Campbell discovers that "all sorts of architectural concepts sprout up in his mind in that jazz jungle," allowing his "fancy" to become "as luxuriant as a tropical forest."[29] Three years later, James Weldon Johnson would hesitatingly claim the skyscraper as the exception to the African American monopoly on American artistic production. But *Flamingo* makes the tie between black arts and skyscraper form concrete, figuring Harlem as the uncredited coauthor of these structures.

This revelation ultimately revises Campbell's vertical model of separate spheres, as the Harlem cabaret and the skyscraper became not just mirrored layers within the city but sister spaces built with the same artistic and affective principles. More than just spaces inducing like physiological responses, these two locations are figured by Borden as forming a circuit of architectural exchange. Campbell tries to rationalize and thus control the shifting scales of the city by positioning himself as the mobile thread between subterranean blackness and its twinned towers of existential darkness. But *Flamingo* finally posits these two spaces traditionally marking the edges of the white metropolitan city as acting as one big space absorbing the white metropolitan from all sides. The skyscraper, crucially, does not only make white metropolitans feel black or produce feelings like those induced by blacks—it is ultimately revealed to be a product of blackness itself. The white metropolitan is merely the vessel transubstantiating black essence into architectural form.

As an architect, Campbell originally seems like the character best equipped to manage the city's unruly spaces. But the novel's belief in his capacity to form and control these spaces ultimately dissolves. Campbell fails to maintain his own ground within the metropolis, let alone transform the ground of others. No longer even the "sole" father of the skyscraper, Campbell's expendability and lack of sovereignty finally overwhelms him. At the novel's conclusion, he kills himself by flinging himself from a skyscraper, crystallizing the white metropolitan's extinction fantasy in the darkening city. "When he jumped," Borden writes, "no one heard his tiny cry or saw him fall, a whirling speck, rolling over and over, down the immense stone precipice, past the many tiers of dark, vacant windows."[30] Campbell exits the novel much as he entered it, his body swallowed by the "eternal night of space" besieging him from all sides. The understanding of white subjects as inherently self-possessed, granting them the natural right to dispossess allegedly less-sovereign racial others professed by advocates of empire and expansion, is unsteadied by the conclusion of *Flamingo*. Borden's white metropolitans ultimately end up suspended within an ether of blackness, unable to spatially or emotionally orient themselves within its ambient urban presence.

Le Corbusier's Black Caves

A few years later, another transatlantic white metropolitan would sample from similar tropes of antebellum bondage and postbellum primitivism to depict the mixture of subjugation and liberation he found the skyscraper to induce. Swiss architect Le Corbusier arrived in the United States in 1935 to much fanfare, already internationally famous for his ideas about moving toward an architecture designed for modern subjects, as the title of his 1923 manifesto proclaimed.[31] After embarking upon a four-month tour of the East Coast and the Midwest to see the architecture of the states, as well as delivering lectures at several universities along the way, Le Corbusier reflected on his visit in his 1936 book *When the Cathedrals Were White*, which could be described as part travelogue, part architectural manifesto, part arch critique of America's buildings and persons.[32] Although Le Corbusier moved across a large swathe of the Eastern seaboard during his visit, the skyscraper remains at the center of his fascination as he, like Borden, constantly returns to the structure in his prose to try to capture what made it feel both so wrong and so right to him.

Blackness forms a large part of his descriptive arsenal for the skyscraper. Though Le Corbusier's attraction to blackness predates his US visit given his embrace of African art in the 1920s alongside a host of other European artists, African American culture particularly fascinated Le Corbusier, architectural historian Mardges Bacon notes, as an example of "a synthesis of the folk and the mechanical."[33] But Le Corbusier's primitivist vocabulary in *When the Cathedrals Were White* migrates beyond denoting subjects, objects, and spaces explicitly marked as black to serve as the explanatory register for the sensory experience of urban modernity at large. He begins the book by establishing a binary between the "honkey-tonks and juke box joints, in Harlem and on Broadway"—places where "life seeks nourishment," on one end—and the "mechanic calculation" of the skyscraper and its inhabitants forming the other end featuring "millions of people undergoing the diminution of life imposed by devouring distances."[34] Though he marks sites of black sound as escaping such diminution through their life-affirming qualities, Le Corbusier observes that, in the rest of the city, "seven million people are bound in the chains of New York."[35] Le Corbusier's throwaway line here invoking metaphorical subjugation becomes explicitly raced as he describes black sites of affective escape on the city's fringes. Whereas New York binds contemporary white metropolitans in chains, Le Corbusier describes the Negro's relationship to bondage as belonging only to the past. The Negro may have been "taught on the plantations of Louisiana [. . .] hymns and folk songs," he writes, but despite currently living "crowded together, in Harlem or Chicago, in slums near the skyscraper," Le Corbusier observes that Negroes of the present "well know that the heart liberated by intoxication opens itself to the effusion of music."[36] Like Borden's reference to "darkies," who, "once bitten twice shy," know to steer clear of modernity's enslaving rhythms, Le Corbusier, too, finds the white metropolitan's struggle for willfulness and meaningful self-presence akin to slavery, while framing the Negro as inspiringly fugitive.

Where skyscrapers stifle and diminish bodies in Le Corbusier's account, black bodies and art forms emerge once more in his text to reflate the body from the inside out. Le Corbusier describes black sound as something that "enters the bosoms of men and women, fixes itself there, carries with it the flow of blood, puts dynamism into the whole body."[37] This music, Le Corbusier implores, "has to be heard in the midst of the clamor of the skyscrapers and roaring subways," filling the body where the skyscraper threatens to empty it out. But if blacks at first escape a diminished mechanized state that the book associates earlier with urban whiteness, they are ultimately figured as firmly within its orbit later on as Le Corbusier defines Negroes in the second half of the book as "an effect of the machine." Upon watching Louis Armstrong's orchestra perform, Le Corbusier remarks that "the men are tireless, like a smoothly running turbine," before finding a similar "rigor of exactitude" in black tap dancers. Armstrong is described as neither human, animal, nor machine but "a black cave," appearing "demoniac, playful and massive, from one second to another, in accordance with an astounding fantasy."[38] Armstrong—cavernous, spectacular, capable of moving the body— evokes a similar response from Le Corbusier as the feelings he experiences amid skyscrapers, which, despite referring them to earlier in terms of mechanic calculation, he most persistently positions as "fairy catastrophes" inspiring romantic flights of feeling despite their structural harshness. In a moment of evening rapture, beholding "the thousand lights of each skyscraper," Le Corbusier describes the sensory experience of their mass. "Splendor, scintillation, promise, proof, act of faith, etc. Feeling comes into play; the action of the heart is released; crescendo, allegro, fortissimo. We are charged with feeling, we are intoxicated, legs strengthened, chest expanded, eager for action, we are filled with great confidence."[39] Just as his description of Armstrong as "demoniac, playful and massive" and a "fantasy" could easily fit with his description of the skyscraper, Le Corbusier's description of the musical experience of the skyscraper resembles the psychic and physiological response he has to Armstrong's jazz.

If Armstrong becomes a fantastic black cave that impishly resonates inside the white body, the skyscraper appears as another kind of cavern of feeling that envelops the white body, causing it to pulsate, expand, and fill with energy. Though originally set in opposition to one another, black subjects and their sounds structure the experiential encounter with the skyscraper, each causing the white metropolitan's body to physically reverberate. Blackness emerges in *Cathedrals* as much more than a subject position—it is treated as an effect, a spectacle, and a location. Just as skyscrapers prove to be more than just buildings, Negroes are more than just bodies; their shared capacities to move white metropolitans make them spaces, agents, and effects all at once. Le Corbusier himself concretizes the connection between blackness and skyscrapers as sites of excess, proclaiming that "jazz, like the skyscrapers, is an *event* and not a deliberately conceived creation."[40] As an event, jazz and by extension its African American originators exist, like the skyscraper, beyond the framework of subject and agent to become atmospheric and temporal ephemera. The skyscraper and the black body are defined in terms of bodily excess while the white metropolitan can only experience excess, leaving him to perform the role of the "overemotional racialized subject" vulnerable to "external control," to recall Ngai's definition of animatedness. The white metropolitan takes up the position of the slave while the black subject oscillates between vibrancy and careful withdrawal, two characteristics framed by these Jazz Age urban narratives as being increasingly lost to the white metropolitan.

It is within this context that Le Corbusier ultimately declares himself the singular white metropolitan daring to fight back against the paralyzing city, positioning himself—as architects Louis Sullivan and Frank Lloyd Wright did before him—as the lone rogue agent up to the task of wrangling the city's excesses into a rational form. Unlike *Flamingo's* bleak conclusion about the white metropolitan in the black city, culminating in the suicide of its male protagonist, Le Corbusier emerges from *When the Cathedrals Were White* with a sense that he can rehabilitate the skyscraper. Within the context of the right plan, as Le Corbusier had already demonstrated in his 1922 Ville Contemporaine plan envisioning a city four times the size of Manhattan organized around sixty uniform skyscrapers, this architecture could bring the modern city into order rather than facilitate form's dissolution.[41] Finding America to be, in the words of architectural historian Mabel Wilson, "a culture churning with racialized bodies and unbridled feminine figures," Le Corbusier's response to this experience of difference was to understand it in terms of his concept of the Ville Radieuse, or the Radiant City, his idea for the systematic restoration of the physical and metaphorical "white cathedrals" of Western civilization's past by placing skyscrapers on a Cartesian grid. Wilson shows how Le Corbusier throughout *Cathedrals* both fears and desires blackness, imagining his dream of the Radiant City to be simultaneously animated by its presence while also serving as a force for containing it.[42]

But Le Corbusier's encounters with New York's black and blackening spaces would prove to have an even longer afterlife. The affiliation between tall buildings and black bodies would be recast once more in the midcentury with the emergence of high-rise housing projects. Le Corbusier's plan for the Radiant City would influence the design of American public housing after World War II, particularly those projects taking the form of clustered towers spatially isolated from the surrounding city by swathes of green space.[43] These large housing projects, inadvertently helping to consolidate and cordon off their largely black populations from downtown centers and other residential hubs, would come to mark a new chapter in the skyscraper's association with racial sensation. Whereas white metropolitans in the 1920s and 1930s linked skyscrapers and black bodies together as forms of excess that caused them to feel dwarfed and unsovereign, a decade later white metropolitans would flee the city's vertiginous verticality for suburbs offering a seemingly endless bounty of horizontal space. The white metropolitans of the 1920s would eventually join the ranks of the nation's expanding suburban population for whom the city was reducible to its downtown centers of work and leisure, positioning themselves to ignore the towering new housing projects racially recoding verticality once more.

Fitzgerald's Dissolving White Sugar Lumps

Feelings of bodily dispossession associated with the experience of skyscrapers were not only articulated in relationship to blackness during the 1920s and 1930s. They also surfaced in connection to broader racial imaginaries. To return briefly to Mary Borden's *Flamingo*, although an earlier draft of the novel depicts blacks as modern-day abolitionists equipped to resist modernity's enslaving scales and distractions, elsewhere in the published manuscript protagonist Peter Campbell situates blacks as belonging to a much larger ethnic conglomeration helplessly enraptured by the skyscraper. He offers the following racial portrait of the city enervated by skyscrapers:

> Every Polack and Slovak and Italian and Dago is aware in his tenement, every Chinese boy in Chinatown, every Swede in her kitchen, every nigger in Harlem, and the Jews on Fifth Avenue, they are all under the influence, they all feel the daring, the defiance of these buildings, their massive lightness, their exultation, the miracle of the immense weight that seems to float upward; and they respond, and it drives them crazy, though they don't know it. It's because the poor boobs take part in the fantastic drama of New York architecture that they're all in the state of perpetual excitement, have monstrous dreams, believe in miracles and get drunk. By God! It's grand! It's crazy! It's terrible![44]

Campbell begins this passage by claiming of skyscrapers that "everyone" in New York must be "aware of them all the time," but the constituency of the aware he goes on to list here reads far more selectively, excluding the category of what Campbell identifies elsewhere in the novel as "Real Americans"—the "Anglo Saxon [. . .] descendants of English Gentlemen."[45] At the passage's start, Campbell fully embodies his role as a "Real American," presenting himself as a dispassionate observer of the various racial and ethnic others he declares "under the influence." However, by the end of this passage, increasingly punctuated by clipped exclamations about the ethnic fervor Campbell is witnessing, he seems far closer to the writhing bodies he tries to represent. His movement in this paragraph from interested yet detached observer to frenzied participant mirrors his larger emotional arc across the novel. Once imagined in his positions as both an architect and a white man to have a certain amount of control over the city and himself, Campbell ultimately proves to be the foremost victim of the vertical city. These ethnic exultants survive their experience of the skyscraper, whereas Campbell does not.

Contrast the linked spatial and emotional landscapes Campbell traverses in *Flamingo* with the environments described by perhaps the most famous white metropolitan protagonist of the Jazz Age—Nick Carraway, the narrator of *The Great Gatsby*. The narrators of *Flamingo* and *When the Cathedrals Were White* excitedly describe feeling continually "moved" against their will in the blackening city, striving to scale the city's vertical extremes of skyscraper peaks and underground Harlem valleys. *Gatsby's* Nick Carraway, by contrast, is a far less excitable guide. We know Nick spends considerable time alone wandering through the city, but he gives the reader very few descriptions of what he experiences on these jaunts. In fact, there are almost no references in *Gatsby* to the spatial iconography most associated with the Jazz Age: skyscrapers make a single appearance in his version of events, briefly described once by Nick as white sugar lumps, while Harlem does not appear at all. As opposed to Borden's and Le Corbusier's vertically oriented narratives of urban living, Fitzgerald primarily structures *Gatsby* in terms of gradual horizontal movement, allowing Nick to accrue knowledge about others—emotional, social, and racial—in paced increments. From the multiple car rides through the city's ashen borderlands to the novel's epic closing lines in which the first Dutch sailors approach the "fresh, green breast of the new world" by boat, the novel's most dramatic moments involve arresting landscapes or symbols cresting into view from across the horizon.[46] There are no aerial perspectives described in *The Great Gatsby*; Nick's real and imaginary gaze tends outward rather than upward.

Given Nick's restrained narration and disinterest in the skyscraper, *The Great Gatsby* sits oddly next to the other novels in this section that more explicitly detail the skyscraper's effects on the white metropolitan's capacity to feel raced. Besides his drunken sexual encounter at Myrtle's party with another man, Nick's sense of self-sovereignty remains largely intact throughout the novel. But we do observe Nick as he begins to question the racial sanctity of Gatsby's performance as a "Real American," a performance that appears least convincing when situated against an urban backdrop. Walter Benn Michaels has most notably shown how Gatsby falls short of being white within the novel's logic, explicating how Fitzgerald figures him as a racial minority whose relationship with Daisy is essentially one of miscegenation. But Gatsby's blackness emerges within the distinct spatial context of the skyscraper; his absorption into the "monstrous" city making his performance of whiteness appear strange to its beholders.[47] *The Great Gatsby* incorporates the skyscraper into a larger narrative sequence that begins with Nick and Gatsby's trip from West Egg into New York City and ends with a different coupling, this time of Nick and Tom who ultimately distinguish themselves from Gatsby. His distinct tics, which appear in the context of West Egg as eccentric and mysterious, accrue a new racial sheen in the skyscraper's shadow. Accused of being both overly willful and not willful enough, too single-minded in his passion for Daisy in a way that causes him to resemble the ethnic exultants of Borden's novels, Gatsby most egregiously fails to perform whiteness when he is stripped of his obscuring suburban extravagances and plunged into a starker—and darker—urban context. Akin to the ways Borden and Le Corbusier correlate their experience of the skyscraper with the experience of black bodies, Fitzgerald crafts a connection between the dazzling white skyscraper, which turns out to have a darker racial source, and Gatsby's false façade, similarly masking his concealed racial alterity. Compared to the other narratives in this section or even other works by Fitzgerald, the skyscraper's presence in *The Great Gatsby* is relatively minuscule. But as with Nella Larsen's *Passing* published a few years later in 1929, skyscrapers help produce the conditions around which some of *Gatsby's* key foreground events—particularly those revolving around racial sight and feeling—unfold.

When Nick and Gatsby decide to drive into Manhattan together during the early stages of their acquaintance, Gatsby's control over his performance as a white man of standing is compromised from the outset. Nick, observing Gatsby up close and in the daylight for the first time, describes the "disconcerting" collage emerging from the juxtaposition of Gatsby's material and gestural accoutrements. The gaudiness of Gatsby's car of "monstrous length," the garishness of his outfit, and the "unfinished" form of his sentences paint for Nick a disorienting portrait of a man managing to both overdo and underdo his self-presentation all at once.[48] No longer hidden behind the large-scale distractions of his West Egg parties, the details of Gatsby's performance, newly observable within the intimacy of Gatsby's sedan, begin to announce to Nick the unsoundness of Gatsby's performance.

Before more of these cracks can accrue, Nick's attention is diverted from the "disconcerting" particularities of Gatsby's behavior to the breathtaking appearance of the Manhattan skyline at the entrance to Queensboro Bridge. Nick cinematically narrates his vision of the skyline as a series of descriptive clauses lacking a predicate. "Over the great bridge, with the sunlight through the girders making a constant flicker upon the moving cars, with the city rising up across the river in white heaps and sugar lumps all built with a wish out of nonolfactory money."[49] The vision Nick narrates is abstract and ephemeral—a city of sweetness and light built with money that has no smell. The skyscraper from afar, like Gatsby, appears to Nick as an unsullied dream, allowing him to conclude from this distant vantage that "the city seen from the Queensboro Bridge is always the city seen for the first time, in its first wild promise of all the mystery and beauty in the world." He easily fits this picture of the white, light city into the archetypal narrative of wondrous and mythic first encounter to which he repeatedly returns across the novel.

As Nick moves closer to the city, however, the stench of money and its correlated racial entanglements overwhelm him. The original virgin urban scene of "mystery and beauty" is famously dashed in the next paragraph when a hearse "heaped with blooms" and "the tragic eyes and short upper lips of southeastern Europe" passes them in one car before they are passed again by a limousine "driven by a white chauffeur, in which sat three modish negroes [. . .] laugh[ing] aloud as the yolks of their eyeballs rolled toward us in haughty rivalry."[50] The world of nonolfactory money and whimsical white sugar lumps Nick glimpses at a distance as a graspable totality immediately collapses once they cross the bridge and enter into a world of fragmented smell and color. Nick's sweeping scene of modernity's fairy-like totality bursts into pieces that he struggles to recollect from the passenger seat of Gatsby's car. Having crossed over from the city's white exterior to its dark interior, Nick imagines "anything could happen now that we've slid over this bridge. [. . .] Even Gatsby could happen, without any particular wonder."

Nick's earlier hypothetical about Gatsby turns out to be accurate—not only does Gatsby "happen" in the city but the city abets his becoming in concrete ways. Unlike the other skyscraper narratives in this section, Nick's sense of himself as a "Real American" does not waver as they approach the skyscraper. But his perception of Gatsby and his performance of whiteness does. Jimmy Gatz's transformation into Jay Gatsby "happens" in the city with the support of what the novel treats as unsavory and racially suspect sources. Nick confronts the city's racialized core over the course of the next several paragraphs when they enter "a well-fanned Forty-second Street cellar" in the heart of midtown. Within this cellar, Nick meets Gatsby's business partner Wolfsheim ensconced within a subterranean layer of scent and sense, a figure whose marked Jewishness and dubious business tactics does irreparable damage to Gatsby's performance as a white subject. Nick's earlier vision of white skyscrapers and, it seems, a white Gatsby, rising effortlessly "with a wish" from "non-olfactory money," are conclusively dashed once he meets Wolfsheim, the real *macher* of modernity at the city's center. In contrast to his nonolfactory vision of the skyline, Nick's depiction of Wolfsheim centers entirely on his stereotypical Jewish nose. From his summation of Wolfsheim as "a small, flat-nosed Jew," Nick continues to fixate on Wolfsheim's nose in the passage that follows, noting in the course of their brief encounter the "two fine growths of hair which luxuriated in either nostril," the way "Mr. Wolfsheim's nose flashed at me indignantly," and observing how "his nostrils turned to me in an uninterested way."[51] Even Nick's phonetic spelling of Wolfsheim's pronunciation of the words "gonnegtion" and "Oggsford" evokes their nasal ring. All of the disconcerting details about Gatsby that Nick earlier observed—his "monstrous" car, garish outfit, and unpolished sentences—become magnified in the embodied form of Wolfsheim. The symbolic chain initiated by the white skyscraper of no scent culminates with the revelation of Wolfsheim, who is all scent, at the base of the skyscraper.

When Nick sees and greets Tom Buchanan in the same Forty-Second Street cellar after his encounter with Wolfsheim, Tom demands to know of Nick, "how'd you happen to come up this far to eat?"—identifying him as out of place in this locale.[52] Together they position themselves as mere observers in this dark underground space, implicitly situating Wolfsheim, explicitly perceived as a racial other, and Gatsby, now racialized by association, as more organic members of the cellar's suspect constituency. Tom and Nick in general maintain a more distant and hesitant relationship to the city throughout the novel, careful to exercise the kind of control that distinguishes them from the raced masses Campbell describes in *Flamingo* as being helpless to the skyscraper's clarion call. Nick slums through skyscraper country during the summer, but always cloaked in solitude and secrecy. He moves through the city in the same way he exits it, voyeuristically accruing a story, while maintaining the privilege to easily leave it behind without doing any permanent damage to his own white metropolitan status. Tom's slumming is done under similar terms, though he can afford even more transparency in his movements than Nick. Even his breaking of Myrtle's nose is framed as an act of cold control rather than one of unwilled outburst. By comparison, up until the novel's calamitous ending where his "passing" is revealed, Gatsby smartly avoids journeying to the city in the company of the Buchanans, where his difference might appear in a new light against the backdrop of the dark, sensual city. Gatsby astutely does much of his business over the phone in order to avoid the association with the tainted skyscraper, racialized by its association with new-money dreamers, Jewish schemers, and Harlem deviants.

Taken together, these Jazz Age works present a pessimistic portrait of the white metropolitan's ability to thrive in the vertical city that end in either suicide within the city or spatial retreat from it. *The Great Gatsby*, however, asserts a lingering belief in the white metropolitan's affective fortitude with its famous closing lines. Following the main narrative's tale of urban disillusionments, Nick adopts a mythic tone at the novel's end, positioning himself once more as the detached white observer reporting on modernity from a distant vantage point. He displaces the fragmented portrait of the modern city that has accrued across the novel with a historical vista of Manhattan as an undiscovered romantic frontier. While the white sugar lumps of the skyscraper, once holding the promise of mystery and promise, ultimately collapse around Nick into the fragments of black and brown bodies, the dreamy landscape of first colonial encounter he invents to replace this fractured image of the city holds no such surprises. Nick imagines how New York must have looked when "the old island here [. . .] flowered once for Dutch sailors' eyes—a fresh, green breast of the new world."[53] He cloaks this scene in wonder, proclaiming this "transitory enchanted moment" of discovery to be the last time the white metropolitan "held his breath in the presence of this continent" in enraptured and innocent "aesthetic contemplation." Nick ultimately survives the modern city by disassociating from it, displacing his earlier image of the falsely glittering white city with this imagined scene of a transparently majestic and prelapsarian landscape enticing and enervating the weary white settler.

But in conjuring this fantasy of an unfallen Manhattan, Nick has to ignore the lessons his earlier moment of skyscraper awe might have taught him. After all, the modern skyline, too, once presented itself as a "transitory enchanted moment" that took his breath away. Nick at the novel's end tries to conjure a final scene of pure experience anchored in an imagined landscape not yet tainted by illusory bodies and buildings. With this closing vista, he rejects the kind of close looking that overwhelms him earlier in the novel when entering the city with Gatsby, scaling back in the end to describe this more totalizing scene of "aesthetic contemplation" unsullied by shape-shifting races or spaces. Just as Nick writes out racial others when staring at the skyscraper from afar, he similarly writes out the presence of America's aboriginal population from his portrait of the "fresh, green breast of the new world." But unlike his experience with the skyscraper, this time Nick will not be forced to directly engage with this vista up close; it remains an idealized and abstracted fantasy located in the imagined past. The form of "aesthetic contemplation" Nick engages in here involves turning away from the modern city—now entangled with the experience of racial alterity—and insulating himself within the safe and more distant forms of gazing he most prefers.

Contrast Nick's abstracting and ultimately self-protecting gaze with Gatsby's blinding focus on Daisy, a form of gazing that serves as one more symptom of Gatsby's racial otherness. The portrait Nick paints of Gatsby by the novel's end resembles a less extreme version of Borden's depiction of the skyscraper's ethnic exultants. The racial others Borden describes as "under the influence," unknowingly "crazy," believers in "miracles" in a state of "perpetual excitement," and harboring "monstrous dreams," are not that far from Nick's depiction of a Daisy-infatuated Gatsby. Like the black and ethnic subjects framed by these Jazz Age texts as unable to see beyond the sphere of their bodies and their immediate desires, Gatsby obsesses over Daisy to the detriment of his own livelihood. Nick survives the novel where Gatsby does not by recognizing, as Le Corbusier does a few years later, the proper distance needed to temper the kinds of close looking that imperils his sense of self-sovereignty—demonstrating a capacity for abstraction claimed by figures like Theodore Roosevelt to be distinct to Anglo Americans. Rather than flinging himself from a skyscraper like the sad white youths Fitzgerald mourns in "Echoes of the Jazz Age," Nick ensconces himself within an invented apparition of the frontier, untarnished by either the black bodies or the blackening skyscrapers Fitzgerald and his Jazz Age compatriots feared were collectively leaching white subjects of their distinct spirit.

Together, Nick Carraway, Peter Campbell, and Le Corbusier form a trio of white male metropolitans who cannot imagine themselves or others like them lasting much longer within the overwhelming American cities of the present. Whereas eugenicist Lothrop Stoddard expressed his concerns in 1920's *The Rising Tide of Color against White World-Supremacy* that "the Nordic native American has been crowded out with amazing rapidity by these swarming, prolific aliens," causing this figure's near extinction in cities, we find Borden, Le Corbusier, and Fitzgerald emphasizing the white metropolitan's extinction as a matter of lost inner fortitude rather than external overcrowding.[54] But while skyscrapers stand accused in these texts of provoking too much wild feeling in their male white metropolitan beholders, eventually whittling away their storied resiliency, the white women staffing their interiors appear to face a different problem of feeling in relation to the skyscraper—they love it too fiercely, a love that while brightening their personal lives threaten to jeopardize the integrity of their race.

Free, White, and Twenty-One: The Racial Romance of the Skyscraper

If white metropolitan men were imagined to languish in the shadow of the sky-scraper during the 1920s and 1930s, the form of skyscraper strain most impact-ing white metropolitan women in novels from this period originates from its interior office space. Between 1880 and 1930, the American white-collar work-force underwent a massive expansion. As smaller-scale farming and entrepre-neurial operations were supplanted by larger corporations and industries whose headquarters were more frequently located in downtown offices rather than in spaces adjacent to factories or farms, these enormous new businesses required a growing number of managerial, technical, and administrative workers to handle what sociologist C. Wright Mills in 1951 described as the "paper and money and people" these enterprises increasingly managed.[55]

White middle-class women made up a large percentage of the expanding professional white-collar workforce handling these items and persons during this period.[56] Office work, deemed more respectable and less physically inten-sive than other forms of work, was perceived by many of these women as a gateway to new forms of financial and social independence. The novels of Faith Baldwin—one of the most popular authors writing about and for white-collar women in the early twentieth century—represented the struggles faced by this new demographic. In her genre tales of female struggle, the New Woman's love triangle increasingly involved a plucky woman, a skeptical man, and a dash-ing skyscraper. Baldwin's career spanned most of the twentieth century and over a hundred novels. But the peak of her popularity came in the late 1920s and early 1930s when she became one of the highest-paid writers in America during the Great Depression. Her office-centered novels from this period, featuring ti-tles such as *Skyscraper*, *The Office Wife*, *Wife vs. Secretary*, and *White Collar Girl*, focused on the challenges working white-collar white women faced trying to keep their working and romantic lives simultaneously afloat. Baldwin's books largely center on battles between working women and their disgruntled husbands over the new welcome women were receiving in parts of the white-collar workforce. Her protagonists struggle to "have it all," unable to reconcile their desire to succeed in the career paths newly open to them with their desire to please their male partners who harbor more traditional conceptions of love and marriage.[57]

Though the office girl's whiteness is a given in most of these texts, remaining largely unmarked as the assumed precondition of her employment, Baldwin's novels approach whiteness as a category that, just like gender and sexuality, needed recalibration to accommodate the new demands the white-collar economy was placing on the office girl's body and spirit. Baldwin's novels posit racial origins for the "drive" helping white women to achieve professional success, while simultaneously insisting that white women were uniquely vulnerable to being swept up by the romance of working life. The sensations of enthrallment, awe, and even romance Baldwin's white protagonists experience in their white-collar workplaces lead them to neglect their obligations as daughters, sisters, wives, and, most important in this era concerned with dropping white birthrates, as potential mothers. Baldwin's white working heroines exist in relation to immigrant and black women characters at the perimeter of these novels, who, due to a mixture of "racial instinct" and a hard-earned skepticism of wage labor, are rendered more immune to the temptations of the skyscraper office. These office novels express concern that as more and more white women dedicated themselves to the reproduction of capital, black and immigrant women were busy reproducing their races.

More than just the background scenery against which the office girls' various experiences of becoming and unbecoming happen to be set, the skyscraper proves instrumental to their experience of the workplace as a place of mass intimacy where these women can imagine being specific versions of good and ambitious workers, while fantasizing about their more abstract roles as cogs within the engine of corporate enterprise. Faith Baldwin juxtaposes her plucky white protagonists' romantic experience of the skyscraper's mass intimacies with the experience of racial and ethnic others who lack the same sense of romanticism in relation to their working lives. For the black maids employed by Baldwin's white working girls, the "intimate" domestic sphere where their wage labor is set is far from inspiring or romantic. These black women debunk the skyscraper's grandeur, situating their white bosses as belonging to the same wage-labor economy as them, just with a better view. Baldwin's office girls may often feel downtrodden by the irresolvable tensions between their romantic lives and their working lives, a tension Baldwin often symbolizes using the skyscraper, but this architecture also positively frames their sensation of being "free, white, and 21," a common rejoinder uttered by her characters upon recognizing the possibility and privilege increasingly theirs for the claiming.

The Working White Woman's Burden

The category of the working woman was, of course, not unique to the early twentieth century. African American, immigrant, and working-class white women had long been required to negotiate their work and home lives, laboring as farm laborers, domestic help, factory and mill workers, and, if they had sufficient schooling and standing, teachers. For many of these women, work was not a choice but a necessity, as retirement upon marriage was not a financial option. But as middle-class women's educational opportunities improved and the demand for white-collar workers boomed in the late nineteenth century, the category of working women expanded to include white women of the middle class. Before the 1880s, young white men primarily filled most office jobs with women making up only 2.5 percent of the clerical workforce in 1870. But, by the 1890s, women held 60 percent of all typing and stenography positions, and by 1920, this percentage had climbed to 90 percent. Technology played a large role in facilitating women's entrance into the white-collar workforce. Since typewriting was a new job without an established gendered history, as Ellen Lupton observes in *Mechanical Brides*, women could hold these positions without the perception of taking opportunities away from men.[58] Moreover, the invention of laborsaving technologies in the home and on the farm allowed daughters to become increasingly expendable to the running of the household, leaving them free to acquire more schooling and move to cities where they could put this training to use.[59]

The majority of the women holding white-collar positions in America between 1870 and 1930 were, as historian Lisa Fine describes, "overwhelmingly white, young, single, and native born."[60] The few black women holding white-collar jobs worked almost exclusively for black-owned businesses. One survey conducted in Chicago and Atlanta between 1931 and 1932 found, for instance, that there were no offices in these two cities employing black and white workers simultaneously.[61] Women who were immigrants or the children of immigrants were more likely than black women to be hired for professional positions, but their numbers still paled in comparison to those of native-born Anglo-descended women hired to fill these jobs. In 1920, for example, the overwhelming majority of the women working in professional fields in Chicago derived from the older class of immigrants originating from northern and western Europe or Canada.[62]

Historian Jacqueline Jones describes the system of apartheid that determined the laboring opportunities for women in this period, observing that "while white women of the laboring classes began to find work in textile factories, and unmarried white women of the middle classes took jobs in the emerging clerical sector, black women remained confined to traditional forms of task-oriented labor—agriculture work and, particularly in more urban settings, domestic service."[63]

Language proficiency was commonly cited as a barrier for nonnative women wanting to enter white-collar professions, while space was one of the major obstacles preventing black women's entrance into these fields. Jacqueline Jones observes that "employers of clerical, telephone, and sales personnel had to balance the cheapness of black female labor with the high costs of physical segregation."[64] The segregation Jones refers to here was twofold, denoting the need for different restrooms and lounges for black and white women workers should black women be hired for these jobs but also the need to make sure that black women did not become the public faces of companies with predominantly white customers and clients. Jones notes that the largest employer of black clerical workers in the early twentieth century was Montgomery Ward, which, not coincidentally, processed retail orders through the mail. She details the practical difficulties Ward's black female employees faced dining in local restaurants during their lunch breaks, spurring the company to build its own cafeteria at its own expense in order to "shore up its image and remove its black employees from public view."[65]

In contrast to labor histories that foreground the structures, both physical and social, keeping nonwhite women from white-collar employment, Faith Baldwin provides a counterexplanation as to why white middle-class women singularly pursued this form of work with such dogged intensity. Though nonwhite women appear infrequently in Baldwin's office novels, when they do feature in these texts, their absence from the office is treated as a matter of racial preference rather than one of systematic exclusion. In *Weekend Marriage*, for instance, Baldwin suggests that the character Connie Varesi, the child of Italian immigrants, quits her white-collar job working for the American Life Insurance Company in a forty-six-story skyscraper to marry and start a family because, as one of her friends explains, "she couldn't stand it, couldn't stand being pulled both ways. By her people, her traditions, her racial instincts one way; by her own standards and ambitions and ideals the other."[66] The novel first introduces Connie by explaining her anomalous presence in the office in the first place, telling the reader that despite being the child of immigrants, Connie "had learned English as soon as she had learned Italian."[67] However, Connie's assimilation is continually marked by the novel as imperfect. While her difference is not heard in the novel, it is continually seen, smelled, and described, as the reader is told that her house is "odorous" with the smell of garlic, that her gestures remain "European" despite "all her American standardization," and, in a scene out of a tenement novel, that her youngest sibling appears unweaned, soiled, and bears protruding ribs. Baldwin emphasizes the un-Americanness of the Varesis at every turn.

While the white Lola Davis, the primary protagonist of *Weekend Marriage*, makes a similar choice to Connie's at the novel's end to quit her job and be a stay-at-home wife, the novel is careful to distinguish between Lola's choice, treated as courageous and selfless, and the one made by the Italian Connie, whose choice to stop working originates from what Lola describes as her "complacent" character, rendering her "placid, with the placidity of her race."[68] Connie quits her job to please her domineering Italian family, whereas Lola insists at the novel's end that, although she is giving up her corporate job, she nonetheless retains her ambition. Lola insists to her husband, "I can't just sit home and rust out, help mother with the housework, sew a little, and pay calls," intending to manage the books and the typing for her husband's burgeoning car repair business.[69] The novel frames Connie's decision to marry as an antimodern and crude act of racial determinism in comparison to Lola's bold sacrifice rooted in considered compromise. Connie seems to exist in the novel to make Lola's capitulation appear fully modern, shrewd, and even feminist in comparison, marking her as a sovereign white woman free to use her gifts of ambition and intelligence how she sees fit—even as Baldwin emphasizes the negative consequences of these gifts being used for professional advancement alone.

Baldwin's depiction of Connie as the negative image of the sovereign white working woman fits with her belief emerging across all of her novels from this period that white women should prioritize love and family over their careers. Baldwin, however, does not idealize this choice, framing it as the best of the imperfect and untenable options available to them. While her novels generally discourage women from working after marriage, they appealed to women in the 1920s and 1930s because their entreaties did not come from places of rote nostalgia or moralism. Rather, Baldwin insistently foregrounds the economic and emotional sacrifices required of women no matter whether they married or remained single, worked, or stayed at home. Her novels reflect the reality for white women of the middle class that marriage was becoming a less reliable stepping-stone to financial security. This was particularly true following the Great Depression, but even before the crash, the rise of consumer culture meant that being contentedly middle class, particular in urban areas, required having more expendable income. Baldwin's novels always end in either marriage or a recommitment to marriage, but all of her protagonists remain conflicted about this decision, hoping up until the final page of the novel that their marriages are ultimately worth the sacrifice and that they can survive the financial blow of the loss of a second income. Baldwin insists that there was nothing simple or quaint about any of the possible divisions of labor now available to modern white couples. The nonwhite characters in her novels highlight the relative freedom white middle-class women possessed in the modern economy, unshackled from cultural and racial inhibitors holding back the antimodern Connie Varesis of the world. And yet, as Baldwin demonstrates, this new freedom was also circumscribed.

The Seductive Skyscraper

The anguish Faith Baldwin's working white heroines experience when forced to choose between their careers and their romantic partners had much to do with the modern office's appeal as both space and symbol. Invoking feelings of romance, grandeur, and pleasing industriousness in Baldwin's protagonists, skyscrapers leave many of her characters unsure as to whether, as one woman explains to her boss, they were "in love with my first job, which you symbolize, or with you."[70] Despite the growing gap between the dazzling exteriors of modern skyscrapers and their pared-down interiors increasingly streamlined for Taylorist efficiency, Baldwin's protagonists report feeling contentedly useful in these offices—a sensation they describe in terms akin to the experience of feeling loved. Despite the depersonalization of office architecture, Baldwin's protagonists experience their workplaces as sites of intrigue, enthrallment, and even romance.

As the newest initiates into the free market, white middle-class women appear in Baldwin's novels as especially vulnerable to the office's charms. Enraptured by the new forms of mass intimacies found within busy skyscrapers, her characters chronically collapse work with love, the earning of wages with freedom, and surveillance with devotion. Compared to the buzzing modern workspaces capturing their hearts, their home lives appear impersonal and static. When at home, these women report missing the feeling of being a part of a larger entity, of being proximate to power despite wielding little of it themselves. Their restless disinterest in the domestic sphere affects their relationships not only with their male love interests but also with the black women they hire to help run their households. Beyond reminding readers that the home was also a site of wage labor, Baldwin's black domestic laborers index the naïveté of their white bosses under the spell of the office's duplicitous appeal, while simultaneously marking the privilege their bosses possess in holding jobs with which it was possible to fall in love. The liberating intimacies ascribed to the skyscraper in these novels emerge in contradistinction to the more confined and less starry-eyed intimacies found in domestic workplaces.

Baldwin renders skyscrapers as sites of high glamour. Just about all of Faith Baldwin's novels about white-collar work include a scene in which the female protagonist marvels at the skyscraper's enchanting exterior. Her protagonists are described as admiring details such as the "long strange beauty of its vertical shadows," its "astonishing reaches of steel and masonry, gilded and hazed in gold," their attraction to the sense of "supremacy and challenge" and the "wild, triumphant aspiration" they find radiating from the skyscraper. The swelling emotions Baldwin's protagonists experience in this architecture's presence reflect the broader architectural consensus at the time that skyscraper façades were growing more stirring with each new decade. In his 1930 monograph *The New World Architecture*, architectural critic Sheldon Cheney, for instance, lauded the skyscraper's "aspiring finials" and "stirring masses" before noting the structure's capacity to "enchant."[71] Critic Talbot Hamlin uses similarly dreamy language to describe skyscrapers in his 1926 monograph *The American Spirit in Architecture*, supplying the following caption to an image of the Manhattan skyline: "Serried towers, lavish, carefully designed, give a fairy, fantastic quality of piling, aspiring form. The unreality and romance of this great mass of office buildings furnish perfect, if unconscious, expression to those dreams, and that vague sentimentality, which so frequently underlie that American worship of business which made the whole possible."[72] If skyscrapers serve as "vernaculars of capitalism," as architectural historian Carol Willis has observed, they increasingly spoke in a dialect of softness, enchantment, and romance.[73]

The "fantastic" and "aspiring" exteriors of skyscrapers, however, masked the growing banality of the office spaces covered over by their external "fairy form." Within the skyscraper, office managers were paring down its workaday interior spaces for maximum efficiency and more total surveillance. The field of office management, adapting Frederick Taylor's ideas regarding factory optimization for white-collar spaces, first emerged as a vocation in the early twentieth century. Manuals on office efficiency called for changes such as the elimination of private offices and the adoption of simpler desks. "The desk is no longer a storage place—or even ornamental—but a tool for making the quickest possible turnover of business papers," wrote Lee Galloway in 1918, one of the early gurus of office management. He advocated swapping the rolltop desk of the nineteenth century for a simpler model with a smooth, flat surface, "trained down to fighting trim."[74] This description of the workspace of protagonist Lynn Harding in Faith Baldwin's 1931 novel *Skyscraper* echoes the new realities of the modern office:

> The room was flanked with files. It was a strictly utilitarian room. There were no splendid draperies, no massive furniture, no murals, no inches-thick carpet in this room; nor were there any little quiet anterooms where tactful men and women interviewed swathed, draped, and sometimes weeping widows or bewildered orphans. Yet in this room where Lynn worked were filed the futures of widows and orphans; row upon row of green metal files.[75]

For Lynn, working as an insurance saleswoman in a fictionalized version of the Empire State Building, the romance of the office does not lie in its trappings, marked here as "utilitarian" form and serving its "tactful" employees. Lynn dutifully redirects her sense of romance instead to the imagined lives of her clients represented in neat abstract rows by the files in her cabinet.[76]

For early twentieth-century office management manuals, there was seemingly no detail too small nor a task too simple that could not stand to be optimized. Lee Galloway's manual for office management discouraged managers from leaving the arrangement of individual desks to "each girl's fancy," insisting that such an arrangement was "not conducive to orderliness and economy of effort."[77] His monograph includes elaborate diagrams laying out the best way to divide drawers, detailing the ideal configuration of office supplies down to the placement of paper clips. The bodies of employees also faced increased scrutiny. Citing studies conducted in factories in which workers were taught "to perform the necessary motions in the easiest possible way" to achieve maximum productivity, Galloway relays to his reader that similar "motion studies" were being undertaken in office settings to bring this level of precision to the posture of office girls. The best way to manage an office, he insists, is to think of it as "a huge machine with many delicate parts" in which "every individual in it is either a help or a cog."[78]

Reading these manuals, we find the roots of the cynical responses to the drudgery of office life emerging in the midcentury, such as David Riesman's *The Lonely Crowd* and William H. Whyte's *The Organization Man*, depicting the white male middle-class office worker as unmanned and lacking individuality. But in contrast to these disillusioned treatises, Faith Baldwin's novels for and about white middle-class women newly entering the workforce in the early twentieth century depict the office as a place of financial and emotional liberation. Being a cog, as protagonist Lola Davis suggests in *Weekend Marriage*, is a desirable prospect, affirming her importance to the operation of something larger than the self. Upon quitting her office job to more fully commit herself to her marriage, Lola laments losing "the feeling of being something, the tiniest cog in the amazing machine."[79] Even when white-collar spaces are impersonal, mechanized, or oppressive, they are nonetheless cast as places where Baldwin's protagonists forge deep intimacy with peers, bosses, customers, and the abstract corporation at large.

Corporations, in fact, actively encouraged workers to consider their offices as intimate places. Managers embraced a feminized rhetoric of love, intimacy, and emotion as a means of pursuing increased productivity. Of course, intimacy had long been understood as a part of capital's technic of expansion. Marx's description of capital as "vampire-like," living "by sucking living labour," indexes not only capital's reliance on "dead labour" but also its desire to gain closer proximity to its subjects and objects.[80] The worker's alienation from his labor increases with capital's push to inhabit more aspects of the production process, breaking down binaries of inside and outside, public and private, along the way.[81] With the expansion of the white-collar workforce, new empirical methods were applied to facilitate intimacy between colleagues as well as between the worker and the idea of work itself. Corporations hired psychologists to study the emotional relationship between workers and their employers. In *Cold Intimacies: The Making of Emotional Capitalism*, sociologist Eva Illouz charts the rise of "emotional capitalism" in the early American twentieth century, which she defines as "a culture in which emotional and economic discourses and practices mutually shape each other."[82] She charts the ways "affect is made an essential aspect of economic behavior and in which emotional life—especially that of the middle classes—follows the logic of economic relations and exchange."[83] Illouz details the adoption of psychoanalytic language and techniques of emotional management within early twentieth-century office spaces emerging from the broader therapeutic culture of the 1920s. Office managers encouraged "feminized attributes" in the office as a way of urging workers to begin "paying attention to emotions, controlling anger, and listening sympathetically to others."[84]

Though Baldwin's protagonists jokingly refer to their work as slavery, with Joan Armstrong in *Career by Proxy* going as far as claiming her boss "looked like a slave driver" before comparing him to Simon Legree, her characters appear generally enthralled by their metaphorical bondage to their places of work. For instance, when one of her peers accuses the ambitious Lynn Harding in *Skyscraper* of "slaving her life away in the toils of a soulless corporation," she responds with a laugh, confessing that "I like my slavery."[85] Lynn works in the Seacoast Building, a thinly veiled version of Empire State. She positively describes the "hurry and confusion" of its dining room and the anonymous camaraderie she experiences in the building's thirtieth-floor women's lounge, complete with trained nurse and library. "Here," the narrator suggests, "friendships were made, here enmities were established, and here the gossip of the day filtered through hundreds of pale or lipsticked mouths, talk of twenty, of forty offices, each with its different activities."[86] By contrast, in the business club for girls where Lynn lives, she describes having "no intimates" at her residence, whose "intangible atmosphere of caged femininity," she insists, "made her melancholy." Lina Lawrence, the working protagonist of *Men Are Such Fools!*, is similarly described as having "liked the great offices high over Park Avenue, she liked the activity, the sense of excitement, alertness . . . the space salesmen waiting in the reception room, the telephones ringing, the discussion of campaigns, consumer reaction, feminine angles, all the jargon of the business."[87] When at home, despite having hired the "indispensable Kate" as a part-time maid, Lina and her husband eat takeout from the local deli most nights and bicker over the division of labor and bills.

Faith Baldwin's novels are works of female complaint, a genre Lauren Berlant describes as foregrounding "a view of power that blames flawed men and bad ideologies for women's intimate suffering, all the while maintaining some fidelity to the world of distinction and desire that produced such disappointment in the first place."[88] Despite being organized around the emotional impasses faced by their female protagonists, complaint novels, as Berlant notes, "provide tremendous pleasure in their vigilance toward recording how other women manage."[89] Her description of the genre as "a space of disappointment, but not disenchantment" maps onto Baldwin's novels, which, like all middle-brow genre fiction, as Berlant insists, revolve around "the management of ambivalence."[90]

But beyond providing a useful description of what Baldwin's novels *do*, Berlant's description of the intimate public of readers consuming such narratives also serves as an apt description of the materialized intimate public hosted by the interiors of Baldwin's skyscrapers. Berlant defines an intimate public as "a place of recognition and reflection" in which "emotional contact, of a sort, is made." She continues:

> A public is intimate when it foregrounds affective and emotional attachments located in fantasies of the common, the everyday, and a sense of ordinariness, a space where the social world is rich with anonymity and local recognitions, and where challenging and banal conditions of life take place in proximity to the atten-

tions of power but also squarely in the radar of a recognition that can be provided by other humans.[91]

The skyscraper, as the physical setting for this laboring public, fosters experiences of what Berlant calls "mass intimacy" for Baldwin's protagonists who enjoy feeling both vague (cogs in a skyscraper "machine" employing thousands) and specific (a devoted worker in love with her boss) within their skyscraper workplaces. Her characters describe the ordinary "hum" and "buzz" of the office as fulfilling sites of emotional attachment. These women are known and relied upon by their bosses, but in the hallways, lobbies, lounges, and elevators of massive skyscraper, Baldwin's protagonists relish their anonymity as organisms belonging to a larger corporate entity. It is this mixture of feeling immediately recognized—a sensation described at times as akin to being loved—while also relishing the pleasing anonymity they also experience as versions of general industrious workers within the skyscraper's expansive interior that these working female protagonists most value.

The source of complaint for Baldwin's protagonists stems from having to choose between their skyscraper workplaces where they can engage in a form of mass intimacy in which they feel both anonymous and local, ordinary and extraordinary, recognized and self-sovereign, and what comes to feel in comparison like the compact and oppressive sites of their domestic lives whose intimacies are too familiar and ordinary. The demands made on them within their homes lack the accompanying gratifying abstraction available to them in their skyscraper offices. Whether they live with their parents, their husbands, or a business club for girls, all of these protagonists experience their home lives as negative spaces in relation to the skyscraper's enchanting intimacy. Unable to reconcile the mass intimacy offered by the skyscraper with the more personal demands made on her within the domestic sphere, "the young business woman of today," Baldwin writes, "is a misfit."[92]

Baldwin's novels make it easy to forget that the homes of her protagonists were also sites of wage labor and management. Most of the married women who work in Baldwin's novels employ some sort of domestic help, a good many of whom are marked as black. Unable to secure work in manufacturing or clerical fields, most black women employed in the North in the early twentieth century found employment as domestic laborers. Though the home has historically been theorized as the more intimate sphere in contrast to other more public ones, Jones notes that black women worked hard to limit their intimacy with their white employers, who often implemented "a variety of ruses to wring more labor from them at cheap prices." Wary of the familial frameworks defining their laboring relations in the South, black women who migrated North at the turn of the century insisted on forging more professional relationships with their white bosses. They generally refused whenever possible to "live in" with their white employers, hoping to retain a sense of separation between their work and home lives.[93] Whereas Baldwin's white protagonists experience their workplaces as places of pleasurable intimacy—hence, the term "office wife" used by many of Baldwin's novels to describe the unique relationship between a male boss and his female secretary—we might note the conditions leading black women in the North to feel suspicious of workplace intimacy given the historical exploitation of their time and labor, physical and affective.

The most extended appearance by a black maid in Baldwin's office novels is in 1939's *Career by Proxy.* White working protagonist Joan Armstrong hires Lily, the niece of her family's "invaluable colored laundress," to help her keep home upon moving out of her family's home to live the life of a sovereign working woman. Lily pops up throughout the novel to serve coffee to Joan's guests, carry in her packages, put flowers in water, and "broil a chicken to perfection." But more importantly to the social economy of the novel, Lily serves as a chaperone to the unmarried Joan, making it acceptable for her to entertain male guests without questions of sexual impropriety. Lily's domestic activities are logged across the narrative, but she does not speak until late in the novel, after Joan has given up her office job due to her untenable romantic entanglement with her boss and has decided to take a trip out west. Breaking the news of her forthcoming trip to Lily, Joan asks her if she'd like a "little vacation."[94] Unsure of whether this is a polite way of being fired, Lily replies, "I'd like it swell" before rolling her eyes, a gesture the reader is unsure Joan sees. Joan then explains to Lily that she has already lined up a new job for herself for when she gets back, news to which Lily exclaims, "But you just got this one," an utterance followed by a description of Lily's unspoken thoughts: "However her own intimates moved from job to job with startling regularity so perhaps there was nothing unusual in this. She had never been able to figure out just why Miss Joan wanted to work anyway. If Lily had had her choice she wouldn't have done a hand's turn." Lily attempts to imagine Joan's career mobility as analogous to that of her black female peers before settling on the chasm between Joan's desire to work despite being financially well off and her own lack of choice in the matter.

It is hard to tell whether Lily's responses to Joan are meant to appear naïve or insightful. Barred from white-collar work, Lily is denied the chance to fall in love with the forms of mass intimacy Baldwin's white working protagonists find so fulfilling within the skyscraper. Lily, unable to fathom Joan's choices, appears in some ways as a stock version of the sage black woman ahistorically immune to the "modern" complications that so trouble Joan. Baldwin seems to share Lily's opinion to a certain degree that it is ultimately unnecessary for white middle-class women to work. But unlike Lily, Baldwin takes great pains to articulate her empathy for women like Joan who wanted to work. Baldwin's solution is for these women to reroute this energy toward helping their husbands succeed. As with Connie Varesi in *Weekend Marriage*, Baldwin has Lily express the "right" opinion that white women should forgo the corporate workplace while also suggesting that Lily's and Connie's judgments derive from the "wrong" place.

The misrecognitions between Lily and Joan in this scene continue to accrue. Joan tells Lily that she'll be closing the apartment during her trip west, explaining to Lily that she "can run in once a week or so and see things are back in order." Lily, unsure as to whether she is being asked as a friend to do Joan a favor or being offered new terms of employment, initially responds to this request by "looking at her sidewise" before demurely replying that "it's okay by me, Miss Joan, except I can't rightly afford it." Joan, sensing that Lily is fishing as to whether her efforts will be paid, starts laughing before proceeding to call her an "an old fake" and assuring her that "I'll pay you, of course." This exchange between Lily and Joan is simultaneously easy and tense, friendly and cutting, agreeable and suffocating. Lily's glances subvert her more formal utterances of empathy designed to ensure she'll be paid. Lily cannot financially afford to be something other than an "old fake" in her articulated performances of deference and passivity. Having mentioned the precarity of her "intimates" moving "from job to job with startling regularity" due to, presumably, the instability of their working situations, Lily's "faking" seems financially sound given the circumstances.

Nowhere does the novel suggest that Lily and Joan have a relationship that could survive either one letting her guard down with the other completely. Though Lily's gestures conflict with her utterances, she accurately maps her unsteady place within Joan's household. Unlike Joan, who spends most of the novel wondering whether she fell in love with "a man or a job" and questioning the nature of her fidelity to the skyscraper, Lily exists as a reminder of the relative privilege of Baldwin's white protagonists who can negotiate their relationship to the various familiarities and abstractions they experience within the skyscraper. Like the Italian Connie Varesi in *Weekend Marriage*, Lily places the skyscraper's affective pull on white professional women into relief, framing her boss's affective confusion about her love for her work as an updated version of the white woman's burden.

Vanishing Americans

Whiteness exists primarily in Baldwin's novels as the assumed precondition of her protagonists. Their race is most directly visible when they are in proximity to black and ethnic women whose struggles are depicted as deriving from different sources. Baldwin reflects just once across all these novels on what her protagonists' enchantment with the skyscraper might mean for the white race in the long term. This moment takes place in 1944's *Weekend Marriage* through the character of Jameson, Lola Davis's older white male boss. Having observed Lola's struggle to have a career while maintaining her marriage from a distance, her boss privately contemplates the scope of Lola's predicament, which he imagines to affect an entire generation of young white women. Jameson openly recognizes the inherent conservatism underlying his belief that women should prioritize their families over their careers, readily admitting that "any smart-aleck modernist, any avid feminist, any, perhaps, dispassionate and impersonal bystander could shoot his argument full of holes." But he nonetheless goes on to defend his stance as originating from a more enlightened place than one might assume:

> It wasn't the alleged looseness of the younger generation that bothered him. He didn't think they were any looser than other generations. More open about it, that's all. A bad egg's a bad egg, no matter what date is stamped on it. There are bolters in every generation. This wasn't the first era openly to discount chastity. No, he wasn't bothered by the morals of the youngsters. He was bothered by their lack of responsibility toward—what was it—an ideal? . . . the race? . . .
>
> Family man. Family woman. Terms, nowadays, not exactly of approbation. Still . . . "Vanishing Americans!" said Jameson aloud, and stumped belligerently to the door.[95]

Baldwin's novels are filled with ellipses and clipped sentences used to mark thoughts glimpsed but not fully articulated and feelings experienced but not fully understood. She often deploys ellipses when women face structural barriers either at work or at home that are impossible for them to individually overcome. Here, however, this choppy syntax is used to present this character's raced concerns about "vanishing Americans" as halting and unformed, a performance of hesitation that paradoxically gives his thoughts even more validity as innocent speculations about an intuited impasse. An older and peripheral character, Jameson periodically appears to empathize with Lola's predicament and places it within a broader historical and social context. Closest in age and inclination to Baldwin, he gives voice to anxieties about whiteness circulating within the broader public sphere at the time. While the term "vanishing Americans" was commonly used to describe the plight of Native Americans in the late nineteenth century, it was co-opted by Anglo Americans in the twentieth century to name their own fears of losing ground to immigrants with higher birthrates. In Jameson's reflections, we hear echoes of concerns originating in the 1900s voiced by Theodore Roosevelt and sociologists such as Edward Alsworth Ross about the falling birthrates of Anglo American women potentially leading to what Ross coined in 1901 as "race suicide." Alarm about white birthrates continued to circulate well into the 1930s, bolstered by the growing national appetite for eugenics. The fact that the Italian Connie Varesi has two children over the course of the novel whereas Lola has none would not have been lost on her middle-class readers likely familiar with what would have been a long-standing fear at that point that, as Alexander Graham Bell wrote of white American women in 1920, "the spirit of avoiding maternity is on the increase," while "the immigrant races are increasing at a much greater rate than our own."[96]

In the closing pages of *Weekend Marriage*, Lola expresses her uncertainty about whether she and her husband will thrive, either financially or emotionally, following her decision to give up her professional ambitions. She ultimately clings to the repeated hope that she and her husband will be able to "make good." All of Baldwin's white-collar heroines express a version of this desire in their attempts to figure out how to "make good" as a wife, a daughter, a mother, and most recently, a worker. But for Baldwin, making good also involves being a good racial subject, sacrificing what was imagined to be their innate racial aptitude for self-sovereignty and independence symbolized and facilitated by the skyscraper in order to better serve the greater white good by renouncing these enticements and staying at home.

When taken together, these Jazz Age works seem to present a pessimistic picture regarding the white metropolitan's survival within the city increasingly dotted by more and taller skyscrapers. Peter Campbell dies; Nick, Tom, and Daisy abandon the city to return to the Midwest; Le Corbusier returns to Europe to imagine new models for urban design capable of correcting the vertical city's chaotic irregularities; Baldwin's novels all end in ambivalence. Her female characters sacrifice some modicum of their professional ambitions for romantic love but remain uncertain whether this gamble will pay off. If the skyscraper was making it harder to feel white and imagine the long-term endurance of its privileges, a new spatial solution to this conundrum was on the horizon. Although I insist early in the book on placing the skyscraper within the context of the long nineteenth century and its attendant theories of race, I end it by resituating the structure once again, this time within this longer twentieth-century narrative of urban decay and white flight as the skyscraper's failure to make room for whiteness ultimately paved the way for white metropolitans to carve this space out elsewhere.

Epilogue

From Skyscraper to Suburb

> The consciousness of Bigger Thomas, and millions of others more
> or less like him, white and black, according to the weight of the
> pressure we have put upon them, forms the quicksands upon which
> the foundations of our civilization rests. Who knows when some
> slight shock, disturbing the delicate balance between social order
> and thirsty aspiration shall send the skyscrapers in our cities
> toppling? Does that sound fantastic?
>
> —*Richard Wright*, Native Son, 1940

The final third of Richard Wright's *Native Son* consists mostly of the courtroom speech that lawyer Boris Max delivers in defense of his client Bigger Thomas who faces the death penalty for murder. Max uses his time before the court not to deny Bigger's culpability for his crimes but to implicate the nation for its role in creating Bigger and the "millions" like him capable of committing such acts. In one of the speech's most rousing moments, Max juxtaposes the skyscraper— used here to symbolize an exclusive version of the American dream accessed only by the few—with the broad yet vulnerable foundation of the many on which it rests. While Bigger himself never describes beholding a skyscraper within the course of the novel nor imagines himself in relation to one despite living only six miles from the skyscraper's birthplace in Chicago's downtown Loop, Max artfully frames their interdependence. Prophesizing the coming of what literary critic Ira Wells describes as "a kind of social earthquake—a 'natural' disaster—in which our celebrated symbols of modernity are flattened by a force that is simultaneously beyond our control and somewhat self-induced," Max suggests both that without the Bigger Thomases of the world there would be no skyscrapers and, simultaneously, that the skyscraper is part of the ontology of Bigger.[1]

Although Wright's rendering of the skyscraper in *Native Son* appears ten years after the end of the early skyscraper era in 1931 as I've marked it, his efforts through Max to mark the structure's social embeddedness resonate with how earlier writers understood this architecture. In Max's speech, we hear not only the echo of Harlem Renaissance writers who found similar resonances between skyscraper architecture and the lives of marginalized subjects but also the sentiments of writers such as Henry James approaching the skyscraper as a symptom of a changing physical and social American scene. Whereas Ayn Rand's *The Fountainhead,* published three years after *Native Son* in 1943, would laud the skyscraper as the perfect symbol of the exceptional individual, praising this structure for refusing to pander "to the humble level of the observer" to stand in its fully erect glory as a "statement of what man had conceived and made possible," Wright's vision of the symbiotic skyscraper is more in keeping with earlier representations of this architecture, figuring it not as a proud symbol of individual exceptionalism but as an emblem of growing concerns about the consequences of exclusion.[2]

While Wright's choice to situate the skyscraper in *Native Son* as part of a broader social geography connecting Bigger to the millions resonates with how earlier writers represented this structure, his understanding of the skyscraper's causal relationships within the social differs from that of this preceding generation. In Max's image of the skyscraper grinding down the consciousness of the many on which it rests, these subterranean frictions only become visible when manifested through the skyscraper's aboveground toppling. Writers working in the early skyscraper era, however, depicted this architecture less as a *symptom* of underlying social tectonics and more as an eruption in its own right, disrupting the existing social worlds and perceptival practices preexisting it, which had to be reorganized in its wake. While the skyscraper stands accused by this earlier generation of writers of abstracting the human figure, the writers I have focused on in this book do not understand the skyscraper in primarily abstract or symbolic terms. They attend instead to how this architecture's concrete materiality directly impacted the perception and experience of the world in, around, and above it. Whereas Max uses the skyscraper to symbolically represent the "delicate balance" between those who want and those who have, his predecessors viewed this structure as an obstacle to representation itself.

If we understand the skyscraper not as a symbol of social relations as Wright does but as a catalyst directly altering these relations—an architecture affecting the experience of the social as opposed to a mere representation of its ills—the afterlife of skyscraper is best understood not by charting its material and discursive evolution into the twenty-first century but by tracking the alternative architectural forms and spatial practices that emerged to counter its muddling effect on racial perception. This is not to say, however, that race does not inform this structure's later histories. Whereas the skyscraper was once heralded as both the sign for and the evidence of American exceptionalism, it has since been transformed into a symbol of a form of global capitalism capable of operating in any place and, even, in spite of place. Max's indictment of the skyscraper in 1940's *Native Son* finds a more literal analogue, perhaps, in contemporary Dubai where towering structures projecting wealth and power mask the exploitative labor contracts and hot and dangerous working conditions faced by the indentured labor of migrants primarily from Pakistan, Bangladesh, and China.[3] Within the United States, one of the most prominent examples of the ongoing racial story of the skyscraper lies in attempts to narrate the destruction of the World Trade Center Towers on September 11, 2001, through a focus on the deaths of white working-class first responders rather than those of the more racially diverse blue- and white-collar workers occupying the buildings when they were brought down. This narrative was echoed and reaffirmed by the 2010 fervor surrounding the "Ground Zero Mosque," in which white firefighters and their families served as the public face of the opposition to the project.[4]

The impact of the early skyscraper's effects on racial perception and feeling is most generatively located not in the skyscraper's later trajectories, however, but in the formation of the midcentury mass suburb drawing people out of the city and the alternative strategies of racial perception that emerged therein. Postwar representations of the suburbs positioned these new sites not only as respites from the racial confusion associated with the density, scale, and multiplying vantage points yoked to the early skyscraper but as incubators of new practices for differently seeing and knowing race. If, as Dianne Harris writes, representations of postwar suburban houses "continuously and reflexively created, re-created and reinforced midcentury notions about racial ethnic and class identities—specifically the rightness of associating white identities with homeownership and citizenship," these efforts to recreate, reinforce, and, by extension, stabilize whiteness by yoking it more strongly to homeownership in these new third spaces was, in part, a response to the effects of the previous era of skyscraper-oriented urbanization that destabilized whiteness's distinction.[5] Whereas many of the early skyscraper narratives I've detailed in this book highlight the difficulties writers faced in trying to locate race either on the surfaces of other bodies or within one's own sensation of feeling like a raced subject in this architecture's shadow, the development of the suburbs partially relocated the labor of perceiving race away from individuals and toward institutions. Government agencies such as the Federal Housing Authority and the Home Owner's Loan Corporation that insured mortgages in coordination with local networks of banks, realtors, and appraisers took up some of the labor of racially vetting bodies and neighborhoods in advance, intentionally steering potential residents into homogeneous neighborhoods. White suburban homebuyers at midcentury could largely take for granted the security of their financial and, by extension, racial investment in their new neighborhoods backed by institutions equally eager to reinforce the color line. Drawing upon "scientific" methods of racial appraisal to create comprehensive redlining maps, these agencies used racialized mechanisms of financialization to counter the perceptual fallibility associated with the built environments of urban centers.

For suburban residents commuting to and from city centers to offices housed within downtown skyscrapers, the Federal-Aid Highway Act of 1956, along with large-scale urban renewal and slum clearance projects in US cities at midcentury, remade downtown urban centers so they functioned less like the kinetic sites of racial encounter described by earlier writers and more like closed systems that were within yet still somewhat separate from the greater city. Black and brown neighborhoods that once abutted urban downtown centers were variously dismantled, displaced, and destroyed as urban renewal, famously referred to by James Baldwin in a 1963 interview with Kenneth Clark as being synonymous with "negro removal," freed up land for other types of occupancy.[6] New highways severed and bypassed preexisting minority communities, allowing their suburban users to zip past these neighborhoods without having to stop to see them in any detail.[7] The growing African American population within towering public housing complexes—the new black skyscrapers of their time—increasingly located in isolated pockets of the city far from where suburban commuters were likely to pass through, further decreased the chances that the middle-class office workers moving between the skyscraper and the suburbs would have the same experience of their own racial alterity earlier writers described in relation to the skyscraper. In the suburban tales of John Cheever, Richard Yates, and Sloan Wilson, for instance, the urban workplaces and environs of their white-collar protagonists are equally as staid and homogeneous as the places they return each evening. Racial others are glimpsed in the interstitial spaces between the city and the suburbs—a quick view of a slum on a train here, an occasional Negro chauffeur or elevator man there, a cameo made by a Polish-speaking housekeeper within a suburban milieu—but there is little anxiety in these stories about the accuracy or viability of racial perception in these spaces. Concerns about racial passers in possession of secret blood or unease about the inability to delineate between the multiple varieties of racial and ethnic difference prevalent in early skyscraper narratives are largely absent from later suburban stories. In these latter tales, one's physical proximity to and ownership of certain architectures join invisible blood and visible skin as a metric for adjudicating race.

White flight, generally framed as a postwar phenomenon, has historically been understood to be a product of developments such as the GI Bill, the Highway Administration, and the FHA, as well as the second wave of the Great Migration after 1940. But contextualizing these midcentury phenomena in relation to early skyscraper narratives allows us to recognize the term *white flight* as a misnomer of sorts. Presuming whiteness to be a preexisting and stable category that simply moved from one location to another, the descriptor *white flight* gives the false impression that whiteness at midcentury was a concrete identity whose subjects simply relocated in reaction to the growing presence of racial others in cities. But representations of the skyscraper from its early era reveal the extent to which whiteness was already being actively reconstituted in this preceding moment. White metropolitans in the early skyscraper era continually ran up against the problem of how to preserve whiteness in hostile perceptual and spatial conditions that made it difficult to separate the ethnic, the racial, and the merely "urban." These turn-of-the-century narratives illustrate how impractical a narrow definition of whiteness rooted in Anglo-Saxon superiority had become in crowded urban centers in which the ability to perceive and differentiate between so many types of difference felt increasingly untenable. Carl Van Vechten's depiction of the skyscraper as the tombstone for a version of whiteness that I began this book with proved true to a certain extent. The midcentury mass suburbs became a place to forge a broader coalition of whiteness—assimilating ethnic variances into a broader racial umbrella through systems of redlining. The suburbs were not vessels receiving whiteness—rather, these spaces helped to remake this category by tethering whiteness more strongly to homeownership and making it a financial asset belonging to specific protected neighborhoods. Although the title of this book is *The Black Skyscraper*, it is part of a broader narrative about the changing definition and experience of whiteness.

"No building type or architectural style creates inequality as such," as architectural theorists Jacob Moore and Susanne Schindler note. "Assuming so," they continue, "would be to grossly over-estimate architecture's power."[8] To extend this line of thought, there is nothing inherent to the high-rise skyscraper, or the low-rise suburbs for that matter, that makes these structures inevitable sites for contemplating or revising notions of race.[9] The skyscraper assumes this role in the late nineteenth and early twentieth centuries as the material frame through which writers saw, imagined, and managed the uneasy confluence of demographic shifts, geographic migrations, infrastructure revolutions, and changing racial policies coming to a head within US cities. Architecture alone can neither produce nor correct for the inequities accompanying capitalist exploitation and structural racism; but while we may overestimate architecture's power to remedy these systems, we have historically underestimated its role in shaping how we perceive, experience, and negotiate these systems. Boris Max in *Native Son* dramatically summons an image of a toppled skyscraper—once the stuff of fantasy, now recast as the inevitable end to an unjust structure—to illustrate the shared consequences of condemning a generation of Biggers to lives of poverty and disappointment. But understanding the skyscraper as it stood and was perceived around offers us a story rooted not in inevitability but malleability, in which race is approached not only as a matter of skin or blood but of scale.

Chapter 1 · Introduction

1. Cited in Kathleen Pfeiffer's introduction to Carl Van Vechten, *Nigger Heaven* (Urbana: University of Illinois Press, 1926) xxiv.

2. Meir Wigoder, "The 'Solar Eye' of Vision: Emergence of the Skyscraper-Viewer in the Discourse on Heights in New York City, 1890–1920," *Journal of the Society of Architectural Historians* 61.2 (June 2002) 152–159. See also Merrill Schleier's two books, *The Skyscraper in American Art, 1890–1931* (New York: Da Capo Press, 1990), and *Skyscraper Cinema: Architecture and Gender in American Film* (Minneapolis: University of Minnesota Press, 2008), which consider the skyscraper's simultaneous rise with key works of visual media as well as forms of masculinity and class identity.

3. Henry James, *The American Scene* (London: Chapman and Hall, 1907) 83.

4. Barbara Hochman writes that in the late nineteenth century this phrase "was applied indiscriminately to plants and trees, new towns, tiled roofs, musical instruments, the post office, the government of Chicago, the British Empire, modern battleships, and Thanksgiving Day." *Uncle Tom's Cabin and the Reading Revolution: Race, Literacy, Childhood, and Fiction, 1851–1911* (Amherst: University of Massachusetts Press, 2011) 152.

5. "The Human Ant Heap," *Independent* (20 Aug 1920) 221.

6. Rosemarie Haag Bletter, "The Invention of the Skyscraper: Notes on Its Diverse Histories," *Assemblage* no. 2 (Feb 1987) 110.

7. Although no longer considered the first skyscraper by most architectural historians, the ten-story Home Insurance Building designed by William Le Baron Jenney remains central to the structure's popular mythology. This structure's status as the first steel-skeleton-supported building and, consequently, as the first skyscraper has been a point of controversy for almost a century now. In 1931, a group appointed by the Western Society of Engineers ruled that the building was not entirely supported by its steel skeleton—only its uppermost floors. Some architectural historians insist that Chicago engineer Frederick Baumann actually beat Jenney to the idea of steel construction. But as architectural historian Donald L. Miller argues, though we lack concrete evidence about who had the idea first, "it was Jenney who actually built a skeleton frame, albeit a partial one. (344). Even if Jenney did not technically build the first skyscraper, the Home Insurance remains an important origin story for this structure within American architectural history. Donald L. Miller, *City of the Century: The Epic of Chicago and the Making of America*

(New York: Simon & Schuster, 1997). For contestations of Home Insurance's status as the first skyscraper, see Winston Weisman, "New York and the Problem of the First Skyscraper," *Journal of the Society of Architectural Historians* 12.1 (Mar 1953) 13–21; Carl Condit, "The Two Centuries of Technical Evolution Underlying the Skyscraper," *The Second Century of the Skyscraper*, ed. Lynn S. Beedle (New York: Springer, 1988) 11–24; Theodore Turak, "Remembrances of the Home Insurance Building," *Journal of the Society of Architectural Historians* 44.1 (Mar 1985) 60–65; Gerald R. Larson and Roula Mouroudellis Geraniotis, "Toward a Better Understanding of the Evolution of the Iron Skeleton Frame in Chicago," *Journal of the Society of Architectural Historians* 46.1 (Mar 1987) 39–48; and Robert Bruegman, "Myth of the Chicago School," *Chicago Architecture: Histories, Revisions, Alternatives*, ed. Charles Waldheim and Katerina Ruedi Ray (Chicago: University of Chicago Press, 2005) 17.

8. Carol Willis, *Form Follows Finance* (New York: Princeton Architectural Press, 1995).

9. Ibid.

10. Ibid., 9.

11. Ann Douglas, *Terrible Honesty: Mongrel Manhattan in the 1920s* (New York: Farrar, Straus and Giroux, 1995) 436.

12. William Starrett, *Skyscrapers and the Men Who Build Them* (New York: Charles Scribner's Sons, 1928) 3.

13. See Harold L. Platt, *Shock Cities: The Environmental Transformation and Reform of Manchester and Chicago* (Chicago: University of Chicago Press, 2005) xiii.

14. Starrett, *Skyscrapers and the Men Who Build Them*, 1; Claude Bragdon, "Architecture in the United States III: The Skyscraper," *Architectural Record* 26.2 (1909) 84–96. See also architectural critic Harry Desmond's statement in 1934 in the same journal that "the greatest contribution of America to architecture is the skyscraper."

15. Thomas Sugrue, *Sweet Land of Liberty: The Forgotten Struggle for Civil Rights in the North* (New York: Random House, 2008).

16. Ellison DuRant Smith, *Congressional Record, 68th Congress, 1st Session* (Washington DC: Government Printing Office, 1924) 65:5961–5962.

17. Stuart Chase, "The Future of the Great City," *Harper's Magazine* 160 (Dec 1929) 84.

18. For more on the complicated history of American cities, see Paul Boyer, *Urban Masses and Moral Order in America, 1820–1920* (Cambridge: Harvard University Press, 1978); Lisa Krissoff Boehm and Steven H. Corey, eds., *America's Urban History* (New York: Routledge, 2015); Gunther Barth, *City People: The Rise of Modern City Culture in Nineteenth-Century America* (Oxford: Oxford University Press, 1980); Charles N. Glaab, *The American City: A Documentary History* (Homewood: Dorsey Press, 1963); Peter Hall, *Cities of Tomorrow: An Intellectual History of Urban Planning and Design in the Twentieth Century* (Oxford: Basil Blackwell, 1988); Platt, *Shock Cities*; and Andrew Lees, *Cities Perceived: Urban Society in European and American Thought, 1820–1940* (Manchester: Manchester University Press, 1985).

19. Boyer, *Urban Masses and Moral Order*, 123.

20. See Boehm and Corey, *America's Urban History*, 145.

21. Boyer, *Urban Masses and Moral Order*, 189.

22. Stephen Grant Meyer, *As Long as They Don't Move Next Door: Segregation and Racial Conflict in American Neighborhoods* (New York: Rowman & Littlefield, 1999) 16. See also Marcy S. Sacks, *Before Harlem: The Black Experience in New York City before World War I* (Philadelphia: University of Pennsylvania Press, 2013).

23. James Smethurst, *The African American Roots of Modernism* (Chapel Hill: University of North Carolina Press, 2011) 13.

24. For a more detailed account of these factors, see Paul Boyer, Andrew Lees, J. Philip Gruen, Lisa Krissoff Boehm, and Steven H. Corey.

25. J. Philip Gruen, *Manifest Destinations: Cities and Tourists in the Nineteenth-Century American West* (Norman: University of Oklahoma Press, 2014) 161.

26. Hall, *Cities of Tomorrow*, 34.

27. Arguing in *Working toward Whiteness* that ethnicity is an ahistorical term when discussing the late nineteenth and early twentieth centuries, David Roediger insists that the term *ethnic* doesn't become a systematized term of analysis distinct from race until the 1940s. *Working toward Whiteness: How America's Immigrants Became White: The Strange Journey from Ellis Island to the Suburbs* (New York: Basic Books, 2006).

28. Michael Omi and Howard Winant, *Racial Formation in the United States*, 3rd ed. (New York, Routledge, 2014) 25–26.

29. Ibid.

30. John T. Buchanan, "How to Assimilate the Foreign Element into Our Population," *Forum* 32 (1901–1902) 689. Cited in Roy Lubove, *The Progressives and the Slums: Tenement House Reform in New York City, 1890–1917* (Pittsburgh: University of Pittsburgh Press, 1962).

31. Richard Mayo-Smith, *Emigration and Immigration: A Study in Social Science* (New York: Charles Scribner's Sons, 1901) 71. See also John Higham, *Strangers in the Land: Patterns of American Nativism, 1860–1925* (New Brunswick: Rutgers University Press, 1998).

32. Boyer, *Urban Masses and Moral Order*, 253.

33. Edward T. Devine, *Misery and Its Causes* (New York: Macmillan, 1920) 11.

34. Cited in Boyer, *Urban Masses and Moral Order*, 189.

35. See St. Clair Drake and Horace Cayton, *Black Metropolis: A Study of Negro Life in a Northern City* (Chicago: University of Chicago Press, 1945), and Robert Park and Ernest W. Burgess, *The City: Suggestions for Investigation of Human Behavior in the Urban Environment* (Chicago: University of Chicago Press, 1925).

36. Cited in Hall, *Cities of Tomorrow*, 35.

37. Robert Hunter, *Tenement Conditions in Chicago* (Chicago: City Homes Association, 1901) 52.

38. Allan Forman, "Some Adopted Americans," *American Magazine* 9.1 (1888) 46. In the first scholarly book about immigration, written in 1901 by Richard Mayo-Smith, found tenement occupants "huddled together, in miserable apartments, in filth and rags, without the slightest regard to decency or health" to "present a picture of squalid existence degrading to any civilization." Mayo-Smith, *Emigration and Immigration*, 133.

39. Jacob Riis, *How the Other Half Lives* (New York: Charles Scribner's Sons, 1890) 21.

40. Ibid.

41. Ibid., 22.

42. Peter Bacon Hales, *Silver Cities: Photographing American Urbanization, 1839–1939* (Albuquerque: University of New Mexico Press, 1984) 279. For more on the role of

race in Riis's work, see Reginald Twigg, "The Performative Dimension of Surveillance: Jacob Riis' *How the Other Half Lives*," *Text and Performance Quarterly* 12.4 (1992) 305–328, and, most helpfully, Bonnie Yochelson and Daniel Czitrom, *Rediscovering Jacob Riis: Exposure Journalism and Photography in Turn-of-the-Century New York* (New York: New Press, 2007), and Shawn Michelle Smith, "The Half of Whiteness," *English Language Notes* 44.2 (Fall–Winter 2006) 189–194.

43. Jacob Riis, *The Making of an American* (New York: Macmillan, 1901) 268.

44. Allan Sekula, "The Body and the Archive," *October* 39 (Winter 1986) 7.

45. Riis, *How the Other Half Lives*, 55.

46. Ibid., 56.

47. Ibid.

48. Ibid., 60.

49. Henry Blake Fuller, *The Cliff-Dwellers* (New York: Harper & Brothers, 1893) 53.

50. Ibid., 54.

51. Ibid.

52. Ibid.

53. Ibid., 55.

54. Elizabeth Grosz, "Bodies-Cities," *Sexuality & Space*, ed. Beatriz Colomina (New York: Princeton Architectural Press, 1996) 248. Grosz goes on to highlight the ways vertically informed forms of lived spatiality in particular "effect the ways we live space, and thus our comportment and corporeal orientations" (249).

55. James Oppenheim, *The Olympian* (New York: Harper & Brothers, 1912) 15.

56. Ibid., 418.

57. Max Bodenheim, "North Clark Street, Chicago," qtd in "Introducing Irony," *The Measure: A Journal of Poetry* 10 (Dec 1921) 18.

58. Wallace Thurman, *Infants of the Spring* (Boston: Northeastern University Press, 1992).

59. For arguments about the skyscraper's phallic properties, see Dolores Hayden, "Skyscraper Seduction / Skyscraper Rape," *Heresies* 1 (May 1977) 108–115; Leslie Kanes Weisman, "Women's Environmental Rights: A Manifesto," *Heresies* 2.11 (1981) 6–9; Elizabeth Lindquist-Cock and Estelle Jussim, "Machismo and Architecture," *Feminist Art Journal* 3 (Spring 1874) 8–10; and Douglas, *Terrible Honesty*.

60. Anne Cheng, *Second Skin: Josephine Baker & the Modern Surface* (New York: Oxford University Press, 2010) 14.

61. I approach skyscrapers in much the same vein that Jonathan Crary considers the nineteenth-century visual apparatuses of the camera obscura and the stereoscope: as "points of intersection where philosophical, scientific, and aesthetic discourses overlap with mechanical techniques, institutional requirements, and socioeconomic forces." *Techniques of the Observer: On Vision and Modernity in the Nineteenth Century* (Cambridge: MIT Press, 1993) 8.

62. See F. James Davis, *Who Is Black?: One Nation's Definition* (University Park: Penn State Press, 1991) 54–58. See also David L. Brunsma and Kerry Ann Rockquemore, "The End of Race?," *Race and Ethnicity: Across Time, Space, and Disciplines*, ed. Rodney D. Coates (Boston: Brill, 2004) 73–92.

63. For more on the "one-drop rule" and its northern application see Davis, *Who Is Black*, 5; Joel Williamson, *New People: Miscegenation and Mulattoes in the United States*

(Baton Rouge: Lousiana State University Press, 2005) 1–2; and Elizabeth M. Smith-Pryor, *Property Rites: The Rhinelander Trial, Passing, and the Protection of Whiteness* (Durham: University of North Carolina Press, 2009) 185.

64. Jerrold M. Packard, *American Nightmare: The History of Jim Crow* (New York: Macmillan, 2003) 98–99.

65. Elizabeth M. Smith-Pryor makes note of this regional problem with the one-drop rule in *Property Rites*: "In an increasingly urbanized North, shifting populations of African American migrants and foreign immigrants made it difficult to apply a 'one-drop' rule of race. The one-drop rule, based on notions of blood as race, required societal knowledge of African ancestry, no matter how inexact" (185).

66. Legal scholar Ian Haney Lopez has studied the fifty-two court cases between 1878 and 1952 in which defendants argued their claim to "whiteness" in order to become naturalized citizens as was required by the laws of the time. The two most commonly invoked justifications by the court when denying the status of whiteness was the language of "common knowledge" and the evidence provided by scientific racism actively working to reify white supremacy. See Lopez, *White by Law: The Legal Construction of Race* (New York: New York University Press, 1997).

67. Takao Ozawa v. United States, Certificate from the Circuit Court of Appeals for the Ninth Circuit, No. 260. Argued October 3 and 4, 1922. Decided November 13, 1922.

68. United States v. Bhagat Singh Thind, Certificate from the Circuit Court of Appeals for the Ninth Circuit, No. 202. Argued January 11, 12, 1923. Decided February 19, 1923, United States Reports, v. 261, the Supreme Court, October term, 1922, 204–215.

69. Ibid.

70. Ibid.

71. Quoted in Roger Celestin and Elaine DalMolin, *France from 1851 to the Present: Universalism in Crisis* (New York: Palgrave Macmillan, 2007) 113.

72. Fredric Jameson, *Postmodernism, or, The Cultural Logic of Late Capitalism* (Durham: Duke University Press, 1990) 39.

73. See, for instance, Nicholas Mirzoeff's charting of the ways, since Thomas Carlyle, revolution from below gets coded as inherently black. Because of blackness's association with "Anarchy and disorder," Mirzoeff continues, "it is precisely, then, with 'blackness' and slavery that a counterhistory of visuality must be concerned" (13). Nicholas Mirzoeff, *The Right to Look: A Counterhistory of Visuality* (Durham: Duke University Press, 2011).

74. Dyer, in acknowledging whiteness's historical fungibility, importantly acknowledges that this fungibility has been key to its operation, insisting that the "instabilities of whiteness also constitute its flexibility and productivity, in short, its representational power." Richard Dyer, *White: Essays on Race and Culture* (New York: Routledge, 1997) 40.

75. These scholars include Theodore W. Allen, David Roediger, Matthew Frye Jacobson, Noel Ignatiev, Michael Omi and Howard Winant, Karen Brodkin, Thomas Guglielmo, and Nell Painter, in addition to Jacobson's *Whiteness of a Different Color: European Immigrants and the Alchemy of Race* (Cambridge: Harvard University Press, 1998), and Roediger's *Working toward Whiteness*. The explosion of work around whiteness in the late 1990s, including Noel Ignatiev, *How the Irish Became White* (New York: Routledge, 1995); Grace Elizabeth Hale, *Making Whiteness: The Culture of Segregation in the South, 1890–1940* (New York: Vintage, 1998); and George Lipsitz, *The Possessive Investment in Whiteness: How*

White People Profit from Identity Politics (Philadelphia: Temple University Press, 1998) helped to shape the historical methods and theoretical claims of critical whiteness studies.

76. Jacobson, *Whiteness of a Different Color*, 5. My understanding of whiteness and racial categories writ large in this period has been deeply influenced by the careful work of Jacobson and Roediger to establish what Jacobson calls the "fluidity of race," combating the notion that "'race' did not really *mean* 'race'" in this period when it came to divisions between Hebrews, Celts, Teutons, and so forth (6).

77. Jacobson, *Whiteness of a Different Color*, 6.

78. See Sara Ahmed, "Declarations of Whiteness: The Non-Performativity of Anti-Racism," *Borderlands* 3.2 (2004); Eva Cherniavsky, *Incorporations: Race, Nation, and the Body Politics of Capital* (Minneapolis: University of Minnesota Press, 2006); Hamilton Carroll, *Affirmative Reaction: New Formations of White Masculinity* (Durham: Duke University Press, 2011); and Robyn Wiegman, "Whiteness Studies and the Paradox of Particularity," *boundary 2* 26.3 (1999) 115–150.

79. Ahmed, "Declarations of Whiteness."

80. Eva Cherniavsky has also warned against emphasizing whiteness's invisibility, arguing that the popularity of this now commonplace claim has caused us to overlook "the way in which it is precisely the boundedness of white embodiment vis-à-vis capital that confers on white personhood an interior core" (*Incorporations*, xxii).

81. There are more works than I can list here that not only take up this theme but also have influenced my own thinking on the subject. In addition to the works already referenced throughout this chapter, some of these include Irene Tucker, *The Moment of Racial Sight: A History* (Chicago: University of Chicago Press, 2012); Colleen Lye, "Introduction: In Dialogue with Asian American Studies," *Representations* 99.1 (Summer 2007) 1–12; Martin Berger, *Sight Unseen: Whiteness and American Visual Culture* (Berkeley: University of California Press, 2005); Kobena Mercer, *Welcome to the Jungle: New Positions in Black Cultural Studies* (New York: Routledge, 1994); Paul Gilroy, *Against Race* (Cambridge: Harvard University Press, 2000); Elizabeth Abel, *The Visual Politics of Jim Crow* (Berkeley: University of California Press, 2010); Sharon Holland, *The Erotic Life of Racism* (Durham: Duke University Press, 2012); and Sara Ahmed, *Queer Phenomenology: Orientations, Objects, Others* (Durham: Duke University Press, 2006).

82. Nicole Fleetwood, *Troubling Vision: Performance, Visuality, and Blackness* (Chicago: University of Chicago Press, 2011) 7.

83. Irene Tucker describes racial perception in a similar way: "If race is conceived as a response or a solution to a set of historically specific problems, then it might continue to be 'useful' even as its logic is revealed to be constructed or historically contingent. The persistence of racial perception would then stand as evidence of that usefulness, rather than as a mark of irrationality or bad faith" (*The Moment of Racial Sight*, 13). Tucker offers a history of the racial sign as marking "the shifting epistemologies encompassing [its] qualities and functions" (6). In relation to Tucker, I am less interested in the history of the racial sign itself and more in the history of the means of its apprehension. In other words, to follow Crary, I hope to track the "techniques" of racial perception rather than its changing subject.

84. For the emergence of ethnicity as racial category, see Omi and Winant, *Racial Formation in the United States*, 12; Richard W. Rees, *Shades of Difference: A History of Eth-*

nicity in America (Lanham: Rowman & Littlefield, 2007); and John Stanfield, *Philanthropy and Jim Crow in American Social Science* (Westport: Greenwood, 1985). Of these three, Stanfield comes closest to recognizing the material conditions of the city as a driver of ethnicity theory, noting that "radical changes in perception and real changes in black status, wrought by capitalist interest in black labor and the dramatic black migration north in the 1910s, sowed the seeds of the environmental paradigms that would dominate social scientific and race relations research" (11).

85. Barbara Fields and Karen Fields similarly refer to the "taxonomic nightmare" that loomed before William Z. Ripley in his 1899 book *The Races of Europe* in which he attempts to compile thousands of measurements to make racial distinctions. "Fitting actual humans to any such grid inevitably calls forth the busy repertoire of strange maneuvering that is part of what we call *racecraft*" (16). *Racecraft: The Soul of Inequality in American Life* (London: Verso, 2012).

86. See Jonathan Crary, *Techniques of the Observer* and *Suspensions of Perception: Attention, Spectacle, and Modern Culture* (Cambridge: MIT Press, 2001); Martin Jay, *Downcast Eyes: The Denigration of Vision in Twentieth-Century French Thought* (Berkeley: University of California Press, 1994); David Levin, ed., *Modernity and the Hegemony of Vision* (Berkeley: University of California Press, 1993); and Michel Foucault, *Discipline and Punish: The Birth of the Prison* (New York: Vintage Books, 1995).

87. Robyn Wiegman, *American Anatomies: Theorizing Race and Gender* (Durham: Duke University Press, 1995) 8.

88. I want to name just a few of the many books engaged in this work: Simon Gikandi, *Slavery and the Culture of Taste* (Princeton: Princeton University Press, 2011); Robin Bernstein, *Racial Innocence: Performing American Childhood from Slavery to Civil Rights* (New York: New York University Press, 2011); Mark Smith, *How Race Is Made* (Durham: University of North Carolina Press, 2007); Fred Moten, *In the Break: The Aesthetics of the Black Radical Tradition* (Minneapolis: University of Minnesota Press, 2003); Daphne Brooks, *Bodies in Dissent: Spectacular Performances of Race and Freedom, 1850–1910* (Durham: Duke University Press, 2006); Moten, "Black Kant," A Theorizing Lecture at the Kelly Writers House, Feb 27, 2007; Kyla Wazana Tompkins, *Racial Indigestion: Eating Bodies in the Nineteenth Century* (New York: New York University Press, 2012).

89. Crary, *Suspensions of Perception*, 3.

90. "Race has always been a profoundly visual rhetoric," as art historian Jennifer González writes, citing the "complex vocabularies developed to delineate social hierarchies based on variations in skin color and phenotype" (380). See "Morphologies: Race as Visual Technology," *Only Skin Deep: Changing Visions of the American Self*, ed. Coco Fusco and Brian Wallis (New York: Harry N. Abrams, 2003).

91. Coco Fusco, "Racial Time, Racial Marks, Racial Metaphors," in *Only Skin Deep*, ed. Fusco and Wallis, 19.

92. Shawn Michelle Smith notes the differing ways such nineteenth-century photographic practices shaped processes of racial perception relative to the subject being captured. "As scientists made race observable in bodies of color, using photography to encode and inscribe race in physiognomy and physiology, commercial studio photographers made the whiteness of their subjects pass unnoticed as 'normal' and 'natural.'"

Smith describes how these different photographic practices ultimately "converged to distinguish blackness from whiteness, making one increasingly visible as 'race' and the other increasingly invisible as 'race.'" Shawn Michelle Smith, *At the Edge of Sight: Photography and the Unseen* (Durham: Duke University Press, 2013) 16.

93. "The photograph became a prime locus of the performance of the racialized index," as Nicholas Mirzoeff notes, since "each time a photograph is looked at, a viewer consciously or unconsciously decides whether and how it indexes the race of its object." Nicholas Mirzoeff, "The Shadow and the Substance: Race, Photography, and the Index," in *Only Skin Deep*, ed. Fusco and Wallis, 111.

94. Joseph Entin, "'Unhuman Humanity': Bodies of the Urban Poor and the Collapse of Realist Legibility," *Novel: A Forum on Fiction* 34.3 (Summer 2001) 316. See also Michael Tavel Clarke's reading of Alvin Langdon Coburn's photography and the links Coburn drew between the practice of photography and the invention of the skyscraper. Clarke insists of these structures that "like photography, they enable new places of mental residence, new forms of consciousness." *These Days of Large Things: The Culture of Size in America, 1865–1930* (Ann Arbor: University of Michigan Press, 2007) 156.

95. Mirzoeff, "The Shadow and the Substance," 112.

96. Some of the most important of these works to my project, in addition to the ones mentioned elsewhere in this chapter, include Peggy Deamer, *Architecture and Capitalism: 1845 to the Present* (New York: Routledge, 2013); Paul Goldberger, *Skyscraper* (New York: Knopf, 1983); Neal Bascomb, *Higher: A Historic Race to the Sky and the Making of a City* (New York: Broadway Books, 2004); Rem Koolhaas, *Delirious New York: A Retroactive Manifesto for Manhattan* (New York: Monacelli Press, 1997). Jim Rasenberger, *High Steel: The Daring Men Who Built the World's Greatest Skyline* (New York: HarperCollins, 2004); George H. Douglas, *Skyscrapers: A Social History of the Very Tall Building in America* (Jefferson: McFarland, 2004); Thomas Leslie, *Chicago Skyscrapers, 1871–1934* (Urbana: University of Illinois Press, 2013); Thomas A. P. van Leeuwen, *The Skyward Trend of Thought: The Metaphysics of the American Skyscraper* (Cambridge: MIT Press, 1990); Benjamin Flowers, *Skyscraper: The Politics and Power of Building New York City in the Twentieth Century* (Philadelphia: University of Pennsylvania Press, 2009); Joseph J. Korom Jr., *Skyscraper Facades of the Gilded Age: Fifty-One Extravagant Designs, 1875–1910* (New York: McFarland, 2013); Scott Charles Murray, *Contemporary Curtain Wall Architecture* (New York: Princeton Architectural Press, 2009); Kenneth Turney Gibbs, *Business Architectural Imagery in America, 1870–1930* (Ann Arbor: UMI Research Press, 1984); Robert Prestiano, *The Inland Architect: Chicago's Major Architectural Journal, 1883–1908* (Ann Arbor: UMI Research Press, 1985); Deborah Pokinski, *The Development of the American Modern Style* (Ann Arbor: UMI Research Press, 1984). Alice Sparberg Alexiou, *The Flatiron: The New York Landmark and the Incomparable City That Arose with It* (New York: St. Martin's Griffin, 2013), and Sarah Bradford and Carl Condit, *Rise of the New York Skyscraper: 1865–1913* (New Haven: Yale University Press, 1996).

97. Daniel Bluestone, *Constructing Chicago* (New Haven: Yale University Press, 1993) 2.

98. Robert Bruegmann, *The Architects and the City: Holabird & Roche of Chicago, 1880–1918* (Chicago: University of Chicago Press, 1997); Katherine Solomonson, *The Chicago Tribune Tower Competition: Skyscraper Design and Cultural Change in the 1920s* (Chicago: University of Chicago Press, 2003); Willis, *Form Follows Finance*; Joanna Merwood-Salisbury, *Chicago 1890: The Skyscraper and the Modern City* (Chicago: Univer-

sity of Chicago Press, 2009); Roberta Moudry, ed., *The American Skyscraper: Cultural Histories* (New York: Cambridge University Press, 2005); and Gail Fenske, *The Skyscraper and the City: The Woolworth Building and the Making of Modern New York* (Chicago: University of Chicago Press, 2008).

99. Fenske, *The Skyscraper and the City*, 9.

100. Steven Holl, Juhani Pallasmaa, and Alberto Perez-Gomez, eds., *Questions of Perception: Phenomenology of Architecture* (New York: William K. Stout, 2007) 36.

101. http://prospect.org/article/architectures-diversity-problem-o.

102. See Craig Barton's edited collection, *Sites of Memory: Perspectives on Architecture and Race* (New York: Princeton Architectural Press, 2001); Lesley Naa Norle Lokko, ed., *White Papers, Black Marks: Architecture, Race, Culture* (Minneapolis: University of Minnesota Press, 2000); Dianne Harris, *Little White Houses: How the Postwar Home Constructed Race in America* (Minneapolis: Minnesota University Press, 2013); William Gleason, *Sites Unseen: Architecture, Race, and American Literature* (New York: New York University Press, 2011); Cheng, *Second Skin*; Mabel O. Wilson, *Negro Building: Black Americans in the World of Fairs and Museums* (Berkeley: University of California Press, 2012), and Joanna Merwood-Salisbury, *Chicago 1890*.

103. Gleason, *Sites Unseen*, 3.

104. Harris, *Little White Houses*, 13.

105. W. J. T. Mitchell, *Seeing through Race* (Cambridge: Harvard University Press, 2012) xii–xiii.

106. W. E. B. Du Bois, *The Souls of Black Folk* (Chicago: A. C. McClurg, 1903) vii.

107. Ibid., 3. In *Photography on the Color Line: W. E. B. Du Bois, Race, and Visual Culture* (Durham: Duke University Press, 2004), Shawn Michelle Smith importantly illustrates the ways that Du Bois's work at the turn of the century "conceptualized the racialized dynamics of the Jim Crow color line as visual culture" in order to reclaim him as an "early *visual* theorist of race and racism" (25). I am deeply indebted to Smith's work on this subject, but I insist not only on Du Bois's interest in the visual but also on the ways architecture shapes his understanding of vision as well as other modes of sensing and perceiving.

108. Du Bois, *Souls of Black Folk*, 138.

Chapter 2 · Architecture and the Visual Fate of Whiteness

1. Matthew Frye Jacobson, *Whiteness of a Different Color* (Cambridge: Harvard University Press) 10.

2. This work includes Noel Ignatiev, *How the Irish Became White* (New York: Routledge, 1995); David Roediger, *The Wages of Whiteness: Race and the Making of the American Working Class* (New York: Verso, 2007); Karen Brodkin, *How Jews Became White Folks and What That Says about Race in America* (New Brunswick: Rutgers University Press, 1998); and Thomas A. Guglielmo, *White on Arrival: Italians, Race, Color, and Power in Chicago, 1890–1945* (New York: Oxford University Press, 2004). Guglielmo diverges from this literature slightly in his insistence on the centrality of dual systems of race (Irish, Italians, Jews) but also color (black, white, yellow) that did different work at the turn of the twentieth century.

3. Frederick Olmsted, "Public Parks and the Enlargement of Towns: Read before the American Social Science Association at the Lowell Institute, Boston, Feb. 25, 1870"

(Cambridge: printed for the American Social Science Association at the Riverside Press, 1870) 18.

4. Ibid., 18–19.

5. Roy Rosenzweig and Elizabeth Blackmar, *The Park and Its People: A History of Central Park* (Ithaca: Cornell University Press, 1992) 232. While they note that "some nativists were unhappy they had to share the park with immigrants," Rosenzweig and Blackmar detail a range of other observers who viewed both the crowds and their diversity more "indulgently" (411). It should be mentioned that African Americans were largely left out of celebrations of Central Park's diversity. A mostly black settlement, Seneca Village, was forcibly cleared to make way for the park.

6. See Rosenzweig and Blackmar, *The Park and Its People*, 377, and Frederick Olmsted Jr., "The Park in Relation to the City Plan," *Forty Years of Landscape Architecture: Central Park* (New York: Putnam, 1928) 205.

7. Frederick Law Olmsted, *The Papers of Frederick Law Olmsted, Volume 3* (Baltimore: Johns Hopkins University Press, 1983) 314.

8. Henry Adams, *The Education of Henry Adams* (Boston: Houghton and Mifflin, 1918) 499.

9. Ibid.

10. Alan Trachtenberg, "Image and Ideology: New York in the Photographer's Eye," *Reading American Art*, ed. Marianne Doezema and Elizabeth Milroy (New Haven: Yale University Press, 1998) 304; 303–349.

11. O. Henry, "Psyche and the Skyscraper," *New York World Sunday Magazine* 15 (Jan 1905) 3.

12. See Jacobson, *Whiteness of a Different Color.*

13. Mary Borden, *Flamingo: A Novel* (New York: Doubleday, Page, 1927) 14.

14. Madison Grant, *The Passing of the Great Race* (New York: Charles Scribner's Sons, 1916) 81.

15. Lothrop Stoddard, *The Rising Tide of Color against White World-Supremacy* (New York: Scribner's, 1922) 165.

16. American panic about the vanishing white race was, of course, not unique to either this particular time or place, with the western frontier serving as a popular antidote to whiteness's vulnerabilities for most of the preceding century, culminating in Theodore Roosevelt and Frederick Turner's 1890s theses about frontier exceptionalism.

17. This is true for books explicitly about race science and aesthetics, such as Walter Benn Michaels, *Our America: Nativism, Modernism, and Pluralism* (Durham: Duke University Press, 1997), and Daylanne English, *Unnatural Selections: Eugenics in American Modernism and the Harlem Renaissance* (Chapel Hill: University of North Carolina Press, 2003), but also for books more broadly on ethnic modernism, such as Werner Sollors, *Ethnic Modernism* (Cambridge: Harvard University Press, 2002), and Rita Keresztesi, *Strangers at Home: American Ethnic Modernism between the World Wars* (Lincoln: University of Nebraska Press, 2005), and more recent books on "melting pot modernism," such as Sarah Wilson, *Melting-Pot Modernism* (Ithaca: Cornell University Press, 2010).

18. "When Is a Caucasian Not a Caucasian?," *Independent* 70 (2 Mar 1911) 478–479.

19. Lewis Mumford, *Sticks and Stones: A Study of American Architecture and Civilization* (New York: Horace Liveright, 1931).

20. Cleveland Moffett, "Mid-Air Dining Clubs," *Century* 62 (1901) 642. For a discussion of midair dining clubs and photographic vision, see Meir Joel Wigoder, "The 'Solar Eye' of Vision: Emergence of the Skyscraper-Viewer in the Discourse on Heights in New York City, 1890–1920," *Journal of the Society of Architectural Historians* 60.2 (June 2002) 152–169. For more on this phenomenon from the period, see also "Dining Clubs in Office Buildings; Large Number of Them Located on Upper Floors of Down-Town 'Skyscrapers'—Lawyers' Club the Pioneer," *New York Times* (4 Jan 1903) SMA2.

21. Peter Bacon Hales, *Silver Cities: Photographing American Urbanization, 1839–1939* (Albuquerque: University of New Mexico Press, 2005).

22. Angela Blake, *How New York Became American, 1890–1924* (Baltimore: Johns Hopkins University Press, 2006) 101.

23. For more on the genre of weird fiction, see Marshall B. Tymn and Mike Ashley, *Science Fiction, Fantasy, and Weird Fiction Magazines* (Westport: Greenwood Press, 1985). Also see S. T. Joshi, *The Modern Weird Tale* (Jefferson: McFarland Press, 2001).

24. Two other adventurous if not exactly fantastic skyscraper stories from the period include Gardner Hunter's "A Common-Sense Heroine," *Youth's Companion* 29 (July 1915) 89, 30, and "A Modern Cliff-Dweller's Experience," *Youth's Companion* 26 (Apr 1906) 3. Both stories feature kids who get stuck atop a skyscraper and have to survive the elements until their rescue.

25. Nick Yablon, *Untimely Ruins: An Archaeology of American Urban Modernity, 1819–1919* (Chicago: University of Chicago Press, 2010).

26. I will be quoting from its final book-length edition. George Allan England, *Darkness and Dawn* (Boston: Small, Maynard, 1914) 11.

27. A. J. Liebling, "To Him She Clung," *New Yorker* (12 Oct 1963). See also Mark Pittenger, "Imagining Genocide in the Progressive Era: The Socialist Science Fiction of George Allan England," *American Studies* 35.1 (Spring 1994) 91–109, and Max Page, *The City's End: Two Centuries of Fantasies, Fears, and Premonitions of New York's Destruction* (New Haven: Yale University Press, 2010) 54–59. Page compares the story's protagonists to the "white suburbanites who already were fleeing cities to escape the flood of racial suspects" (59).

28. England, *Darkness and Dawn*, 22.

29. Ibid., 94.

30. Murray Leinster, "The Runaway Skyscraper," *Argosy and the Railroad Man's Magazine* (22 Feb 1919). All subsequent references are to the electronic version of this essay (Project Gutenberg, 2005), http://www.gutenberg.org/files/17355/17355-h/17355-h.htm.

31. Ibid.

32. Ibid.

33. Ibid.

34. Ibid.

35. Ibid.

36. Ibid.

37. Theodore Roosevelt, *American Ideals* (New York: G. P. Putnam's Sons, 1920) 327, quoted in Gail Bederman, *Manliness & Civilization* (Chicago: University of Chicago Press, 1995) 184.

38. Leinster, "The Runaway Skyscraper."

39. Ibid.

40. Frank Norris, "A Plea for Romantic Fiction," *Boston Evening Transcript* (18 Dec 1901) 14.

41. William Dean Howells, *Criticism and Fiction* (New York: Harper & Brothers, 1891) 131.

42. "The Upward Movement in Chicago," *Atlantic* 80 (Oct 1897) 534–547. Qtd from Henry Blake Fuller's *The Cliff-Dwellers*, ed. James Dimuro (Toronto: Broadview Editions, 2010) 307; Henry James, *The American Scene* (London: Chapman and Hall, 1907) 136; William Dean Howells, *Literary Friends and Acquaintance: A Personal Retrospect of American Authorship* (New York: Harper & Brothers, 1910) 77.

43. Both "monstrous phenomena" and "multiplication" appear in *The American Scene*.

44. This idea of the particular body versus any body resembles what Jacques Rancière describes when he presents democracy as a government of chance. Rancière argues that what "grounds the power of rule in a community" is that "there is no ground at all" for determining who rules. He explicates this using book 3 of Plato's *Laws* and the idea of the "drawing of lots" to determine who rules, suggesting "qualification without qualification," or "the government of chance" as a means of democratic politics. See *Dissensus: On Politics and Aesthetics* (New York: Continuum, 2010) 50–51.

45. Kenneth Warren, *Black and White Strangers: Race and American Literary Realism* (Chicago: University of Chicago Press, 1995).

46. We might, again, consider Henry Blake Fuller as a precursor to James's and Howells's concerns about the viability of race in skyscrapered city. In the introduction, I described the difficulty the protagonist of *The Cliff-Dwellers* has navigating the dense and diverse city. But Howells and James more pointedly tie these concerns about racial differentiation to the skyscraper's particular effects, not just on density but on vantage point and scale.

47. Henry James, *The American Scene*, 81.

48. William Dean Howells, *The World of Chance* (New York: Harper, 1893) 12.

49. William Dean Howells, *The Letters of an Altrurian Traveler* (Gainesville: Scholars' Facsimiles & Reprints, 1961) 70.

50. Howells, *Literary Friends and Acquaintance*, 77. Qtd in Shaun O'Connell, *Remarkable, Unspeakable New York: A Literary History* (Boston: Beacon Press, 1995) 40. O'Connell references both of these quotes, considering them as the impressions of a youthful Howells pre–New York City move.

51. Amy Kaplan, *The Social Construction of American Realism* (Chicago: University of Chicago Press) 63.

52. Paul Abeln, *William Dean Howells and the Ends of Realism* (London: Routledge, 2005) 4.

53. See Ambrose Bierce's 1892 assessment of realism as "absolutely destitute of that supreme and sufficient literary endowment, imagination," finding Howells as someone who "does not what he would, but what he can; takes notes with his eyes and ears and writes them up as any other reporter" and his fans as "fibrous virgins, fat matrons, and oleaginous clergymen." Bierce, "Sharp Criticism of Mr. Howells," *New York Times* 23 (May 1892) 5.

54. In addition to Nancy Bentley, Christophe Den Tandt, Christopher Raczkowski, and Carrie Tirado Bramen also challenge this claim by situating Howells within visual

traditions of the sublime, in the case of Den Tandt and Raczkowsi, and the picturesque for Bramen. Bramen, for instance, in contrast to critics who depict Howells as a "curmudgeon, repelled by the city streets and wary of the increasing heterogeneity of the metropolis," recuperates Howells as a modern flaneur who repeatedly sought out scenes of impoverishment in his novels and urban sketches even as they punctured the "ethical limits" of a realist project. Bramen, "William Dean Howells and the Failure of the Urban Picturesque," *New England Quarterly* 73.1 (Mar 2000) 84; Christophe Den Tandt, *The Urban Sublime in American Literary Naturalism* (Urbana: University of Illinois Press, 1998) 28; Christopher Raczkowski, "The Sublime Train of Sight in *A Hazard of New Fortunes*," *Studies in the Novel* 40.3 (Fall 2008) 300–301. See also Lance Rubin, *William Dean Howells and the American Memory Crisis* (Amherst: Cambria Press, 2008).

55. Paul Petrie's reading of pragmatism, for instance, suggests that Howells's interest in embedded situations of local vision and providing pragmatist solutions is more admirable than we have given him credit for, as critics taking a more distanced stance critique him for the evasive and conservative-seeming actions of his protagonists. "Racial Duties: Toward a Pragmatist Ethic of Race in W. D. Howells's *An Imperative Duty*," *Nineteenth-Century Literature* 63 (2008) 223–254.

56. Kaplan, *The Social Construction of American Realism*, 63.

57. William Dean Howells, Editor's Easy Chair, *Harper's Monthly* (Feb 1909) 479. See also William Dean Howells, *Imaginary Interviews* (New York: Harper & Brothers, 1910) 87–96. All page numbers quoted will be from the version in *Imaginary Interviews*.

58. See Rob Davidson, *The Master and the Dean: The Literary Criticism of Henry James and William Dean Howells* (Columbia: University of Missouri Press, 2005) 228.

59. Ibid.

60. Howells, *Imaginary Interviews*, 89.

61. Ibid.

62. Ibid., 89–90.

63. Ibid., 95.

64. Howells, *Criticism and Fiction*, ii.

65. For more on Howells's evolving relationship to photography, see Owen Clayton's article "London Eyes: William Dean Howells and the Shift to Instant Photography," *Nineteenth-Century Literature* 65.3 (2010) 374–394.

66. Howells, *Imaginary Interviews*, 95.

67. Ibid., 91.

68. Ibid., 92.

69. Ibid.

70. Ibid.

71. Ibid., 96.

72. Paul Abeln also finds Howells engaged in a similar struggle, though in more generic terms: "Later in his life, Howells would see his legacy linked rhetorically to 'realism' and would find himself unable to project a personal or professional image powerful enough to break the connection." *William Dean Howells and the Ends of Realism*, 6.

73. William Dean Howells, *An Imperative Duty* (New York: Harper & Brothers) 1891.

74. James, *The American Scene*, 107, 85.

75. Ibid., 79.

76. Bill Brown, *A Sense of Things: The Object Matter of American Literature* (Chicago: University of Chicago Press, 2003) 177–188. See also J. Michelle Coghlan's meditation on taste, Henry James, and historical memory, "Aftertastes of Ruin: Uncanny Sites of Memory in Henry James's Paris," *Henry James Review* 33.3 (Fall 2012) 239–246.

77. James, *The American Scene,* 76.

78. Ibid., 89.

79. Brown, *A Sense of Things,* 183.

80. James, *The American Scene,* 89.

81. Ibid.

82. Ibid., 81.

83. Ibid., 162.

84. Michael Tavel Clarke reads this scene similarly, finding "James's inward retreat in *The American Scene*" here and elsewhere to represent "his desire for seclusion, isolation, and privacy, which he finds everywhere thwarted in American buildings and American culture generally" (149). But whereas Clarke finds a desire for retreat emerging from most of James's American spatial engagements, I draw distinctions between James's reaction to spaces of bigness he finds interesting and at times inspiring and his response to the skyscraper where he fails to see any representative possibilities, either aesthetic or democratic. *These Days of Large Things: The Culture of Size in America, 1865–1930* (Ann Arbor: University of Michigan Press, 2007).

85. Janet Wolf Bowen, "Architectural Envy: 'A Figure Is Nothing without a Setting' in Henry James's *The Bostonians,*" *New England Quarterly* 65.1 (March 1992) 5.

86. James, *The American Scene,* 241.

87. Ibid.

88. Ibid., 95.

89. Ibid., 62; Gary Levine, *The Merchant of Modernism: The Economic Jew in Anglo-American Literature, 1864–1939* (New York: Routledge, 2014) 91.

90. James, *The American Scene,* 81.

91. Ibid., 82.

92. Ibid., 83.

93. Ibid.

94. Ross Posnock, *The Trial of Curiosity: Henry James, William James and the Challenge of Modernity* (New York: Oxford University Press, 1991) 74.

95. Sara Blair notes James's mixture of "nativist anxiety about American immigration and the policy of the 'open door'" as well as his feeling of "further openness" in the "canny linking of the sons of the bourgeoisie in Cambridge" with Ellis Island's "foreign matter." With his "documentary images," Blair finds James asking "what cultural forms . . . will frame, document, manage the making of Americans, the 'recruiting of national body'" (164). The fact that James can even ask these questions about representation at Ellis Island marks its difference from James's insistence that such framing, documenting, and managing are doomed to fail amid the skyscraper. *Henry James and the Writing of Race and Nation* (New York: Cambridge University Press, 1996).

96. James, *The American Scene,* 388.

97. Ibid.

98. But if James the storyteller can inhabit these northern and southern sites of racial contact and mixture with varying degrees of security, James the democrat recog-

nizes that the discriminatory pleasure he experiences in the South as a storyteller comes at the expense of his democratic interests. He marks the moral tension of his tranquility in Virginia, when James finds himself at Jefferson Davis's home, reminding his reader of the ugly discriminatory capacities that lie beneath the South's genteel veneer.

99. Adeline Tintner, *The Twentieth-Century World of Henry James: Changes in His Work after 1900* (Baton Rouge: Louisiana State University Press, 2000) 9.

100. Henry James, *The New York Stories of Henry James* (New York: New York Review of Books, 2006) 465.

101. Ibid., 466.

102. Ibid., 467.

103. Ibid.

104. Ibid., 478.

105. Ibid., 494.

106. Ibid., 500.

107. Warren, *Black and White Strangers*, 129.

108. Nicola Nixon, "'Prismatic and Profitable': Commerce and Corporate Person in James's 'The Jolly Corner,'" *American Literature* 76.4 (2004) 819. Whereas Nixon reads the story in terms of the dangerous sameness growing corporate monopolies imposed upon the American people, Hsuan Hua reads the story, on the other hand, as a cipher for anxiety-provoking difference. Hua writes that Brydon's "obsessive opening of doors, by obliterating boundaries and establishing continuities between rooms, actively transforms the old apartment into an architectural version of America itself: his 'policy' of keeping vistas clear is Brydon's own version of the nation's controversial Open Door Policy." "Post-James and the Question of Scale," *Henry James Review* 24.3 (2003) 233–243.

Chapter 3 · *Miscegenated Skyscrapers and Passing Metropolitans*

1. Other work on how aesthetics were informed by evolution and eugenics in the United States includes Christina Cogdell, *Eugenic Design* (Philadelphia: University of Pennsylvania Press, 2004); Daylanne English, *Unnatural Selections: Eugenics in American Modernism and the Harlem Renaissance* (Durham: University of North Carolina Press, 2004); Barbara Larson and Fae Brauer, eds., *The Art of Evolution: Darwin, Darwinisms, and Visual Culture* (Dartmouth: Dartmouth University Press, 2009); and Dana Seitler, *Atavistic Tendencies: The Culture of Science in American Modernity* (Minneapolis: University of Minnesota Press, 2008).

2. Anne Cheng, *Second Skin: Josephine Baker and the Modern Surface* (Oxford University Press, 2013) 13.

3. George H. Douglas, *Skyscrapers: A Social History of the Very Tall Building in America* (New York: McFarland, 2004), is one such architectural historian highlighting the "multitude of technologies" that allowed the skyscraper to be realized in the form it was in the late nineteenth century (61).

4. Race-based competition was germane to many industrial fields. Labor historian John Commons observed back in 1907 that the tactic of "playing one race against the other" was a "symptom of originality" distinct to American employers. But of these employers, steel corporations were inordinately successful in their strategy of what Commons called "divide and conquer" by encouraging racial discord within its interracial

workforces. John Commons, *Race and Immigrants in America* (London: Macmillan, 1907) 150. See also David R. Roediger and Elizabeth D. Esch, *The Production of Difference: Race and the Management of Labor in U.S. History* (New York: Oxford University Press, 2015) 5.

5. Bruce Nelson, *Divided We Stand: American Workers and the Struggle for Black Equality* (Princeton: Princeton University Press, 2002) 145–184. Steel industries did not unionize until 1937, when the Steel Workers Organizing Committee finally signed a collective bargaining agreement with U.S. Steel. For more on the history of race and steel, see John Hinshaw, *Steel and Steelworkers: Race and Class Struggle in Twentieth-Century Pittsburgh* (Albany: State University of New York Press, 2002); Dennis C. Dickerson, *Out of the Crucible: Black Steelworkers in Western Pennsylvania, 1875–1980* (Albany: State University of New York Press, 1986); Thomas Misa, *A Nation of Steel: The Making of Modern America, 1865–1925* (Baltimore: Johns Hopkins University Press, 1998); Lizabeth Cohen, *Making a New Deal: Industrial Workers in Chicago, 1919–1939* (New York: Cambridge University Press, 2008); and Joe Trotter and Jared Day, *Race and Renaissance: African Americans in Pittsburgh since World War II* (Pittsburgh: University of Pittsburgh Press, 2010).

6. Arno Dosch, "Just Wops," *Everybody's Magazine* 25.5 (Nov 1911) 579.

7. See Arthur B. Reeve, "Men Monkeys Who Build Our Towers," *Scrapbook* 5 (May 1908) 759–767, and Cromwell Childe, "The Structural Workers," *Frank Leslie's Popular Monthly* (July 1901) 268.

8. The pamphlet was titled *Miscegenation: The Theory of the Blending of the Races, Applied to the American White Man and Negro* and published in 1863. For more of the history of this pamphlet and the origins of the word *miscegenation*, see Elise Lemire, *Miscegenation: Making Race in America* (Philadelphia: University of Pennsylvania Press, 2002), and Tavia Nyong'o, *The Amalgamation Waltz: Race, Performance and the Ruses of Memory* (Minneapolis: University of Minnesota Press, 2009).

9. See St. Clair Drake and Horace Cayton, *Black Metropolis: A Study of Negro Life in a Northern City* (Chicago: University of Chicago Press, 1945).

10. Nativist concerns rooted in eugenics and race science about white "race suicide" and miscegenation also informed the debates leading to the passage of various immigration quotas passed in the United States in the 1920s. Mark Largent has traced the ways that laws preventing interracial marriage laid the legal groundwork for forced sterilization programs in *Breeding Contempt: The History of Coerced Sterilization in the United States* (New Brunswick: Rutgers University Press, 2009) 64–65. Resistance to school desegregation coming to a head in the 1950s was based in part on miscegenation fears. Michael Klamen in *Brown v. Board of Education and the Civil Rights Movement* (New York: Oxford University Press, 2007) 87, writes, for instance, that Supreme Court Justice Felix Frankfurter made sure the court's opinion in *Brown* emphasized access to public education over condemning racial classification as a way of avoiding the question of miscegenation altogether.

11. In this, I follow Daniel Bluestone, who argues that "the nineteenth-century skyscraper fits more comfortably with its own contemporaries than with twentieth-century successors; nineteenth-century skyscrapers appear less exceptional, more grounded in the past. It follows that parks, churches, and civic and cultural institutions reflected nineteenth-century Chicago as truly as skyscrapers did—and even, I will argue, in much the same way." *Constructing Chicago* (New Haven: Yale University Press, 1991) 2.

12. This includes not only books by Carol Willis and Thomas Leslie as well as Benjamin Flowers's *Skyscraper: The Politics and Power of Building New York City in the Twentieth Century* (Philadelphia: University of Pennsylvania Press, 2009) but also accounts of singular buildings that track the evolution of these structures in light of fuller contexts cited in the introduction.

13. Donald Hoffmann, *Frank Lloyd Wright, Louis Sullivan, and the Skyscraper* (New York: Dover Publications, 1998) 9.

14. This is the ethos shared by many of the essays in Peggy Deamer's edited collection *Architecture and Capitalism: 1845 to the Present* (New York: Routledge, 2013).

15. Thomas Leslie, "Dankmar Adler's Response to Louis Sullivan's 'The Tall Office Building Artistically Considered': Architecture and the 'Four Causes,'" *Journal of Architectural Education* 64.1 (Sept 2010) 83.

16. Thomas Leslie, *Chicago Skyscrapers, 1871–1934* (Urbana: University of Illinois Press, 2013) xiv.

17. Joanna Merwood-Salisbury, *Chicago 1890: The Skyscraper and the Modern City* (Chicago: University of Chicago Press, 2009) 27. See also Charles Davis, "Viollet-le-Duc and the Body: The Metaphorical Integrations of Race and Style in Structural Rationalism," *Architectural Research Quarterly* 14.4 (2010) 341–348; Mabel O. Wilson, *Negro Building: Black Americans in the World of Fairs and Museums* (Berkeley: University of California Press, 2012).

18. For work on the role of bodies in architectural design, see Richard Sennett, *Flesh and Stone: The Body and the City in Western Civilization* (New York: W. W. Norton, 1996), and George Dodds and Robert Tanner's edited volume, *Body and Building: Essays on the Changing Relation of Body and Architecture* (Cambridge: MIT Press, 2002).

19. Vitruvius Pollio, *The Ten Books on Architecture* (Cambridge: Boston University Press, 1914) 72.

20. William Gleason writes, for instance, about the presence of slaves in Andrew Jackson Downing's pattern books in *Sites Unseen: Architecture, Race, and American Literature* (New York: New York University Press, 2011). For more on blackness and the formation of an American architectural practice designed around an understanding of the white autonomous US subject, see Irene Cheng's "Race and Architectural Geometry: Thomas Jefferson's Octagons," *J19: The Journal of Nineteenth-Century Americanists* 3.1 (Spring 2015) 121–130.

21. Joanna Merwood-Salisbury uses this phrase to describe the thinking of architect William Le Baron Jenney, an idea that had traction for many American architects, in her chapter "Western Architecture: Regionalism and Race in the *Inland Architect*," *Chicago Architecture: Histories, Revisions, Alternatives*, ed. Charles Waldheim and Katerina Ruedi Ray (Chicago: University of Chicago Press, 2005) 6.

22. These are the words of Frederic Ward Putnam, director of Harvard's Peabody Museum of American Archaeology and Ethnology and one of the organizers of the 1893 Chicago World's Fair. Frederic Ward Putnam, "An Interesting Suggestion for the Columbian Exposition," *Chicago Tribune* (30 May 1890) 13. For more on the fair's racial organization, see Robert Rydell, *All the World's a Fair: Visions of Empire at American International Expositions, 1876–1916* (Chicago: University of Chicago Press, 1987), and Wilson, *Negro Building*.

23. N. Clifford Ricker, "Possibilities for American Architecture," *Inland Architect and News Record* 11.5 (Nov 1885) 63.

24. Irving Pond, "Architectural Kinships," *Inland Architect and News Record* 17.2 (Mar 1891) 22–29.

25. Ibid.

26. Merwood-Salisbury, "Western Architecture," 9. See also Irving Pond's article "Home" in which he writes that "the development of architecture has gone on hand in hand with the development of the social character of the race." *Inland Architect and News* 10.6 (Nov 1887) 63. For more on Pond's race-based theories, see Jonathan Massey's *Crystal and Arabesque: Claude Bragdon, Ornament, and Modern Architecture* (Pittsburgh: University of Pittsburgh Press, 2009) 173–175. Massey notes Pond's efforts to "prevent such architectural miscegenation" Bragdon would better embrace (175).

27. Cogdell, *Eugenic Design*, 5.

28. Carl Condit, *The Chicago School of Architecture: A History of Commercial and Public Building in the Chicago Area, 1875–1925* (Chicago: University of Chicago Press, 1964) 79.

29. "Freed of its load-bearing responsibilities," as architectural historian Scott Charles Murray writes, "the exterior became a blank canvas." *Contemporary Curtain Wall Architecture* (New York: Princeton Architectural Press, 2009) 11.

30. Montgomery Schuyler, "Modern Architecture," *Architectural Record* 4 (July–Sep 1894) 9. Originally delivered at Union College, New York, 1894.

31. Barr Ferree, "An American Style of Architecture," *Architectural Record* 1 (July 1891) 39.

32. Ibid., 42.

33. Ibid., 45.

34. Allen B. Pond, "The Evolution of an American Architecture," *Inland Architect and News* 10.9 (Jan 1888) 98.

35. Deborah Pokinski tracks the development and expansion of what she calls "the new eclecticism" between 1905 and 1922, which she argues was at first much more narrowly defined before expanding by the early 1920s to tolerate increasingly "radical" styles in *The Development of the American Modern Style* (Ann Arbor: UMI Research Press, 1984). "By 1922," she writes, "the evolutionary process that characterized the development of Modernism in American architecture had reached the crucial point where original and nonhistorical styles were preferred to styles based on historical precedent in the minds and on the buildings of American architects" (50).

36. Robert Kerr, "The Problem of National American Architecture," *Architectural Record* 3.2 (Oct–Dec 1893) 123.

37. Henry Rutgers Marshall, "The Legitimate Design for the Casing of Steel-skeleton Structures," *Proceedings of the 37th Annual Convention: American Institute of Architects* (Providence: R. A. Johnson, 1898) 101. For more on "academic eclecticism," see Richard W. Longstreth, "Academic Eclecticism in American Architecture," *Winterthur Portfolio* 17. 1 (Spring 1982) 55–82. See also Pokinski, *The Development of the American Modern Style*.

38. C. H. Blackall, "The Legitimate Design for the Casing of Steel-Skeleton Structures," *Proceedings of the 37th Annual Convention: American Institute of Architects* (Providence: R. A. Johnson, 1898) 106.

39. Henry Van Brunt, *Discourses on Architecture* (Boston: James R. Osgood, 1875) x. Not only did European eclecticism provide "a new national architecture that seemed appropriate to the modern age," as art historian Martin Berger argues, but it also "helped European-Americans to transcend the oppressive cultural and racial weight of European, Near Eastern and, later, Asian architectural precedents." See *Sight Unseen: Whiteness and American Visual Culture* (Berkeley: University of California Press, 2005) 104.

40. John Root, "A Great Architectural Problem," *Inland Architect and News Record* 15.5 (June 1890) 67–71.

41. Schuyler, "Modern Architecture," 13.

42. Herbert Croly, "An American Architecture," *Architectural Record* 23.2 (Feb 1908) 111.

43. N. Clifford Ricker, "Architectural Grammar," *Inland Architect and Builder* 13.8 (Dec 1886) 66.

44. For more on the American reception of evolutionary theory and race science, see Stephen Jay Gould, *The Mismeasure of Man* (New York: Norton, 1996); Cogdell, *Eugenic Design*; Carl Degler, *In Search of Human Nature: The Decline and Revival of Darwinism in American Social Thought* (New York: Oxford University Press, 1991); Richard Hofstadter, *Social Darwinism in American Thought* (Boston: Beacon Press, 1992); John S. Haller, *Outcasts from Evolution: Scientific Attitudes of Racial Inferiority, 1859–1900* (Carbondale: Southern Illinois University Press, 1996); Paul Lawrence Farber, *Mixing Races: From Scientific Racism to Modern Evolutionary Ideas* (Baltimore: Johns Hopkins University Press, 2010); Thomas Gossett, *Race: The History of an Idea in America* (Oxford: Oxford University Press, 1997); and Ann Fabian, *The Skull Collectors: Race, Science, and America's Unburied Dead* (Chicago: University of Chicago Press, 2010).

45. Elizabeth Cabot and Cary Agassiz, eds., *Louis Agassiz: His Life and Correspondence* (Boston: Houghton, Mifflin, 1893) 601–602.

46. Cited in Gould, *The Mismeasure of Man*, 80.

47. Ibid., 81.

48. Blackall, "Steel-Skeleton Structures," 107.

49. Sheldon Cheney, *The New World Architecture* (New York: Longmans, Green, 1930) 135.

50. John Beverly Robinson, *Architectural Composition: An Attempt to Order and Phrase Ideas which hitherto have been only Felt by the Instinctive Taste of Designers* (New York: D. Van Nostrand, 1908) 68.

51. Louis Sullivan, *Kindergarten Chats and Other Writings* (New York: Dover, 1979) 30.

52. Ibid., 195.

53. See, for instance, Scottish anatomist Robert Knox, *The Races of Men: A Fragment* (Philadelphia: Lea & Blanchard, 1862) in which he describes "a ruffianly mixed population of blacks and browns" becoming "extinct in time, as all mixed races must" (256). American race scientist Samuel Morton would hazard similar claims in 1850, suggesting that mixed-race women had a harder time conceiving. See Morton, "Additional Observations on Hybridity in Animals and on Some Collateral Subjects," *Charleston Medical Review* (Nov 1850).

54. David S. Andrew, *Louis Sullivan and the Polemics of Modern Architecture: The Present against the Past* (Urbana: University of Illinois Press, 1985) 35. See also Charles Davis, "On Physiognomic Difference in Sullivan's The Autobiography of an Idea," a conference

paper he delivered at the Southeast Chapter Society of Architectural Historians in 2012 and posted to his website: https://raceandarchitecture.wordpress.com/2013/03/07/the -poetics-of-identity-in-louis-sullivans-memoir-the-autobiography-of-an-idea/. For more on Sullivan's interest in degeneracy, see Sherman Paul, *Louis Sullivan: An Architect in American Thought* (Englewood Cliffs: Prentice-Hall, 1962), and Cogdell, *Eugenic Design*.

55. For more on Sullivan's contradictions, see Robert C. Twombly, *Louis Sullivan: The Poetry of Architecture* (New York: W. W. Norton, 2000); Andrew, *Louis Sullivan*; and John Shannon Hendrix, *The Contradiction between Form and Function in Architecture* (New York: Routledge, 2013).

56. For more on Sullivan and eclecticism, see Mario Maneiri-Ella, *Louis Henry Sullivan* (New York: Princeton Architectural Press, 1995), and Twombly, *Louis Sullivan*.

57. John Ruskin, *The Seven Lamps of Architecture* (New York: Dover, 1989, based on the original in 1889). Sullivan's organicism was also shaped by an American transcendentalist tradition routed through Ralph Waldo Emerson and Horatio Greenough. For more on this, see in addition to the other Sullivan historiography cited here, Narciso G. Menocal, *Architecture as Nature: The Transcendentalist Idea of Louis Sullivan* (Madison: University of Wisconsin Press, 1981), and Naomi Tanabe Uechi, *Evolving Transcendentalism in Literature and Architecture: Frank Furness, Louis Sullivan, and Frank Lloyd Wright* (New York: Cambridge University Press, 2014).

58. This quote comes from Sullivan's essay "The Tall Office Building Artistically Considered," *Lippincott's Magazine* 57 (Mar 1896) 48–49. For more on Sullivan's organicism, see Hugh Morrison, *Louis Sullivan: Prophet of Modern Architecture* (New York: W. W. Norton, 1998); Twombly, *Louis Sullivan*; Lauren S. Weingarden, *Louis H. Sullivan and a 19th-Century Poetics of Naturalized Architecture* (New York: Ashgate, 2009); and Menocal, *Architecture as Nature*.

59. Sullivan, "The Tall Office Building Artistically Considered," 48.

60. Ibid.

61. Louis Sullivan, "The Young Man in Architecture," *The Public Papers* (Chicago: University of Chicago Press) 139.

62. Philip Steadman, *The Evolution of Designs: Biological Analogy in Architecture and the Applied Arts* (New York: Routledge, 1979) 59. See George Cuvier and Edward Griffith, *The Animal Kingdom Arranged in Conformity with Its Organization, Volume 8* (London: Whittaker, Treacher, 1929) 249.

63. For more on the magnetism of skyscraper construction, see Jim Rasenberger, *High Steel: The Daring Men Who Built the World's Greatest Skyline* (New York: HarperCollins, 2004); Col. William A. Starrett, *Skyscrapers and the Men Who Build Them* (New York: Scribner's 1928); Gail Fenske, *The Skyscraper and the City: The Woolworth Building and the Making of Modern New York* (Chicago: University of Chicago Press, 2008); and David Nye's *American Technological Sublime* (Cambridge: MIT Press, 2008).

64. George Ethelbert Walsh, "Modern Towers of Babel in New York," *Harper's Weekly* (12 Jan 1907) 206.

65. Sullivan, *Kindergarten Chats*, 30.

66. "The Poetry of Skyscrapers," *Chicago Defender* 6 (Jan 1912) 8.

67. H. A. Caparn, "The Riddle of the Tall Building: Has the Skyscraper a Place in American Architecture?," *Craftsman* 10 (July 1906) 477.

68. H. Toler Booraem, "Significance of Architectural Form," *Architectural Record* 25.3 (Mar 1909) 200.

69. Ann Douglas, *Terrible Honesty: Mongrel Manhattan in the 1920s* remains a landmark work placing this time and place on the map in terms of racial mixture (New York: Farrar, Straus and Giroux, 1996).

70. "Census of 1920 Shows Less Increase than in Previous Decade," *New York Times* (15 May 1921).

71. Douglas, *Terrible Honesty.*

72. Allyson Hobbs, *A Chosen Exile: A History of Racial Passing in American Life* (Cambridge: Harvard University Press, 2014). The *Oxford English Dictionary* lists *Nigger Heaven* as originating the term *passing*, but a version of the term appears in James Weldon Johnson's *Autobiography of an Ex-Colored Man*, first published in 1912: "For I did indeed pass into another world. From that time I looked out through other eyes, my thoughts were colored, my words dictated, my actions limited by one dominating, all-pervading idea which constantly increased in force and weight until I finally realized in a great, tangible fact" (New York: Hill and Wang, 1991) 20–21.

73. Louis Fremont Baldwin, *From Negro to Caucasian, or How the Ethiopian Is Changing His Skin* (San Francisco: Pilot Publishing, 1929) 14.

74. Karen Halttunen, *Confidence Men and Painted Women: A Study of Middle-Class Culture in America, 1830–1870* (New Haven: Yale University Press, 1986).

75. Robert Park, "The City: Suggestions for the Investigation of Human Behavior in the Urban Environment," *American Journal of Sociology* 20.5 (1915) 608.

76. "White but Black," *Century Magazine* (Feb 1925) 498. Qtd in Elizabeth M. Smith-Pryor, *Property Rites: The Rhinelander Trial, Passing, and the Protection of Whiteness* (Durham: University of North Carolina Press, 2009) 90.

77. Lester Walton, "'Pride of Place' Powerful Play," *New York Age* (20 Jan 1916) 1, col. 7. Qtd in Smith-Pryor, *Property Rites,* 90.

78. Ibid.

79. Cheng, *Second Skin.*

80. Ibid., 98.

81. Nella Larsen, *Passing: A Norton Critical Edition,* ed. Carla Kaplan (New York: W. W. Norton, 2007) 76.

82. Nella Larsen, "To Charles S. Johnson," Aug 1926, Walter White Correspondence, NAACP Papers, Library of Congress. Cited in Larsen, *Passing,* 158–160.

83. Ewa Plonowska Ziarek writes about this letter in *Feminist Aesthetics and the Politics of Modernism* (New York: Columbia University Press, 2013) 202.

84. Larsen's interest in literary representation untethered to evidentiary surfaces even emerges in the name of one of her protagonists. The name *Clare* derives from the Latin *clarus*, which, as Ewa Plonowska Ziarek points out, denotes not only clarity but brightness. But Clare proves to be a highly ironic choice for this character given that nothing about her—her race, her intentions, even the causes of her death—can be made clear. Her brightness, as Ziarek further notes, ultimately blinds Irene rather than produce illumination. *Feminist Aesthetics and the Politics of Modernism,* 207.

85. Larsen, *Passing,* 7.

86. Ibid.

87. W. C. Clark and J. L. Kingston, *The Skyscraper: A Study in the Economic Height of Modern Office Buildings* (New York: American Institute of Steel Construction, 1930) 118.

88. Hugh Ferriss, *The Metropolis of Tomorrow* (New York: Ives Washburn, 1929) 18.

89. Ibid.

90. Ibid.

91. Lewis Mumford, *Sticks and Stones: A Study of American Architecture and Civilization* (New York: Horace Liveright, 1924) 176.

92. Ibid.

93. Ibid.

94. Ibid.

95. Jennifer DeVere Brody connects this vision of the city to the Red Summer Riots of 1919, denoting a type of social instability. "Clare Kendry's 'True' Colors: Race and Class Conflict in Nella Larsen's *Passing*," *Callaloo* 15.4 (Fall 1992) 1053–1065.

96. Larsen, *Passing*, 7.

97. Ibid.

98. Ibid., 8.

99. See George Simmel, "The Metropolis and Mental Life," *The Sociology of Georg Simmel*, trans. Kurt Wolff (New York: Free Press, 1950) 409–424.

100. For a reading of a different Nella Larsen novel, 1928's *Quicksand*, in relation to urban sociology see Mary Esteve, *The Aesthetics and Politics of the Crowd in American Literature* (Cambridge: Cambridge University Press, 2003).

101. Thadious Davis, however, raises the possibility of the nearby Morrison Hotel, which also had a popular rooftop restaurant similar to the one featured in the novel, as a match. Thadious Davis, *Nella Larsen: Novelist of the Harlem Renaissance* (Baton Rouge: Louisiana State University Press, 1993).

102. Dianne Harris and D. Fairchild Ruggles, eds., *Sites Unseen: Landscape and Vision* (Pittsburgh: University of Pittsburgh Press, 2007) 24. This specific claim is more explicitly yoked via the skyscraper to De Certeau's reading of the view from the World Trade Center, which I engage in more depth in chapter 4. Michel De Certeau, *The Practice of Everyday Life*, trans. Steven F. Rendell (Berkeley: University of California Press, 2011) 92.

103. Larsen, *Passing*, 11.

104. Ibid., 18.

105. Ibid.

106. Smith-Pryor, *Property Rites*, 209.

107. Ibid.

108. For more on the print history of this ending, see Mark Madigan, "'Then Everything Was Dark'?: The Two Endings of Nella Larsen's *Passing*," *Papers of the Bibliographical Society of America* 83.4 (Dec 1989) 521–523.

109. Larsen, *Passing*, 82.

110. Anne duCille, *The Coupling Convention* (New York: Oxford University Press, 1993); Miriam Thaggert, "Racial Etiquette: Nella Larsen's *Passing* and the *Rhinelander Case*," *Meridians: Feminism, Race, Transnationalism* 5.2 (2005) 1–29.

111. Larsen, *Passing*, 82.

112. Baldwin, *From Negro to Caucasian*, 36.

Chapter 4 · The Black Skyscraper

1. James Baldwin, *Notes of a Native Son* (Boston: Beacon Press, 1955) 7.

2. James Weldon Johnson, *The Book of American Negro Poetry* (New York: Harcourt, Brace, 1922) vii.

3. James Weldon Johnson, *The Book of American Negro Poetry*, rev. ed. (New York: Harcourt, Brace, 1931).

4. James Weldon Johnson, *Along the Way: The Autobiography of James Weldon Johnson* (New York: Viking Press, 1933) 328.

5. Kelly Miller, *Race Adjustment [and] The Everlasting Stain* (New York: Arno Press, 1968) 129.

6. Mary White Ovington, *Half a Man: The Status of the Negro in New York* (New York: Negro Universities Press, 1969) 83.

7. See Dianne Harris, ed., "Race, Space, and the Destabilization of Practice," *Landscape Journal* 37.1 (2007) iv–174; Craig Barton, ed., *Sites of Memory: Perspectives on Architecture and Race* (New York: Princeton Architectural Press, 2001); Lesley Naa Norle Lokko, ed., *White Papers, Black Marks: Architecture, Race, Culture* (Minneapolis: University of Minnesota Press, 2000); William Gleason, *Sites Unseen: Architecture, Race, and American Literature* (New York: New York University Press); Anne Cheng, *Second Skin: Josephine Baker & the Modern Surface* (Oxford: Oxford University Press); Charles Davis, "Viollet-le-Duc and the Body: The Metaphorical Integrations of Race and Style in Structural Rationalism," *Architectural Research Quarterly* 14.4 (2010) 341–348; and Mabel O. Wilson, *Negro Building: Black Americans in the World of Fairs and Museums* (Berkeley: University of California Press, 2012).

8. Melvin L. Mitchell, *The Crisis of the African-American Architect: Conflicting Cultures of Architecture and (Black) Power* (New York: Writer's Advantage, 2003) 67.

9. Farah Jasmine Griffin, *"Who Set You Flowin'?": The African-American Migration Narrative* (New York: Oxford University Press, 1996); and Lawrence Rodgers, *Canaan Bound: The African-American Great Migration Novel* (Urbana: University of Illinois Press, 1997).

10. Horkheimer decried the structure's height in the late 1920s for masking the fact that its "basement is a slaughterhouse." See *Dawn & Decline: Notes 1926–1931 and 1950–1969*, trans. Michael Shaw (New York: Seabury Press, 1978) 67.

11. Ronald A. T. Judy, "Introduction: On W. E. B. Du Bois and Hyperbolic Thinking," *boundary 2*, 27.3 (Fall 2000) 10.

12. W. E. B. Du Bois, "The Criteria of Negro Art," *Crisis* 32 (Oct 1926) 297.

13. Ibid., 296.

14. Du Bois's "art," most often taking the form of politically engaged genre fiction, formally and thematically diverged in places from fellow Marxist Georg Lukacs's prescriptions for a realist literary style that measured the totality of capitalism by discovering "the underlying essence" in subjective experience revealing "the hidden social forces that produce them." Ross Posnock uses Du Bois's 1928 novel *Dark Princess* to demonstrate the incompatibility of his fictional practice with Lukacs's ideas about realism, remarking that "Georg Lukacs would find the lavish attention Du Bois pays to interior life a symptom of modernism's decadent 'ontologism,'" to be a "flight from historical reality." But despite Du Bois's deep dive into many of his protagonists' subjective worlds, his writing still treaded closer to Lukacsian realism than the more openly experimental

forms of modernism and expressionism that Lukacs opposed. Ultimately, both Du Bois and Lukacs advocated for an artistic practice wherein abstraction was only acceptable when in the service of, as Lukacs describes, "penetrat[ing] the laws governing objective reality." See Georg Lukacs, "Realism in the Balance," *Aesthetics and Politics*, ed. Theodor Adorno et al. (New York: Verso Books, 2010); and Ross Posnock, *Color and Culture: Black Writers and the Making of the Modern Intellectual* (Cambridge: Harvard University Press, 2009).

15. Open any leftist novel or magazine set in New York City in the early twentieth century and you are likely to stumble upon multiple references to the skyscraper as a symbol of capitalistic dastardliness. Left-leaning and even reform-minded writers were quick to refute the free-market triumphalism inherent in much of the structure's mainstream praise with its own schema of villainous iconography. Loaded with ominous skyscraper synecdoche, this work was quick to situate the skyscraper as the unapologetic center of capital's all-encompassing spider web. See, for instance, Max Eastman, *Venture* (New York: Boni & Liveright, 1927), which concludes with a scene of an evil capitalist looking down from the top of the Woolworth Building to find its "generalizing" picture in line with his own "scientific view" of the city ripe for exploitation (384). Or the poem "Woolworth Building," published in the *New Masses*, which indicts the structure for funding its erection with "blood-soaked and vice-stained pennies" and "trickling nickels of dimes" that were "squeezed out of weak and pitiful girls" and "levied on needy families," with no mention of the workers who too were "squeezed" in the act of its building. See "Woolworth Building," *New Masses* (Apr 1916) 20.

16. W. E. B. Du Bois, *The Souls of Black Folk* (Chicago: A. C. McClurg, 1903) 12.

17. Fredric Jameson, *Archaeologies of the Future: The Desire Called Utopia and Other Science Fictions* (London: Verso, 2011) 16.

18. Nicholas Mirzoeff, *The Right to Look: A Counterhistory of Visuality* (Durham: Duke University Press, 2011).

19. W. E. B. Du Bois, "Sociology Hesitant," *boundary 2*, 27.3 (Fall 2000) 38.

20. Judy, "Introduction," 10.

21. Du Bois, "Sociology Hesitant," 38.

22. Ibid.

23. Ibid.

24. Ibid., 39.

25. Ibid.

26. Ibid., 42.

27. W. E. B. Du Bois, "The Princess Steel," W. E. B. Du Bois Papers (MS 312), Special Collections & University Archives, University of Massachusetts Amherst Libraries.

28. Britt Rusert and I have since published this story. "W. E. B. Du Bois's 'The Princess Steel,'" *PMLA* 130.3 (May 2015) 819–829. All citations taken from this version.

29. Du Bois, "Princess Steel," 822.

30. Ibid.

31. Ibid.

32. Ibid.

33. Ibid.

34. Ibid.

35. Ibid., 823.

36. Ibid.

37. Ibid.

38. Ibid.

39. Ibid., 824.

40. Ibid., 829.

41. Ibid.

42. W. E. B. Du Bois, *Darkwater: Voices from the Veil* (New York: Harcourt, Brace and Howe, 1920).

43. Susan Gillman and Alys Weinbaum use the phrase "politics of juxtaposition" to talk about Du Bois's prose style in their introduction to *Next to the Color Line: Gender, Sexuality and W. E. B. Du Bois* (Minneapolis: University of Minnesota Press, 2007) 6.

44. Du Bois, *Darkwater*, 243.

45. Ibid., 253.

46. James Smethurst, *The African American Roots of Modernism* (Chapel Hill: University of North Carolina Press, 2011) 13.

47. Du Bois, *Darkwater*, 224.

48. Ibid. See also Russ Castronovo's discussion of Du Bois's relationship to cinematic experience in *Beautiful Democracy* (Chicago: University of Chicago Press, 2007) 152–156.

49. Du Bois, *Darkwater*, 256.

50. Ibid., 257.

51. Ibid., 224.

52. Ibid., 262.

53. Thomas Bender, *The Unfinished City: New York and the Metropolitan Idea* (New York: New Press, distributed by W. W. Norton, 2002) 53.

54. For a longer reading of this scene of communication technologies, see my article, "The Black Skyscraper," *American Literature* 85.3 (2013) 541–561, and Amy Kaplan, *The Anarchy of Empire in the Making of U.S. Culture* (Cambridge: Harvard University Press, 2005).

55. Du Bois, *Darkwater*, 268.

56. Ibid.

57. Ibid.

58. Ibid., 269.

59. Ibid.

60. Alys Weinbaum, "Interracial Romance and Black Internationalism," in *Next to the Color Line*, ed. Gillman and Weinbaum, 104.

61. Nick Yablon argues, like Alys Weinbaum, that Du Bois foregrounds interracial sex as the solution to humanity's survival, while also suggesting that Du Bois's use of the Met Life Building may have been a critique of the insurance company's discrimination against African Americans. See Yablon, *Untimely Ruins: An Archaeology of American Urban Modernity, 1819–1919* (Chicago: University of Chicago Press, 2008) 327–329.

62. Du Bois, *Darkwater*, 270.

63. Ibid.

64. Ibid.

65. Ibid., 271.

66. Ibid., 272.

67. Ibid., 273.

68. Ibid.

69. Weinbaum, "Interracial Romance," 107.

70. W. E. B. Du Bois, "The Browsing Reader, review of *Home to Harlem*," *Crisis* 35 (June 1928) 202; W. E. B. Du Bois, "Books, review of *Nigger Heaven*," *Crisis* (Dec 1926) 81.

71. Du Bois, "The Browsing Reader," 374.

72. See "Miss Cynthie" and "Harlem, the Negro Metropolis" in *The City of Refuge: The Collected Stories of Rudolph Fisher*, ed. John McCluskey (Columbia: University of Missouri Press, 2008) 97–107, 328–331.

73. Rudolph Fisher, "Ezekiel Learns," *The City of Refuge*, ed. McCluskey, 74–77.

74. Fisher, "Ezekiel Learns," 74.

75. Ibid.

76. Michel De Certeau, *The Practice of Everyday Life* (Berkeley: University of California Press, 2011) 92.

77. Wallace Thurman, *Infants of the Spring* (Boston: Northeastern University Press, 1992).

78. Wallace Thurman, "High, Low, and Present: Review of *The Walls of Jericho, Quicksand, and Adventures of a Slaver*." Originally published in *Harlem: A Forum of Negro Life*, Nov 1928. Reprinted in *The Collected Writings of Wallace Thurman: A Harlem Renaissance Reader* (New Brunswick: Rutgers University Press, 2003) 219.

79. Thurman, *Infants of the Spring*, 240.

80. On the usefulness of Thurman's "bad modernism," see Monica Miller's essay "The Black Dandy as Bad Modernist," *Bad Modernisms*, ed. Douglas Mao and Rebecca Walkowitz (Durham: Duke University Press, 2006) 179–205.

81. See Judith Brown's reading of this scene in *Glamour in Six Dimensions: Modernism and the Radiance of Form* (Ithaca: Cornell University Press, 2009) 129. She quotes David Levering Lewis from *When Harlem Was in Vogue* (New York: Penguin Books, 1997) 331: "The novel's ending is conceptually well done and exhibits its most skilled and unencumbered prose."

82. Thurman, *Infants of the Spring*, 280.

83. Elisa F. Glick, "Harlem's Queer Dandy: African-American Modernism and the Artifice of Blackness," *Modern Fiction Studies* 49.3 (Fall 2003) 423.

84. In addition to the elsewhere-referenced essays of Monica Miller, see Granville Ganter's "Decadence, Sexuality and the Bohemian Vision of Wallace Thurman," *MELUS* 28.2 (Summer 2003) 83–104; Glick, "Harlem's Queer Dandy," 414–44; Stephen Knadler, "Sweetback Style: Wallace Thurman and a Queer Harlem Renaissance," *Modern Fiction Studies*, 48.4 (Winter 2002) 899–936; Michael Cobb, "Insolent Racing, Rough Narrative: The Harlem Renaissance's Impolite Queers," *Callaloo* 3.1 (2000) 328–351; and Kevin J. Mumford's "Homosex Changes: Race, Cultural Geography, and the Emergence of the Gay," *American Quarterly* 48.3 (1996) 395–414.

85. Thurman, *Infants of the Spring*, 206.

86. Ibid., 206–207.

87. Ralph Ellison, Alfred Chester, and Vilma Howard, "Ralph Ellison: The Art of Fiction No. 8," *Paris Review* 8 (Spring 1955), www.theparisreview.org/interviews/5053/the-art-of-fiction-no-8-ralph-ellison.

88. This is the case in Amy Helene Kirschke's biography of Douglas, *Aaron Douglas: Art, Race and the Harlem Renaissance* (Jackson: University of Mississippi, 1995). Art historian Richard J. Powell is the exception who reads Douglas's skyscrapers more dynamically. But even Powell falls back on insisting on the skyscraper as a mere metaphor of "human striving, social progress, and spiritual transcendence" (114). "Paint That Thing! Aaron Douglas's Call to Modernism," *American Studies*, 46.1/2 (2010) 107–119.

89. Cited in Eleonore van Notten, *Wallace Thurman's Harlem Renaissance* (New York: Rodopi, 1995) 158–159.

90. Kirschke, *Aaron Douglas*, 83.

91. Ibid.

92. Thurman, *Infants of the Spring*, 20.

93. Ibid., 208.

94. Ibid., 284.

95. Scott Herring, "The Negro Artist and the Racial Manor: *Infants of the Spring* and the Conundrum of Publicity," *African-American Review* 35.4 (2001) 581–596.

96. Brown, *Glamour in Six Dimensions*, 132.

97. Hugh Ferriss, *The Metropolis of Tomorrow* (New York: Ives Washburn, 1929).

98. "William Sells Books to Harlem," *Publishers Weekly* (15 Apr 1928) 1623.

99. Caroline Goeser, *Picturing the New Negro: Harlem Renaissance Print Culture and Modern Black Identity* (Lawrence: University Press of Kansas, 2007) 137.

100. "William Sells Books to Harlem," *Publishers Weekly*.

101. See the following passage from the "Walking in the City" chapter of *The Practice of Everyday Life*: "The ordinary practitioners of the city live 'down below,' below the thresholds at which visibility begins. They walk—an elementary form of this experience of the city; they are walkers, *Wandersmänner*, whose bodies follow the thicks and thins of an urban 'text' they write without being able to read it. [. . .] The networks of these moving, intersecting writings compose a manifold writing that has neither author nor spectator, shaped out of fragments of trajectories and alterations of spaces: in relation to representations, it remains daily and indefinitely other" (93).

Chapter 5 · Feeling White in the Darkening City

1. Mary Borden, *Flamingo: A Novel* (New York: Doubleday, Page, 1927).

2. Louis Sullivan, *Kindergarten Chats (Revised 1918) and Other Writings* (New York: Wittenborn, Schultz, 1947) 49.

3. Alain Locke, "The New Negro," *The New Negro: Voices of the Harlem Renaissance*, ed. Alain Locke (New York: Albert and Charles Boni, 1925) 4.

4. F. Scott Fitzgerald, "Echoes of the Jazz Age," *Scribner's Magazine* (Nov 1931) 463.

5. Ibid.

6. Theodore Roosevelt, *The Naval War of 1812* (New York: G. P. Putnam's Sons, 1900) 35.

7. Theodore Roosevelt, "The Expansion of the White Races," *National Edition: The Works of Theodore Roosevelt*, ed. Hermann Hagedorn, vol. 18 (New York: Charles Scribner's Sons, 1926).

8. For more on changing mores of American masculinity at the turn of the century, see Gail Bederman, *Manliness and Civilization* (Chicago: University of Chicago Press, 1995).

9. Guy Emerson, *The New Frontier: A Study of the American Liberal Spirit, Its Frontier Origin, and Its Application to Modern Problems* (New York: Henry Holt, 1920).

10. William Allen Johnston, "Skyscrapers While You Wait," *Harper's Weekly* (11 June 1910) 9. See also architectural critic Randolph Sexton's related remarks claiming the skyscraper as "an American institution, planned to meet modern American requirements and serve modern American purposes, built of materials of modern manufacture in methods peculiarly American, has finally been made to express Americanism in its design" (2). *American Commercial Buildings of Today* (New York: New York Architectural Book Publishing, 1928).

11. For more on the history of skyscraper suicides, see George H. Douglas, *Skyscrapers: A Social History of the Very Tall Building in America* (New York: McFarland, 2004) 161–174; Max Page, *The City's End: Two Centuries of Fantasies, Fears, and Premonitions of New York's Destruction* (New Haven: Yale University Press, 2003) 61–100; and Joanna Merwood-Salisbury, *Chicago 1890: The Skyscraper and the Modern City* (Chicago: University of Chicago Press, 2009) 92–93.

12. Milo Milton Quaife, *The Development of Chicago, 1674–1914* (Chicago: Caxton Club, 1916) 254.

13. Edna Worthley Underwood, "Invitation to Judge the First Opportunity Contest," *Opportunity* (May 1925) 130. For more on American and transatlantic strands of primitivism, see Michael North, *The Dialectic of Modernism: Race, Language, and Twentieth Century Literature* (New York: Oxford University Press, 1994); Heather Hathaway, Josef JaYab, and Jeffrey Melnick, eds., *Race and the Modern Artist* (New York: Oxford University Press, 2003); and Sieglinde Lemke, *Primitivist Modernism: Black Culture and the Origins of Transatlantic Modernism* (New York: Oxford University Press, 1998).

14. Sianne Ngai, *Ugly Feelings* (Cambridge: Harvard University Press, 2007) 91.

15. For instance, see Ariela Freedman, "Mary Borden's *Forbidden Zone*: Women's Writing from No-Man's Land," *Modernism/Modernity* 9.1 (Jan 2002) 109–124; and Laurie Kaplan, "Deformities of the Great War: The Narratives of Mary Borden and Helen Zenna Smith," *Women and Language* 27.2 (Fall 2004) 35–44.

16. This bit of fiction mirrors Borden's own biography, since she, too, married a British diplomat.

17. Louis Kronenrenilk, "In 'Flamingo' a Sweeping Panorama of New York," *New York Times* (16 Oct 1927) BR2.

18. Borden, *Flamingo*, 18, 217.

19. Ibid., 2.

20. Ibid., 124, 102.

21. Ibid., 112, 113.

22. Ibid., 294.

23. Ibid., 18.

24. Ibid.

25. Ibid., 131.

26. Ibid., 7.

27. Borden, "Flamingo," manuscript draft, Howard Gottleib Archival Research Center, Boston University, Box 13, 21–22.

28. Borden, *Flamingo*, 18.

29. Ibid.

30. Ibid., 416.

31. Le Corbusier, *Toward an Architecture*, trans. John Goodman (Los Angeles: Getty Research Institute, 2007).

32. The definitive account of Le Corbusier's relationship to America and the details of his trip is Mardges Bacon's *Le Corbusier in America: Travels in the Land of the Timid* (Cambridge: MIT Press, 2001).

33. Ibid., 221. For more on Le Corbusier's specific interest in folk and vernacular cultures as extensions of his interest in the primitive, see also Francesco Passante, "The Vernacular, Modernism and Le Corbusier," *Journal of the Society of Architectural Historians* 56.4 (Dec 1997) 438–451; and Anne Cheng, *Second Skin: Josephine Baker & the Modern Surface* (New York: Oxford University Press, 2010). For more on primitivism in European art more broadly, see Simon Gikandi, "Picasso, Africa, and the Schemata of Difference," *Modernism/Modernity* 10.3 (2003) 455–480.

34. Le Corbusier, *When the Cathedrals Were White* (New York: McGraw-Hill, 1947) xiv, xv.

35. Ibid., 40.

36. Ibid., 158, 159.

37. Ibid.

38. Ibid., 160.

39. Ibid., 90.

40. Ibid., 161.

41. For some, but certainly not all, that has been written about this plan, see Jean-Louis Cohen, *Le Corbusier, 1887, 1965: The Lyricism of Architecture in the Machine Age* (Cologne: Taschen, 2005) 32–33; Bacon, *Le Corbusier in America*, 171; and John R. Gold, *The Experience of Modernism: Modern Architects and the Future City, 1928–53* (New York: Taylor & Francis) 41.

42. Mabel O. Wilson, "Dancing in the Dark: The Inscription of Blackness in Le Corbusier's Radiant City," *Places through the Body*, ed. Heidi J. Nast and Steve Pile (New York: Routledge, 1998).

43. For some of the literature regarding Le Corbusier's influence on American public housing, see Alexander Von Hoffman, "High Ambitions: The Past and Future of American Low-Income Housing Policy," *Housing Policy Debate* 7.3 (1996) 423–446; Richard Plunz, *A History of Housing in New York City* (New York: Columbia University Press, 2016); Jane Jacobs, *The Death and Life of Great American Cities* (New York: Vintage Books, 1961); H. Peter Oberlander and Eva Newbrun, *Houser: The Life and Work of Catherine Bauer* (Vancouver: University of British Columbia Press, 2000); and Bacon, *Le Corbusier in America*, chap. 6.

44. Borden, *Flamingo*, 165.

45. Ibid., 187.

46. Bruce Barnhart writes about the irony of Fitzgerald's association with the Jazz Age given the paucity of his writings on the subject of jazz, writing that "Fitzgerald's engagement with any music that could meaningfully be referred to as 'jazz' was in many ways quite shallow" (97). *Jazz in the Time of the Novel: The Temporal Politics of American Race and Culture* (Tuscaloosa: University of Alabama Press, 2013).

47. Walter Benn Michaels, *Our America: Nativism, Modernism, Pluralism* (Durham: Duke University Press, 1995).

48. F. Scott Fitzgerald, *The Great Gatsby* (New York: Scribner, 1999) 68–69.

49. Ibid., 68.

50. Ibid., 69.

51. Ibid.

52. Ibid., 74.

53. Ibid., 180.

54. Lothrop Stoddard, *The Rising Tide of Color against White World-Supremacy* (New York: Scribner's, 1922) 165.

55. C. Wright Mills, *White Collar: The American Middle Classes* (New York: Oxford University Press, 1951) 65.

56. Angel Kwollek-Folland, *Engendering Business: Men and Women in the Corporate Office, 1870–1930* (Baltimore: Johns Hopkins University Press, 1994).

57. Sociologist C. Wright Mills excludes the work of Faith Baldwin from his literary genealogy of the white-collar girl in his classic 1951 study, *White Collar: The American Middle Class*. He focuses instead on the "office girl" novels of male authors, including Christopher Morley, John Dos Passos, Booth Tarkington, and Sinclair Lewis. Recent cultural histories of the rise of the office have, however, rectified this slight. Nikil Saval's *Cubed: A Secret History of the Workplace* (New York: Doubleday, 2014) and Julie Berebitsky's *Sex and the Office* (New Haven: Yale University Press, 2012) consider Faith Baldwin's novels as narratives that chart the changing sexual politics of the modern office. Both Saval and Berebitsky note in their books that Baldwin's novels did not merely represent white-collar women but were written for white-collar women. They approach her novels affective guides for actual working women in this period who identified with these working heroines who looked and lived like them.

58. Ellen Lupton, *Mechanical Brides: Women and Machines from Home to Office* (New York: Princeton Architectural Press, 1996) 43.

59. Lisa M. Fine, *The Souls of the Skyscraper: Female Clerical Workers in Chicago, 1870–1930* (Philadelphia: Temple University Press, 1990).

60. Ibid., xvii.

61. Kwollek-Folland, *Engendering Business*, 33.

62. Fine, *Souls of the Skyscraper*, 34.

63. Jacqueline Jones, *Labor of Love, Labor of Sorrow: Black Women, Work, and the Family, from Slavery to the Present* (Philadelphia: Basic Books, 2010) 78.

64. Ibid., 148. See also Jacqueline Jones, *American Work: Four Centuries of Black and White Labor* (New York: Norton, 1998) 313.

65. Jones, *Labor of Love, Labor of Sorrow*, 178.

66. Faith Baldwin, *Weekend Marriage* (New York: Triangle, 1944) 95.

67. Ibid., 5.

68. Ibid., 209.

69. Ibid., 309.

70. Faith Baldwin, *Career by Proxy* (New York: Warner Paperback Library, 1939) 141.

71. Sheldon Cheney, *The New World Architecture* (New York: Tudor, 1930) 18.

72. Talbot Hamlin, *The American Spirit in Architecture* (New Haven: Yale University Press, 1926).

73. Carol Willis, *Form Follows Finance: Skyscrapers and Skylines in New York and Chicago* (New York: Princeton Architectural Press, 1995) 19.

74. Lee Galloway, *Office Management: Its Principles and Practice* (New York: Ronald Press, 1919) 90. As Alexandra Lange writes, "'Something is wrong,' Galloway quotes one office manager as saying, 'if a clerk, in seven seconds, cannot put his hand on any paper or article needed which is temporarily in his possession.' The operative words in this statement are *seven seconds*—time sheets accounted for every minute in the worker's day, with or without the manager's stopwatch—and *temporarily*, for nothing is the clerk's to keep." Alexandra Lange, "White Collar Corbusier: From the Casier to the cités d'affaires," *Grey Room* 9 (Fall 200) 58–79.

75. Faith Baldwin, *Skyscraper (Femme Fatales: Women Write Pulp)* (New York: Feminist Press at CUNY, 2003) 13–14.

76. For a brief reading of this novel, which is the lead-in to a deeper analysis of its film adaptation, *Skyscraper Souls*, see Lawrence Rainey, "Office Politics: *Skyscraper* (1931) and *Skyscraper Souls* (1932)," *Critical Quarterly* 49.4 (Winter 2007) 71–88.

77. Galloway, *Office Management*, 188.

78. Ibid., 447. In a different office manual by Henry Leffingwell, another office Taylorite, the author rails against using humanist language to discuss the office's functionality. He writes that approaching the workplace in terms of the "good" or "fair" treatment of employees was "superfluous," preferring "the scientific method" for "handling human beings and their work." In this vein, he insists elsewhere in the manual that "excitement of any kind is a condition that should be guarded against" because "the efficiency of an office, for example, can be utterly destroyed, for the time being, by such a common accident as the fainting of a girl." The girl's fainting is not treated as a matter of health and safety or employee morale but as an example of a malfunctioning operating line. See Henry Leffingwell, *Office Management: Principles and Practice* (New York: A. W. Shaw, 1926) 42.

79. Baldwin, *Weekend Marriage*, 310.

80. Karl Marx, *Capital*, vol. 1 (New York: Penguin Classics, 1990) 342.

81. While Marx extensively describes the alienation of physical laborers in the first volume of *Capital*, the white-collar worker's increasing sense of alienation within the expanding professional-managerial class during the early twentieth century was something Marx wrote little about. Later Marxist critics such as C. Wright Mills and Barbara and John Ehrenreich begin to work out a theory of class, alienation, and the professional managerial class starting around the midcentury. See C. Wright Mills, *White Collar: The American Middle Classes* (New York: Oxford University Press, 1951); and Barbara and John Ehrenreich's essay "The Professional-Managerial Class," *Between Labor and Capital*, ed. Pat Walker (Boston: South End Press, 1979).

82. Eva Illouz, *Cold Intimacies: The Making of Emotional Capitalism* (Cambridge: Polity Press, 2007) 5.

83. Ibid., 5.

84. Ibid., 16.

85. Baldwin, *Career by Proxy*, 11.

86. Baldwin, *Skyscraper*, 31.

87. Faith Baldwin, *Men Are Such Fools!* (New York: Sun Dial Press, 1936) 55–56.

88. Lauren Berlant, *The Female Complaint: The Unfinished Business of Sentimentality in American Culture* (Durham: Duke University Press, 2008) 2.

89. Ibid., 2.

90. Ibid., 5.

91. Ibid., 10.

92. Faith Baldwin, *The Office Wife* (Philadelphia: Triangle Books, 1929) x.

93. Jones, *Labor of Love, Labor of Sorrow*, 133.

94. All citations from this scene from Baldwin, *Career by Proxy*, 192–193.

95. Baldwin, *Weekend Marriage*, 285.

96. Alexander Graham Bell, "Is Race Suicide Possible?," *Journal of Heredity* 11.9 (11 Nov 1920) 340.

Epilogue

1. Ira Wells, *Fighting Words: Polemics and Social Change in Literary Naturalism* (Tuscaloosa: University of Alabama Press, 2013) 128.

2. Ayn Rand, *The Fountainhead* (New York: Signet, 1996) 37.

3. The abusive labor practices on skyscraper work sites in Dubai have been detailed in a number of places. See Shaheen Pasha, "Dubai's Towering Skyscrapers Are Built by a 'Horrifically Exploitative Labor System,'" *Quartz* 27 (May 2013), http://qz.com/88278 /dubais-towering-skyscrapers-are-built-by-a-horrifically-exploitative-labor-system/. A 2011 *Guardian* article talks about these abuses as "a place where the worst of western capitalism and the worst of Gulf Arab racism meet in a horrible vortex." See Nesrine Malik, "Dubai's Skyscrapers, Stained by the Blood of Migrant Workers," *Guardian* (27 May 2011), http://www.theguardian.com/commentisfree/2011/may/27/dubai-migrant-worker -deaths.

4. Brendan O'Connor, "The Sad, True Story of the Ground Zero Mosque," *The Awl* (1 Oct 2015), http://www.theawl.com/2015/10/the-sad-true-story-of-the-ground-zero-mosque.

5. Dianne Harris, *Little White Houses: How the Postwar Home Constructed Race in America* (Minneapolis: University of Minnesota Press, 2013) 1.

6. The quote in full: "A boy last week, he was sixteen, in San Francisco, told me on television—thank God we got him to talk, maybe somebody thought to listen. He said, 'I got no country. I got no flag.' Now, he's only 16 years old, and I couldn't say, 'you do.' I don't have any evidence to prove that he does. They were tearing down his house, because San Francisco is engaging . . . most cities are engaged . . . in something called urban renewal, which means moving Negroes out: it means Negro removal, that is what it means. The federal government is an accomplice to this fact." See James Mossman, "Race, Hate, Sex and Colour: A Conversation with James Baldwin and Colin MacInnes," *Conversations with James Baldwin*, ed. Fred R. Standley and Louis H. Pratt (Jackson: University Press of Mississippi, 1989) 41–42.

7. For more on this history, as well as the creative strategies residents of these neighborhoods under siege developed to combat them, see Eric Avila, *The Folklore of the Freeway: Race and Revolt in the Modernist City* (Minneapolis: University of Minnesota Press, 2014).

8. Reinhold Martin, Jacob Moore, and Susanne Schindler, eds., *The Art of Inequality: Architecture, Housing and Real Estate: A Provisional Report* (New York: The Temple Hoyne Buell Center for the Study of American Architecture, 2015) 60.

9. Just as, as Katherine G. Bristol argues, there was nothing inherent within the form of the densely vertical public housing projects emerging in the midcentury that made them prone to the kinds of physical and social deterioration associated with these

spaces. Such a focus on the architecture alone, she writes, "denies the existence of larger problems endemic to St. Louis' public housing program. By attributing more causal power to architecture than to flawed policies, crises in the local economy, or to class oppression and racism, the myth conceals the existence of contextual factors structuring the architects' decisions and fabricates a central role for architecture in the success or failure of public housing. It places the architect in the position of authority over providing low-income housing for the poor." Katherine G. Bristol, "The Pruitt-Igoe Myth," *Journal of Architectural Education* (May 1991) 163–171.

Abel, Elizabeth. *The Visual Politics of Jim Crow*. Berkeley: University of California Press, 2010.

Abeln, Paul. *William Dean Howells and the Ends of Realism*. London: Routledge, 2005.

Adams, Henry. *The Education of Henry Adams*. Boston: Houghton and Mifflin, 1918.

Ahmed, Sara. "Declarations of Whiteness: The Non-Performativity of Anti-Racism." *Borderlands* 3.2 (2004).

———. *Queer Phenomenology: Orientations, Objects, Others*. Durham: Duke University Press, 2006.

Alexiou, Alice Sparberg. *The Flatiron: The New York Landmark and the Incomparable City That Arose with It*. New York: St. Martin's Griffin, 2013.

Andrew, David S. *Louis Sullivan and the Polemics of Modern Architecture: The Present against the Past*. Urbana: University of Illinois Press, 1985.

Avila, Eric. *The Folklore of the Freeway: Race and Revolt in the Modernist City*. Minneapolis: University of Minnesota Press, 2014.

Bacon, Mardges. *Le Corbusier in America: Travels in the Land of the Timid*. Cambridge: MIT Press, 2001.

Baldwin, Faith. *Career by Proxy*. New York: Warner Paperback Library, 1939.

———. *Men Are Such Fools!* New York: Sun Dial Press, 1936.

———. *The Office Wife*. Philadelphia: Triangle Books, 1929.

———. *Skyscraper (Femme Fatales: Women Write Pulp)*. New York: Feminist Press at CUNY, 2003.

———. *Weekend Marriage*. New York: Triangle, 1944.

Baldwin, James. *Notes of a Native Son*. Boston: Beacon Press, 1955.

Baldwin, Louis Fremont. *From Negro to Caucasian, or How the Ethiopian Is Changing His Skin*. San Francisco: Pilot Publishing, 1929.

Barnhart, Bruce. *Jazz in the Time of the Novel: The Temporal Politics of American Race and Culture*. Tuscaloosa: University of Alabama Press, 2013.

Barth, Gunther. *City People: The Rise of Modern City Culture in Nineteenth-Century America*. Oxford: Oxford University Press, 1980.

Barton, Craig, ed. *Sites of Memory: Perspectives on Architecture and Race*. New York: Princeton Architectural Press, 2001.

Bascomb, Neal. *Higher: A Historic Race to the Sky and the Making of a City.* New York: Broadway Books, 2004.

Bederman, Gail. *Manliness and Civilization.* Chicago: University of Chicago Press, 1995.

Bell, Alexander Graham. "Is Race Suicide Possible?" *Journal of Heredity* 11.9 (11 Nov 1920): 339–341.

Bender, Thomas. *The Unfinished City: New York and the Metropolitan Idea.* New York: New Press distributed by W. W. Norton, 2002.

Berebitsky, Julie. *Sex and the Office.* New Haven: Yale University Press, 2012.

Berger, Martin. *Sight Unseen: Whiteness and American Visual Culture.* Berkeley: University of California Press, 2005.

Berlant, Lauren. *The Female Complaint: The Unfinished Business of Sentimentality in American Culture.* Durham: Duke University Press, 2008.

Bernstein, Robin. *Racial Innocence: Performing American Childhood from Slavery to Civil Rights.* New York: New York University Press, 2011.

Bierce, Ambrose. "Sharp Criticism of Mr. Howells." *New York Times* (23 May 1892): 5.

Blackall, C. H. "The Legitimate Design for the Casing of Steel-Skeleton Structures," *Proceedings of the 37th Annual Convention: American Institute of Architects.* Providence: R. A. Johnson, 1898.

Blair, Sara. *Henry James and the Writing of Race and Nation.* New York: Cambridge University Press, 1996.

Blake, Angela. *How New York Became American, 1890–1924.* Baltimore: Johns Hopkins University Press, 2006.

Bletter, Rosemarie Haag. "The Invention of the Skyscraper: Notes on Its Diverse Histories." *Assemblage* 2 (Feb 1987): 110–117.

Bluestone, Daniel. *Constructing Chicago.* New Haven: Yale University Press, 1993.

Bodenheim, Max. "North Clark Street, Chicago." Quoted in "Introducing Irony." *The Measure: A Journal of Poetry* 10 (Dec 1921): 17–18.

Boehm, Lisa Krissoff, and Steven H. Corey, eds. *America's Urban History.* New York: Routledge, 2015.

Booraem, H. Tolder. "Significance of Architectural Form." *Architectural Record* 25.3 (Mar 1909): 193–202.

Borden, Mary. *Flamingo: A Novel.* New York: Doubleday, Page, 1927.

———. "Flamingo." Manuscript Draft. Howard Gottleib Archival Research Center, Boston University, Box 13.

Boyer, Paul. *Urban Masses and Moral Order in America, 1820–1920.* Cambridge: Harvard University Press, 1978.

Bradford, Sarah, and Carl Condit. *Rise of the New York Skyscraper: 1865–1913.* New Haven: Yale University Press, 1996.

Bragdon, Claude. "Architecture in the United States: III. The Skyscraper." *Architectural Record* 26.2 (1909): 84–96.

Bramen, Carrie Tirado. "William Dean Howells and the Failure of the Urban Picturesque." *New England Quarterly* 73.1 (Mar 2000): 82–99.

Bristol, Katherine G. "The Pruitt-Igoe Myth." *Journal of Architectural Education* (May 1991): 163–171.

Brodkin, Karen. *How Jews Became White Folks and What That Says about Race in America.* New Brunswick: Rutgers University Press, 1998.

Brody, Jennifer DeVere. "Clare Kendry's 'True' Colors: Race and Class Conflict in Nella Larsen's *Passing*." *Callaloo* 15.4 (Fall 1992): 1053–1065.

Brooks, Daphne. *Bodies in Dissent: Spectacular Performances of Race and Freedom, 1850–1910*. Durham: Duke University Press, 2006.

Brown, Adrienne. "The Black Skyscraper." *American Literature* 85.3 (2013): 541–561.

Brown, Bill. *A Sense of Things: The Object Matter of American Literature*. Chicago: University of Chicago Press, 2003.

Brown, Judith. *Glamour in Six Dimensions: Modernism and the Radiance of Form*. Ithaca: Cornell University Press, 2009.

Bruegmann, Robert. *The Architects and the City: Holabird & Roche of Chicago, 1880–1918*. Chicago: University of Chicago Press, 1997.

———. "Myth of the Chicago School." *Chicago Architecture: Histories, Revisions, Alternatives*, edited by Charles Waldheim and Katerina Ruedi Ray, 15–29. Chicago: University of Chicago Press, 2005.

Brunsma, David L., and Kerry Anne Rockquemore. "The End of Race?" *Race and Ethnicity: Across Time, Space, and Disciplines*, edited by Rodney D. Coates, 73–92. Boston: Brill, 2004.

Buchanan, John T. "How to Assimilate the Foreign Element into Our Population." *Forum* 32 (1901–1902): 689–694.

Cabot, Elizabeth, and Cary Agassiz, eds. *Louis Agassiz: His Life and Correspondence*. Boston: Houghton, Mifflin, 1893.

Caparn, H. A. "The Riddle of the Tall Building: Has the Skyscraper a Place in American Architecture?" *Craftsman* 10 (July 1906): 476–488.

Carroll, Hamilton. *Affirmative Reaction: New Formations of White Masculinity*. Durham: Duke University Press, 2011.

Castronovo, Russ. *Beautiful Democracy*. Chicago: University of Chicago Press, 2007.

Celestin, Roger, and Elaine DalMolin. *France from 1851 to the Present: Universalism in Crisis*. New York: Palgrave Macmillan, 2007.

"Census of 1920 Shows Less Increase than in Previous Decade." *New York Times* (15 May 1921): 85.

Chase, Stuart. "The Future of the Great City." *Harper's Magazine* 160 (Dec 1929): 82–90.

Cheney, Sheldon. *The New World Architecture*. New York: Longmans, Green, 1930.

Cheng, Anne. *Second Skin: Josephine Baker & the Modern Surface*. New York: Oxford University Press, 2010.

Cheng, Irene. "Race and Architectural Geometry: Thomas Jefferson's Octagons." *J19: The Journal of Nineteenth-Century Americanists* 3.1 (Spring 2015): 121–130.

Cherniavsky, Eva. *Incorporations: Race, Nation, and the Body Politics of Capital*. Minneapolis: University of Minnesota Press, 2006.

Childe, Cromwell. "The Structural Workers." *Frank Leslie's Popular Monthly* 52.3 (July 1901): 262–274.

Clark, W. C., and J. L. Kingston, *The Skyscraper: A Study in the Economic Height of Modern Office Buildings*. New York: American Institute of Steel Construction, 1930.

Clarke, Michael Tavel. *These Days of Large Things: The Culture of Size in America, 1865–1930*. Ann Arbor: University of Michigan Press, 2007.

Clayton, Owen. "London Eyes: William Dean Howells and the Shift to Instant Photography." *Nineteenth-Century Literature* 65.3 (2010): 374–394.

Cobb, Michael. "Insolent Racing, Rough Narrative: The Harlem Renaissance's Impolite Queers." *Callaloo* 3.1 (2000): 328–351.

Cogdell, Christina. *Eugenic Design: Streamlining America in the 1930s.* Philadelphia: University of Pennsylvania Press, 2004.

Coghlan, J. Michelle. "Aftertastes of Ruin: Uncanny Sites of Memory in Henry James's Paris." *Henry James Review* 33.3 (Fall 2012): 239–246.

Cohen, Jean Louis. *Le Corbusier, 1887, 1965: The Lyricism of Architecture in the Machine Age.* Cologne: Taschen, 2005.

Cohen, Lizabeth. *Making a New Deal: Industrial Workers in Chicago, 1919–1939.* New York: Cambridge University Press, 2008.

Commons, John. *Race and Immigrants in America.* London: Macmillan Company, 1907.

Condit, Carl. *The Chicago School of Architecture: A History of Commercial and Public Building in the Chicago Area, 1875–1925.* Chicago: University of Chicago Press, 1964.

———. "The Two Centuries of Technical Evolution Underlying the Skyscraper." *The Second Century of the Skyscraper,* edited by Lynn S. Beedle, 11–24. New York: Springer, 1988.

Crary, Jonathan. *Suspensions of Perception: Attention, Spectacle, and Modern Culture.* Cambridge: MIT Press, 2000.

———. *Techniques of the Observer: On Vision and Modernity in the Nineteenth Century.* Cambridge: MIT Press, 1993.

Croly, Herbert. "An American Architecture." *Architectural Record* 23.2 (Feb 1908): 111–122.

Cuvier, George, and Edward Griffith. *The Animal Kingdom Arranged in Conformity with Its Organization.* Vol. 8. London: Whittaker, Treacher, 1929.

Davidson, Rob. *The Master and the Dean: The Literary Criticism of Henry James and William Dean Howells.* Columbia: University of Missouri Press, 2005.

Davis, Charles. "Viollet-le-Duc and the Body: The Metaphorical Integrations of Race and Style in Structural Rationalism." *Architectural Research Quarterly,* 14.4 (2010): 341–348.

Davis, F. James. *Who Is Black?: One Nation's Definition.* State College: Pennsylvania State University Press, 1991.

Davis, Thadious. *Nella Larsen: Novelist of the Harlem Renaissance.* Baton Rouge: Louisiana State University Press, 1993.

Deamer, Peggy. *Architecture and Capitalism: 1845 to the Present.* New York: Routledge, 2013.

De Certeau, Michel. *The Practice of Everyday Life,* translated by Steven F. Rendell. Berkeley: University of California Press, 2011.

Degler, Carl. *In Search of Human Nature: The Decline and Revival of Darwinism in American Social Thought.* New York: Oxford University Press, 1991.

Den Tandt, Christophe. *The Urban Sublime in American Literary Naturalism.* Urbana: University of Illinois Press, 1998.

Devine, Edward T. *Misery and Its Causes.* New York: Macmillan, 1920.

Dickerson, Dennis C. *Out of the Crucible: Black Steelworkers in Western Pennsylvania, 1875–1980.* Albany: State University of New York Press, 1986.

Dodds, George, and Robert Tanner, eds. *Body and Building: Essays on the Changing Relation of Body and Architecture*. Cambridge: MIT Press, 2002.

Dosch, Arno. "Just Wops." *Everybody's Magazine* 25.5 (Nov 1911): 579–589.

Douglas, Ann. *Terrible Honesty: Mongrel Manhattan in the 1920s*. New York: Farrar, Straus and Giroux, 1995.

Douglas, George H. *Skyscrapers: A Social History of the Very Tall Building in America*. New York: McFarland, 2004.

Drake, St. Clair, and Horace Cayton. *Black Metropolis: A Study of Negro Life in a Northern City*. Chicago: University of Chicago Press, 1945.

Du Bois, W. E. B. "Books, review of *Nigger Heaven*." *Crisis* 33 (Dec 1926): 81–82.

———. "The Browsing Reader, review of *Home to Harlem*." *Crisis* 35 (June 1928): 202.

———. "The Browsing Reader, review of *The Walls of Jericho*." *Crisis* 35 (June 1928): 374.

———. "The Criteria of Negro Art." *Crisis* 32 (Oct 1926): 290–297.

———. *Darkwater: Voices from the Veil*. New York: Harcourt, Brace and Howe, 1920.

———. *The Philadelphia Negro: A Social Study*. Philadelphia: University of Pennsylvania Press, 1899.

———. "The Princess Steel." W. E. B. Du Bois Papers (MS 312). Special Collections & University Archives. University of Massachusetts Amherst Libraries.

———. "Sociology Hesitant." *boundary 2* 27.3 (Fall 2000): 37–44.

———. *The Souls of Black Folk*. Chicago: A. C. McClurg, 1903.

———. "W. E. B. Du Bois's 'The Princess Steel.'" *PMLA* 130.3 (May 2015): 819–829.

DuCille, Anne. *The Coupling Convention*. New York: Oxford University Press, 1993.

Dyer, Richard. *White: Essays on Race and Culture*. New York: Routledge, 1997.

Eastman, Max. *Venture*. New York: Boni & Liveright, 1927.

Ehrenreich, Barbara, and John Ehrenreich. "The Professional-Managerial Class." *Between Labor and Capital*, edited by Pat Walker, 5–45. Boston: South End Press, 1979.

Ellison, Ralph, Alfred Chester, and Vilma Howard. "Ralph Ellison: The Art of Fiction No. 8." *Paris Review* 8 (Spring 1955). www.theparisreview.org/interviews/5053/the-art-of-fiction-no-8-ralph-ellison.

Emerson, Guy. *The New Frontier: A Study of the American Liberal Spirit, Its Frontier Origin, and Its Application to Modern Problems*. New York: Henry Holt, 1920.

England, George Allan. *Darkness and Dawn*. Boston: Small, Maynard, 1914.

English, Daylanne. *Unnatural Selections: Eugenics in American Modernism and the Harlem Renaissance*. Chapel Hill: University of North Carolina Press, 2004.

Entin, Joseph. "'Unhuman Humanity': Bodies of the Urban Poor and the Collapse of Realist Legibility." *Novel: A Forum on Fiction* 34.3 (Summer 2001): 313–337.

Esteve, Mary. *The Aesthetics and Politics of the Crowd in American Literature*. Cambridge: Cambridge University Press, 2003.

Fabian, Ann. *The Skull Collectors: Race, Science, and America's Unburied Dead*. Chicago: University of Chicago Press, 2010.

Farber, Paul Lawrence. *Mixing Races: From Scientific Racism to Modern Evolutionary Ideas*. Baltimore: Johns Hopkins University Press, 2010.

Fenske, Gail. *The Skyscraper and the City: The Woolworth Building and the Making of Modern New York*. Chicago: University of Chicago Press, 2008.

Ferree, Barr. "An American Style of Architecture." *Architectural Record* 1 (July 1891): 39–45.

Ferriss, Hugh. *The Metropolis of Tomorrow.* New York: Ives Washburn, 1929.

Fields, Barbara, and Karen Fields. *Racecraft: The Soul of Inequality in American Life.* London: Verso, 2012.

Fine, Lisa M. *The Souls of the Skyscraper: Female Clerical Workers in Chicago, 1870–1930.* Philadelphia: Temple University Press, 1990.

Fisher, Rudolph. *The City of Refuge: The Collected Stories of Rudolph Fisher,* edited by John McCluskey. Columbia: University of Missouri Press, 2008.

Fitzgerald, F. Scott. "Echoes of the Jazz Age." *Scribner's Magazine* (Nov 1931): 459–464.

———. *The Great Gatsby.* New York: Scribner, 1999.

Fleetwood, Nicole. *Troubling Vision: Performance, Visuality, and Blackness.* Chicago: University of Chicago Press, 2011.

Flowers, Benjamin. *Skyscraper: The Politics and Power of Building New York City in the Twentieth Century.* Philadelphia: University of Pennsylvania Press, 2009.

Forman, Allan. "Some Adopted Americans." *American Magazine* 9.1 (1888): 46–53.

Foucault, Michel. *Discipline and Punish: The Birth of the Prison,* translated by Alan Sheridan. New York: Vintage Books, 1995.

Freedman, Ariela. "Mary Borden's *Forbidden Zone*: Women's Writing from No-Man's Land." *Modernism/Modernity* 9.1 (Jan 2002): 109–124.

Fuller, Henry Blake. *The Cliff-Dwellers.* New York: Harper & Brothers, 1893.

Fusco, Coco. "Racial Time, Racial Marks, Racial Metaphors." *Only Skin Deep: Changing Visions of the American Self,* edited by Coco Fusco and Brian Wallis, 13–48. New York: Harry N. Abrams, 2003.

Galloway, Lee. *Office Management: Its Principles and Practice.* New York: Ronald Press, 1919.

Ganter, Granville. "Decadence, Sexuality and the Bohemian Vision of Wallace Thurman." *MELUS* 28.2 (Summer 2003): 83–104.

Gibbs, Kenneth Turney. *Business Architectural Imagery in America, 1870–1930.* Ann Arbor: UMI Research Press, 1984.

Gikandi, Simon. "Picasso, Africa, and the Schemata of Difference." *Modernism/Modernity* 10.3 (2003): 455–480.

———. *Slavery and the Culture of Taste.* Princeton: Princeton University Press, 2011.

Gillman, Susan, and Alys Weinbaum, eds. "Introduction." *Next to the Color Line: Gender, Sexuality and W. E. B. Du Bois,* 1–36. Minneapolis: University of Minnesota Press, 2007.

Gilroy, Paul. *Against Race.* Cambridge: Harvard University Press, 2000.

Glaab, Charles N. *The American City: A Documentary History.* Homewood: Dorsey Press, 1963.

Gleason, William. *Sites Unseen: Architecture, Race, and American Literature.* New York: New York University Press, 2011.

Glick, Elisa F. "Harlem's Queer Dandy: African-American Modernism and the Artifice of Blackness." *Modern Fiction Studies* 49.3 (Fall 2003): 414–444.

Goble, Mark. *Beautiful Circuits: Modernism and the Mediated Life.* New York: Columbia University Press, 2010.

Goeser, Caroline. *Picturing the New Negro: Harlem Renaissance Print Culture and Modern Black Identity.* Lawrence: University Press of Kansas, 2007.

Gold, John R. *The Experience of Modernism: Modern Architects and the Future City, 1928–53*. New York: Taylor & Francis, 2013.

Goldberger, Paul. *Skyscraper*. New York: Knopf, 1983.

González, Jennifer. "Morphologies: Race as Visual Technology." *Only Skin Deep: Changing Visions of the American Self*, edited by Coco Fusco and Brian Wallis, 379–393. New York: Harry N. Abrams, 2003.

Gould, Stephen Jay. *The Mismeasure of Man*. New York: Norton, 1996.

Grant, Madison. *The Passing of the Great Race*. New York: Charles Scribner's Sons, 1916.

Griffin, Farah Jasmine. *"Who Set You Flowin'?": The African-American Migration Narrative*. New York: Oxford University Press, 1996.

Grosz, Elizabeth. "Bodies-Cities." *Sexuality & Space*, edited by Beatriz Colomina, 241–253. New York: Princeton Architectural Press, 1996.

Gruen, J. Philip. *Manifest Destinations: Cities and Tourists in the Nineteenth-Century American West*. Norman: University of Oklahoma Press, 2014.

Guglielmo, Thomas A. *White on Arrival: Italians, Race, Color, and Power in Chicago, 1890–1945*. New York: Oxford University Press, 2004.

Hale, Grace Elizabeth. *Making Whiteness: The Culture of Segregation in the South, 1890–1940*. New York: Vintage, 1998.

Hales, Peter Bacon. *Silver Cities: Photographing American Urbanization, 1839–1939*. Albuquerque: University of New Mexico Press, 1984.

Hall, Peter. *Cities of Tomorrow: An Intellectual History of Urban Planning and Design in the Twentieth Century*. Oxford: Basil Blackwell, 1988.

Haller, John S. *Outcasts from Evolution: Scientific Attitudes of Racial Inferiority, 1859–1900*. Carbondale: Southern Illinois University Press, 1996.

Halttunen, Karen. *Confidence Men and Painted Women: A Study of Middle-Class Culture in America, 1830–1870*. New Haven: Yale University Press, 1986.

Hamlin, Talbot. *The American Spirit in Architecture*. New Haven: Yale University Press, 1926.

Harris, Dianne. *Little White Houses: How the Postwar Home Constructed Race in America*. Minneapolis: Minnesota University Press, 2013.

———, ed. "Race, Space, and the Destabilization of Practice." *Landscape Journal* 26.1 (2007): iv–174.

Harris, Dianne, and D. Fairchild Ruggles, eds. *Sites Unseen: Landscape and Vision*. Pittsburgh: University of Pittsburgh Press, 2007.

Hathaway, Heather, Josef JaYab, and Jeffrey Melnick, eds. *Race and the Modern Artist*. New York: Oxford University Press, 2003.

Hayden, Dolores. "Skyscraper Seduction / Skyscraper Rape." *Heresies* 1 (May 1977): 108–115.

Hendrix, John Shannon. *The Contradiction between Form and Function in Architecture*. New York: Routledge, 2013.

Henry, O. "Psyche and the Skyscraper." *New York World Sunday Magazine* 15 (Jan 1905): 3.

Herring, Scott. "The Negro Artist and the Racial Manor: *Infants of the Spring* and the Conundrum of Publicity." *African-American Review* 35.4 (2001): 581–596.

Hinshaw, John. *Steel and Steelworkers: Race and Class Struggle in Twentieth-Century Pittsburgh*. Albany: State University of New York Press, 2002.

Hobbs, Allyson. *A Chosen Exile: A History of Racial Passing in American Life*. Cambridge: Harvard University, 2014.

Hochman, Barbara. *"Uncle Tom's Cabin" and the Reading Revolution: Race, Literacy, Childhood, and Fiction, 1851–1911*. Amherst: University of Massachusetts Press, 2011.

Hoffmann, Donald. *Frank Lloyd Wright, Louis Sullivan, and the Skyscraper*. New York: Dover, 1998.

Hofstadter, Richard. *Social Darwinism in American Thought*. Boston: Beacon Press, 1992.

Holl, Steven, Juhani Pallasmaa, and Alberto Perez-Gomez, eds. *Questions of Perception: Phenomenology of Architecture*. New York: William K. Stout, 2007.

Holland, Sharon. *The Erotic Life of Racism*. Durham: Duke University Press, 2012.

Horkheimer, Max. *Dawn & Decline: Notes 1926–1931 and 1950–1969*, translated by Michael Shaw. New York: Seabury Press, 1978.

Howells, William Dean. *Criticism and Fiction*. New York: Harper & Brothers, 1891.

———. "Editor's Easy Chair." *Harper's Monthly* (Feb 1909): 479–481.

———. *Imaginary Interviews*. New York: Harper & Brothers, 1910.

———. *An Imperative Duty*. New York: Harper & Brothers, 1891.

———. *The Letters of an Altrurian Traveler*. Gainesville: Scholars' Facsimiles & Reprints, 1961.

———. *Literary Friends and Acquaintance: A Personal Retrospect of American Authorship*. New York: Harper & Brothers, 1910.

———. *The World of Chance*. New York: Harper, 1893.

Hua, Hsuan. "Post-James and the Question of Scale." *Henry James Review* 24.3 (2003): 233–243.

"The Human Ant Heap." *Independent* (20 Aug 1920): 221.

Hunter, Gardner. "A Common-Sense Heroine." *Youth's Companion* (29 July 1915).

———. "A Modern Cliff-Dweller's Experience." *Youth's Companion* (26 Apr 1906).

Hunter, Robert. *Tenement Conditions in Chicago*. Chicago: City Homes Association, 1901.

Ignatiev, Noel. *How the Irish Became White*. New York: Routledge, 1995.

Illouz, Eva. *Cold Intimacies: The Making of Emotional Capitalism*. Cambridge: Polity Press, 2007.

Jacobs, Jane. *The Death and Life of Great American Cities*. New York: Vintage Books, 1961.

Jacobson, Matthew Frye. *Whiteness of a Different Color: European Immigrants and the Alchemy of Race*. Cambridge: Harvard University Press, 1999.

James, Henry. *The American Scene*. London: Chapman and Hall, 1907.

———. *The New York Stories of Henry James*. New York: New York Review of Books, 2006.

Jameson, Fredric. *Archaeologies of the Future: The Desire Called Utopia and Other Science Fictions*. London: Verso, 2011.

———. *Postmodernism, or, the Cultural Logic of Late Capitalism*. Durham: Duke University Press, 1990.

Jay, Martin. *Downcast Eyes: The Denigration of Vision in Twentieth-Century French Thought*. Berkeley: University of California Press, 1994.

Johnson, James Weldon. *Along the Way: The Autobiography of James Weldon Johnson*. New York: Viking Press, 1933.

———. *Autobiography of an Ex-Colored Man*. New York: Hill and Wang, 1991.

———. *The Book of American Negro Poetry*. New York: Harcourt, Brace and Company, 1922.

———. *The Book of American Negro Poetry*. Rev. ed. New York: Harcourt, Brace, 1931.

Johnston, William Allen. "Skyscrapers While You Wait." *Harper's Weekly* (11 June 1910): 9–10.

Jones, Jacqueline. *American Work: Four Centuries of Black and White Labor*. New York: W. W. Norton, 1998.

———. *Labor of Love, Labor of Sorrow: Black Women, Work, and the Family, from Slavery to the Present*. Philadelphia: Basic Books, 2010.

Joshi, S. T. *The Modern Weird Tale*. Jefferson: McFarland, 2001.

Judy, Ronald A. T. "Introduction: On W. E. B. Du Bois and Hyperbolic Thinking." *boundary 2* 27.3 (Fall 2000): 1–35.

Kaplan, Amy. *The Anarchy of Empire in the Making of U.S. Culture*. Cambridge: Harvard University Press, 2005.

———. *The Social Construction of American Realism*. Chicago: University of Chicago Press, 1988.

Kaplan, Laurie. "Deformities of the Great War: The Narratives of Mary Borden and Helen Zenna Smith." *Women and Language* 27.2 (Fall 2004): 35–44.

Keresztesi, Rita. *Strangers at Home: American Ethnic Modernism between the World Wars*. Lincoln: University of Nebraska Press, 2005.

Kerr, Robert. "The Problem of National American Architecture." *Architectural Record* 3.2 (Oct–Dec 1893): 121–132.

Kirschke, Amy Helene. *Aaron Douglas: Art, Race and the Harlem Renaissance*. Jackson: University of Mississippi, 1995.

Klamen, Michael. *Brown v. Board of Education and the Civil Rights Movement*. New York: Oxford University Press, 2007.

Knadler, Stephen. "Sweetback Style: Wallace Thurman and a Queer Harlem Renaissance." *Modern Fiction Studies* 48.4 (Winter 2002): 899–936.

Knox, Robert. *The Races of Men: A Fragment*. Philadelphia: Lea & Blanchard, 1862.

Koolhaas, Rem. *Delirious New York: A Retrospective Manifesto for Manhattan*. New York: Monacelli Press, 1997.

Korom, Joseph J., Jr. *Skyscraper Facades of the Gilded Age: Fifty-One Extravagant Designs, 1875–1910*. New York: McFarland, 2013.

Kronenrenilk, Louis. "In 'Flamingo' a Sweeping Panorama of New York." *New York Times* (16 Oct 1927): BR2.

Kwollek-Folland, Angel. *Engendering Business: Men and Women in the Corporate Office, 1870–1930*. Baltimore: Johns Hopkins University Press, 1994.

Lange, Alexandra. "White Collar Corbusier: From the Casier to the cités d'affaires." *Grey Room* 9 (Fall 2002): 58–79.

Largent, Mark. *Breeding Contempt: The History of Coerced Sterilization in the United States*. New Brunswick: Rutgers University Press, 2009.

Larsen, Nella. *Passing: A Norton Critical Edition*, edited by Carla Kaplan. New York: W. W. Norton, 2007.

Larson, Barbara, and Fae Brauer, eds. *The Art of Evolution: Darwin, Darwinisms, and Visual Culture*. Hanover: Dartmouth University Press, 2009.

Larson, Gerald R., and Roula Mouroudellis Geraniotis. "Toward a Better Understanding of the Evolution of the Iron Skeleton Frame in Chicago." *Journal of the Society of Architectural Historians* 46.1 (Mar 1987): 39–48.

Le Corbusier. *Toward an Architecture*, translated by John Goodman. Los Angeles: Getty Research Institute, 2007.

———. *When the Cathedrals Were White*. New York: McGraw-Hill, 1947.

Lees, Andrew. *Cities Perceived: Urban Society in European and American Thought, 1820–1940*. Manchester: Manchester University Press, 1985.

Leffingwell, Henry. *Office Management: Principles and Practice*. New York: A. W. Shaw, 1926.

Leinster, Murray. "The Runaway Skyscraper." *Argosy and the Railroad Man's Magazine* (22 Feb 1919): 59–82.

Lemire, Elise. *Miscegenation: Making Race in America*. Philadelphia: University of Pennsylvania Press, 2002.

Lemke, Sieglinde. *Primitivist Modernism: Black Culture and the Origins of Transatlantic Modernism*. New York: Oxford University Press, 1998.

Leslie, Thomas. *Chicago Skyscrapers, 1871–1934*. Urbana: University of Illinois Press, 2013.

———. "Dankmar Adler's Response to Louis Sullivan's 'The Tall Office Building Artistically Considered': Architecture and the 'Four Causes.'" *Journal of Architectural Education* 64.1 (Sep 2010): 83–93.

Levin, David, ed., *Modernity and the Hegemony of Vision*. Berkeley: University of California Press, 1993.

Levine, Gary. *The Merchant of Modernism: The Economic Jew in Anglo-American Literature, 1864–1939*. New York: Routledge, 2014.

Lewis, David Levering. *When Harlem Was in Vogue*. New York: Penguin Books, 1997.

Liebling, A. J. "To Him She Clung." *New Yorker* (12 Oct 1963): 143–168.

Lindquist-Cock, Elizabeth, and Estelle Jussum. "Machismo and Architecture." *Feminist Art Journal* 3 (Spring 1874): 8–10.

Lipsitz, George. *The Possessive Investment in Whiteness: How White People Profit from Identity Politics*. Philadelphia: Temple University Press, 1998.

Locke, Alain. "The New Negro." *The New Negro: Voices of the Harlem Renaissance*, edited by Alain Locke, 3–18. New York: Albert and Charles Boni, 1925.

Lokko, Lesley Naa Norle, ed. *White Papers, Black Marks: Architecture, Race, Culture*. Minneapolis: University of Minnesota Press, 2000.

Longstreth, Richard W. "Academic Eclecticism in American Architecture." *Winterthur Portfolio* 17.1 (Spring 1982): 55–82.

Lopez, Ian Haney. *White by Law: The Legal Construction of Race*. New York: New York University Press, 1997.

Lubove, Roy. *The Progressives and the Slums: Tenement House Reform in New York City, 1890–1917*. Pittsburgh: University of Pittsburgh Press, 1962.

Lukacs, Georg. "Realism in the Balance." *Aesthetics and Politics*, edited by Theodor Adorno, Walter Benjamin, Ernst Bloch, Bertold Brecht, and Georg Lukacs, 28–59. New York: Verso Books, 2010.

Lupton, Ellen. *Mechanical Brides: Women and Machines from Home to Office*. New York: Princeton Architectural Press, 1996.

Lye, Colleen. "Introduction: In Dialogue with Asian American Studies." *Representations* 99.1 (Summer 2007): 1–12.

Madigan, Mark. "'Then Everything Was Dark'?: The Two Endings of Nella Larsen's *Passing*." *Papers of the Bibliographical Society of America* 83.4 (Dec 1989): 521–523.

Malik, Nesrine. "Dubai's Skyscrapers, Stained by the Blood of Migrant Workers." *Guardian* (27 May 2011). http://www.theguardian.com/commentisfree/2011/may/27/dubai-migrant-worker-deaths.

Maneiri-Ella, Mario. *Louis Henry Sullivan.* New York: Princeton Architectural Press, 1995.

Marshall, Henry Rutgers. "The Legitimate Design for the Casing of Steel-Skeleton Structures." *Proceedings of the 37th Annual Convention: American Institute of Architects.* Providence: R. A. Johnson, 1898.

Martin, Reinhold, Jacob Moore, and Susanne Schindler, eds. *The Art of Inequality: Architecture, Housing and Real Estate; A Provisional Report.* New York: The Temple Hoyne Buell Center for the Study of American Architecture, 2015.

Marx, Karl. *Capital,* translated by Ben Fowkes. Vol. 1. New York: Penguin Classics, 1990.

Massey, Jonathan. *Crystal and Arabesque: Claude Bragdon, Ornament, and Modern Architecture.* Pittsburgh: University of Pittsburgh Press, 2009.

Mayo-Smith, Richard. *Emigration and Immigration: A Study in Social Science.* New York: Charles Scribner, 1901.

Menocal, Narciso G. *Architecture as Nature: The Transcendentalist Idea of Louis Sullivan.* Madison: University of Wisconsin Press, 1981.

Mercer, Kobena. *Welcome to the Jungle: New Positions in Black Cultural Studies.* New York: Routledge, 1994.

Merwood-Salisbury, Joanna. *Chicago 1890: The Skyscraper and the Modern City.* Chicago: University of Chicago Press, 2009.

———. "Western Architecture: Regionalism and Race in the *Inland Architect.*" *Chicago Architecture: Histories, Revisions, Alternatives,* edited by Charles Waldheim and Katerina Ruedi Ray, 3–14. Chicago: University of Chicago Press, 2005.

Meyer, Stephen Grant. *As Long as They Don't Move Next Door: Segregation and Racial Conflict in American Neighborhoods.* New York: Rowman & Littlefield, 1999.

Michaels, Walter Benn. *Our America: Nativism, Modernism, Pluralism.* Durham: Duke University Press, 1995.

Miller, Donald L. *City of the Century: The Epic of Chicago and the Making of America.* New York: Simon & Schuster, 1997.

Miller, Kelly. *Race Adjustment [and] the Everlasting Stain.* New York: Arno Press, 1968.

Miller, Monica. "The Black Dandy as Bad Modernist." *Bad Modernisms,* edited by Douglas Mao and Rebecca Walkowitz, 179–205. Durham: Duke University Press, 2006.

Mills, C. Wright. *White Collar: The American Middle Classes.* New York: Oxford University Press, 1951.

Mirzoeff, Nicholas. *The Right to Look: A Counterhistory of Visuality.* Durham: Duke University Press, 2011.

———. "The Shadow and the Substance: Race, Photography, and the Index." *Only Skin Deep: Changing Visions of the American Self,* edited by Coco Fusco and Brian Wallis, 111–126. New York: Harry N. Abrams, 2003.

Misa, Thomas. *A Nation of Steel: The Making of Modern America, 1865–1925.* Baltimore: Johns Hopkins University Press, 1998.

Mitchell, Melvin L. *The Crisis of the African-American Architect: Conflicting Cultures of Architecture and (Black) Power.* New York: Writer's Advantage, 2003.

Mitchell, W. J. T. *Seeing through Race*. Cambridge: Harvard University Press, 2012.

Moffett, Cleveland. "Mid-Air Dining Clubs." *Century* 62 (1901): 642–652.

Morrison, Hugh. *Louis Sullivan: Prophet of Modern Architecture*. New York: W. W. Norton, 1998.

Morton, Samuel. "Additional Observations on Hybridity in Animals and on Some Collateral Subjects." *Charleston Medical Review* (Nov 1850).

Mossman, James. "Race, Hate, Sex and Colour: A Conversation with James Baldwin and Colin MacInnes." *Conversations with James Baldwin*, edited by Fred R. Standley and Louis H. Pratt, 46–58. Jackson: University Press of Mississippi, 1989.

Moten, Fred. "Black Kant." A Theorizing Lecture at the Kelly Writers House, 27 Feb 2007.

———. *In the Break: The Aesthetics of the Black Radical Tradition*. Minneapolis: University of Minnesota Press, 2003.

Moudry, Roberta, ed. *The American Skyscraper: Cultural Histories*. New York: Cambridge University Press, 2005.

Mumford, Kevin J. "Homosex Changes: Race, Cultural Geography, and the Emergence of the Gay." *American Quarterly* 48.3 (1996): 395–414.

Mumford, Lewis. *Sticks and Stones: A Study of American Architecture and Civilization*. New York: Horace Liveright, 1931.

Murray, Scott Charles. *Contemporary Curtain Wall Architecture*. New York: Princeton Architectural Press, 2009.

Nelson, Bruce. *Divided We Stand: American Workers and the Struggle for Black Equality*. Princeton: Princeton University Press, 2002.

Ngai, Sianne. *Ugly Feelings*. Cambridge: Harvard University Press, 2007.

Nixon, Nicola. " 'Prismatic and Profitable': Commerce and Corporate Person in James's 'The Jolly Corner.' " *American Literature* 76.4 (2004): 807–831.

Norris, Frank. "A Plea for Romantic Fiction." *Boston Evening Transcript* (18 Dec 1901): 14–18.

North, Michael. *The Dialect of Modernism: Race, Language, and Twentieth-Century Literature*. New York: Oxford University Press, 1994.

Nye, David. *American Technological Sublime*. Cambridge: MIT Press, 2008.

Nyong'o, Tavia. *The Amalgamation Waltz: Race, Performance and the Ruses of Memory*. Minneapolis: University of Minnesota Press, 2009.

Oberlander, H. Peter, and Eva Newbrun. *Houser: The Life and Work of Catherine Bauer*. Vancouver: University of British Columbia Press, 2000.

O'Connell, Shaun. *Remarkable, Unspeakable New York: A Literary History*. Boston: Beacon Press, 1995.

O'Connor, Brendan. "The Sad, True Story of the Ground Zero Mosque." *The Awl* (1 Oct 2015). http://www.theawl.com/2015/10/the-sad-true-story-of-the-ground-zero-mosque.

Olmsted, Frederick. *The Papers of Frederick Law Olmsted*. Vol. 3. Baltimore: Johns Hopkins University Press, 1983.

———. *Public Parks and the Enlargement of Towns: Read before the American Social Science Association at the Lowell Institute, Boston, Feb. 25, 1870*. Cambridge: printed for the American Social Science Association at the Riverside Press, 1870.

Olmsted, Frederick, Jr. "The Park in Relation to the City Plan." *Forty Years of Landscape Architecture: Central Park*. New York: Putnam, 1928.

Omi, Michael, and Howard Winant. *Racial Formation in the United States.* 3rd ed. New York: Routledge, 2014.

Oppenheim, James. *The Olympian.* New York: Harper & Brothers, 1912.

Ovington, Mary White. *Half a Man: The Status of the Negro in New York.* New York: Negro Universities Press, 1969.

Packard, Jerrod M. *American Nightmare: The History of Jim Crow.* New York: Macmillan, 2003.

Page, Max. *The City's End: Two Centuries of Fantasies, Fears, and Premonitions of New York's Destruction.* New Haven: Yale University Press, 2003.

Park, Robert. "The City: Suggestions for the Investigation of Human Behavior in the Urban Environment." *American Journal of Sociology* 20.5 (1915): 577–612.

Park, Robert, and Ernest W. Burgess. *The City: Suggestions for Investigation of Human Behavior in the Urban Environment.* Chicago: University of Chicago Press, 1925.

Pasha, Shaheen. "Dubai's Towering Skyscrapers Are Built by a 'Horrifically Exploitative Labor System.'" *Quartz* (27 May 2013). http://qz.com/88278/dubais-towering-sky scrapers-are-built-by-a-horrifically-exploitative-labor-system.

Passante, Francesco. "The Vernacular, Modernism and Le Corbusier." *Journal of the Society of Architectural Historians* 56.4 (Dec 1997): 438–451.

Paul, Sherman. *Louis Sullivan: An Architect in American Thought.* Englewood Cliffs: Prentice-Hall, 1962.

Petrie, Paul. "Racial Duties: Toward a Pragmatist Ethic of Race in W. D. Howells's *An Imperative Duty.*" *Nineteenth-Century Literature* 63 (2008): 223–254.

Pittenger, Mark. "Imagining Genocide in the Progressive Era: The Socialist Science Fiction of George Allan England." *American Studies* 35.1 (Spring 1994): 91–109.

Platt, Harold L. *Shock Cities: The Environmental Transformation and Reform of Manchester and Chicago.* Chicago: University of Chicago Press, 2005.

Plunz, Richard. *A History of Housing in New York City.* New York: Columbia University Press, 2016.

"The Poetry of Skyscrapers." *Chicago Defender* (6 Jan 1912): 8.

Pokinski, Deborah. *The Development of the American Modern Style.* Ann Arbor: University of Michigan Research Press, 1984.

Pollio, Vitruvius. *The Ten Books on Architecture.* Cambridge: Boston University Press, 1914.

Pond, Allen B. "The Evolution of an American Architecture." *Inland Architect and News* 10.9 (Jan 1888): 98–99.

Pond, Irving. "Architectural Kinships." *Inland Architect and News Record* 17.2 (Mar 1891): 22–29.

Posnock, Ross. *Color and Culture: Black Writers and the Making of the Modern Intellectual.* Cambridge: Harvard University Press, 2009.

———. *The Trial of Curiosity: Henry James, William James and the Challenge of Modernity.* New York: Oxford University Press, 1991.

Powell, Richard J. "Paint That Thing! Aaron Douglas's Call to Modernism." *American Studies* 46.1/2 (2010): 107–119.

Prestiano, Robert. *The Inland Architect: Chicago's Major Architectural Journal, 1883–1908.* Ann Arbor: UMI Research Press, 1985.

Putnam, Frederic Ward. "An Interesting Suggestion for the Columbian Exposition." *Chicago Tribune* (30 May 1890): 13.

Quaife, Milo Milton. *The Development of Chicago, 1674–1914*. Chicago: Caxton Club, 1916.

Raczkowski, Christopher. "The Sublime Train of Sight in *A Hazard of New Fortunes*." *Studies in the Novel* 40.3 (Fall 2008): 285–307.

Rainey, Lawrence. "Office Politics: *Skyscraper* (1931) and *Skyscraper Souls* (1932)." *Critical Quarterly* 49.4 (Winter 2007): 71–88.

Rancière, Jacques. *Dissensus: On Politics and Aesthetics*. New York: Continuum, 2010.

Rand, Ayn. *The Fountainhead*. New York: Signet, 1996.

Rasenberger, Jim. *High Steel: The Daring Men Who Built the World's Greatest Skyline*. New York: HarperCollins, 2004.

Rees, Richard W. *Shades of Difference: A History of Ethnicity in America*. Lanham: Rowman & Littlefield, 2007.

Reeve, Arthur B. "Men Monkeys Who Build Our Towers." *Scrapbook* 5 (May 1908): 759–767.

Ricker, N. Clifford. "Architectural Grammar." *Inland Architect and Builder* 13.8 (Dec 1886): 66–67.

———. "Possibilities for American Architecture." *Inland Architect and News Record* 11.5 (Nov 1885): 62–63.

Riis, Jacob. *How the Other Half Lives*. New York: Charles Scribner's Sons, 1890.

———. *The Making of an American*. New York: Macmillan, 1901.

Robinson, John Beverly. *Architectural Composition: An Attempt to Order and Phrase Ideas which hitherto have been only Felt by the Instinctive Taste of Designers*. New York: D. Van Nostrand, 1908.

Rodgers, Lawrence. *Canaan Bound: The African-American Great Migration Novel*. Urbana: University of Illinois Press, 1997.

Roediger, David. *The Wages of Whiteness: Race and the Making of the American Working Class*. New York: Verso, 2007.

———. *Working toward Whiteness: How America's Immigrants Became White: The Strange Journey from Ellis Island to the Suburbs*. New York: Basic Books, 2006.

Roediger, David, and Elizabeth D. Esch. *The Production of Difference: Race and the Management of Labor in U.S. History*. New York: Oxford University Press, 2015.

Roosevelt, Theodore. *American Ideals*. New York: G. P. Putnam's Sons, 1920.

———. "The Expansion of the White Races." *National Edition: The Works of Theodore Roosevelt*, edited by Hermann Hagedorn. Vol. 18. New York: Charles Scribner's Sons, 1926.

———. *The Naval War of 1812*. New York: G. P. Putnam's Sons, 1900.

Root, John. "A Great Architectural Problem." *Inland Architect and News Record* 15.5 (June 1890): 68.

Rosenzweig, Roy, and Elizabeth Blackmar. *The Park and Its People: A History of Central Park*. Ithaca: Cornell University Press, 1992.

Rubin, Lance. *William Dean Howells and the American Memory Crisis*. Amherst: Cambria Press, 2008.

Ruskin, John. *The Seven Lamps of Architecture*. New York: Dover, 1989.

Rydell, Robert. *All the World's a Fair: Visions of Empire at American International Expositions, 1876–1916*. Chicago: University of Chicago Press, 1987.

Sacks, Marcy S. *Before Harlem: The Black Experience in New York City before World War I.* Philadelphia: University of Pennsylvania Press, 2006.

Saval, Nikil. *Cubed: A Secret History of the Workplace.* New York: Doubleday, 2014.

Schleier, Merrill. *The Skyscraper in America Art, 1890–1931.* New York: Da Capo Press, 1990.

———. *Skyscraper Cinema: Architecture and Gender in American Film.* Minneapolis: University of Minnesota Press, 2008.

Schuyler, Montgomery. "Modern Architecture." *Architectural Record* 4 (July–Sep 1894): 1–13.

Seitler, Dana. *Atavistic Tendencies: The Culture of Science in American Modernity.* Minneapolis: University of Minnesota Press, 2008.

Sekula, Allan. "The Body and the Archive." *October* 39 (Winter 1986): 3–64.

Sennett, Richard. *Flesh and Stone: The Body and the City in Western Civilization.* New York: W. W. Norton, 1996.

Sexton, Randolph. *American Commercial Buildings of Today.* New York: New York Architectural Book Publishing, 1928.

Simmel, George. "The Metropolis and Mental Life." *The Sociology of Georg Simmel,* translated by Kurt Wolff, 409–424. New York: Free Press, 1950.

Smethurst, James. *The African American Roots of Modernism.* Chapel Hill: University of North Carolina Press, 2011.

Smith, Ellison DuRant. *Congressional Record, 68th Congress, 1st Session.* Vol. 65. Washington, DC: Government Printing Office, 1924.

Smith, Mark. *How Race Is Made.* Durham: University of North Carolina Press, 2007.

Smith, Shawn Michelle. *At the Edge of Sight: Photography and the Unseen.* Durham: Duke University Press, 2013.

———. "The Half of Whiteness." *English Language Notes* 44.2 (Fall–Winter): 189–194.

———. *Photography on the Color Line: W. E. B. Du Bois, Race, and Visual Culture.* Durham: Duke University Press, 2004.

Smith-Pryor, Elizabeth M. *Property Rites: The Rhinelander Trial, Passing, and the Protection of Whiteness.* Chapel Hill: University of North Carolina Press, 2009.

Sollors, Werner. *Ethnic Modernism.* Cambridge: Harvard University Press, 2002.

Solomonson, Katherine. *The Chicago Tribune Tower Competition: Skyscraper Design and Cultural Change in the 1920s.* Chicago: University of Chicago Press, 2003.

Stanfield, John. *Philanthropy and Jim Crow in American Social Science.* Westport: Greenwood, 1985.

Starrett, William. *Skyscrapers and the Men Who Build Them.* New York: Charles Scribner's Sons, 1928.

Steadman, Philip. *The Evolution of Designs: Biological Analogy in Architecture and the Applied Arts.* New York: Routledge, 1979.

Stoddard, Lothrop. *The Rising Tide of Color against White World-Supremacy.* New York: Scribner's, 1922.

Sugrue, Thomas. *Sweet Land of Liberty: The Forgotten Struggle for Civil Rights in the North.* New York: Random House, 2008.

Sullivan, Louis. *Kindergarten Chats and Other Writings.* New York: Dover, 1979.

———. "The Tall Office Building Artistically Considered." *Lippincott's Magazine* 57 (Mar 1896): 48–49.

————. "The Young Man in Architecture." *The Public Papers*, edited by Robert Twombly, 131–143. Chicago: University of Chicago Press, 1988.

Takao Ozawa v. United States, Certificate from the Circuit Court of Appeals for the Ninth Circuit, No. 260. Argued October 3 and 4, 1922. Decided November 13, 1922.

Thaggert, Miriam. "Racial Etiquette: Nella Larsen's *Passing* and the Rhinelander Case." *Meridians: Feminism, Race, Transnationalism* 5.2 (2005): 1–29.

Thurman, Wallace. "High, Low, and Present: Review of *The Walls of Jericho, Quicksand,* and *Adventures of a Slaver.*" Originally published in *Harlem: A Forum of Negro Life* (Nov 1928). Reprinted in *The Collected Writings of Wallace Thurman: A Harlem Renaissance Reader*. New Brunswick: Rutgers University Press, 2003.

————. *Infants of the Spring*. Boston: Northeastern University Press, 1992.

Tintner, Adeline. *The Twentieth-Century World of Henry James: Changes in His Work after 1900*. Baton Rouge: Louisiana State University Press, 2000.

Tompkins, Kyla Wazana. *Racial Indigestion: Eating Bodies in the Nineteenth Century*. New York: New York University Press, 2012.

Trachtenberg, Alan. "Image and Ideology: New York in the Photographer's Eye." *Reading American Art*, edited by Marianne Doezema and Elizabeth Milroyk, 302–349. New Haven: Yale University Press, 1998.

Trotter, Joe, and Jared Day. *Race and Renaissance: African Americans in Pittsburgh since World War II*. Pittsburgh: University of Pittsburgh Press, 2010.

Tucker, Irene. *The Moment of Racial Sight: A History*. Chicago: University of Chicago Press, 2012.

Turak, Theodore. "Remembrances of the Home Insurance Building." *Journal of the Society of Architectural Historians* 44.1 (Mar 1985): 60–65.

Twigg, Reginald. "The Performative Dimension of Surveillance: Jacob Riis' *How the Other Half Lives.*" *Text and Performance Quarterly* 12.4 (1992): 305–328.

Twombly, Robert C. *Louis Sullivan: The Poetry of Architecture*. New York: W. W. Norton, 2000.

Tymn, Marshall B., and Mike Ashley, *Science Fiction, Fantasy, and Weird Fiction Magazines*. Westport: Greenwood, 1985.

Uechi, Naomi Tanabe. *Evolving Transcendentalism in Literature and Architecture: Frank Furness, Louis Sullivan, and Frank Lloyd Wright*. New York: Cambridge Scholars, 2014.

Underwood, Edna Worthley. "Invitation to Judge the First Opportunity Contest." *Opportunity* (May 1925): 130.

United States v. Bhagat Singh Thind, Certificate from the Circuit Court of Appeals for the Ninth Circuit., No. 202. Argued January 11, 12, 1923. Decided February 19, 1923, *United States Reports*, v. 261, The Supreme Court, October Term, 1922, 204–215.

Van Brunt, Henry. *Discourses on Architecture*. Boston: James R. Osgood, 1875.

Van Leeuwen, Thomas A. P. *The Skyward Trend of Thought: The Metaphysics of the American Skyscraper*. Cambridge: MIT Press, 1990.

Van Notten, Eleonore. *Wallace Thurman's Harlem Renaissance*. New York: Rodopi, 1995.

Van Vechten, Carl. *Nigger Heaven*. Urbana: University of Illinois Press, 1926.

Von Hoffman, Alexander. "High Ambitions: The Past and Future of American Low-Income Housing Policy." *Housing Policy Debate* 7.3 (1996): 423–446.

Walsh, George Ethelbert. "Modern Towers of Babel in New York." *Harper's Weekly* (12 Jan 1907): 206–207.

Warren, Kenneth. *Black and White Strangers: Race and American Literary Realism*. Chicago: University of Chicago Press, 1995.

Weinbaum, Alys. "Interracial Romance and Black Internationalism." *Next to the Color Line: Gender, Sexuality and W. E. B. Du Bois*, edited by Susan Gillman and Alys Weinbaum, 96–123. Minneapolis: University of Minnesota Press, 2007.

Weingarden, Lauren S. *Louis H. Sullivan and a 19th-Century Poetics of Naturalized Architecture*. New York: Ashgate, 2009.

Weisman, Leslie Kanes. "Women's Environmental Rights: A Manifesto." *Heresies* 2.11 (1981): 6–9.

Weisman, Winston. "New York and the Problem of the First Sky- scraper." *Journal of the Society of Architectural Historians* 12.1 (Mar 1953): 13–21.

Wells, Ira. *Fighting Words: Polemics and Social Change in Literary Naturalism*. Tuscaloosa: University of Alabama Press, 2013.

Wells-Barnett, Ida B. *Southern Horrors and Other Writings: The Anti-lynching Campaign of Ida B. Wells, 1892–1900*. Boston: Bedford Books, 2007.

"When Is a Caucasian Not a Caucasian?" *Independent* 70 (2 Mar 1911): 478–479.

"White but Black." *Century Magazine* (Feb 1925): 498.

Wiegman, Robyn. *American Anatomies: Theorizing Race and Gender*. Durham: Duke University Press, 1995.

———. "Whiteness Studies and the Paradox of Particularity." *Boundary 2* 26.3 (1999): 115–150.

Wigoder, Meir. "The 'Solar Eye' of Vision: Emergence of the Skyscraper-Viewer in the Discourse on Heights in New York City, 1890–1920." *Journal of the Society of Architectural Historians* 61.2 (June 2002): 152–159.

"William Sells Books to Harlem." *Publishers Weekly* (15 Apr 1928): 1623.

Williamson, Joel. *New People: Miscegenation and Mulattoes in the United States*. Baton Rouge: Louisiana State University Press, 2005.

Willis, Carol. *Form Follows Finance*. New York: Princeton Architectural Press, 1995.

Wilson, Mabel O. "Dancing in the Dark: The Inscription of Blackness in Le Corbusier's Radiant City." *Places through the Body*, edited by Heidi J. Nast and Steve Pile, 133–152. New York: Routledge, 1998.

———. *Negro Building: Black Americans in the World of Fairs and Museums*. Berkeley: University of California Press, 2012.

Wilson, Sarah. *Melting-Pot Modernism*. Ithaca: Cornell University Press, 2010.

Wolf Bowen, Janet. "Architectural Envy: 'A Figure Is Nothing without a Setting' in Henry James's *The Bostonians*." *New England Quarterly* 65.1 (Mar 1992): 3–23.

"Woolworth Building." *New Masses* (Apr 1916): 20.

Yablon, Nick. *Untimely Ruins: An Archaeology of American Urban Modernity, 1819–1919*. Chicago: University of Chicago Press, 2010.

Yochelson, Bonnie, and Daniel Czitrom. *Rediscovering Jacob Riis: Exposure Journalism and Photography in Turn-of-the-Century New York*. New York: New Press, 2007.

Ziarek, Ewa Plonowska. *Feminist Aesthetics and the Politics of Modernism*. New York: Columbia University Press, 2013.

Page locators in italics signify figures.

Printed in Great Britain
by Amazon